Full Sails Ahead

Full Sails Ahead

Nadia Yassine

Translated from French
by Farouk Bouasse

Justice and Spirituality Publishing
Iowa City, Iowa, USA • 2006

Printed in the U.S.A.

Published by
Justice and Spirituality Publishing
P.O. Box 5235
New Britain, PA 18901
U.S.A.

Web site: http://www.JSpublishing.net

ISBN 0-9675795-2-X

Library of Congress Catalog Card Number 20-04102894

Printed on acid-free paper

The front cover reflects a passage in the introduction: "Raising 'full sails' is intended to lift all the thick veils that obstruct the view of Islam in its pure and original form." The original image of Islam is illustrated here by traditional Islamic artwork on a yellow background. Yellow, a warm color, communicates the youth, hope, and dynamism of Islam. Gold refers to the golden days of Islam. The intensifying yellow and complex geometric pattern point to the diversity of the Muslim world. The warm orange of the drapery suggests the coming change that will unveil the beautiful and shining look of Islam.

CONTENTS

TRANSLATOR'S FOREWORD

NADIA YASSINE is the eldest daughter of Imam Abdessalam Yassine, the renowned Muslim scholar and theorist whose thinking is gradually becoming known to the English-speaking audience now that two of his books (out of more than 30) have been translated into English: *Winning the Modern World for Islam,* translated from the French in 2000; and *The Muslim Mind on Trial: Revelation versus Secular Rationalism,* translated from the Arabic in 2003.

Nadia Yassine is a prominent figure of Islamic renascence not only in her native Morocco, but internationally as well. Through interviews with international newspapers, magazines, and TV channels, she has expounded the views of the movement *Jama'at al-'Adl wa'l-Ihsan* (Justice and Spirituality Association, hereafter JSA) regarding domestic and foreign issues of concern to the Muslim world.

In *Full Sails Ahead* Yassine invites her readers—Westerners in particular but Muslims as well—to set out on a voyage aboard a fictional boat towards Islam as originally revealed.

Two major concerns motivate the book. The first and main concern is to call to mind the meaning of our transient passage on earth what awaits us after death, and especially how we can win the eternal bliss of the other life, the true life. The second concern is to rectify an image of Islam heavily skewed by a multitude of misconceptions. Such misconceptions prevent the Western mind from appreciating the true nature of the Islamic Message, the last message destined for mankind from the God of mankind.

Dispelling firmly entrenched misconceptions is no easy task. Their powerful grip on the Western collective memory owes largely to the assiduous work of a particularly malevolent orientalism. To this has been coupled the singularly dishonorable image of Islam given by its official and unofficial representatives.

The author relies on her readers' temerity and determination to know the secret of their existence, even as she relies on them to engage in this opened avenue of dialog. Only through such dialog can misgivings and apprehension toward the Other be relieved, and a foundation laid for a future relationship founded on mutual respect, solidarity, and altruistic work for the common good of humanity.

The book opens with a preface responding to the attacks of September 11, 2001. The introduction then sets the stage for the argument of the book and explains the author's motivations in writing it.

Part I, **Waverings**, casts light on the environment that imprisons the Western mind. The first chapter diagnoses the evident evil of unbridled modernity and draws attention to its various manifestations. The chapters that follow discuss the powerful aspects of that world and the ways in which it weakens receptivity to the Message of a truly just society, and curbs the will to progress.

In Part II, **Turbulent Collisions**, Yassine takes on the obstacles to understanding erected by a Western tradition maintained out of fear or hatred of Islam. She examines certain attitudes and contests the arguments maintained by a particular line of thought.

In Part III, **New Horizons,** the author strives to present Islam as it originally was. Historical deviations are recalled, particularly as they have affected the development of Muslim societies. Yassine comments broadly on the roots of decadence and endeavors to rid Islam of the scars of Muslim history. Sustained self-criticism, she maintains, is called for: it is all too easy an evasion to cast responsibility upon others for maintaining the fog that envelops the Islamic Message and deceives the inquisitive mind.

The epilog is a re-invitation to read *islam* with new eyes and a new heart. In it we are reminded of the stations of *islam (islam, iman, ihsān)* and are urgently called to save the destiny of humankind through mutual cooperation and understanding, rather than conflicts and hostilities.

Clearly, *Full Sails Ahead* comes within the scope of the missionary work of the Justice and Spirituality Association, which proposes to Moroccan society and to the whole Muslim world a communitarian and humanitarian project. This project would direct the efforts of the Islamic renascence to reconstructing the shattered edifice of the Muslim nation.

According to the JSA, Muslims are living in a positively critical period. Throughout the Islamic world, the rebirth of Islam is the harbinger of a total awakening. The Islamic world is heading for the promise of the last of the Prophets. Muhammad (grace and peace upon him) informed Muslims that their dismembered Islamic world would be reunited. He gave the glad tidings of the coming, after centuries of despotic rule, of a second caliphate.

The ordeals the Muslim world is now undergoing are divine tests intended to shake it out of its current torpor and prepare it to undertake once again the sublime mission of which it has been the depository. Victory and unity will surely come about, but Muslims must pay its price through their diligent work and boundless sacrifice. That is why the book primarily enjoins Muslims to know the truths of Islam, their history, and the roots of the evils that have brought about their decline. The author urges them, once they know these evils and the means to combat them, to take part in the slow but sure effort of reconstruction. The details of the methods to be used, the phases to be covered, and the conditions to be met are elaborately expounded in the books of the author's father, Imam Abdessalam Yassine.

The author appeals as well to the wise people of the West to learn the universal dimension of the Islamic Message and to take part in establishing justice and peace worldwide. The West, as evidenced, for instance, by demonstrations there (as indeed elsewhere around the world) against the unjust and ill-intentioned war on Iraq, deservedly boasts countless people of good will who desire to live in peace with their brothers and sisters in humanity, irrespective of their religious creeds, races, cultures, and civilizations.

The challenge ahead is for sincere people everywhere to work in unison to curb the evil intentions of fanatics and lunatics of all stripes—enemies of mankind who wreak mischief on earth and sow discord between peoples, warmongers animated by sentiments of hatred and rancor who thrive only in periods of unrest, self-centered people who sacrifice the peace of humanity and world stability on the altar of their parochial interests.

I wish to express my gratitude here to many friends in England and America whose assistance was invaluable. I wish to thank in particular my Muslim brothers: Ahmed Dallal, Hassan Elannani, and Muhammad Hjaoua. Special thanks as well to Imad Benjelloun, my Muslim brother and Justice and Spirituality Publishing President, for the interest and care he has commendably accorded to publishing this book. I am also indebted to the author, Nadia Yassine, for her remarkably precious counsels. Finally, I address singular thanks to respected Professor Martin Jenni for his remarkable vetting of the translation.

To you, dear reader, I wish an agreeable voyage in the company of the author towards the original nature of Islam.

—FB

EDITOR'S FOREWORD

IT IS FITTING that the English-language version of a book inviting both Muslims and non-Muslims on a voyage toward new horizons should have engaged the labors of both a Muslim translator and a non-Muslim editor. My role as the latter was to prepare the text for an American readership.

The task, despite my colleague's diligent translation, was a challenging one. As Nadia Yassine herself admits, the argument of the book was largely directed at a distinctly literate francophone readership, both in Europe and in the former French colonies of North Africa; and while the two groups differ in many ways—as colonizers and colonized, globalists and (all too frequently) the victims of globalization—they share in a common culture that on many fronts stands in marked contrast to the American experience, both before and after the decisive events of September 11, 2001. Thus, a good deal more than translation from one language to another (demanding enough in itself) is at stake here.

A language such as French or English (or our author's native Arabic) brings with it an entire world of contexts and associations. Madame Yassine's eloquent command of "the language of Voltaire" is everywhere evident in the original, not only in the amazing breadth of her sources, current and classical, but also, and particularly, in the nature of her argumentation, the omnivorous scope of her reading, by her very personal response to the (sometimes bitter) lessons of her distinctly French education.

While Yassine's penetrating assessment of the West, especially as the purveyor of materialist and spiritually rootless modernity, speaks plainly and forcefully, her discussion of Western secularism is directed almost exclusively to the peculiarly French development of *laïcité*. Her statistical evidence for the radical decline in the West in the number of practicing Christians, while more broadly representative of much of Europe, stands in marked contrast with the American scene, where polls swing wildly in the opposite direction. The situation in the United States, particularly at present, is one of a broadly based and politically active population of Christian conservatives with unprecedented representation in public office.

Yassine's comparative study of the Bible and the Qur'ān is founded, with regard to the former, on well-established (chiefly Germanic) critical scholarship; still, its findings would offend the large number of American adherents of biblical inerrancy—though these are, alas, unlikely to be reading a book whose major thrust is to present, with conviction and remarkable candor, the serene Message of Islam. More receptive non-Muslim readers will surely wish to explore the topic further; in this respect, the chapter titled "The Islamic View of Christianity" in Murad Hoffmann's *Islam: The Alternative* (2nd enlarged ed., Amana Publications, 1999) will be of particular interest.

In presenting this Message Madame Yassine demonstrates that she has deeply absorbed the wisdom of her revered and erudite father, Imam Abdessalam Yassine, from whom especially she has acquired a profound understanding of the Qur'ān as well as a passion for a just and spiritually reawakened Islamic community. But upon this solid foundation she has been able to erect a compelling and remarkably enlightening argument of her own. Her frank analysis of Islamic history and the bold lessons she draws from it will surely astonish and encourage both Muslim and non-Muslim readers alike.

One of these lessons in particular, namely the restoring of Islamic womanhood to its full and original role—"a generation of responsible and free women . . . the equal of men in the eyes of God and of his Messenger"—is breathtaking and inspiring. It is a long-awaited restoration Yassine not only advocates but embodies.

What is perhaps most remarkable about this book is that its author really has two distinct readerships in mind and that she has been able to reach both in ways that intersect to their mutual advantage. To the Muslim it is a clear call for profound renewal of the Islamic vision and vocation; to the reflective Westerner it is an illuminating and engaging lesson. To both it extends an invitation to journey together in mutual understanding toward a singular goal.

—MJ

PREFACE

THIS IS NOT the preface I had intended. It is what the attack perpetrated against the American superpower on September 11, 2001, compelled me to write. That colossal event has probably changed the course of contemporary history and so, too, that of my modest book, already completed before that fateful day.

After the ultimatum issued by George W. Bush—"You are either with us or against us"—I am enjoined, like everyone else on the planet, to take a stand with respect to the "event." Take a stand I shall indeed, but out of respect for nuance and depth, and not in response to this "hold-up" so typical of a country reputed to be the "fastest draw in the West."

I am neither for nor against the United States. I am for wisdom and level-headedness. It does not seem to me that this nation bases its policy on these two particular concepts. Even granting the margin of cynicism and Realpolitik that can be conceded to any political entity, this nation widely surpasses that standard. There, legitimate coolness in political dealings has become a frost impervious to humanistic concerns, a self-declared and unprecedented imperialism. I do, of course, feel sympathy for those thousands of victims at the World Trade Center, among whom were hundreds of Arabs and Muslims. Yet how quickly Arabs were made to take responsibility for what happened, through the fabrication of stupidly transparent evidence. The passport alone, reportedly found in the rubble, should surely have driven humanity in a stampede to find the perpetrators of the attack, whatever the cost. (Or hasn't the formula for inferno-proof paper been discovered yet?)

Intelligent as the nature of its power enables it to be, the United States seemed to have a handy culprit at the ready. It was urgent that American opinion be galvanized into action by giving a face to whoever had struck Olympia: the thunderbolt of the gods had to fall somewhere. So the case already present in the mind of the superpower was hastily set forth; the misfortune would at least help achieve reconciliation between a recalcitrant Pakistan and an equally rebellious India, both nuclear powers too close to certain sources of energy. There was thus nothing to lose in once again displaying its might in that sensitive corner of the globe—especially now that it had a legitimate and devastating alibi.

Let me make clear at this point that I am a member of the Islamic world America has decided to punish, and that I belong to a movement that has been accused of being radically Islamist. It is not a label I recognize myself by, for I am keenly aware of the murderous power of words in a media-driven era like ours.

It would indeed be much to our credit if by "Islamist" was meant that particular determination to return to our true Muslim origins. But alas, the term has been so loaded with negative connotations as to have become synonymous with extremism and fanaticism. When Islamist is further described as "radical," it becomes a euphemism for barbarian.

Labels like these arise from a determination to convince the world that all Islamists are barbarians appearing out of nowhere to occupy and dominate Muslim societies. Thus all social movements that further the cause of Islam have opprobrium heaped on them by being defined as agents of disruption. Projects for the recovery of Muslim society—the sole means we have of linking our fragmented societies—are thereby damaged. Economic imperialism, increasingly facilitated by globalization, requires standardization, and this is inevitably compromised by the unifying spirit the renewal of *islam* inevitably inspires. The upsurge of a reawakening *islam,* seen as having too federating an identity, further compromises the ill-gotten gains of colonization, with its arbitrary borders and designated spokesmen.

Any Islamist movement is therefore presented as being extraneous to the natural development of history on the move. So skillfully is the campaign waged that what should have been a return to the universal values of dignity, equity, dialog, and tolerance lapses into an identity crisis that can only conceive itself in a relationship of conflict with a hostile world.

The cultural aggression to which the Muslim world has been subjected has caused a toughening of stands, of which the attack on the Trade Center is perhaps only an initial expression.

The West, having already destabilized, impoverished, degraded, fragmented, and "deculturated" the colonized populations through its support of the most ignoble tyrannies, has brought on this renewal—a natural destiny of the Muslim world—and has driven both sides into drifts that are dangerous for everyone. By persistently opposing even the most modest proposals, the West has encouraged a sort of extremism that is deaf to any discourse or dialog.

This was the mistake they made in Egypt with El Banna, founding father of the Muslim Brotherhood. They made it again with the Islamic Salvation Front [Front Islamique de Salut] in Algeria, and they continue to adopt this mistaken response to the problem.

My movement, for instance, which has on many occasions proved its popularity and credibility in its respect of nonviolence (one of its basic principles), is nonetheless labeled radical because it opposes a regime that guarantees the well-being of everyone but Moroccans. Our interpretation of *islam* is far from reductionist; yet they will hear none of it. We are—and will always be—extremists simply because we do not meet the required standards laid down for the security and superiority of the West.

Planning a future beyond what the West allows us through the elites in power is deemed unacceptable. We must go where the Northern hemisphere insists on leading us or we will go nowhere. We must adopt policies that secure the stability of global capitalism. The outrages of the international monetary authorities, their policies of structural adjustments, and other, more barbaric strategies are to be borne without breathing a word. Viewed from amid the suffering, such policies and strategies deny the majority access to primary medical care and a decent system of education that differs from the current one, more effective in deadening minds than in educating them. A vicious cycle of poverty permeates our society, leaving it without recourse. Already overwhelmed by its domestic history—the successive powers that have debased, exploited, manipulated, betrayed, and eventually sold it—the Muslim community grapples with a ruthless modernity[1] in which it finds a place only in garrets, on the fringes of the opulent city of globalizing capitalism.

Since we know that it is only our Islamic values of unfailing solidarity that prevent us from sinking into total chaos, why should it surprise us that the retreat from these values has had so radical a result? *Islam* feels set upon for the simple reason that it has lost its identity as the self-confident bearer of a tranquil Message, assuming instead a wounded identity as the last hold-out in the face of unspeakable barbarity. No longer a serene entity, Islam has become a solitary refuge in a deteriorating society where there is no room for others, where outsiders are considered to be wily adversaries no one seeks any longer to convince.

The ancient domination of the political over the spiritual in our Muslim history has thus joined forces with modern cultural domination; the result has incited our community to extremism. Yet even that is redeemable, if we are prepared to pay the price of the undertaking.

"Extremists are lost, extremists are lost, extremists are lost," the Prophet (grace and peace be upon him) repeated in a *hadīth*.[2] He taught us to be a justly balanced community; but it is a balance we still cannot find, and one that we must diligently strive to find. But how are we to advance in this quest in an atmosphere as electric as that at the beginning of this new century?

It is high time for our modern world to make radical changes by striving to regard humankind not merely as a worthless workforce serving the interests of a small minority, but as an ultimate value. The challenge will be to do less Realpolitik and more real politics, political activity in its noblest sense.

It is surely political activity in the latter sense that the movement to which I belong, and which my father founded, attempts to promote. Ours is a movement of society. Some have accused it of being radical; others have described it as quietist, since for three decades it has advocated non-violence.

The reawakening of faith in the Muslim world is much more complicated than some would wish to pretend. Its true dynamic exists in our sense of community.

The crisis of conscience engendered by September 11 may perhaps help reposition the interpretations that have up to now issued from a singular way of thinking. In light of what happened, the West may perhaps acknowledge the right of the Muslim world to find its own antidotes, its own equilibrium.

Returning to Mr. Bush's demand that I identify and define myself, I am obliged to mention the work of education that is under way in the Moroccan society. It is a work inaugurated by my father thirty years ago, of which Western observers know only scraps. That is because his books are written in Arabic—only two of his books are in French. This fact requires a certain calling that is in ever more desperately short supply on Northern shores.

Of the two works in French, *Islamiser la modernité*[3] defends the idea that Muslims must not reject or destroy modernity, but rather tame it and win it for *islam* so that they may further offer to humanity the gift of *islam*'s liberating message. Among those who deigned to read the book, many saw in it an insult to modernity. The best of them, conceiving *islam* and modernity as opposing sides, indulged in the childish polemics of which side would win. The last echoes of this game-like reaction appeared in 2001 in an article in *Le Nouvel Observateur* by Jean Daniel in which, commenting on the September attacks, the author ironically asserted that "for want of winning the modern world for *islam*, we ought to suppose instead that we shall one day have to face the necessity of modernizing *islam*."[4]

In the same issue, Josette Alia, a symbol of that sort of Western condescendence that so many of us find exasperating, and the personification of the certitude that *islam* alone needs self-criticizing, left me brief space to write what I thought of the events of September 11. This represented immense progress: the last time I had received Alia at home, her interview resembled a multiple-choice exam. Everything must have a beginning, and I think that for such a newspaper, albeit with a style of its own, it is already very good to have begun what might one day become a real dialog.

From here on out, such dialog is inevitable; it will no longer be a matter of pretending to give it a start while merely taking bids over *islam* and modernity. If in the Muslim world there are serious proposals to win the modern world for *islam*, then the West, rather than condemning the idea or rejecting it disdainfully, must get used to the fact that from now on the renewal of *islam* is an inescapable component of the future, and of the values of one third of humanity.

It will be for the West, through the policies it adopts, to decide the nature of this key partner in a globalizing society. Those values can either be a source of tolerance and openmindedness, as already evidenced in Muslim history, or the breeding ground of unprecedented violence, if the West, as attested by the events of September 11, persists in fermenting revolt.

The call will probably go a long time without response. At least, that is what is suggested by the longstanding American tradition of turning a deaf ear to the outside world. The American will to power has become so immense that it no longer bothers (at least not until September 11) to hide it with even a small veil of decency.

The July 2001 issue of *Le Monde diplomatique*, just a few weeks before the attacks, revealed the extent of what might be obsessive self-importance. With a kind of crazed megalomania, Senator Jesse Helms declared, "We are in the center, and we must stay there," and further, "The United States must rule the world by bearing the moral, political and military torch by law and by force, and serve as an example to all the other peoples."[5] Charles Krauthammer expressed the American vertigo in these terms: "America straddles the world like a giant. . . . Ever since Rome destroyed Carthage, no power has reached the summits we have attained."

John Bolton, U.S. Secretary of State Colin Powell's assistant, betrayed that madness in more direct and less literary political terms, saying, "international law does not exist." Since the advent of Bush junior at the head of the Empire, contempt for the international law has grown increasingly, as any serious and beneficial treaty, whether in the military, environmental, or economic domain, is systematically trampled. What happened in Manhattan should not be read in the context of a clash between enemy civilizations, but as the expression of exasperation before so much arrogance.

Moreover, such haughtiness is far from new: the explosion of hatred on September 11 is only the latest act of a drama that has long been brewing. The roots of that evil are certainly political, but they trace their rootlets deep in the philosophical subconscious that determines the West's sociological choices.

The United States is merely the incarnation of a Prometheus whose raging fury is boundless, embarked as he is on an unprecedented technologized adventure. Misadventure is perhaps the more appropriate word: history would not have needed Bin Laden to warn the spearhead nation of its Promethean progress on fatal slopes. As early as 1943, Saint Exupéry, posted at an American base in Tunisia, described what he perceived as the expression par excellence of a "terrible human desert." His presence on that base aroused in him existential questions that ought to be posed even more urgently in light of the century that has just begun. "Where is the United States going?" he wondered. "And where are *we* going?"

Some may wish at any cost to read the events of September 11 as a break in a long-foreseeable development, rather than its outcome. It has been characterized as a break between two worlds, an absolutely astonishing event—but it is an illusion to present the event in that light.

If it is true that *islam* still holds sufficient fighting spirit to attempt the impossible, the malaise is total before the megalomaniacal turn the superpower's relations with the rest of the world have taken. While it is true that Bin Laden did what he did in the name of *islam,* many would have wished to demonstrate their anger in the name of the malaise generated by so much power and so much ignorance of the Other.

Some thirty years ago, Georges Friedman, to cite but one source, expressed the faint impression that the United States was treading dangerous waters. He described it as the most propitious locus for the fatal development of what he called the Great Imbalance:

> Each time I set foot on its soil—as I have done for some twenty years now—I am convinced that an enormous game is being played there on which the fate of the human race may perhaps depend. It is there that the greatest progress has been made in daring exploits of technology, despite its inherent difficulties. . . . It is there that conquests, wealth, efficiency, power, mistakes, misfortunes, fears, and vices are most openly paraded—through pride? candor? rashness? It is there that the contrast between economic development and moral underdevelopment is set forth in the most dazzling fashion. . . . No other country is better equipped to scourge the world. . . . I have never considered settling in that land, and I am upset to find myself there again. A complex curiosity—enormous, unsatisfied, not merely intellectual—impels me towards this nation (is it one in fact?), the explorations of the technological jungle with which it

surrounds itself, and which it has made further dense, such that it sinks into itself, subject at each moment to cruel losses of its physical and psychic substance, and risks its own defeat.[6]

I know full well that the American people are not all brutes. The law of averages alone suggests that there is an imposing number of lucid and level-headed Americans. Although majority rule, along with the economic and political pressure of certain lobbies, may prevent them from giving another face to their nation, still they are there. Evidence of such lucidness is provided by a report in the September 19, 2001, edition of *Le Monde,* in which an American painter declared:

> It is difficult to say such a thing today, but I think we asked for it. New York represents the domination of a center that imposes its law on other countries, orders coffee from Costa Rica, oil from the Middle East. If we no longer want coffee, we tell them: fuck off! Our democracy is based on falsehood. It is sustained by an incredible consumption of energy. Yet we want the rest of the world to believe they could live like us. If that were the case, the planet would die.

If only the politicians could hear such voices of wisdom! Stanley Hoffmann was saying the same thing back in 1968 in a more academic style, in a book whose title, *Gulliver in Chains,* needs no comment. According to him, the will to dominate for the sake of domination will end up neutralizing even the principle of efficiency to which American policy claims to adhere, as "efficiency is the art of achieving one's goals in a way that serves one's interests."

Had it heeded the warning signs, America might have saved face. The wisdom to which Hoffmann appeals might have prevented the events of September 11. The psychosis vis-à-vis Islamism—that terrifying bugbear they thought they had dammed up at home—is likely to degenerate into a terror that may annihilate any hope for a serene dialog with this movement, now that it is believed to be determined to make its *jihād* à la Bin Laden.

Rather than let itself be persuaded by its material power, the West should perhaps go back to its archives to search for treasures of wisdom. We may still turn back and stop the megamachine that, in its frantic race toward whatever goal, produces the wake of a colossal percussion. The determining mechanism is situated in the North—more exactly, in that great power, the United States.

Those who imagine our world can be easily divided up in the era of globalization are making, in my opinion, a serious error of judgment. I close this preface by recalling a metaphor of Hoffmann's that I find in keeping with the style of the day—the same Stanley Hoffman who never ceases to denounce America's "pyromaniac penchants":

If I had to choose a metaphor for the current international system, I would say that the system is like a bar to which a number of galley-slaves are chained. Some of these are small, two of them are enormous, and several of them handle explosives. Each has his own personality, but no one can do much with it. Anyone trying to break the line would bruise his ankles; dragging along his chained companions could easily blow up the works. So, despite their differences in weight, musculature and the size of their fists, despite their murderous hatred and jealousy, and whatever their grievance, they are all bound together, alive but powerless.[7]

Recent developments in international politics do not render the metaphor obsolete. Although the configuration of the international society has changed, we are increasingly the victims of the interdependence Hoffman described.

We might say that these bonds have grown tighter yet in our global-village world, and I see no way of getting rid of them. The only chance left for us is to choose the nature of those bonds. Given our options, we can either make them chains that alienate us all, or instead forge privileged relationships that respect the difference of our identities, which need not become identical.

If we persist in the path of alienation, there will always be a galley slave who, according to Hoffmann's metaphor, will seek to become a Spartacus and will plunge friends and foes alike into bloodshed. It would not matter to him—not even the state of chaos would disturb him. With nothing to win, he has, he assumes, nothing to lose.

Salé, October 24, 2001

NOTES

1. TN: Modernity, from the French *modernité*, refers in this book to the set of values—philosophical, cultural, political, economic and social—that represent the modern, and particularly the Western, world-view of man, society, life, science, etc. The topic figures largely in a recent major study by the author's distinguished father (see n. 3 below).

2. TN: Saying of the Prophet (grace and peace be upon him).

3. Abdessalam Yassine, *Islamiser la modernité*, al Ofok, 1998, contains an author's list of 19 titles, two written in French and 17 in Arabic. An English translation of this work was published in 2000 by Justice & Spirituality Publishing under the title *Winning the Modern World for Islam*.

4. *Le Nouvel Observateur*, no. 1926, Oct. 4–10, 2001, p. 26.

5. Philip S. Golub, "Rêves d'empire de l'administration américaine" [the American Administration's dreams of empire], *Le Monde diplomatique*, July 2001.

6. Georges Friedman, *La puissance et la sagesse* [Power and wisdom], Gallimard, 1970, p. 13.

7. Stanley Hoffman, *Gulliver enchaîné: essai sur la politique étrangère des États-Unis* [Gulliver in chains: essay on United States foreign policy], du Seuil, Paris, 1971, p. 95.

INTRODUCTION

Travel teaches many a bitter lesson.
Théophile Gautier

Rubbing and filing our brain against the brain of others
Michel de Montaigne

The disciple of wisdom ought to have a great and courageous heart.
The burden is heavy and the journey is long.
Confucius

Why the title *Full Sails Ahead?* [1] Autosuggestion, certainly; self-encouragement in order to brave a stormy sea.

Why *Full Sails Ahead*? To invite you on a voyage of sincerity—perhaps also of severity. At a time when the media strive to make bloody lunatics of all on board, such an invitation will surely seem naïve. Yet they will be raising full sails all the same.

It will not be seen as pure coincidence if the word *voiles* appears in the title of a book written by a veiled woman. Freudians will not fail to sniff out in that title the metaphor for an abortive attempt. Let me defuse from the outset any such psychoanalytical sallies. My use of the word *voile* has nothing at all to do with repression! It is well and truly a clear allusion that I proclaim in all consciousness, one that I assume in my title as well as in my life.

But this book, I hasten to reassure my reader, is in no way intended as a panegyric to the scarf. *Islam,* [2] whatever we may think of its enemies—or indeed of its supporters—is more than a square of fabric. If the former consider the veil an ostentatious and menacing sign, the latter all too often fall into an opaque vision of *islam.* For them, *islam* is reduced to a show of clothing, and the dress of the veiled woman becomes for them a veritable obsession.

Hoisting high my sails, I too can be provocative, for French, the language that I have borrowed to write in, has waged war on "three girls and a scarf." [3] I hoist them because I know that in a world where the image reigns, being provocative is the only way to hold people's attention.

I will use and misuse what Colette once called the "tyranny of words" with the intention of attracting eyes that have become disillusioned by too much communication, and of shaking consciences made languid by too much conformity. Self-important minds will find my words insolent noise, but that may draw their attention. They may indeed wake up on the wrong foot—the words will perhaps have been a bit too acrid—yet an awakening, no matter how it comes about, is always more fitting than comatose lethargy.

The reader will not fail to notice my fury against France, more than any other Western country. The reason for this attitude should not be hard to understand; many parameters may be taken into account. The first of these is my education. Of all the western countries I know France the best, since I have been in steady contact with its culture. Besides, there is always a tendency—indeed an interest—to take on what one knows full well.

The second parameter is that France has effectively played a primordial and central role in the formation of western culture. According to Anne-Marie Thiesse,[4] the primary cause behind European nationalism was a desire to escape from French cultural hegemony. Speaking of the European struggle against the French cultural model that invaded European circles, she writes:

> The struggle against conventionality merges indeed with an offensive against French cultural hegemony. In eighteenth-century Europe, French is not only the language of Versailles, but that of most European circles. French culture was able to assert itself as being the most accomplished expression of the literate, a model that could be imitated but never equaled. The brilliance of the French sun allows for mere reflections elsewhere.[5]

Criticizing France therefore amounts to criticizing the leader of Western culture and thus rends honor to whom honor is due.

Full Sails Ahead. I therefore hoist my sails in order to "speak up" following Pierre Bourdieu's advice in his dialog with Günter Grass.[6] I will bear this precious advice in mind, even though I may seem obnoxious to many because I belong to a category of persons whom some would not like to have a say at all.

Full Sails Ahead. In particular I hoist my sails for love of the high seas of the mind. I hoist them on the mast of an imaginary ship in order to offer a change of scene to those who have grown bored. I hoist them for those whose life resembles that of a draught animal endlessly pulling and turning the millstone.

I then write for those who no longer have the courage to go round in circles and have at last the audacity to gaze at themselves in the mirror, those who have the nerve to think differently. I write for albatrosses, those who feel to be in their element only in the heights of unknown skies.

I am writing for you, Sisyphus.

Is it not time to rid yourself of your burdens and the punishment no god inflicted upon you—one in fact, you imposed on yourself? Hasn't the time come to free yourself of evil forces that hold you without holding you back, forces that bleed you white but do not kill you, that use you but do not exhaust you, that burn you but do not consume you?

Sisyphus of all nations, revolt! make the effort! You are dangerously draining yourself. Your wound is open and your truth is fleeing from you.

Full Sails Ahead. I am neither the first nor the last to use the metaphor of a voyage. Many before me have done so, and many will surely do so after me. This is perhaps because no matter who we are, where we are, or which time we live in, we think of ourselves as voyagers by vocation.

Initiated by the Creator, the Prophet Muhammad (grace and peace be upon him) knew our profound nature and advised his disciples, "Live this life as voyagers."

Supreme wisdom! Wisdom itself!

Writing in a most secular language in order to establish contact with a certain frame of mind, I will content myself for the moment with this saying of the Messenger. I am forcing myself for the same reasons by using references that are closer to the French-speaking subconscious. Aware of the fact that some minds will only respond to imagery drawn from Greek mythology, I will use it time and again while praying God to pardon me the blasphemy inherent in pagan mythologies. There is no god but God. Once having inhaled a breath of fresh air in this pure saying from the mouth of the Prophet, I dive with no breathing apparatus into the inanity of Greek "wisdom."

One can scarcely speak of voyaging without evoking Ulysses. I cannot, on the other hand, remember the account of the episodes of this hero without thinking of what I read between the lines. While Homer retraced for me Ulysses' steps, it was, strangely enough, the image of Penelope that made an impression on me. My regard for this woman came more from a profound existential feeling than from a quibbling feminist point of view. As I read further, I told myself that no matter what setbacks that hero faced, he was surely happier than his alter ego languishing in his absence. All the while he was collecting the trophies of wisdom, in the end, the only thing his wife cultivated and reaped was fidelity. The spirit of endurance and patience that Penelope symbolizes is much to her credit; still, forging ahead in life and changing will eternally remain an attitude more meritorious than suffering the assaults of time and suitors.

I firmly believe that the secret of life is progress. For while Ulysses' poor wife sat at her loom weaving and undoing her weaving, he was braving, enduring, bearing, combatting, transforming and being transformed, confronting, breathing the air of the open sea—in a word, he was living.

With the tale of these two spouses in mind, I invite my readers to journey with me with full sails ahead against wind and waters, against one-sided views and small-minded notions!

If you feel more like Penelope than Ulysses, read no further. Content yourself with weaving and undoing your weaving. Long for an alter ego who will never return. But if you feel more like Ulysses—then full sails ahead toward a new horizon!

I might have written instead, *Lifting all veils,* for I write not only from the desire to deal with objections and protests, but out of every Muslim's duty to lift the obscuring veils that prevent the other from catching the message of the Qur'ān, the ultimate Message intended and sent to all humankind by our Creator.

Thus chapter by chapter we shall progress step by step in a world where duplicities skew our sight and impoverish our being, so as to overcome them. However vehemently I may plead the case, it is out of love for all humankind that I write, love for all the citizens of the modern world whose accumulated misunderstandings threaten to deprive them of a ticket to a reenchanted world, a world reinhabited by humankind, the true humankind. One cannot help but sympathize deeply with the kind of person who has become a shadow of himself, a prisoner of his ego, deliberately oblivious to his essence and bereft of meaning.

My precise objective is to destroy the barriers that stand between this person and his primordial right to know the secret of his existence by recognizing God.

Before embarking, I must point out that this book has no academic pretensions. I conceive of it first as a cry from the heart for which arguments serve as resonance chamber. It is no more and no less than a passionate invitation to a voyage toward meaning.

NOTES

1. TN: The French title, *Toutes voiles dehors,* the author plays on the French homonyms *voile* m. (veil) and *voile* f. (sail). For the voyage to which she invites her readers, raising "full sails" is intended to lift all the thick veils that obstruct the view of *islam* in its pure and original form.

2. Throughout this book, I use italicized form *islam* to designate the Islamic faith. By "Islam" I refer to its sociopolitical or geostrategic reality.

3. TN: For elaboration of this French-style secular war, see Part II, Chapter II.

4. Research director at the *Centre National de la Recherche Scientifique* [national center for scientific research], and alumnus of the *École Normale Supérieur* [college for training teachers].

5. Cf. Anne-Marie Thiesse, *La création des identités nationales, Europe XVII–XX siècles* [the creation of national identities in 17th- through 20-century Europe], UH, Seuil, 1997, p. 29.

6. Pierre Bourdieu, "La tradition 'd'ouvrir sa gueule' " [the tradition of "opening one's yap"], in "Horizons, entretiens," *Le Monde,* Dec. 3, 1999: p. 16.

I.
WAVERINGS

I. 1. A PARTICULAR THIRST

The truth of a man is first of all what he hides.
André Malraux

What a pity it is I must be what I am,
A man who has strayed, not knowing whither he goes.
Charles d'Orléans

All men who get bored on one planet spend their wretched lives in search of another.
Charles Nodier

The Need for an Out There

In March of 1997 the French Public Opinion Research Institute, in collaboration with the television channels France 2 and France 3, conducted a poll among young people between 14 and 25 years of age in order to learn what was currently high on the charts. Nineteen per cent named *The X Files;* the American TV serial that always begins with the assertion: "The truth is Out There."

In fact, the result of this investigation largely surpasses expectations. As this book goes to press, *The X Files* is the subject of a real cult that is spreading ever more widely, with all the passion and the profound motivation that "cult" implies.

The serial offers more than a mere hour of intrigue between FBI agents and picturesque aliens—the fantastic adventures of mutants of all stripes. It is above all a special occasion offered by mass television to visit the irrational—the very domain Western civilization has definitively banned from its official point of view, and one that it tolerates only in certain areas of artistic expression.

The success of *The X Files* may also be due to the fact that it betrays the unspeakable anguish of modern man's subconscious—a subconscious that rings hollow, devoid as it is of any presence of the sacred. The culture of the eerie is surely a substitute for the faith that is enchained by the taboos of the modern world. It has become a sort of mysticism of modern times, one that those who no longer have the right to a true belief may well fall back on.

This thirst for an "Out There," hardly unique to a French public opinion poll on *The X Files,* can be found as well in many other domains besides the movies or television, although these are surely the cultural media in which it is most spectacularly expressed. Heading the Top Ten is a series of movies similar in their subjects to the theme developed by that TV series. The public is ready to pay anything for a remarkable moment, an instance of the extraordinary, a second of belief in an Out There—be it better or worse than reality.

Want some? Here you are! Anything will do to slake the thirst for the marvelous or supernatural, to respond to an apprehension of death—of all that our mortal senses cannot perceive. The coin of fascination has another, darker side: a predilection for the strange belies the anxiety of existence.

The cinema is at one's service. Those *Men in Black,* initiated into the mysteries of weird-looking aliens, see what others do not. A little boy is endowed with an extraordinary *Sixth Sense* that enables him to have unusual friends. A doll is haunted by dark forces, a mummy rises from its wrappings to execute a posthumous curse. In *Jumanji,* an infernal game imprisons its participants in a nightmarish world. The film is particularly revealing: all the Old Testament themes are taken up, from the Diaspora to the Flood, and even the Redemption.

Man makes a travesty of faith besotting himself with such childish fantasies. Through its perfect mastery of special effects, the ever more competitive and spectacular movie industry offers a grand voyage. Speaking of the cinema, we come to be more and more like the people shown in *Les Rêveurs,* the science fiction film in which men who have destroyed their environment live on, linked to a dream-machine from which they disconnect themselves only in order to feed on a synthetic greenish jelly.

In the domain we are discussing, the preeminence of image is absolute. Special effects offer extraordinary possibilities for the spectator's fantasy. The image is an ideal medium for expressing the inexpressible; the box office of the best movies explodes whenever the subject is strange or fantastic.

So insistent is the need of an Out There that it will go any lengths to be satisfied.

A Re-enchanted World

Despite the utter preeminence of the cinema in a world where image rules supreme, writing has not yet lost its accustomed privilege in recounting mankind's anxieties and dreams. Since Gutenberg, writers' pens have never ceased to be powerful fixatives of prevailing emotions, collective sentiments, and society's popular illusions.

As such, New Age Literature is particularly revealing of a latent anxiety before an accomplished and disenchanted world, a world that races towards collision with postmodernity. That world's uneasiness is readily evident from a scan of current popular culture and the literary preferences of the moment.

The themes of the bestsellers of recent years offer irrefutable proof that mankind dreams of—indeed, demands—curling up with the marvelous and the irrational. I doubt whether all those who queued up before bookstores until midnight in a cold night of December 2000 to get their copy of the latest *Harry Potter* have the excuse of children. This cult serial, a veritable social phenomenon, fascinates not only schoolboys but also those eternal children, the adults of the modern world. When we pause to probe the themes of currently successful books, the future looks anything but rosy.

Books serve as secret passages leading to unordinary worlds that even the most serious person delights in visiting. The imaginary has come to be the gentle retreat of those who no longer believe in anything, at least for those whose human drives are not entirely spent.

For the modest price of a book, modern writers offer the reader an encounter with extraordinary characters with whom he will happily identify. For a furtive moment, free from the restraints of inquisitive reason, he will believe in extraordinary powers, in the spirit of things!

Within the space of a book, and in just the time it takes to read it, literature will re-enchant for him, even more subtly than the cinema, a world that is becoming desperately void of magic. The modern bestseller also raises its fist in the face of that very modern tyranny: the worship of reason.

Today's successful book puts reason to flight, or at least muzzles it by making *it* "see reason," by giving a privileged place of honor to feelings and instincts, to the passions, to sixth sense. In exchange for the stifling dimensions of rational despair, it offers the fourth dimension.

New Age literature takes its admiring public on a toboggan ride of the imaginary, the fantastic, the unusual—all the way to psychic disintegration. New Age bestsellers are confessionals in which the reader admits his weakness for the absurd and his complicity with the author who unveils for him the splendors of the occult. The titles alone are expressive. Just reading them erases any doubts we might have about the nature and increasingly invasive emergence in postmodern literatures of the thirst for an Out There, the thirst for oneself, the hunger for spirituality.

According to *Le Petit Larousse*, alchemy is defined as

> an occult science that witnessed a great development between the twelfth and eighteenth centuries, a spiritual and esoterically inspired search for a universal remedy (elixir, panacea, philosopher's stone) capable of effecting the transmutation of being and matter (notably the transmutation of base metals into gold).

Thus the very title of Paulo Coelho's bestseller *The Alchemist* invites the purchaser to cross the threshold of a unique world where the base is transmuted into the precious, where there is a balm for all ailments, where matter is controled, where the philosopher's stone is kept. For the price of the book, the author offers his reader mental escape, a tour of Wonderland, where he will play Alice with great delight.

Modern man has thus a universal and insatiable desire for an imaginary world. Remembrances of a lost paradise, perhaps? No doubt! But such recollections are painful. Like some ecchymosis of the soul, they unleash a spreading pain in the cold heart of one imprisoned in the icy cells of rational understanding, one who has become rigid and exclusionary. Jealous, fierce, and narrow-minded, modernity is the prison warden that allows the inmates to speak with the supernatural only through channels, the grids of the understanding it supports, the only means it approves of. The poor prisoner is mercilessly fed on raw rationality. His only contact with faith in God is through books stolen and read in solitude: another Papillon[1] hurling himself against concrete walls. Modern literary penchants attest to such frustration and tragedy.

First published in 1988, *The Alchemist* continues to gild the drab everyday life of those who languish wearily in despair of having lost the capacity for asking the primordial questions of being and meaning.

The popular Brazilian author has more recently published another bestseller, *By the River Piedra, I Sat Down and Wept.* Wearing a vaguely religious perfume, the novel has made literary news. It owes its triumph not so much to its title as to its evocation of the Virgin Mary (may God bless her) that pervades the book.

Susanna Tamaro, another seller of "Out There," is in her way to becoming the best author in the genre; offering her readers a wide gamut of the occult, she knows how to touch a sensitive nerve. A new book, *Follow Your Heart,* is in vogue across Europe. An initiatory story besotted with spiritism, karma and astrology, the novel is a sickly sweet cocktail done up with a dash of violence. Despite its mediocre reviews, the book has brought its author a record-breaking sales rate even among bestsellers.

That ought to teach us that style means nothing to the modern reader who cares only for illusions and thrilling feats of the imagination. Few people nowadays buy a book for its grammar exercises or to enrich their vocabulary, as was widely the case some decades ago. Instead they buy it as if it were subway fare or an airline ticket to a better world, a world rejected in reality.

Yet this world, on sale by the authors of screen plays and novels, this world so sought after, so often encountered in New Age pages, is nonetheless often very harrowing. It owes the infatuation it enjoys to the limits within which the rationalistic mind, narrow and blind to the interests of the soul, confines modern man. The realities of that world, where the atmosphere is often dreary and breathing comes hard, are disturbing. What New Age novels promise us is alarming—so alarming that we must pray that the imaginary is not transmuted into reality.

Gloomy Premonitions

It is chilling to note how often futuristic novels of the past have proved premonitory. Who among the readers of the past generation did not revel in Aldous Huxley's *Brave New World,* content as they were to be living in another world, where genetic engineering existed only in novels? How reassuring it was to attribute Huxley's fictions to his failed career as biologist!

We used to thank God that the world where eugenics was brazenly practiced and where genetics was used to create social classes on demand, existed only in the texts and minds of writers who had attended the school of Mendel. Those were the good old days: Dolly, the cloned ewe, was not yet bleating!

With the birth of Dolly, however, assurances of a world kept safe from the horrors Huxley described have vanished. When ethics committees prove ineffective, all the assurances of human wisdom disappear, for nothing will curb the hegemonic ambitions of the dark and mysterious powers that rule the world. Assurances die completely when what goes on backstage in the modern world (read: the Third World) is laid to view: experiments in drug control, in biotechnology.

Our strides toward the *Brave New World* grow ever longer and more confident. Already the human genome lies under microscopes that are not always well-intentioned—and even when they are! Let us recall that Einstein, researching the atom, never for a moment thought of Hiroshima, Nagasaki, or Chernobyl!

Was Huxley a visionary after all? So it would seem—but the postmodern curses predicted by current science fiction are far more disturbing. We must, however, read them attentively, for they are candid courtrooms where the trial of modernism is ongoing—and God knows that the unbridled modernism we live in needs to be put on trial!

Rather than shrugging their shoulders, those who do not take seriously the warnings of visionary authors should revise their thinking. Authors like Huxley have more than an aroused and vivid imagination; they often start from experience as much as from intuition.

Pierre Thuilier is one such thinker who uses the fabulous to set off alarms. In a fictitious report[2] from the year 2081, he anticipates the cataclysm that supposedly overtook the West between 1999 and 2002. His depiction of things is far from the exclusive product of a fruitful imagination. Jacques Decornoy describes the author of the imaginary report as:

> a pillar of the periodical *La Recherche,* rising up against current pretensions of running societies "scientifically," opposed to the strategy of expelling poetry, legends, culture; against "purifying" in the name of a certain conception of "reason," in the name of an inadmissible "appalling form of violence" the roots of which he detects and whose effects he dissects under five aspects of Western man: Homo Urbanus, Homo Economicus, Homo Corruptus, Homo Technicus, Homo Scientificus.[3]

Decornoy then summarizes the book:

> In his novel describing the human condition of the twenty-first century, Pierre Thuilier, after a few "preliminary reflections," goes straight to the heart of the matter. Recalling the suffering endured by "ordinary citizens" at the close of this century, he asks himself: "They often grumbled, they laid claims whenever their material interests appeared to be menaced, but eventually they accepted the spiritual misery proper to modernity." How is the fact to be explained that such dissatisfaction and frustration found no more energetic expression? As for "the political, economic and cultural elite," they "behaved as if the gravity of the situation escaped them"; "they desperately attempted to solve on an ad hoc basis masses of problems adjudged to be urgent without ever questioning the great principles (explicit or implicit) on which their practices were founded."

This is exactly the image created by the refusal of the United States to go further towards solving the very serious climatic issues raised at the Kyoto Conference in the year of "grace" 2001! "Nothing proves that global warming is caused by pollution," argues this so-pragmatic Nation. Everything leads us to conclude that it is rather the *opposite* that "nothing proves."

The Need for Meaning

Pierre Thuillier and the New Age writers are not the only children of modernity to issue warnings against the disenchantment and folly that seizes our world. They are merely the literary expression of a malaise expressed in a more learned manner by philosophers of the caliber of Edgar Morin, who, describing what he calls scientific obscurantism,[4] writes:

> Unfortunately, a mutilating and one-dimensional vision claims a cruel price in the human realm: mutilation maims the flesh, spills blood, spreads suffering. An inability to conceive of the complexity of the anthroposocial reality in its microdimension (the individual being) and macrodimension (all mankind) has led to endless tragedies and is leading us to the supreme tragedy.[5]

"Mutilating" is apt indeed; it is high time that the savants of the West take note. In the cultural milieu of a history forged in the face of the divine, wisdom itself has become muzzled by other, more highly rated values. The most virtuous remain conditioned in the depths of their wisdom. The taboos are firmly established, and even the boldest among the wise cannot overstep the boundaries set by the "right-thinking trend" without risking being branded as visionaries or revisionists.

However urgent the desire for an Out There, discussing it will remain cautious and incremental. The modern thinker who does not wish to be labeled ephemeral and romantic must resort to ingenious allegories when speaking of the absolute. Should he ever dare to unleash its ancient demons, he will be declared *persona non grata* and banished to the fringes of the clan of the philosophically correct.

Censure goes hand in glove with self-censure. While the secular environment keeps vigil on "correct thinking," its schools are equally alert to banish from understanding anything that does not jibe with secularism, relativity, triviality, and whim. The secular Medusa that Enlightenment philosophy gently but carefully locked in the mind will never tolerate being looked at straight in the eye.

In the kingdom of Holy Secularity and Relativity, declaring one's belief in the absolute is lèse-majesté. God is confined to an empty heart or the cold desert of a church, where a space is made for the rare type who occasionally kneels down before Him. The modern mind looks condescendingly on those Sunday lovers of the sacred Flesh and Blood. It will scarcely tolerate them licking their chops in public at the end of the mass. Beyond the doorstep of the church, the absolute is to be conscientiously folded up and consigned to the closet like the "Sunday best" of yesteryear.

The Absolute makes its appearance once a week among the most faithful, less often among others, but never among the more illumined who have bathed in "Enlightenment" to the point of intoxication and even drowning. And it is these who enjoy the dubious advantage of being in the majority.

The fashion of rejecting the absolute has become a law that is not transgressed with impunity; spoil-sports must at best content themselves with beating about the bush moaning buzz-words. Albert Jacquard desperately entitles his book *Voici le temps du monde fini* [the time of the finished world is here]. Bernard Cassen bids higher by introducing his book *Il n'y a plus d' 'ailleurs' sur cette planète* [there are no more "Out Theres" on the planet].[6]

False Paradises

The need for absolutes—the search for an Out There—has become a profitable market. The movie industry mines it feverishly; so does the book trade. More sinister industries also profit from this need, producing daytime nightmares and plunging their takers into bottomless pits.

Readily mistaking mirages for water, the thirsty are the easy prey of false prophets and vendors of illusions. Ever increasing in number, these find in destabilized minds a fertile field in which the evil seeds of their ideas take root and flourish. Sects indulge in a novel trade where the absolute is the product on offer to modern man, more disoriented than ever before on the planet.

If there have always been persuasive Rasputins of all stripes, "is this not simply because man, since time immemorial, has gone in search of explanations that would lessen his fundamental anxiety about what exists behind life—about what lies beyond?"[7]

Such anxiety is stronger now than ever before. Despite the frenzied masquerades and giddy thrills, anxiety bores through the subconscious and penetrates uncertain certitudes. Modern man, whose spiritual dimension has been mutilated, does his utmost to reestablish links with a world that he bears in his depths and that the deafening noises of unbridled modernism prevent him from communicating with. Deprived of what is essential (in the literal sense of the word), he finds refuge in the company of false apostles who take pains to empty his pockets as well as his brain before they convince him to simply put an end to his life in an ultimate collective delirium.

God (exalted be He) said in the Qur'ān:[8] *Oh man! What is it that misleads you from your Generous Lord?*[9]

Who has hurled you into the hands of sects that worsen your distress and incite you to commit suicide, to violence, if not to cannibalism or other atrocities? It is surely the icy cold of the modern, blasé world. Surely it is the senselessness of an exclusively consumerist life.

According to Danielle Hervieu-Léger and the French team of sociologists of religion who take Max Weber's analysis as reference, sects are "emotional communities where one can observe a considerable affective investment on the part of members and a strong attachment to a leader called 'the shepherd.'" They serve as well as a palliative for the conventional churches discredited since May of 1968.

The sects open their arms, promising false paradises to those no longer able to bear the hell of solitude and indifference. The market of false spirituality is widespread, and it attracts a wide clientele. It varies from sects that slightly tweak Christian dogmas, to breathe new life into them, to such pernicious and highly dangerous sects as the Order of the Solar Temple, the Mandarom, or the Church of Scientology. Their programs offer a whole range of possibilities, from precepts not far from conventional teachings of charity and fraternity to the practices of black magic, unspeakable debauchery, or the consumption of hard drugs.

Chased out the door, Christian spirituality returns through the window—sometimes through the sewer pipes! Modern societies' general fascination with black magic is very significant. Michael Jordan writes:

> The black mass made popular by fiction writers like Denis Weathly is little more than a travesty of the Roman Catholic mass where the Eucharistic host, stolen from a church, is desecrated or replaced by an object like a turnip painted black. For a black mass to be performed according to the rules, a defrocked priest must be present. The presence of such a person is improbable today, but it is known that at a particular time clergy members took active part in certain acts of sorcery and satanism.[10]

A travesty of sacred gestures, black magic is a sort of a reversed religion that is recruiting an increasing number of followers. Its faithful are numerous and growing in number, since, unlike the sects, spirituality enjoys the privilege of publicity. Even in France—an underdeveloped country in this regard compared to the U.S.A—more than ten million persons consult clairvoyants and healers, and one person out of two claims to be sensitive to paranormal phenomena.[11]

Fascination with the occult has become a social phenomenon, accepted as such by political powers as well as public opinion. If in certain hard-line secular countries it is no longer conceivable to introduce a political program founded on religious membership, it is nonetheless quite acceptable to establish parties whose objectives are quirkily fashionable. During the 1993 elections in the U.K. there appeared a Natural Law Party to advocate the development of Transcendental Meditation and the encourage of "flying yoga."[12]

If in the land of Voltaire the Islamic veil is deemed an ostentatious sign and spirituality merely irritating sanctimoniousness, an initiative such as that of Jack Lang, the former Minister of Culture who as the mayor of Blois undertook to build a National Center for the Art of Magic and Illusion, is quite in vogue.

So it goes with modern man, who whether governing or governed "can't see the forest for the trees." He may think he is soaring toward the Truth—toward the Face of God, but it is Satan's grin that welcomes him at the borders of reality. So it goes with modern man, happy enough with any haven of the mind that satisfies the need of an Out There that torments him.

Membership in sects is one way or other to reestablish links with the mysteries of being. It is a way to search for a vision, a way to put the pieces back together of a fleeting, disintegrating world.

The popular rap artist Bambi Cruz gives vent to his distress in the face of a shattered world in the rhythmic and unnuanced language of rappers. Not everyone appreciates the crude language of rap music, though it is perhaps a sign of the profound distress of our young people. *Ouvre les yeux* [open your eyes] is the title of one of Cruz's songs. The first verse is enough to suggest that the malaise *is* far from being some kind of "make-believe" in rappers' language:

> We're nothing but a bunch of modern slaves,
> Prisoners of a system that keeps making fools of us,
> Our brains are washed and rinsed out like a tee-shirt,
> We're spun, programmed, formatted from the cradle . . .
> Don't tell me I'm the only one who's trying
> To put to this puzzle's pieces back together.

In fact, the world of music clearly reveals the lack of an Out There; devoid of meaning, it seeks substitutes in all kinds of madness—fetishism, for instance, or neo-idolatry.

The phenomenon of groupies and spaced-out fans is another sign of the grand dismantling of the modern world. For want of faith in God, people invent defective gods whose only claim to fame is knowing how to strum a guitar or sway their hips and roar obscenities!

The famous crystallization Stendhal describes in *Sentimental Education* has begun to attain tragic proportions. In the novel, Stendhal likens the sublimation that passion aroused in the beloved to the transformation of a branch into a sparkling jewel when plunged into a salt mine, where it is covered with crystals that transfigure its harmless nature into one that is sacred and superior.

The nothingness in people's hearts turns the merest public bawler into a deity worthy of adoration—and often adored. Thus the crisis of values has become a breeding ground for gods.

It is no mere coincidence that the Beatles phenomenon, which never ceases to have minds in its sway, developed rapidly in 1968, the very year that rebellious young people no longer wanted god or master. Musical expression in the West has always been closely allied with religion; thus the upheaval in its values is a sign of the times, an easily deciphered attestation of rebellion and crisis.

Each century has the music it merits. Classical music was initially intended to give rise to spiritual enthusiasm. The great beauty of its harmony and movement aided the faithful Christian's perception of other harmonies, other beauties.

If music indicates the height of the inner flight of the generation that adopts it, then the music prized by our current youth is the expression of a fatal flight at low altitude. The music today's young people like is a dreadful story in three D's—distress, disorder, and disharmony.

Techno music is metallic din, a load of clanging trash dumped on a scrap heap; it's like environment pollution, the Gulf War, starvation in the southern Sahara. Rap is a monotone succession of desperate yelps: Rock, hysteria; Hard Rock, insanity.

If music is any indication of the state of mind of the generations that practice it, then our young are sending an unmistakable SOS.

A World of Ugliness

Music is certainly no longer a means of communication among souls, as Proust[13] would have it. Unable to fulfill this noble function, music often becomes the catalyst for aggressive and pornographic impulses.

When it is not a springboard to spiritual heights, music is transformed into an unhealthy outlet. For a youth that is disoriented and without secure values, the need of an Out There is transformed into a will for the power to smash everything: it favors the return of Nazism. The electric atmosphere maintained by infernal music downloads hatred into excited minds.

The so-called Skinheads, devotees of such music, have become professionals in the crime against humanity, where violent action crowns their musical trance. These shaved-heads easily pass from syncopated rage to galvanizing action: think of the Turkish families who lost their lives in Germany in a crime premeditated in music!

Endsieg, whose name is very significant (Ultimate Victory), is a German group that advocates the extermination of "Kanaks."[14] Members of this group of thugs scream their vile racism before an overexcited public:

> They come to Germany chomping garlic
> They dirty all they touch
> We've got to beat them up; we've got to kill them
> Let's throw them in jail
> Let's put them in camps.

Endsieg is hardly an exception. The gangs determined to beat up Kanaks are growing in number, and the hatred in their hearts is enormous.

Violence, ugliness, and pitilessness is the message such trendy music conveys, whether it sings of racism, sex, or whatever. Such music has become an explicit hymn to obscenity, a canticle of bad taste and fanaticism.

Art (musical or otherwise), once an expression of the divine, is forced by the curse of the modern times to become a subterfuge, a palliative for the latent lack of the absolute. Like the sects, it has its own gurus and false prophets.

Music is not the sole domain that has plunged from harmonious summits to the bottom of the well of dubious estheticism, the distinctive sign of the perdition of man who turns his back on his God. The art of modern man is no longer capable of capturing the beauty of the heavens or the smile of a Mona Lisa. Instead, all the venom that fills him is flung at the canvas, reproducing in his "art" the utter darkness of a soul bereft of any source of light.

If art is the reflection of the inner being, then it is no mere coincidence if paintings such as Malevitch's monochrome squares are so admired these days with their "fascinating" and chilling simplicity. These immaculate squares aptly represent the absolute void of the modernist mind. A black square posed on a red background: what an expression of the bleakness of the human mind in the face of an uncertain future, without prospects! Isn't red the color of the latent feeling of an impending danger, the reflection of a flame that resists and will not be extinguished?

The fascist critics of modern art were not so indulgent: they labeled it degenerate. But it doesn't take a fascist to distinguish between the art of the harmonious and the esthetic dislocations that we are made to ingest by giving them flattering names like Cubism, Surrealism, the Plastic Arts. If we really believe that art is first and foremost a matter of taste, then modern art, whatever the ism, remains tasteless and odorless. The art modern man takes refuge in is non-art.

Still another sign of the times is revealed by such "art" and the shoals of being it bears witness to. Not only denatured by perverted tastes, it has also become devalued by its all-too-intimate tie to market values—the only values recognized by the liberalizing and globalizing world. Art is no more than a means among others for exploiting multimillionaires yearning for an Out There. In the more modest circles, the merchants of arts will exploit their clientele's snobbery to sell them whatever.

The confession of Picasso, the father of fragmented art, dispenses us from further critiquing the artistic insanity that seems to have infected Northern man. Earlier in his artistic life Picasso painted wonders. But mankind seems to need an Out There, even if—especially if—it is ugly, fragmented, and diverting. Will modern man recognize the mirror of his soul in such "diversion"?

Bearing witness to such modern folly, the great pope of modern painting declares:

> People no longer look to art for consolation and exaltation. The refined, the wealthy, the idle, the distillers of quintessence search for what is new, bizarre, original, extravagant, scandalous. As for me, ever since Cubism and beyond it, I have contented these masters and critics with every peculiar whim that came into my head, and the less they understood it, the more they admired me. By dint of having fun with such games, such nonsense, all those puzzles and stylistic ornaments, I became very quickly famous. Now fame for a painter means sales, profits, fortune, wealth. Today, as you know, I am famous and rich. But when I am by myself I haven't the courage to consider myself an artist in the great and ancient sense of the term. Giotto, Titian, Rembrandt, Goya—those were truly great painters. I am only a public entertainer who understood his time and mined as best he could the idiocy, vanity and cupidity of his contemporaries. This is a bitter confession, more painful than it might seem to be, but it has the merit of being sincere.[15]

From Guernica to Caesar's scrapheap, such is modern art, the expression of a grand malaise generated by an increasingly directionless world. Artists, as Picasso admits, have become public entertainers and, somewhere deep down, miserable clowns as well.

Fatal "Out Theres"

Purchasing the work of a famous painter may be fatal for a bank account. Other purchases of the new and unusual are fatal altogether. I am speaking here of that other scourge of the modernizing world, drugs. For those who are driven by a search for the wondrous, drugs present the deadliest snare. Officially banned, the need of an Out There is otherwise obliging, opening dangerous windows that peer out into illusional spaces and endless labyrinths.

The right to an Out There was once forfeited by the likes of Auguste Comte as being among the most primitive and outmoded expectations in a society aspiring to inhabit the heights of the rational sciences. It has, alas, come once again to be the order of the day, but in the form of substitutes that are diverse, ruinous and mephitic.

Drugs are the most destructive path in the quest of mysticism, a quest that is natural to man but one that has been confiscated by a culture that is exclusive, violent and authoritarian. As La Bruyère aptly wrote, "Men want in part to be slaves, and they draw on that to enable themselves to dominate elsewhere." Drugs, by far more noxious than philosophy, art, or membership in sects and gangs, are nonetheless the surest way to reach in record time phantasmagoric "Out Theres."

If the promotion of all sorts of art is in the hands of certain dubious magnates, even governments have begun to reckon drugs as an irrepressible phenomenon which post-modernity must inevitably embrace. Already, those who are supposed to protect their citizens interpret the evidence such that the need that drives young people to take drugs must be included in the global management of societies—societies that are inevitably declining.

Having waged war in vain against easy profits, they now opt for condoning drugs and managing their distribution in a rational manner so as to limit the damage.[16]

The speeches used to promote such a policy are "noble" and realistic, drawing would-be lessons from the ultimately unsuccessful Prohibition. Better to anticipate events in order to best have them under control. (Why not precipitate them while we are about it?) Countries that know how to draw lessons from the history of this insane world would say, "Let's authorize drugs! We have only to keep an eye on the way they are distributed and, presto, the virtuous political conscience is clear and pleased with itself!"

They call that modernity!

Wise pens dry up in amazement before such decisions that have nonetheless become widespread in the so-called civilized world. Among moderators of opinion, those who try to cry Fire—those who oppose the official absurdity that reigns in their countries—must ultimately resign themselves before the capitulations of the highest echelons of power.

In the Southern Hemisphere the drift of "realistic" governments is not conditioned by neo-humanist considerations, but rather by the will, legitimate in a competitive world, to invigorate public coffers desperately drained by underdevelopment. If it is true that taking drugs has become commonplace and that the practice is very difficult to curb, it is also true that entire economies are based on trafficking in hard drugs, and that serious anti-drug policies pose tremendous risks to unbridled economic liberalism. The drug phenomenon and its tragic repercussions on the human plane belong to the cruel logic of a most vicious cycle.

Where Is Man?

Never has mankind made such pretty speeches and had the means for spreading them so far and wide as now. The most intoxicating speech is surely the one that pretends to defend human rights.

The more these rights are rehashed, the more they are trotted out, the more uncertain and fuzzy they become. The more we depart from man's essence and lose direction, the more we speak of such rights. The greater man's oppression, the livelier the debate. The baser his exploitation, the more his value becomes. The more he is crushed by savage global liberalism, the more it preaches human rights.

Who are these humans with rights? Where are they? Is it that citizen of modernity, bewildered, blasé, frustrated that he cannot seem to consume as much as his neighbor? Is it the drug addict, hooked on his illusions, visiting in tears the infernal paradises that course in his veins? Or might they be the wretched devils of the South, ignorant, indigent, desperate, without a hunk of bread to chew on? Are we *so* remote from one another?

Who is man? Where is he? Few would take the time to pose such crucial questions. We think it sufficient to know the secret of certain equations, to ply the sciences to our ends. Modernist reflection knows only "bicycle logic": how to ride without asking questions, especially questions about the wheels that make the world turn—the world that has become a politico-economic machine!

Pretty speeches anesthetize the conscience: humanity is sinking into a hypnotic state from which only tragic reality can make it come back. Thus drugged—figuratively and literally—man gradually loses his identity and denies the values that characterize his status as human being.

If from our relationship with the world virtue continues to be exiled, our future is seriously compromised. A *human* future, that is. Uncertain futures lurk in the darkness, awaiting the chance to trip us up. Pessimism begins to spread, gently and silently, even in the best of minds—especially in such minds. Well-disposed minds yield to the disastrous passions that seem to have imposed their will.

Only a "square" with a conscience will be shocked by the words of Christian de Brie in the respectable pages of *Le Monde diplomatique:*

Narcostates and narcodemocracies, narcoterrorism and narcoguerillas, narcotourism and narcodollars: drugs have infested every sphere of political, economic and social life. They spread with globalization of the economy and market democracy. They finance terrorism and guerilla warfare. . . . They are the means of survival—if not the sole economic activity—of numerous peasants throughout the South, as well as of the outcasts of urban ghettos. But they are also a precious lubricant of the capitalist financial system and those who operate it. Drugs have multiple functions. It is time to unmask the hackneyed prohibitionist policies used for all ends except for public health; it is time, in view of the realities, to make necessary and long-overdue changes.[17]

Are there no other solutions than abandoning ourselves to this fleeting world's decline? Is there a life more miserable than that of one who, having lost all moral reference, loses his identity in the bargain? Is any lot more wretched than that of man, blinded by the passions of this life, who will rise up blind from the dead?

He who chooses to be blind in this life will rise [from the dead] *blind in the Ultimate Life and will be all the more lost.*[18]

NOTES

1. The famous convict who never despaired of escaping and who broke records attempting to do so.

2. Pierre Thuilier, *La grande implosion: rapport sur l'effondrement de l'Occident 1999–2002* [the big implosion: report on the collapse of the West 1999–2002], Fayard, Paris, 1995.

3. *Le Monde diplomatique*, January 1996, p. 14.

4. Edgar Morin, *Introduction à la pensée complexe* [introduction to complex thought], E.S.F., p. 20.

5. Ibid.

6. Cf. *Le Monde diplomatique*, August 1991, p. 31.

7. Jean-François Raux, in *La société en quête de valeurs* [society in search of values], Maxima, 1996.

8. TN: In my translation of the Qur'ān, I have attempted to remain as close as possible to the author's interpretation of the Holy Book. I say interpretation first because one cannot talk of translation of God's Word revealed in the Arabic language. The second reason or "treason" is elaborately explained by the author in Part III, Chapter V, in the section, "The Qur'ān and Translation." See also *The Holy Qur'ān, Translation and Commentary*, A. Yūsuf Ali, Amana Corp., Brentwood, Md., 1983. In the notes, citations from the Qur'ān (in italics in the text) are identified as in the following note (S. = Sūra, identified by Roman numeral; the Arabic number is that of the verse).

9. Qur'ān: S. LXXXII. 6.

10. Michael Jordan, *Les sectes, prophéties, pratiques et personnalités* [sects, prophecies, practices, and personalities], Ed. PML, 1996, p. 86.

11. *Le Monde*, February 17, 1993. Figures have probably doubled since then.

12. *Le Monde diplomatique*, May 1993, p. 1.

13. Marcel Proust, in *Time Remembered*: "Music is perhaps the unique example of what could have been—had language and word formation not been invented—the communication channel of souls."

14. "Kanaks" refers to Melanesians from New Caledonia, but the term is used symbolically to designate all non-Aryans.

15. Confession made to the writer Giovanni Papini in 1952 and reported by Albert Pilot in *L'art, la science et l'argent* [art, science, and money], La Lyre, Rabat, 1998.

16. Roch Cote, *Drogue: la guerre chimérique* [drugs: the illusory war], *Les Belles Lettres*, Paris, 1996.

17. *Le Monde diplomatique*, April 1996, pp. 22–23.

18. Qur'ān: S. XVII. 72.

I. 2. PHILOSOPHICAL VERTIGO

Just as you do not become healthy by swallowing the dregs of bottles from an ancient pharmacy,
so you do not gather wisdom by muddling your mind with remnants of human philosophies.
Victor Hugo

Certitude, servitude.
Jean Rostand

The rooster does not deviate from his nature—not because he cannot,
but because his pride will not let him.
Lautréamont

THE PHILOSOPHY that defines the ideal around which a society structures its relationships largely determines its composition. Not only does that philosophy set its stamp of approval on anthroposocial relationships, it makes itself the measure of the world and of the leading members of the society. It infests the culture, and it interferes with the sciences in order to use them as it sees fit.

The knowledge a society has of the world and of itself is entirely massed about the prevailing philosophy. Thus it is that when the latter is severed from Revelation—the only source that provides us with a balanced field of vision—it is automatically skewed awry. Philosophical skewing implicates that of the sciences as well; this in turn determines an individual's perception of himself, of life, of his relationships with others, how he manages politics, the economy. When a debased philosophy bears the seal of one in possession of the most impressive arsenal the world has even known, it is even more fatal to humankind. An entire planet, entangled willy-nilly in a deathly labyrinth, finds itself breathing in lethal doses of the fumes of the absurd.

Descartes, the Father of the Modern Malaise

Philosophy is, according to the good old *Grand Larousse*, the "rational study of human thinking, guided by the double point of view of knowledge and action."

Descartes, the uncontested father of the modern illness known as Excessive Rationalism, defined philosophy as "the study of wisdom, and by wisdom I mean not only prudence in affairs, but a perfect knowledge of all things knowable."

In this definition Descartes reveals to us all the confidence he has in himself and in his extraordinary capacity of embracing the whole of human knowledge. Elsewhere he indicates the distinct link between philosophy and science. Descartes himself was both a scientist and a philosopher. In the *Principia philosophiæ* he wrote:

The whole of philosophy can be likened to a tree whose roots are Metaphysics; Physics is the trunk, and the branches that grow out of the trunk are all the other sciences; these can further be reduced to the three principal sciences, Medicine, Mechanics, and Ethics. Ethics, which presupposes complete knowledge of the other sciences, I deem to be the highest and most perfect science and the ultimate degree of wisdom.

Despite the level-headedness behind the thinking that makes Ethics a branch of science, Descartes remains limited in his vision of things, conditioned as he was by the realities of his time. It was then still possible to attempt to embrace all branches of knowledge: the scientific domain had not yet become as complicated as it has since then. In our day one might be tempted to answer him by paraphrasing Shakespeare: "There are more things in heaven and earth, Descartes (Horatio), than are dreamt of in your philosophy."[1] Recent discoveries in Microphysics as well as in Macrophysics have definitely proved that the time of certitudes is well and truly past. Perhaps Shakespeare was more of a philosopher than Descartes!

Philosophical certitudes breed shallow arguments. Surely it was Descartes's certi-tude that all knowledge could be acquired by the philosopher that fired his brain, got his hackles up and made him crow his famous *cogito!*

Descartes is the father of the modern certainties postmodernity means to consign to the scrapheap of History. In comparison with the moderation and majesty of comprehension of a Socrates, the weightlessness of this boastful philosophy demon-strates philosophy's decline. Even the uninitiated person recognizes that Socrates was closer to the truth in advocating modesty in the face of the precariousness of knowledge. His method attests to his conviction that knowledge is not a mere amassing of scattered learning but rather an innate faculty for using this learning in order to gain knowledge.

How are we to rate the whole of Descartes's writings in the face of a single utterance of Plato? Against one breath of Socrates' worthy disciple, what do a thousand computations of Descartes weigh on the scales of wisdom? In a single, brief phrase Plato extracted the quintessence of wisdom: "For this is an experience which is characteristic of a philosopher, this wondering: this is where philosophy begins and nowhere else."[2] Greek paganism had served at least to preserve its philosophers' modesty. The crushing weight of Olympia—populated by a horde of moody gods of unpredictable temperament—allowed them to keep a cool head and a low profile.

Descartes is really of no interest to us here except to note that it was his ideas that, like an underground spring, irrigated all subsequent philosophies. So complex and imposing is his work that all the philosophers who came after him measured themselves by it.[3]

If Malebranche, Spinoza, and Leibniz brought a Christian touch to their writings, Locke, Berkeley, and Hume alike drew their inspiration from Cartesianism. Kant, in his famous Copernican revolution of subject and object, proves himself a

Cartesian in the matter. More recently, Husserl gave his 1929 Paris conferences the title *Méditatations cartésiennes* [cartesian meditations]. Hegel also held up Descartes as a hero.[4]

But the controversies so rich a vein of thought as Descartes's has always raised is not the subject of the present chapter. A critique of Descartes allows us to take indirect aim at a certain manner of thinking that claims to have its roots in his philosophy. Enlightenment Philosophy did not escape the Cartesian tinge that has pervaded subsequent centuries. "Enlightenment" surely expresses a sentiment of well-being of the Europe liberated by such a philosophy from obscurantism. Someone from the South, alas, perceives these luminous effects in a different light, and from another angle. The rising day of the sparkling philosophy, which was to spread its brilliance on cultural nights overseas, would have a blood-red color.

Dark Enlightenment

Nourished by its Cartesian roots, the Enlightenment not only provided the lighting for hunting out the ghosts of the Inquisition; it was also the first spark of the "civilizing" thinking that considered colonizing a humanist *duty*—like a noonday sun shedding light on the dark.

The intellectual flame of Enlightenment's torch would also ignite the stakes erected to the misfortune of other modes of thought. In their academically chaste way, the philosophers of Enlightenment provide legitimacy and a clear conscience to those inveterate arsonists whose impulses are uncurbed before any other way of apprehending the world. Philosophies thought to be the most brilliant often legitimize the darkest of barbarities.

Victor Hugo put it this way, hardly suspecting how well:

Voltaire then reigned; this intelligent ape
sent by the devil on a mission to man[5]

Darwin, capturing a late reflection of Enlightenment splendor, would seek to prove that "ape" can be used in the true sense of the word. The Enlightenment, of which Darwinism is but the extension and the most extreme manifestation, emerged in fact from a cave[6] where men, far from being concerned with the sun, begin to dress themselves in the hides of animals—the cave of the godless.

"Let us crush this infamous thing." So Voltaire used to sign his incendiary letters to d'Alembert. This "infamous thing" was obviously religion. When our "intelligent ape" said "the surest thing is to be sure of nothing,"[7] it was not in reference to the platonistic wisdom of Montaigne, but rather in evidence of Cartesian doubt.

Even though we may accord Voltaire the right to hate a religion that invented tortures in order to save souls, we have also to second Mme. de Deffend, who put this pertinent question to him in a letter: "You are combating and destroying all errors, but what are you putting in their place?"

Passing from methodological doubt into stubborn conviction, Voltaire and many others replaced the "infamy" of the Inquisition with the thorough abomination of pathological navelgazing. They encouraged and promoted the sad reality of human-kind endlessly centered on itself, the hoax of man as an accident of nature.

They freed the mind so as to enslave it the more, "unchaining" Prometheus only to let him swing cruelly over the abyss of nonsense. Buoyed by their corrosive philosophies, the godless man drifts like an anchorless vessel, asea in the infinite anguish of an absurd world. All that might channel man's worse instincts has been destroyed; all questions have been answered—except the essential ones, the questions imposed on us by death and the search for the meaning of life.

Do you sleep content, Voltaire; and your hideous smile,
does it still flash over your fleshless bones?

Thus in the words of de Musset we shall ask Voltaire and all those who advocated nothingness and defended nonsense. None of their dubious doubts have laid our existential anxieties to rest. All conjecture ends in the graves of the philosophers, their corpses as disincarnate as their approaches to man.

A dominating philosophy can therefore be both a culture's framework and its intellectual synthesis. Cartesian thought prepared the Stations of the Cross of future philosophies. A philosophy is always the heir of a history and, when powerful, the source of a dominating mode of thought: a way of life—if not its disarray.

In this perspective of continuity, any philosophy that conceives of humankind without the help of its Creator can only be static, no matter what novelties it introduces. Whatever our illusions concerning the complexity of our world, the eternal human being is a very simple truth. "Homer is new this morning—and nothing is perhaps as old as today's newspaper," said Paul Valéry, wisely.

If our illusions are multiple and tinged, the truth is spotless and ever new. The Prophets alone know how to express the truth in its original purity. In the Scriptures, the parables are strikingly topical: Cain is still slaying his brother; David floors Goliath ever yet, the worship of the Golden Calf goes on; and the "seven plagues of Egypt" nicely describes the scale of current wickedness and modern "Pharaonism."

Unbridled by the absolute, human philosophies become wild imaginings, mad rides of the mind that, rather than bringing us close to the meaning of life and humankind, take us further from it.

Let that be the basis of a salutary epistemology!

All atheist philosophy is a tightrope over the precipice of illogic and nothingness. Any philosophical maneuver that aims to make man annoyed with his eternal truth is merely a transaction that leads inevitably to his spiritual bankruptcy and the decline of human societies.

It is for this reason that the present chapter severely calls into question the thinking of Descartes, which has over the centuries propounded the idea of a mechanistic vision of the world. Wallowing in the bed of history, it rapidly became transformed into a fierce agnosticism.

It may have been a sun, however pale; but it has surely become a black hole opening onto nothingness. Descartes sowed the wind of a philosophical movement that has not ceased to drag down human thinking to the very brink of superficiality and the void. Descartes of course never openly denied the existence of God. Indeed, our philosopher of the triumphal mind used to proclaim that behind this well-oiled machine of a world there surely exists a Sovereign Mechanic.

Within the framework of personal speculation, we may be allowed to think that the confinement of God in a mechanist approach probably sprang from a strategy of diversion in the face of an Inquisition on the look-out. After all, Galileo is Descartes's contemporary. If the former refused to die for Astronomy, our defendant is no more disposed to die for his philosophy, especially since it was hardly worth it.

The comparison is inversely proportional. If by declaring that the earth turned around the sun, Galileo called man's pride into question, Descartes puffed him up again by declaring that the whole world turned around his ego, that all information flowed through his gray matter.

A Unique Mode of Thought

We may in plain language indict Descartes for being the leader of rebellion against a world where God is too present. Had he not, in his youthful writings, admitted that he was hiding his hand? *Larvatus prodeo* [I go forth bewitched] is a mysterious Cartesian phrase that has been the subject of numerous and impassioned commentaries. Some see in it an admission of the esoteric research Descartes had conducted. Others of less vivid imagination content themselves with the thought of our man conducting his works in seclusion and silence.

Blaise Pascal was certainly more perspicacious by asserting in his 77th *Pensée* something we can only share with him as suitably cogitation over the *Cogito*:

> I cannot forgive Descartes; he would have liked to do without God throughout his entire philosophy, but he could not help giving Him a flick of the finger for Him to set the world in motion. After that, he had no further need of God.

Cogito ergo sum: I think, therefore I am! This is the quintessence of Descartes's thinking and the essence that perfumes all the improbable certitudes of the western man of today. Thus thought Descartes; thus spoke Descartes; and thus the modern world that follows him cries "Amen." Having acquired systematic and methodical doubt, man lets himself become lost among the fragile connections of his neurons.

The rational thinking Descartes devoted himself to establishing and refining came to be set up as a universal and exclusive mode of thought, arrogant and scornful of any other. It quickly became the only received, conceived, and acceptable way permitted of understanding the world.

All men and all cultures are enjoined to obey and adopt this mental hypertrophy as a natural state befitting modern and civilized man. Wherever they are, whoever they are, men are either Cartesians or dangerous fundamentalists, unless, as inhabitants of regions of little interest to certain geopolitical strategies, they are merely simple exotic subjects arousing the curiosity of the white man, the cogitating man.

In the latter chapters of this book, we will see that *islam* is in no way a religion of rambling and delirium. It is just the opposite. There is a world of difference between recognizing the rational mind and setting it up as a god, on whose altar any other measure of man is sacrificed. *Islam* encourages man never to make such a leap, never to tame reason so. Cartesian doubt made rationality the absolute initiator of man, who thereby becomes inevitably, dangerously, fatally, and tragically one-dimensional. "Disjunction and reduction" summarize Edgar Morin's description of Cartesian thinking, the origin of the modern and prevailing thought. In his *Introduction à la pensée complexe,* he writes these sound reflections:

> In the history of the West we may diagnose the domination of a paradigm formulated by Descartes. Descartes disconnected the domain of the subject, reserved for philosophy and inner meditation, from the domain of the object, the domain of scientific, measurement, precision. Descartes formulated this disjunction very well, and it has come to prevail in our world. It increasingly separates science from philosophy, the culture of human affairs from that of literature, poetry, the arts and sciences. The former, founded as it is on reflection, can no longer be nourished by objective knowledge. The latter, founded on the specialization of knowledge, cannot reflect on itself by itself.[8]

The culture of the "disconnected man" of meager wingspan, the little man, small-minded and one-dimensional, is nonetheless determined. Bloated with conceit, it intends to convert the world to its narrow and obtuse views. With its weaponry and its media it has, alas, the necessary arsenal to do just that.

For a long time now Descartes has held the world in his clutches, disconnecting and reducing Western man to his sorry, wounded state. We may well wonder why he had so great an impact on succeeding generations. Why has Descartes's name alone endured and had issue? Why has his name garnered such praise and prestige—and not, for example, Pascal's? How is it that rational thought—self-confident, wrapped in certitudes, exact and verifiable to the eye or under the microscope—become synonymous with "Cartesian thinking"?

Why hasn't the adjective "Pascalian" passed into everyday language? Why are certain points of view automatically dismissed? Why is Pascal—and many others more interesting than Descartes—so reluctantly cited in the curriculum, a brilliant mind but for some scruple consigned to oblivion, rather than a reference worthy of being the basis of a general way of thinking?

Pascal (since we have chosen him as a witness of this intellectual isolation) was brilliant enough to have been forgiven his bigotry and not completely rejected.[9] Yet his defect prevented him from becoming *the* reference. His paradigms did not suit the direction Europe would choose in the course of its revolt against the Church—and against the god that Church represented.

Morin's definition of a paradigm allows us to understand the success Cartesian thought has had:

> A paradigm, if it is to be formulated by somebody—Descartes for instance—is basically the product of a whole cultural, historical and civilizational development.[10]

Thus Pascal's thinking would not be chosen to mold culture. It has remained instead a kind of historical property that the likes of Jacques Attali would take pleasure in reshaping, just a few years ago, carefully erasing the aura of saintliness that has clung to the man by denigrating his image with an allusion to his incest with his sister.

Nothing is sacred! There are no more taboos, only totems. Pascal is revised and corrected by Attali for being too religious. Attali's scalpel will perform miracles in order to bring his patient's profile into conformity with the modern esthetic norm. A small incision here, a small addition there and voilà, the face-lift is miraculous! Smeared by this story of incest, Pascal's thoughts will assume a timelier, more spicy allure. "The heart has its reasons that reason knows not," once the expression of faith and mysticism, has strangely become ambiguous. Pascal is updated as mere amusement and nothing more.

Voyeurism and an obsession with the sordid, having become the religion of the godless, make them transfer modern man's baseness even onto the ancients. The ideas of Pascal and others are revisited in a plot against wisdom in its classical sense. The thinking of the past is manipulated, dissected, reordered, revised, denied, and refashioned in order to be foreclosed and cleared of its metaphysical whims. The great ideas of the past are aswarm with new readings tinged with modern man's cultural heritage and the color of his denial.

Even Descartes's thinking, despite its honorable modern reputation, is carefully expurgated and represented as Holy Secularity wishes. It has become divested of its depth, laundered of any sense of the divine. Its principles have been turned upside down so as to become more Cartesian than Descartes, more Catholic than the Pope.

As absolute rebellion against the absolute, the modernist approach not only removes the halo from the divine, it even strips it of its workman's clothes: Descartes's Great Mechanic is no longer welcome.

Lilliput

Manipulator and downright rebel against God, "modernicious"[11] man engages in philosophical disinformation. Denying his past, he no longer presents the ideas that stamped his history without first rearranging and reinventing them so as to appear rational. He has done this so well and so completely that every spiritual incongruity has been purged, and his world has been transformed into a desert where not even the mirage of an absolute remains.

Modern man's vaunted life of the mind has become a cancer of the brain. His crippling headaches have only just begun. His thinking can only be painful, since it is the expression of a contemporary inflammation of the brain, the dizziness of his reeling ego. Now that the age of the great philosophers is over, only the mediocre thoughts of second-rate cogitators remain. Man no longer makes use of the profound reflection that has always made him a creature apart. In the North, he has too many leisure activities; in the South, he does not have the means.

Scattered, dissipated, overinformed, overnourished, the navel-gazing Northener cares only about his outlook, his instincts.

Scattered, dissipated, indigent, misinformed, malnourished, the Southerner submits in resignation to the curse of one-eyed philosophies determining the international policies that inflict on him all sorts of wrongs and outrages.

Between these extremes, it is true that a variety of realities exists in both North and South. Even so, hope in man's humanity often dwells in unsuspected areas. In this equation, the man of the South is the less underprivileged, since he often remains in control of his reason. The opulence of the Northern is usually a curtain that fails to conceal his moral and spiritual indigence. Behind the gilded veil lurks a fearsome moral distress and a fatal lack of meaning.

This caustic criticism of Descartes and the accusation leveled against the citizen of the modern world are not meant to imply that modern man has been wearing himself out poring over the pages of the *Discours de la méthode*. Descartes is merely the instigator of a way of thinking that, within an anthroposocial framework, is internalized by the individual as a kind of second nature and injected by everyone in the consensual management of social issues.

Enlightenment Philosophy was already an internalized and politicized version of Cartesian thinking. Secularism would play a decisive role in popularizing and broadly circulating such thinking. The Cartesian ideal would slowly seep into the intellectual and emotional landscape of the West. Although it was to lose its rigor, abandon its clarity, and become more an alibi than a reflection, it would have an enormous impact.

Faltering already at the outset of that socio-historical shift, the Cartesian idea soon became a mindless habit—and a habitual mindlessness. Putting an idea into practice often weakens its vigor, and popularizing it almost always presupposes its trivialization. Any reliable caricaturist, if asked to represent his modern contemporary, will depict him in the pangs of intellectual birth, his brow wrinkled from excessive cogitation. Jacques Brel, the Belgian singer and poet, splendidly sketches the man of today as a Lilliputian in his "tiny coat, tiny car, tiny hat."[12]

We might amuse ourselves by adding to this list of "tiny" attributes of this dwarfish heir of modernity's stunted philosophies.

Salutary Doubt

It was these supposedly epic philosophies that gave birth to these dwarfish minds. In advocating a *tabula rasa,* Descartes deprived us of many good things that, had he discerned them, might have nourished sound thinking. He might have avoided serving his guests a potluck dinner, where indigestible grub takes the place of gourmet offerings.

Yet Descartes, notwithstanding all we have written about him, was far from shabby! He merely opened a Pandora's box of spiritual aridity for which humankind has paid dearly and will pay even more. His thinking, as great and profound as any mechanistic thinking could be, shriveled up at the scorching breath of the historical hatred that was prepared to hang its clerics with the guts of its kings.

That is regrettable in itself, since even a mechanical understanding of the world, by means of his neurons, remains one of the relatively better ways of doing so. In any case it is a nobler view than the one that prevails today—one that originates in organs other than the brain and thus favors a vision of humankind even more simplistic and utterly bestial.

The object of this chapter is, however, not to reject at all costs the idea of man using his head. The question is whether that is the *only* allowable and honorable way for him to be.

Cogito ergo sum, I think therefore I am, so be it! But perhaps for this expression to have universal validity, that is, to fully express the immutable truth of man in harmony with the scheme of things, we must add, "I am . . . who?"—thus raising questions that would give pause to Cartesian self-satisfaction.

This small addition turns the assertion into a question, opening horizons instead of closing them. The expression so modified will better suit the reality of the modernist man whose cocksure assertions have less resonance for those who are beset by more recent uncertainties. Certain scientific discoveries in the field of quantum physics have surely aroused a new generation of doubts.

Edgar Morin lifts a small corner of the veil on the malaise that touches the few who are concerned about these matters:

> The microphysical breach revealed the interdependence of the subject and the object, the insertion of unknown factors into knowledge, the dereification of the notion of matter, and the eruption of empirical contradiction. The macrophysical breach has joined in the same entity the heretofore absolutely heterogeneous concepts of time and space, and has broken all our concepts once they were taken beyond the speed of light. Yet these two breaches, it was believed, were far from our world: one in the infinitesimal, the other in the infinitely great. We did not want to realize that the moorings of our conception of the world had just been broken in the two infinites, that, between them, we were not on the solid ground of an island surrounded by an ocean, but on a flying carpet.[13]

The world once thought to be well finished, well defined, well covered, well visited, and well recorded begins to undulate beneath our feet. Doubt will likely become the sole wisdom in our days. To doubt is keenly recommended, but not the methodical doubt that is based on nihilism as a guiding principle. Many centuries before Descartes and Morin, Ghazali (Algazel)[14] taught us what kind of methodical doubt is that makes sense instead of losing it. In his work, such doubt takes another dimension and promises the soul healthy food instead of leaving it starve to death around a desperately empty table. Let us read what pure wisdom might be:

> How can you trust perception? Is vision not the best sense to apprehend the world? Does the shadow not appear motionless whereas it moves incessantly? Does not the star seem the size of a dinar whereas in fact it is bigger than earth? I have ceased to believe in sensory perception; should I perhaps believe only in the mind and in the truths it has proved? But who can assure me that the confidence I have in the mind may not also prove to be less valid than the one I had in my senses? Who can assure me that there exists no other power that, should I acquire it, will not discredit my reason just as it made me lose confidence in my sensory perceptions. I clarify the idea by evoking the issue of sleep. Do we not regard our dreams in unreal things? Do we not take them as realities and then awaken to discover that none of it really exists? Who can assure me that what we perceive with our senses or our mind—all that we experience in life—is true? Perhaps one day you may be in a state similar to your waking state in relation to your sleeping state, where the realities of today will seem to you as those in your sleep. [. . .] You will then be certain that all your mind thought to have absorbed will prove to be but pure illusion. For then you will be told: *We have removed your veil and sharp is your sight this Day.*[15]

Death in the Soul

Is it not rational and reasonable to place in the center of any epistemology the sole absolute truth of man, his death? Is death not to be taken into account as a deciding element in any exact or less exact knowledge of man?

Western literature abounds in relatively bitter reflections on death.[16] Yet its relationship to death is one of apprehension and rejection, marked by taboos. When death is spoken of, it is only to be declared defeated, repulsed, delayed; it is never seen serenely, at peace with oneself. At the onset of the postmodern era, talking carelessly about death is a sign of an acutely psychopathic state. Like AIDS, it is something to be shielded against.

"Think positive" is the leitmotif of the moment. It is an extreme negativism, indeed even an extreme negation of the social order, to speak of death, to deal with it, to make of it an art or an affair. Thinking too much of death is the expression of serious behavioral problems, the symptom of obvious mental illness. Modern man is enjoined to brave the idea of death, entitled to flirt sometimes with it in an occasional adrenalin attack, but never invited to espouse it and live in harmony with it. The age of morbid reflection is gone. The longevity realized thanks to modern medicine is inebriating, giving the illusion of a false eternity.

Freud, another pope of mankind rebelling against God, diametrically opposed *Thanatos* with *Eros* in his arguments. *Eros* is raised to the skies while *Thanatos* is devalued. Death's impulse is negative and pathological. To accept death and ask questions about what awaits us after death is a defect, a terrible deviation to be combatted, an illness to be cured. Thus, each day that God makes, Freudianized mankind repels and sterilizes the idea of death: there is no good or bad philosophizing about this subject. Better not think about it at all!

Modern man is a fighter. He is not supposed to mix life and death in the same breath. The dead are dead, their "vital functions" (hollow words to describe life) have ceased; the living go on to conquer the world—period!

Modernity would love to get rid of death once and for all and erase it from our minds. It would have liked to flee from it—yet death dwells in the depths of our being. It haunts us. It is born with us: it never leaves us, it invades our genes, and no miraculous remedy can beat or stop it. It is the only state shared equally by us all.

A philosophy that does not hold death to be crucial is a lie, an illusion, a wild imagining, a vertigo, nausea.

NOTES

1. TN: *Hamlet,* Act I, Scene V.

2. TN: Plato, "Theaetetus" (155d), in the *Complete Works,* ed. John M. Cooper. Indianapolis, Cambridge: Hackett Publishing Company, 1997.

3. *Encyclopedia Universalis*: René Descartes.

4. Ibid.

5. Victor Hugo, *Les Rayons et les ombres* [rays and shadows], 1840.

6. In the Platonic sense of the word.

7. Cf. Voltaire, *Singularités de la nature* [nature's peculiarities].

8. Morin (1990), p. 103.

9. TN: Pascal "turned from preoccupation with the scientific to the study of man and his spiritual problems and found faith as a sounder guide than reason," Dagobert D. Runes, *Dictionary of Philosophy.* Philosophical Library, New York, 1960, p. 226.

10. Morin, ibid.

11. Cf. Claire Bombardier, *Lettre ouverte aux Français qui se prennent pour le nombril du monde* [an open letter to the French who consider themselves the "navel of the world"], Albin Michel, 2001. The term "modernicious" (Fr. *moderniseux*) refers to the unhealthy modernist passion to convert the whole world to the principle of "sameness," a tendency equally denounced by Gilles Deleuze.

12. *"p'tit manteau, p'tite auto, p'tit chapeau."*

13. Morin (1990), p. 27.

14. Ghazali (1058–1111). Jean Calmard describes him in the *Dictionary of Islam: Religion and Civilization,* Albin Michel, 1997, p. 319, as a theologian who abandoned traditional teaching and his position as the caliph's advisor to found a mystic doctrine based on the principle of doubt as a path for reaching certitude. Referring to al-Ghazālī's *Al Munqidh,* the author says, "In the book, there is a sort of intellectual and religious autobiography similar to the *Discours de la Méthode:* indeed like Descartes, Ghazali goes in search of certitude through doubt."

15. Morin (1990); citation from the Qur'ān: S. L. 22.

16. By literature I mean all that is read, ranging from poetry to philosophy.

I. 3. THE SOUL'S RUIN

Since wisdom, according to Solomon the sage, does not enter the malevolent soul,
science without conscience cannot but be the soul's ruin.
François Rabelais

The profit of our study is to become better and wiser.
Michel de Montaigne

Just as a heap of stones is not a house, so the accumulation of facts is not science.
Raymond Poincaré

One can only call science those returns that are always successful. The rest is literature.
Paul Valéry

Better laugh about it!
In this chapter methodical doubt gently draws us alongside a beautiful beach. A fifty-year-old man is seated there alone; his brow is wrinkled, his look is pensive. His profile is vexed, and all his attention is strangely captured by turtles waddling out of water. The vigorous plashing of the waves does not make him lose his concentration.

Hush! Let time suspend its flight, the hours cease their course—for here someone is thinking. Someone is pondering the truth of truths, the secret of secrets. A new science is stirring in the mind of this mysterious character, and, like Athena, is about to burst open the skull of its father and run to announce the good news to all humankind.

Modern man's new religion is being born on the Galápagos Islands. There Darwin is giving birth to the Messiah-like science that he will offer his successors as an eternal Christmas, a pagan Christmas, an anti-Christmas. There on the Galápagos Islands Darwin is inventing the myth of the Superfish that decided to make a revolution by unleashing evolution.

Poets are indeed more sensible than philosophers, even though the latter dress up their "subcortical swoons" as scientific information. With premonitory mockery and pre-Darwinian candor, La Fontaine scoffed at the frog that wanted to look bigger than an ox and, straining to change his shape, exploded.

Who knows? The fables of the old wise Frenchman might have been different had he been born after Darwin. He would surely have changed his tune and gone with the flow. Morality would then have lost a good master, and his fables would also have lost their originality, since Darwin not only surpassed him in imagination but succeeded in doing what he had never managed to do: convincing people of the veracity of his fables.

Let us imagine for a moment that La Fontaine was Darwin's contemporary and supported his theory of evolution. He might have written this:

The Fish That Wanted to Evolve—and Did So

Mister Fish with legs,[1] tired of his pond,
Woke up one morning in a happy mood.
He saw the sun shine murkily outside
And filled his gills with a desire to reach it.

He swelled so much, he nearly killed himself,
But one who does not swell will never molt.
So well he did it that he came to change,
Running about the banks in sheer delight.

But having promised one last backward glance,
He turned to look once more at all his cousins.
They hadn't bothered to evolve—not them!—
Contented to be sluggish spawn forever.

He very nearly reached the shady shores
When first he sprouted such a smart new tail,
and then a bloated muzzle—whereupon
He lost his scales and grew a coat of down.

Intoxicated by this change of state,
He hardly knew which branch he might begin—
Lucy perhaps, Cro-Magnon, Neanderthal—
Or dawdle playfully between two chains.

To be an ape was surely very charming,
But grudgingly he came to give it up,
Unable to resist his grand ambition:
He wanted human shape, and there he headed.

His dreams of power pushed him ever further.
Eager to evolve, he leapt through links
And, out of breath but always perservering,
He got it in his head to be a man!

And so his countless dreams came true at last,
For, having shot down all that stood before him,
Destroying all that blocked his chosen path,
He soon was walking on the moon itself!

Such is the great wisdom of the forests,
Especially when emerging from the swamps:
Whoever would evolve must kill the others,
For Earth is far too small for all mankind.

Let us admit that laughter is not to be taken for serious criticism. But better laugh about it first! We might even have been content to laugh, as if it were a Disney cartoons if only this thesis were merely a thesis. Yet this poisonous philosophy happens to be the blessed daily bread of a deicide civilization as well as the running water it drinks without suspecting its high degree of toxicity.

No criticism, however well founded, has succeeded in ridding the prevailing philosophy of this morbid notion. Although it is a pseudoscience founded on a bestial premise, it endures despite repeated announcements of its imminent demise.

Every God-given day, honest men of science disprove the deception and revile the fraud of Darwinian verbiage—in vain! Every day the sun rises, a new voice den-ounces the falsehood turned into theory and proposes to open a new path for a serious research that proves the opposite of what our modern idiocy swallows whole as the absolute truth of man. No matter how high voices rise, no matter how many sound minds revolt, Darwin is the only one heard, the only one believed, the only one sworn by.

Morin who defines the paradigm as the outcome of a multidimensional process, is absolutely right.[2] If Darwinism had not existed, it certainly would have been invented sooner or later. It is the natural ending of the Promethean myth and the necessary eschatology of the non-believer who killed his gods and overthrew his masters. It is a bitter harvest of a doubly rooted germination: the affiliation attributed to the vanished Greek culture and the one active and contributory to a current and eventful history of a West that wages war on religion.

We will content ourselves here with observing Darwinism from the cultural angle—the only one of interest to us, anyway, since even the exact sciences are culturally based. Ilya Prigogine, the Nobel prize-winning physicist, confirms this fact, making of this idea one of his central arguments: "It is urgent," he maintains, "that the sciences be recognized as an integral part of the culture in which they develop."[3]

For the time being, Darwinism is far from being considered as a cultural expression. It is presented as a scientific absolute.

There is no question whatsoever of dissecting transformism within the realm of science. Others not short of competence and valid arguments have done so in vain. Others well-equipped against the oil slick have strived to remove it from the scientific landscape and consign falsehood to the scrap heap of thinking, but have failed.

We will not, therefore, take part in pursuing the particulars of that grinning-monkey theory, nor do we intend to lose ourselves in the maze of its sad philosophy. The sole aspect to hold our attention is the relationship of cause and effect between

Darwinism and anti-clericalism. Therein resides the secret of the theory's success. It is apparently the *coup de grâce* dealt to the Church's theses, and the scientific legitimation of agnosticism, and perhaps atheism as well.

Darwin against the Church

Christianity, as distorted by the Evangelists and then taught by the Church for long centuries, is rebarbative.[4] Combined with the Church's violent repression against the evangelized society, the unnatural vexation intrinsic to its precepts gradually eroded the power of the Church. The faithful became gradually less faithful in their minds and then in their deeds, first in private life and then public life. The mass refutation of God materialized in the political domain in a long process of rejection that commenced with bloodshed and ended in the rigor of a secularism beyond appeal.

It is interesting in this regard to notice the coincidence between the rigorous application of secularism in a particular nation and the hieratic quality of the Church in its past relations with the said nation. The more intimate the relationship with the latter was in the past, the more furious secularism is today. France, the former eldest daughter of the Church, is today the mother of a rigid secularity and the enemy of religion.[5]

Darwinism as a thesis cannot be isolated from this socio-historical context. It is the philosophical face of the revolt against the Church's absolutism. Excessive "devoutness" and obscurantism soon discredited the faith in a Church from playing an intermediary role between Heaven and earth. The constant reminder to "turn the other cheek," the bullying about sexuality, and the schemes of the clergy became so many nagging invitations to revolt.

Being a good Catholic meant not being human. From this arose the prestige of the men of the Church: they were to be perfect on behalf of others. In their dealings with such obscure and purple-clad men, the faithful had the right to a weekly absolution that amply sufficed as religious practice. They contented themselves with having their sins removed in their purifying confessionals.

Confession serves to relieve the faithful of the burden of their misdeeds, permitting them to savor with clear consciences other wicked actions while awaiting the following week. Their saintly men have in their possession a magic eraser that erases liabilities from the balance sheet: it has the shape of a cross.[6]

The religion that exhorts its churchmen to be angels will be doomed to the hell of humanist philosophies. Rebelling against such a concept of man is all the more justifiable in light of the history of the Church, which is far from being a mere chronicle of choirboys.[7] You have only to leaf through the almanacs of history to be convinced that the Church, while perhaps preoccupied with chastity and absolution, has not busied itself exclusively with these concerns.

It would take much time to dwell on the simonies and intrigues of popes and other senior dignitaries of the Church. As that is not the subject of the present chapter, we will only assert that the Church that sang the praises of the Kingdom of Heaven got blithely involved in some shady business with the kingdom on earth. Some historians assert that the nurseries of this pious hypocrite swarmed with bastards and that its ambitions were merely temporal, hegemonic and sometimes carnal.

Such contradictions provoked schisms in the Roman Church, and the silly faithful that swallowed all its nonsense became scarce. The man of the Church became progressively less admired, more suspected, and subjected to irony.

Literature, the mirror of the times and the teacher of critical thinking, saw to the wearing away of the halos of wingless angels. Ridiculing them on the stage, the inspired comedian Molière, a shrewd observer of the moral standards of his time, brought the critical mind to bear on a heretofore sacrosanct institution. He did so on a broadly popular scale.[8] His theater so much delighted the era where the first signs of total revolution against the absolute (still perceived in the Church) were being felt that the title of one of his plays, *Tartuffe* (a proper name), became a common name describing treachery and hypocrisy.

It was regarded as a duty to drag through the mud the men supposed to represent God and then the idea of God Himself. The obsession and passion aroused by this subject were very clear in all artistic trends ever since the end of the eighteenth century. To display one's atheism was a means of being provocative. To have no belief in God became gradually a sign of intelligence, a stamp of originality that distinguished one from the trivial multitude.

The campaign, it is true, began on the quiet in a mitigated trial of strength with clericalism. Voltaire, for instance, would adopt the narrative genre—despite his contempt for that literary genre—in order to flay kings and clerics in all quietude. In his *Zadig* a certain "Yebor, the most stupid and fanatic of the Chaldreans," who wants to impale the hero for having a poor opinion of griffons, is none other than Bishop Boyer, as Voltaire indicated in a notice preceding a posthumous edition. Yebor is an anagram of the churchman who attempted to prevent Voltaire from entering the French Academy.

Anticlericalism spread slowly but surely. Gradually, tongues were loosened and religious convictions faded; the cold war waged against religion turned into total warfare: the triumphant war rhyme was Positivism, Existentialism, Naturalism, Marxism. . . .

Darwinism takes its place in the onslaught against a suffocating and hypocritical Church.

A chess game began between those who wanted man to assume his humanity and live free and liberated, and those who wanted him to be a spineless character resigned to submit to the powerful authority of the Catholic Church as the servant of an inaccessible God. The game spread over three centuries. Darwinism is eager to call a resounding checkmate. The game is over. The chessboard is even smashed on the back of an absolutist absolute.

The sole force of the rebellious (and revolting) theory is that it has released Prometheus and put an end altogether to a long harangue where the absolutism of the absolute was always the winner. Darwinism is merely the last movement of the requiem in honor (in dishonor) of the confounded Christian. Far from being a scientific—and therefore universal—thesis, it is only a pathetic family story: hatred against a father that ends up in crime. The father is not only murdered but his corpse is fiercely and horribly attacked.

Philosophical murder is the last stage of the emancipation of Christian society, the ultimate weapon for settling scores with the Father in Heaven. With Darwinism, modernity makes of man the smug parricidal heir, the absolute master in a playful and permissive world.

If there are still some children of Christianity who have refused to take part in the crime and who attempt to denounce the damned children, their arguments are weak, their convictions are shaky, and their reasoning is marginalized. The Creationists, the Vitalists, and the other defenders of the Bible find it extremely difficult to defend a Book that swears with science that the neo-Darwinists have no right to defend their beliefs in light of recent paleontologic discoveries.

The War of Religion

Serious and total war began between the two religions. During the first centenary celebrated in Chicago in 1959 in honor of the publishing of *The Origin of Species,* Julian Huxley exultantly expounded the objectives of the new religion that had ousted the old one:

> In the evolutionary scheme of thought there is no longer either need or room for the supernatural. The earth was not created, it evolved. So did all the animals and planets that inhabit it, including our human selves, mind and soul as well as brain and body. . . . At last the evolutionary vision is enabling us to discern, however incompletely, the outline of the new religion which, we can be sure, will arise to serve the needs of the coming era.[9]

It is worth pointing out that the word "fundamentalist" was born exactly in the wake of the war between the Christian religion and the religion of the apes. In 1910 ninety American theologians solemnly ranked Darwinism among heresies and signed a petition aiming to ban its teaching as a scientific truth: "Christian truths must be announced without reducing them in conformity to the current mentality" is an idea, among others, that the document defends.[10] That led William Jenning Bryan to publish, in July of 1923, an article entitled "The Fundamentals," setting forth the common fundamental principles on which these evangelic Protestants refused to compromise in their insistence on condemning "certain repercussions of modernism."[11]

Christianity defended itself with all its might. Already in 1913, under the banner of doctrinal integrity, the Catholic church rejected any notion of evolution from a religious system meant to be kept as a doctrinal whole.

The world of Christianity resists as best it can the assaults of the new religion that wages a crusade on what remains of the faith in its god. Is there the least doubt that the meaning of Darwinism and secularism bears significance only in relationship to Christianity itself? After all, the spirit of the Inquisition, a papal and exclusively Christian invention, provoked hard-line secularism and the isolation of the divine after so many shock waves in the course of history. The Bible, a book with stories fraught with nonsense, gave and still gives legitimation to the theories of man creating himself.[12] Darwinism itself finds a breeding ground in the unintelligible passage of Holy Scripture in which it grows and develops like an indestructible mold that gradually sweeps across everything.

Darwinian pseudoscientists have pledged to make life hard for theism and force it back to its trenches where they hope to keep it in the background. Fair enough—isn't this just the reverse of the trials of science conducted by the church? *Vade retro, Satana!* Darwinism is a theory heated up so as, in Victor Hugo's phrase, "to cauterize hell." That is the logic of war; the positioning is rigid and the defeats of the Former Exterminator are boundless.

In a debate held in 1997, the French sociologist Danielle Hervieu-Léger enumerated the consequences of relegating spirituality to the private sphere. In a rational modern society, the assertion of the individual and a "diversity of spheres of social activity" has, according to her, forced the narrowing of the space of religion. The situation for religion is, as she sees it, likely to deteriorate further, since "from 1959 on the number of priests who die is greater than that those who get ordained," and that "among young people between 18 and 24, religious practice [in France] is less than 4%."[13]

The great defeat is not only reflected in the dwindling number of priests but also in the poor quality of faith. Most believers struggle with themselves to remain confident in their religion.

The fiercest struggles are often mental. Many followers of Christianity—Catholic and Protestant alike—finding the Bible indefensible, accommodate secularism and use cunning with themselves. They indulge in elaborate mental gymnastics to be in the picture with the ape-like and conquering theses. The Holy Book, their reference claimed to be God's Word, is not well put together and cannot ward off the fierce attacks of the modern faith. The subterfuge in vogue consists in con-sidering faith as pertaining to the subjective domain and science to the objective.

In his *Evolution and the Foundation of Ethics,* the perspicacious William Provine, eminent Professor of History at Cornell University asserts that it is impossible to escape conflict between science and religion insofar as no one who maintains his religious beliefs while accepting modern evolutionary biology can do so without checking his brains at the churchhouse door.[14]

Some Christian believers defy antinomy, finding a syncretism that reveals the terrible losses among classical spirituality. Teilhard de Chardin is perhaps the best illustration of such unusual casuistry and the inventor of the Omega Point, a parabola at the crossroads of *nirvana,* the Christian Heaven and Universal Conscience. The name itself has a taste of the fantastic, which confirms the subject developed in the first chapter of this book.

The declaration that follows resembles more a hymn to evolutionary theory than an alleged desire to strike a balance between the abject materialism it spreads and the expiatory spirituality of the Christian faith. It is interesting for us insofar as it is a testament to the landslide victory of the villainous bestial tenet, a dark tenet notwithstanding the touch of brightness that the latter-day mystic wants to put in it:

> Is evolution a theory, a system, or a hypothesis? It is much more—it is a general postulate to which all theories, all hypotheses, all systems must henceforth bow and which they must satisfy in order to be thinkable and true. Evolution is a light which illuminates all facts, a trajectory which all lines of thought must follow—that is what evolution is.[15]

Amen! Others less adamant but no less shaken in their convictions by this philosophical upheaval will say that macroevolution is a possible explanation of the manner in which God created new forms of life! As if God was in need of a "manner" to create or as if He had one and endeavored to make it evident to us.

Oh the boundless vanity of the "ape" that thinks too much, or rather of the "Superfish" bewildered by the infernal blow of evolution!

Happy Conversion

It is a misjudgment of the exclusivism and intolerance of the new clergy to imagine that such a mixture of genres is acceptable to their members. Even the most accommodating among these reconcilers of religions does not merit the indulgence of those who attend to the supremacy of the conquering evolutionist tenet. In this regard, the adventures of the American Scientific Affiliation (ASA) with a cleaning campaign conducted by the Church of Darwin are highly demonstrative.[16] The buried pharisaicisms of the ASA, tolerated for a while by the Darwinism omnipresent and omnipotent in scientific circles, were rejected the moment its speech became clear.

The publication of the booklet entitled "Teaching Science in a Climate of Controversy: a view from the American Scientific Affiliation," in reply to a fascicle published in 1984 by the Academy of Sciences, gave rise to an energetic general outcry in the evolutionist milieu.[17]

William Benetta, well-known devourer of Creationists, organized a reprisal by mobilizing heavy artillery and summoning the help of great scientific figures to shoot down the opuscule. These leading scientists declared the latter to be no more and no less than "an attempt to replace science by a pseudo-scientific system devoted to the confirmation of biblical accounts."[18]

Similar expressions with some closer inversions probably preceded the kindling of the pyres of the Inquisition: "An attempt to replace God with a pseudo-scientific system devoted to the negation of biblical accounts" was probably the public indictment leveled against the accused burnt at the stake. At least the gentle Christians of the ASA will have learned that the principle of "turning the other cheek" has no equivalent in the religion of the apes. If you venture to give them a slap, they will make it a duty to squash you. That's only natural—they are still in the era of the Crusades.

To believe in a god other than the one of natural selection is to merit the hell of the right-thinking guardians. The ASA is not the only institution to have dealt with the new knights of a theory that, for want of being round, goes round in circles. The men of science and the conservatives attached to the British Museum of Natural History have also tasted the torments of the new crusaders who do not loll about and miss no opportunity to lynch non-believers.

The centenary of the building hosting the Museum was celebrated in 1981 by a presentation on Darwin's theory. A welcoming board wrote:

Have you ever wondered why there is such a diversity of human beings? According to one view, all the living beings we see today evolved from a distant ancestor through a process of gradual transformation. How has evolution been able to transform itself into something else? The presentation you are going to hear examines a possible explanation—that of Darwin himself.

Who could think ill of Darwinism while reading such assertions? Nonetheless, Darwinist purists deem as blasphemous any questioning of the bestial tenet—something not to be tolerated. The eyes of naturalist censure quickly detected heresy, especially when an adjacent board brazenly stated: "According to another view, God created all perfect and immutable things."

The Museum's schizophrenia expressed in such dual speech did not move the crusaders of the absurd to pity. This time, the valiant knight launching the offensive was someone named L. B. Halstead. The columns of *Nature,* the main scientific review in Great Britain, opened fire on Kensington's old building, accused of having too heavy an anti-Darwinism record.

The charge was uncompromising and sustained. The lesson to be learned from the capitulation would make itself known in 1987. That year's visitor would find no trace of the misdemeanor that cost the Museum the severe reprisal of the Planet of the Apes philosophers. Converted and well ordered, corrected and docile, the welcoming board, formerly sacrilegious, sang a rousing alleluia to the new and invincible dogma, along with a touching *mea culpa:* "Comparing ourselves to our fossil cousins, we see the proof of our having evolved."

It continued its prostration before the absolute of the moment by invoking the conquering deities, saying: "The works of Darwin have largely supported the understanding according to which all living beings have developed to the forms we see today through a process of gradual transformation spread over very long periods. That is what we call evolution. Many people believe that the theory of evolution is not in conflict with their religious convictions."

The conversion is complete! The one who pretends to have been self-created has all the rights, while the one who pretends to establish links between God and science must hides his hand. The mixture is often thunderous, since it provokes an angry response from the right-thinking guardians of modernity.

Capitulations

On this subject, the book *Dieu et la science* [God and science] offers an excellent illustration of the widespread spiritual and intellectual cowardice before the denseness of evolutionism, an example of the loathsome and general silence before the sustained bawling of the Darwinist choirboys.

In the book, Jean Guitton,[19] much to our good fortune, converses with Igor and Grichka Bogdanov, astrophysicists of great renown. With the evidence to prove it, the two scientists clearly say that life could not have been created by chance. The idea of God as evidence implicitly accompanies the reader along the book. Yet, like a plague-stricken idea, it could not be spelled out, lest there be accusations of incongruity.

The temerity of the title is enough. All the arguments developed in the book support and demonstrate the rational requirement of Creation and the Creator. Yet the laws of the modern decorum are not to be transgressed. The book asserts that the probability of life created by chance is nil. It asserts that billions and billions of tests would have to be made in order to find the right planet, the right temperature, the right stellar moment and a list of other precise conditions in order for life to be. The book concludes that chance needed to have had a decisive and premeditated will in order to create life. The book then draws a discreet veil and revels in silence.

In the same vein, an astrophysicist developing the same idea in the pages of *Paris-Match* was asked by a journalist who was not as "tactful" as Jean Guitton: "Are you saying that God exists?" His answer was edifying: "I am not a priest."

Capitulation before the bestial tenet of Darwinism characterizes modernity. God is either to be ignored or insulted. Its hypocritical language is unnuanced: when heaven is to be vilified, half-tones are not tolerated. Ever since the end of the nineteenth century, the fashion of philosophy has been precisely one of uttering blasphemies.

In a spirit of rivalry, any author wishing credibility must dip his pen more or less in the blood of the god Nietzsche declared dead. Denouncing deity and religion has become a sign of modern cultural nobility that all candidates for visibility must strive to merit, a debt of honor that every staunch cogitator owes his culture.

Darwinism acquires full meaning and deserves to be considered only within the Bacchic objections of a society that rebels against the Church and her God. In a serious thematic library, evolutionary writings would have to be somewhere between philosophies of the absurd and Surrealist literature. Psychoanalysis and Marxism would not be too far away.

Karl Popper, truly inspired, does not fail to establish an effective link among these three (in)disciplines. Very critical of Marxism and Freudism, the two trends of thought which were taught to him as fully-fledged sciences, he defines them along with Darwinism as "a hodge-podge of explanations that account for everything and therefore explain nothing." He asserts: "No matter what, the theory was confirmed. ... A Marxist could not open a newspaper without finding everywhere a confirmation of his interpretation of history. ... Freudian analysts insistently remarked that their theories were constantly verified by their 'clinical observations.'" [20]

The same psychoanalyst, Popper maintained, could put forward exactly the same arguments to explain why A killed and why B sacrificed himself. The methodological grid he set up to classify scientific disciplines would immediately eliminate Marxism, Freudism and Darwinism.

Evolutionism is thus the Church's Brutus. Contrary to what is believed, the Church knows what it takes to survive. To endure, it must make a pact with the devil—nothing new for it. A shrewd diplomat, it knows how to keep a low profile when need be. Didn't Pope John Paul II write in his message to the *Pontifical Academy of Sciences* on October 23, 1996, that "the theory of evolution is more than a hypothesis"?[21] The skillful ambiguity of the phrase lets the defenders of His Holiness pretend that his message was misunderstood, since Darwin was never mentioned by his name.

Even if it were the case, the veiled reference is suggestively made to those who have made a clean sweep of any idea of the Higher Life or any other such impropriety in the kingdom of philosophical correctness. We said earlier that the war was total. In fact it has well and truly ended, and the winner is triumphant and arrogant. The Church and the world of science (whether true or false) have joined battle against each other and the Grand Inquisitor of yesterday is floored by the Cyclops of today.

Casting off a kind of spirituality that is incompatible with modernism and compensating for a lack of priestly vocations, the West teeters dangerously into the banal in its morbid hunger to consume. All investigations, whatever their nature, now serve to encourage people in this direction. It is with the eyes of an evolved ape that the world is now observed and plundered.

Popper rightly indicates that observation is always selective: there must be an object to observe, a specific task to undertake, an interest to pursue, a point of view to maintain, a problem to solve. In league with the skeptical philosophers, among whom is Hume, Francis Bacon invalidates the absolute objectivity of the exact sciences. What can be said then of the back-and-forth process of induction and deduction riddled with missing links that characterize the Darwinian hypothesis? Johnson, very Popperian as far as methodology is concerned, raises the question in his book:

> Scientists were stunned to see the apparently invulnerable edifice of Newtonian physics crumble when modern techniques made it possible to make new kinds of observations. The validity of induction as a basis for science was not only philosophically uncertain, it was also inaccurate. ... In scientific practice, theory normally precedes the experiment or fact-gathering process, rather than the other way around. ... It provides a starting point for investigation when it is set forth with sufficient clar-

ity for it to be evaluated. Progress is made not by searching the world for confirming examples, which can always be found, but by searching out contradictory evidence that reveals the need for a new and better explanation.[22]

Even the exact sciences are thus affected by the culture in general. As for the social sciences, they suffer seriously from cultural biases. Popper evaluates the degree of authenticity of science in proportion to its capacity to evolve in relation to criticism. He says: "The wrong view of science betrays itself by craving to be right."[23]

With respect to this methodology, Darwinism is not only a disastrous conception of science, since it leaves no room for criticism and asserts itself as absolute truth, but is above all a groundless induction that provides pieces of evidence made to order. Here is a good example of fabrication related by P. M. Grand:

> The scientific fact has meaning and value only in relation to the theories that science has at its disposal at the time the fact is observed. In 1856, for instance the discovery of the upper part of a strange skull near Düsseldorf in the Neanderthal was far from fascinating. Vorvich considered it a congenital malformation associated with a kind of idiocy. If the discovery of a brain-pan of a similar type, forty years later at Trinil, resulted in quite different and fruitful discussion, it is because the publication meanwhile of Darwin's book (*The Origin of Species*, 1869) had called man's origins into question and sensitized scientific thinking to the transformist hypothesis.[24]

Gareth Nelson, a Darwinist paleontologist associated with the American Museum of Natural History, epitomizes the scientific reasoning of the evolutionists: "We must find our ancestors. We will indeed choose them . . . since we know they must exist, and these are the best candidates."[25]

"These" are chimpanzees, animals whose genetic code, closest to ours, is a windfall in the search of proof. This quasi-similarity between the genes of the two species has become the knockout argument for those who want us all to ape the apes.

Any trifle reassures Darwinists in their animal hypotheses, and what was only yesterday a circus freak has become the subject of evolutionary wonder. In 1966 two psychologists from the University of Nevada, R. A. and B. T. Gardner, introduced to the public Washoe, a young female chimpanzee that—wonder of wonders—managed to learn a hundred signs of the language of deaf-mutes.[26]

A Pseudo-Science

Scientific illusionism and sustained propaganda are the two basic points of the new dogma's strategy. Proselytism is also founded on a certain occultism necessary to preserve the minds of the faithful from doubt. They are thus left to live with their primary knowledge in the same way the clergy kept believers ignorant of the particulars of religion.

Neanderthal man strangely resembled Cro-Magnon man, though we are sure today that they are of different lineage. But the "Black Eve" calls into question the date and place of man's appearance on earth, thus burying in a mass grave a range of pseudo-ancestors that evolutionists used to swear, by their great (ape-headed) gods, were truly our ancestors.[27]

Why not inform people that Darwinism is merely a series of assumptions, not a science? Why not acknowledge defeat here as in linguistics and say that the origin of man—and of language as well—cannot, scientifically speaking, be determined?[28]

Dawkins answers this question in an edifying manner: "Darwin gives us the means to be intellectually complete atheists."[29] Darwinism thus follows the logic of armament and disarmament. Losing Darwinism as an ideological weapon amounts to exposing oneself to a fatal danger before the enemy of modernity, religion. The memory of the religion that wears the cowl of the iniquitous and narrow-minded torturer, causing nausea and nettle-rash and strengthening the will to power.

Modernity is defined first as a rescuing liberation from the religious shackles. Darwinism is a liberating ideology and has never been a science. The pillars of evolutionist theory continue to undergo scientific revision. Ernst Haeckel's "biogenical" law, for instance, is still studied as a truth despite its having been demolished by embryologists long ago.[30] Gould himself remembers having learned the formula during his university studies fifty years after it had been buried by science.

Everything is shaky on this ground, even the famous molecular clock. The latter is the sophisticated weapon of neo-Darwinism that no layman is susceptible to comprehend or *a fortiori* attack. It is a sort of homing missile, the lethal weapon of what is called today the hard sciences. Biologists for whom it is the privileged tool look down on paleontologists as merely vulgar hunters of debris.

Happy martyrs of the Darwinian cause, the latter will be reassured to see this race of Darwinism's Robocops take over and will gladly give way to them. Reassured by the strength of their rears, they willingly allow themselves to unveil some secrets.

Now that the neo-Darwinists have come to the rescue of the failing theory, Rebecca Cann, Alan Wilson's colleague, admits: "Many paleontologists fear that if they expose the legitimate scientific limits of the certainty of their theories, fundamentalists and creation 'scientists' may misrepresent these data to dispute the fact that evolution occurred."[31] Such is a reality that is to be found, let us recall, at any cost.

The novel religion has its esoterism, its secretive priests and its cunning. It is the same clergic who takes care of keeping secrets who would risk discrediting the dogmas of the initiates. He certainly will not tell *you* that the Beijing Man and Java Man are much debated. Such results are not given media coverage, especially since they ensure a prestige far more remarkable than the one guaranteed by the Catholic religion to its priests.[32] Leakey is reported to be a celebrity. Johanson behaves like a star and has frenzied avidly plying him for his autograph.

But if Darwinism has its priests, it has no ascetics. In our modernist world, smitten with media racket, the grand evolutionist show will long continue to promote the ruination of the soul and the death of the conscience.

NOTES

1. *Nos ancêtres poissons à pattes* [our legged-fish ancestors], *Le Monde,* Oct. 5, 1996.

2. Morin (1990).

3. Mahdi al Mandjra, "Nord/Sud" [north/south], in *Repères,* Toubkal, Casablanca, 1992, p. 176.

4. In III.4 we will see that the Gospels, though defending very just principles, are human writings and belong only in part to Revelation.

5. Secularism, conceived in the beginning as the establishment of a neutral ground, has evolved to an attitude of exclusion and the (symbolical and cultural) persecution of religion.

6. The entire philosophy of absolution lies on the idea that Jesus (peace be upon him) sacrificed himself for humanity. The sign of the cross is a reminder addressed to God that this world has henceforth settled scores with Him during the crucifixion, and that His son paid for the entire humankind.

7. I apologize to all the honest Christian men and women, whose number is great indeed. The Qur'ān attests that you are excellent spokesmen for us. If I vilify the Church, it is as an institution whose wrongdoings are no secret to anyone. [TN: The Church's insistence on clerical chastity and celibacy has been defeated by the supremacy, in humanist philosophy, of man's pursuit of pleasure over other considerations.]

8. Victor Hugo said: "Voltaire speaks to a party; Molière to society; Shakespeare to man."

9. P. E. Johnson, *Darwin on Trial,* Washington: Regnery Gateway, 1991, p. 151.

10. Cf. the prospectivist review *Futuribles,* no. 202, p. 18.

11. Cf. *The Forum* review, no. 70.

12. In contrast to the Qur'ān, whose texts were meticulously written down during the lifetime of the Prophet (grace and peace be upon him), the Bible was subject to deliberate falsification. Out of the 1284 pages of which the Bible is composed, 1012 are very much prior to the birth of Jesus Christ (peace be upon him).

13. *Ecole normale catholique,* April 23, 1997. The debate may be found in the column "Thèmes: Religions et modernité," in *Géoscopie,* Feb. 1998. Web address: www.géoscopie.com.

14. S. L. Goldman, "Science, Technology and Social Progress," Lehigh University Press, Bethlehem, PA, 1989, introduction.

15. Johnson (1991), p. 130.

16. The ASA is an association of teachers of scientific courses and evangelized Christians who are prepared for a scientific comprehension of the natural world up to the theory of evolution. Their sole sin vis-à-vis evolutionism is putting forward that the natural world is ruled by God.

17. The fascicle explains that science used to claim to have control over all the problems related to evolution. It belies such a claim by reporting accounts made by objective scientists who assert that science has not yet solved all the mysteries of evolution.

18. Let us stress that the creationists have quickly left the ranks of the ASA, weary of its conciliatory attitude vis-à-vis certain theories.

19. Contemporary Christian philosopher and author, among others, of *La pensée moderne et le catholicisme* [modern thought and Catholicism].

20. Karl Popper, *Conjectures et réfutations*, Payot, 1985.

21. Cf. *Le Monde*, October 25, 1996, and *Le Figaro*, October 26–27, 1996. *Le Monde* made it the theme of its editorial and put forward that this statement signaled the end of the dogma of sin.

22. Johnson (1991), p. 147.

23. Johnson (1991), p. 147.

24. P. M. Grand, *Découverte de la préhistoire* [discovery of prehistory], Club Français du livre, pp. 19–20.

25. Grand, p. 120.

26. I know people whose dog has done even better: it pulled a chair a few meters, climbed onto it to choose a chocolate bar from a cupboard of food, and then climbed down to eat it behind its master's back! Thank goodness dogs walk on all fours; otherwise, their intelligence would have made them ideal candidates in the compulsory quest of ancestors. We would have had canine ancestors in addition to our ape ancestors: in short, we would have had to suffer an image of ourselves even more flattering than that of the macaques. Darwinists would have barked louder than their enemies.

27. It is a new method, called infallible, that is based on the very latest things where research work is concerned, namely molecular chemistry. According to the molecular clock, Lucy is supposed to be the ancestor of the human race. Consequently, man is said to have appeared in Africa 200,000 years ago. That would imply that the examples of homo erectus found outside Africa are necessarily foreign to the ancestral line since they date back even further.

28. Once again the instruction of silence is imposed, since the *Société linguistique de Paris* [Paris linguistic society] has forbidden its members to give papers on this subject, cf. Vergez and Huisman, *Nouveau cours de philosophie: La connaissance et la raison* [a new course on philosophy: knowledge and the mind], Fernand Nathan, 1980.

29. P. E. Johnson, *Le darwinisme en question* (Fr. trans. of *Darwin on Trial*), p. 15, in the preface by Anne Dambricourt Malassé, researcher at the CNRS.

30. That is, "Ontogenesis recapitulates phylogenesis," by which the embryo presents during its formation different aspects that recapitulate the different phases of our evolution.

31. Cf. Michael H. Brown, *The Search of Eve*, Harper and Row, 1990, p. 239.

32. According to Johnson, Bowden gives an intriguing version of the Piltdown Man hoax and other forgeries. His book is available at Sovereign Publication, P.O. Box 88, Kent BR2, U.K.

I. 4. CREATING THE GLOBAL VILLAGE

Anything believed by everybody has, always and everywhere, every chance of being false.
Paul Valéry

Any uncontrolled power leads to madness.
Alain

The world will only be saved—if at all—by the unsubdued.
André Gide

If we don't start by assuring our own level-headedness, how can we rule the world?
Sseu-ma T'sien

A Fleeting World

From theory to theory, from philosophy to philosophy, we come now to examine a global phenomenon that we call a "deed," although "submission" better suits it. The *Encyclopedia Universalis* defines globalization as follows:

> Globalization, in the general sense of the word, is at once the process and the outcome of the process according to which phenomena of all types (economic, environmental, political, etc.) tend to assume a truly global dimension.

The artful haziness of the definition is not a sign of slackening in the reliability attributed to this encyclopedia. The indecisiveness of the definition is caused by the very nature of the phenomenon. Globalization, the outcome of a multitude of factors that are perhaps interactive but not necessarily interdependent, does not easily lend itself to a precise definition. The definition is also difficult because the phenomenon varies according to the angle from which it is observed, the motivations (or motives) that urge us to analyze it, the country and hemisphere to which we belong, and the education we have received.

The other factor that makes it enigmatic to define globalization satisfactorily is the tremendous speed of its advance. We simply had not seen it coming. History, until recently, had the courtesy to allow us room to guess a forthcoming event, to apprehend it, to await it, to anticipate it—in short, it left time for time to unfold. Thus we could describe a limited phase of its course as being an "event." We used to take part, somehow or other, in its unfolding, having, if not the privilege to have control on it, at least the comforting illusion of doing so.

It did not matter whether we made the "deed" or it made us; the important thing was that we used to dwell in history: events did not completely escape our vigilance. We used to inhabit history, living in a natural connection with events, whether happy or not. The speed of globalization has deprived us of such a beneficial and comforting advantage.

We no longer inhabit history; we are history's orphans. Inhabiting history meant being able to sketch an outline of the future and guide ourselves with a glance at the rearview mirror. Hence the other distinctive feature of globalization is its dangerous novelty. Such specificity makes our future impenetrable; our misted rearview mirror no longer serves us well. Godless man with his hypertrophied brain, history's orphan, heedless of the future, fragmented in his mind, citizen of a bedlam: that is the one who is to face globalization. That is where our path has led us: a turbulent world that prevents us from thinking out our future in serenity. This chapter will examine the different facets of this perversion of meaning and, consequently, of the meaning which globalization imposes on us.

Complex and complicated, globalization requires a long reflection and solid references in the method chosen to investigate it. It is difficult for the hasty man, forged with the fire of the here and now and soaked in a sea of incertitudes, to take stock of such a disconcerting development. "Move along, there's nothing to think about" is the appropriate motto of modernism![1]

Profound reflection is chased out by the barrage of information that hammers at your door, plagues you all day long, pursues you, enters by the ears, exits through the eyes, endlessly harassing you. Serious calm reflection is an inconvenience in the era of information at any price—a very low price indeed.

Nevertheless, even those who resist the groundswell of easy, futile, and distorted information affirm that thinking through globalization is no easy matter. Until recently, thinking through an event meant being in possession of thought processes enabling one to classify it, manage its premises, draw a lesson from it or, often, deduce the possibility or requirement of action.

Thinking means, to begin with, being able to conceptualize the facts. The complexity of globalization aggravates the particular handicap of the modernity's "doxosophers."[2] Unable to form an overview of the situation, they content themselves with fashioning a patchwork of similarly vague concepts—all the more disconcerting for those who deign to search for the roots of events.

Surveying the field of the fragmented conceptual investigation, we easily note that this global phenomenon is discussed as a thing in itself that can only be subjectively defined. The phenomenon has caused a lot of ink to flow, and it is on the agenda of every reflection on the future of man. Economists call it "globalization." Others prefer to speak of it in more elaborate terms, defining it, in Wolfram Eberhart's phrase, as a "global era." Still others define it as a "global breakthrough,"[3] the new era where many data contribute to make it the "colossal event" that has the virtue of "bundling scattered phenomena together."[4]

Some borrow from Karl Jaspers the idea that ours is a pivotal era, a transitional era like the first century B.C. The argument, intending to be comforting, defends the idea of a positive evolution and assures us that we are moving forwards, never backwards. History continues to advance while making some adjustments on the way. Thus we need not worry if it sometimes changes course or proceeds by leaps and bounds. Such swerving is described as pivotal and benefits various social categories. For the merchant, a global market; for the philosopher, a universal mode of thought; for the politician, a new world order.

Alas, this entire theoretical lullaby will not put worries to rest or allay apprehensions. Anyone who tries to have a look at history's rearview mirror will retch. The gap between what it reflects and the way we live is far too wide. History's long calm river begins to boil and foam under our feet. We have come to a real and devilish quagmire.

A Devilish Quagmire

In pursuit of its frantic course, our insensible era refuses to be tamed. The human galley is a drunken boat,[5] a ship of fools swept along by its own wake. Everything moves, shakes, whirls, and boils in the devilish quagmire. Man can only peer into this ferment and pray that the monsters that dwell in the quagmire do not devour him. Among the monsters that have already made a rapacious appearance is the Multilateral Agreement on Investment (MAI).[6] Many others lurk, ready to pounce.

It is clear that the menacing horror is economic.[7] Globalization's economic dimension outweighs every other aspect. The change that has occurred precisely in this domain is the mainspring of globalization's systemic dynamic. This aspect commands our attention because of the crucial role assigned to it by the modern and competitive world. It is also because changes that occur in it are easy to gauge. Zaki Laïdi, a research scholar for the CNRS, underlines this argument:

> On this level, the idea of an accelerated globalization makes indubitable sense since economic interdependence has increased ever since the mid-eighties; trade exchanges between industrialized countries increase at twice the speed of their gross domestic product, whereas in the previous decade the growth of exchange was only one and a half times more than that of production. This phenomenon assumes a global dimension since, for instance, the proportion for Latin America passed from 0.5 between 1975 and 1984 to 2.5 between 1985 and 1994. Economic globalization is particularly indicated by the fact that the exchange dynamic has supplanted the production dynamic. [. . .] This explosion of exchanges is at last visible on the financial level where, here also, the mid-eighties may be considered as a turning point due to the triple effect of advances in technology, the appearance of new financial instruments, and market liberalization.[8]

This citation is from a work from a collection, directed by Laïdi and contributed to by other eminent research scholars, called *Faire sens* [making sense]. The collection takes as its motto Leibniz's provocative sentence, "We thought we had reached port, but we found ourselves thrown back on the open sea."

The times may have changed, but there is something rebellious in man that refuses to be led and always tries to understand. Dating an event has always been a comforting human undertaking. The attempt to locate most precisely the events of our world is a way of "making sense" and reassuring ourselves.

The starting point of globalization has been dated by many as the 1980s, but if you scratch the surface a little, its chronological roots seem more difficult to detect than we may believe. In 1931 Paul Valéry, in his *Regards sur le monde actuel* [views on today's world], makes allegations that could easily pass for an optimistic definition of a nascent globalization:

> The coming of age of the world is beginning. . . . What can be more remarkable and more important than the stock-taking, distribution and linking of the parts of the world? . . . [T]he novel solidarity, excessive and instantaneous, between regions and events is the already very palpable consequence of this great event.

The global "event" was already felt, and even the most loquacious grew speechless before the unprecedented event and baptized it with metaphors. The "coming of age of the world" is Valéry's name for the new era long before the Eighties. The times were naïve enough for it to be assumed that the means of communication would promote solidarity between the races and the quarters of the globe. Living before World War II, he could scarcely have imagined the pernicious side of the Gulf War. Now, certainly, we are in the midst of a global era, yet our difficulty in extrapolating the paradigm is total, and the verbiage of this feverish moment remain uncoordinated.

Those for whom the political aspect of globalization is most important have chosen the Eighties as its chronological starting point. The multidisciplinary consensus on this date makes us suspect at least the precipitousness of the "event" at this particular time. Laïdi proposes a host of events that are not necessarily linked in time or in sense but have played a decisive part in the birth of what he calls the "global era." He cites the coming to power of Margaret Thatcher, who gave a new breath to the neoliberal revolution. The election of the Pope also played a part, as well as the establishment of *solidarnoscść* in Poland. According to Laïki, the event that contributed most to the advent of the "global era" is surely the decline of the Soviet power. Gorbachev's assumption of power was an event within another event that made the event. The global era is not gratuitously described as "complex."

According to the linguist Benveniste, an event becomes one once we have enough words to describe it. The present event is therefore one once the discourse that attempts to define it is illustrated by striking facts with highly symbolic significance. Globalization takes shape in the dramatization brought about by the end of the Cold War. The fall of Communism enables us to distinguish a "post" from a "pre" and to give substance to the event. It enables us in particular to consider the global event as inevitably linked with liberal democracy. The West and its outlook invade the conceptual market as the only valid and imperishable goods. The global era will henceforth keep pace with western modernity.

The fall of the Berlin Wall, generally looked on as a symbolic barrier, provoked the "democratic" flood. Democratization became to some extent a pretext for globalization. It became its leitmotif, just as pacification was an excuse for colonization.

An Ephemeral Link

Democracy, becoming drained of its substance at home, is paradoxically the product fawned upon and exhibited in the global showcase. It is an attractive commodity, an accessory indispensable for winning the benevolence of the powers of the moment. Democracy is globalization's ideological ultimate weapon—another paradox of the global era. It is considered the magic ideological cement that guarantees the stability and cohesion of the system. Those for whom democracy is not a tradition must therefore get in tune with globalization by becoming part of the equation in relation to this common denominator.

A full and deeply rooted tradition for the peoples who have witnessed its gradual birth in their lands, democracy is a magic triangle for those who perceive it as ideological membership and the source of enrichment. Pluralism, the constitutional state, and the respect of human rights constitute an incantational trilogy. The petty dictators who support globalization heap praise on this magic triptych and make of it a talisman. They set up their trophies by creating *ex nihilo* the parties required for the global showcase. They organize elections (whose results are known in advance), set a few political prisoners free, and disclose a few of their private secrets. But only those who go along with the farce will be impressed.

To have a small place in the global sun and ensure the indulgence of the World Policeman depends on how talented you are.

Human rights are a global norm to be respected. In fact, to be accredited you only have to deliver speeches in profusion about their protection. Strangely enough, those who talk more often about human rights are generally the ones who violate them most. The world's Human Rights Policeman is the undisputed champion in their violation.

In this global era, more than ever before, democracy is an empty shell, an undulating point of reference, an attractive mirage for a world frightened of its future. Isabelle Stengers, writing about democracy in a metaphorical style that totally befits our approach, tells us about the ambiguity of this concept:

> The paradigm asserts the homogeneity of the landscape, but it does not reveal the existence of passes and fissures on the paths that join the various regions together; in the official log of the trip it remains silent about the local aid without which anyone who comes along could not manage to find a way through.[9]

The idea of democracy has become a substitute for the social link impossible to establish between the various parts of the global village. Rather than its actual practice, the idea alone serves as a necessary (though fictitious) sociopolitical link to globalization.

Democracy is a lovely and brilliant idea, but this idea, however seductive, has been tarnished in its land of origin by the routine of everyday practice, and among rulers of the South it is merely a buzzword that grants them access to prosperity—their own, of course.

Democracy, as desired and accepted by the managers of globalization, is an ingenuous alibi for murdering other cultures with a clear conscience. In the name of such improvised democracy, global society is required to be homogeneous; its cultures are enjoined to merge.

Global society, as ironically described by Jacques Decornoy, pretends to be idyllic; in it,

> [I]ndividuals, groups, classes, nations fuse together. Everything merges into one single world: amid ceaseless movement and babbling discussion, a utopia is built. But that, if the word has any meaning, signifies the death of roots, for how can anything take root in a country of nowhere?[10]

The traditional varnished image of the brilliant idea of democracy that the great beneficiaries of "the principle of sameness"[11] endeavor to promote obscures a far less resplendent reality. Globalization is not that realization of potential proposed to us, the "Omega Point" attained by a wise and solidarity-oriented mankind. Those who present it or feign to present it as such are either dreamers cut off from the world, or barefaced profiteers and liars.

The ideological coating that varnishes this arrangement needs only to be slightly scraped in order to discover that globalization is a balance of power and a working drawing of a plan of domination, not that of beatific humanism.

We introduced this chapter by stating that globalization is a "submission" more than a "deed." When one really thinks about it, it is both at once since, in every power struggle there are those who do the deed and those who must undergo it. Globalization assumes both aspects; it depends on which side you look at it from.

Globalization is a history of domination: let us be clear to say so. Globalization is the totalization of Western cultural hegemony: let us be courageous enough to acknowledge it. Globalization is a spearhead situated in the United States of America: let us be candid enough to recognize that.

A History of Domination

Wounded at being defeated and surpassed by a younger and more vigorous nation, Europe, that tired old lady, reluctantly recognizes that globalization's real manager is the U.S. Globalization is painful even for a region that is fairly well off in the new line-up.

56

Globalization, well and truly a global confiscation by a single entity, creates an abysmal future for the South, while giving rise to complexes in the North. Europe licks the wounds to its self-esteem by giving globalization intense media coverage in which it presents itself as a member of the cast, rather than a walk-on.

It is time to consider globalizing domination from the point of view of technology. Here the U.S. has taken over the reins from the old continent. Its size and vigor have placed the young nation beyond the competition in this decisive domain.

Half-hearted notions of establishing a universal brotherhood have always accompanied the rapid expansion of technology. "All men are becoming brothers" was the motto solemnly proclaimed at the expositions that succeeded one another after the World's Fair in London in 1851, when the first undersea cable was inaugurated. The series culminated in the Paris Exposition of 1900.

Nineteen-hundred is also the year that marked the end of a century, and it witnessed the landing of the U.S. Marines on the island of Cuba under the pretext of helping the natives free themselves from the moribund Spanish Empire. Stage right: the peaceful aspect of the progress of Western civilization. Stage left: the fury of war and colonial conquest.[12]

Behind a universalist humanism singing the anthem of world brotherhood, a very ambitious new Nation was preparing to assert itself as an invincible and imperial superpower. Europe's two great wars and a marked decline in technological development, embroiled as she was in military concerns, enabled the U.S. to assume a position of power. In particular, World War II occasioned its disclosure to the world of its superpower stature and its title to being the savior of the world. It also saw the American launching of the atomic era, which, as Théodore Monod aptly put it, took over from the Christian era.

With unmatched arrogance and inimitable cowboy-like panache, the United States stormed into the century of modernity. It has without doubt become the most representative pole of modern man, well-armed and well-disposed in its efficient, can-do thinking.

It soon gave birth to advanced technologies that more gently perpetuated the supremacy that began with the combustion of a whole nation. Cultural fusion quickly took over from atomic fusion. Communication has become the most effective weapon for launching another offensive that is otherwise more profitable: the cultural conquest that conceals a purely economic invasion.

Uncle Sam dominates the world with its blessings. Its offer to share the atomic umbrella it has developed is the latest invitation to a security meeting under the protection of the defender of the world, of man, life, and progress.

Globalization is an American word first used at the end of the Sixties. It was enthroned in two books of that period, Marshal McLuhan's *War and Peace in the Global Village* (1969) and Zbigniew Brzezinski's *Between Two Ages: America's Role in the Technetronic Era* (1970). The first of these, occasioned by the Vietnam War, expanded on the benefits of television that enabled its viewers to become active participants rather than passive citizens.[13] Brzezinski[14] used the concept of the global city since connotation of intimacy evoked by the word village was less suited to the new international environment.

The United States, according to Brzezinski, its favorite advisor, is the sole country to propose a global model of modernity through its "techniques, methods and new organizational practices." Brzezinski defends the idea of America as the main propagator of this "technetronic" revolution. The barbarous neologism signifies the network created by the computer, television, and telecommunication.

Further, the United States cuts a figure of a paradise in the face of the hell of the Soviet block and its vexatious societies. By the same pretext it touted the right to convert the whole world to its lifestyle, confining it to its point of view for its own good. The world had to choose between the Gulag and Disneyland.

This sledgehammer argument won it a distinct superiority in communications. Already in 1995, 65% of world communication came from the United States.[15] It then took the lion's share of the cultural landscape leveled by the fall of the Berlin Wall. A real intellectual offensive was soon launched to convince the world of the validity of its mawkish neo-imperialism. In the Eighties the labors of Theodor Levitt, Director of the *Harvard Business Review*, legitimized the worldwide expansion strategies of busi-nesses. The global world gave way to the global marketplace and called into question the traditional Taylorist scheme of business.

Globalization enabled interaction between three levels that had heretofore been independent: the local, the national and the international. Economic management quickly colored politics, as modern and successful management techniques of businesses were transposed to the register of international relations.

Efficiency is far from being a fault in a complex society. But the danger, the whole danger, lies in considering society—national and international—through the eyes of a cold and cynical manager for whom efficiency alone matters. It is immoral, but alas established: politics at the time of globalization not only imitates business, it also conceives human relations in terms of deals and profits.

While it is true that from time immemorial the political domain has obeyed the blunt realism Machiavelli detailed so well, globalization takes such realism to a tragic extreme. Taking the example of colonization, we see how it also aimed to capture new markets and was likewise stimulated by raw realism. The colonizing state had as major concern the well-being of its citizens. As for the colonized entity, it had also the advantage in defending its own people by locating the enemy, or at least by knowing what to hold on to. Even cynical policies had man at its core, and it was still possible to defend oneself.

In the era of globalization we are slowly sliding into a new world order that no longer puts man—or at least a localized citizen—at its logical center, but rather profit first and last. Platitudes of one-world uniformity conceal a monstrous reality in which the individual as well as the group count for nothing beyond the wealth they produce. The Golden Calf is back!

The Megamachine

We are on a sure and inevitable path toward a new stratification of society that will soon be made irrespective of political membership. The increasingly evident dis-semination of poverty is hidden like a disgraceful evil. If, on the one hand, the indigence (both material and psychological) of countries is keenly displayed, the poverty that is rife even at the feet of the Statute of Liberty is carefully concealed.

Serge Latouche, for one, does not think that this overbalancing is to be done in as gentle a manner as we might believe. Latouche aptly depicts globalization as a "megamachine":

> I usually say that we are tearing along in a race car that has lost its driver. The machine seems to me doomed to crash at any moment in its mad run into an obstacle or over a cliff.[16]

"Megamachine" better expresses the scale of globalization as well as its mechanical and implacable nature. For Latouche, the human element on board this device is not a traveler but merely a cog in the machine. The appalling machine snatches him up, whirling him into the works and crushing him to extract its fuel. The means becomes an end. Latouche blacklists modernity:

> The society in which technique is no longer a simple means for attaining the objectives and values of the group but becomes the system's impassable horizon—an objective unto itself—dates back to the period of the emancipation from traditional societal regulations, i.e. to the onset of modernity.[17]

Latouche is not the only one who sees dark clouds looming over the global future. In a highly edifying article published by *Le Monde,* Jacques Attali and Boutros Ghali express similarly bleak views of postmodernity.[18]

For Attali, globalization amounts to a "juxtaposition of connected solitudes" that will lead us, if nothing is done about it, to a global society composed of three groups:

> [First,] a superclass comprising several tens of millions of people who own all the means of connection and creation. . . . Second, the nomads of misery . . . who maintain the technologies and must move from job to job in order to survive—a group of around a billion people. Third, all the rest, a gigantic middle class living in the false hope of joining superclass and in real fear of teetering into global nomadism.

As reported in the *Le Monde* article, the aim of the symposium was to examine the prospects of the twenty-first century. Which of the three categories Europe would come under was of course one of the questions raised.

"The United States," they conclude, "will always be there," and—short of the world blowing up in the meantime—we may take their word on it. Europe will also be a great power provided it severs the umbilical cord with the United States. China and Japan will perhaps find a small place among the future powers. Then, brazenly passing over in silence the lot of the rest of the world, they concluded that "the best way to defend ourselves against the invasion of the poor is simply to help them become less poor." In plainer language, they advise that welfare be given somewhat greater importance at state level while, internationally, hand-outs be given to populations damned by globalization. Such resolutions undoubtedly explain the profusion of charitable nongovernomental organizations (NGOs) in charge of the Third World, and of the plans for integration and development trotted out by local ministers as national undertakings.

The debate, to come back to the symposium, is instructive and interesting. But God alone knows how the international organizations love to talk. Will the evils of globalization be averted for all that? We know that the effectiveness of their action is inversely proportional to the luxuriance and fervor of their speeches. There is no doubt as to their role as *"machins"*[19] in the service of the Great. The moment they overstep the limits set by the supersovereign states, they are stood in the corner.

> During the '70s and the beginning of the '80s, Unesco was the central fo-rum of discussion about communications systems (an idea that originated in the non-aligned countries no one dares mention). The debates were definitely closed by the middle of the '80s with the retreat of Unesco be-fore the delegation of Reagan's America and Thatcher's United Kingdom, under the pretext that the controversy was extremely politicized.[20]

The Unesco debates on the future do not conceal the ever-increasing powerless-ness of international institutions. Boutros Ghali asserts: "The U.N. does not have the means to control the post-cold war period."[21] Jacques Attali informs us that the current international organizations are to be privatized—the North will appropriate them. In a brief burst of honesty, he allows that they will be "even more privatized than they are today."

This seemingly trivial difference, however, indicates a sad reality: the U.N. and all the international institutions are already merely forums in the pay of the North, namely the U.S. We need only remember the price Yemen was forced to pay for its vote against the attack on Iraq by American forces in 1991. Having been naïve enough to imagine he was participating in a truly international forum, the representative of this country of the South dared to say nay. The American ambassador, like some character out of a Western, leaned toward the Yemeni spokesman and said, "This vote is going to cost you." (Bang! bang!) The following day American aid to this poor country was suspended.

History is decided—and will increasingly be decided—elsewhere; the future is coolly concocted in places where we do not philosophize, where we vote even less, and where the heart is kept in one's pocket!

False Friends

Since the second half of the Eighties, the principal debates on globalization have been conducted in more technical organizations. The GATT gave way to the WTO. Even though Mitterand was scandalized by the idea of a single cultural model, the cool and calculating machine —the megamachine—moves forward, unshakable, attaching little importance to the tranquil force of the French president: "It would be disastrous," he declared indignantly, "to help the spreading of a single cultural model. Is what the totalitarian regimes ultimately failed to do to be accomplished by the laws of money in league with the forces of technology?"[22]

A good and wise question! Yet wisdom is not the forte of the global "deed." Mitterand asked the question during a debate held within the WTO that ended, on December 15, 1993, in a strategic defeat of the European Union. The agreement was certainly not concluded in the name of the cultural exception claimed by France. Jack Valenti, official of the MPAA (Motion Picture Association of America), an institution that defends the interests of Hollywood, replied, "This negotiation has nothing to do with culture. . . . The sad truth is that Europe is turning its back to the future."

Forging ahead toward the future means, in the vocabulary of neocolonialism's conclaves, accepting that "today, in all institutions, power swings from the leaders to the shareholders."[23]

If, fearing for and defending its cultural exception, Europe merits a mitigated but polite reply from the shareholders that govern us, the Muslim (that is, more than the quarter of humanity) who asks the essential question of his right to another view of the future is immediately given the answer that "dialog between the satellite and the mosque" will be established.[24] More bluntly, they would say: "You are not well equipped for dialog." More poetically: "A miserable earthenware pot that dares to challenge a pot made of reinforced concrete!" More administratively: "We'll get back to you on that."

Those who live in the destitute world will not even have the right to moan; they will have just the right to watch the "deed" being done. In a word, they will have to undergo it. Fully aware of its total powerlessness, the South must attend in eloquent silence the birth of the cool monsters careened by the Organisation for Economic Cooperation and Development (OECD).

The details of the MAI, for instance, were drafted in utter secrecy. Multinationals, glorious expression of lucrative globalization, discreetly prepared the new manifesto of the global capitalist. Cooked up since 1995 by the 29 richest member states, the treaty is a masterpiece of iniquity. The objective of these long esoteric secret meetings was to reach an agreement before presenting the underdeveloped countries a take-it-or-leave-it treaty. Legislators and citizens were kept in ignorance of the proceedings until 90% of the OECD text had been drawn up.

Only weeds grow in the dark, where vampires are in their element. The MAI is a bloodthirsty vampire indeed: it is *Alien* in person. Like the beast imagined by Hollywood, it gives you no time to realize what is happening to you until it blithely devours you.

The text of the treaty is a masterpiece of ambiguity that can easily mislead you as to the real principles of the agreement. It is crueler than Faust's pact with the Devil: modern demons are more conversant with well-conducted manipulation.

The interests of the investing multinational are its sole concern, the sole policy and the sole truth of the State contracting with the Devil. Specialists affirm that the investor, by means of this treaty, acquires the right to have a say in all the acti-vities of the state in question.

The cornerstone of this satanic pact is the clause dealing with "Rights of Investors." Any such activity adjudged by investors to be against their interests will immediately be cancelled, whether it is carried out for direct public interest[25] or related to a branch of industry that has apparently no direct connection with the investor's activities.

The MAI has not yet bound contracting parties (thank God!). But we are given a foretaste of it from another agreement, currently in force, namely the North American Free Exchange Agreement (NAFTA). Although its terms are far less crushing than those of the MAI, NAFTA allowed the international firm Ethyl to institute proceedings against Canada for having banned a chemical additive hazardous for the environment.[26] The case is pending; if Ethyl wins, Canada will have to pay 251 million dollars to the multinational.

In order to enter NAFTA, Mexico in its turn had to abandon the measures of its Constitution taken in favor of the land reform established after the Revolution. The result of the first four years since the application of the treaty has been the massive destruction of small landowners while the food-processing multinationals were laying their hands on huge farms.

> We can imagine that such a mechanism will have the effect of paralyzing
> any governmental action aimed at protecting the environment, preserv-
> ing natural resources, guaranteeing job security and equal opportunity or
> investment directed toward serving the general interest.[27]

What shall we call such a monster from the "devilish quagmire"? How shall we describe an era that permits such dealings?

The hidden face of such disguised contractual slavery is unmasked thanks to men and women of good will—a race that is fortunately not extinct at the time of a baffling global era. The danger represented by the MAI was signaled by an NGO that launched a large-scale media campaign against this kind of pact.[28] Such NGO demonstrations give rise to a glimmer of hope—though the future is not much brighter.

Fears

During a debate on the subject, Jack Lang, former French Minister of Culture, said: "We don't know who's negotiating what on behalf of whom."

Passing from the politician to the boss, the nature of power has changed; it has become as fluid as water, as elusive as a drop of mercury. In classical democratic societies, power was delegated. In the changes wrought by the global era, power has become a matter of easy appropriation. Economic factors now prevail over the political—as is caricatured in this reply: "Timon, the well-known boss, was recently asked if he intended to go into politics. 'I don't do politics,' he replied. 'I buy it ready-made.' "[29]

Notwithstanding the prevailing syrupy speeches on human rights and democracy, the global era, under scrutiny, is an era where everything is bought and sold with no moral curbs or humanitarian concerns. You may think you have free disposal of your life and deeds, but the State, which is supposed to protect you, deliberately sells you for a handful of dollars. The *Leviathan* of long ago has found its master.

If the arguments of Jacques Attali or Boutros Ghali in one of modernity's boudoirs[30] are not convincing of the dangerousness of post-modernity, let the figures speak for themselves in witness of the inhumanity of the carnage.

The three richest men in the world have wealth greater than the GDP of the poorest 48 countries—that is, a quarter of all the countries of the world. In more than 70 countries, per capita income is less than what it was twenty years ago. On a world scale, half of humanity lives on less than $1.50 a day.[31] In 1960, 20% of the world population living in the world's richest countries had an income 30 times higher than that of 20% of the poorest countries. By 1995, their income was 82 times higher.[32]

Globalization is the "deed" that enables a small number to suck the blood of billions of individuals, reducing them to beggary and slavery. The warning signs of unbearable iniquity are all too evident: the gap between the two worlds is widening. While private dietary clinics are established in the North, a third of humanity suffers from anemia. While the wealthy rejoice and splash about in luxurious swimming pools, one third of humanity has no access to drinking water.

Globalization is the pauperization of the world's overwhelming majority and the increasingly flagrant economic rupture between North and South. The future, according to serious forecasting, will surely be dangerous for North and South alike. Crises will be widespread. The North can still prevent the disaster from taking place, thanks to its political structures; the South can only go under. Most certainly, that is what it is doing. Held hostage by totalitarian powers as stupid and greedy as they are illegitimate, it has no chance, except by some miracle.

If France has deputies like Catherine Lalumière, who made Prime Minister Jospin reconsider this treaty,[33] who among the deputies of the parliaments of the South (if there are any) will report the dangers inherent to globalization? In that part of the world, colonialism has left behind an elite who are immune to intelligence. They rule at sight; the five-year plan is the best they can think of. When they happen to be as bright as Catherine Lalumière, it is in their own interest, never in the interest of those who supposedly elected them.

"Victory over the MAI might foretell others."[34] Let us hope and pray that this is so. That that victory was due essentially to the action of certain NGOs suggests that good will and group action can frustrate the future of the monsters that lurk in the dark. Be that as it may, pessimism is prevalent, and the twentieth century ends with a most negative balance.[35]

NOTES

1. The phrase is Dominique Wolton's, in *Penser la communication* [thoughts on communication], Flammarion, 1997, p. 80.

2. According to a term of Plato's that Pierre Bourdieu renders as "a technician of opinion who thinks he is a scientist" in *Contre-feux* [backfire], *Raisons d'agir,* 1998, p. 15.

3. Cf. Zaki Laïdi, *Le temps mondial* [global time], Complexe, 1997, p. 21.

4. Idem, p. 14 : Pierre Nora's quotation in *Faire l'histoire, nouveaux problèmes* [making history: new problems], Paris: Gallimard, 1974, p. 305.

5. TN: Reference to the famous poem, *Bateau ivre,* by the poet Arthur Rimbaud 1854–91.

6. Further information on the MAI is found at the end of the chapter.

7. Cf. Viviane Forrester's famous book, *L'Horreur économique* [economic horror], Fayard, 1996.

8. Cf. Zaki Laïdi (1997), pp. 17–18.

9. Isabelle Stengers, *L'invention des sciences modernes* [the invention of the modern sciences] Paris: Flammarion, Champs, 1995, p. 136.

10. Jacques Decornoy, "Communication et eugénisme pornographique" [communication and pornographic eugenics] in *Le Monde diplomatique,* December 1992, p. 8.

11. The expression is taken from Gilles Deleuze.

12. Armand Mattelart, "Dangereux effets de la globalisation des réseaux, les nouveaux scénarios de la communication mondiale" [dangerous effects of network globalization: new scenarios of global communication], *Le Monde diplomatique,* August 1995, pp. 24, 25.

13. I do not wish to dwell on the illusion spread by such view of things. We will see that at length in what follows.

14. Political expert who was Director of Research of the Institute on Communist Affairs at Columbia University, and who became security advisor of former U.S. President Jimmy Carter and one of the founders of the Trilateral Commission.

15. Mattelart (1995), p. 25.

16. Serge Latouche, text published Feb. 27, 1998, on the site "Terminal," http:/weblifac. ens-cachan.fr/Terminal/texts/forum64.html.

17. Idem, p. 2.

18. *Le Monde,* Tuesday, April 28, 1998, in the article that covered the third session of *Entretiens du XXIe siècle* [talks on the 21st century] organized in Paris by Unesco: *Un dialogue à l'Unesco pour imaginer le XXIe siècle* [a Unesco dialog for imagining the 21st century].

19. "So-and-so's," as de Gaulle disdainfully used to call the U.N.

20. Mattelart (1995), p. 25.

21. He is well placed to know: he was its Secretary-General.

22. *Le Monde diplomatique,* August 1995.

23. Cf. *L'Événement du jeudi* [the Thursday event] March 17–23, 1994: the assertion is Attali's.

24. Cf. *Le Monde,* April 28, 1998.

25. Such as a constitutional law or reform that aims to provide social security for its citizens, or a law that obliges entrepreneurs to recruit employees among the local population.

26. Because it contains a neurotoxin that can damage the car's antipollution device.

27. *Le Monde,* April 28, 1998.

28. Ralph Nader's "Public Citizen." The United States, which in the beginning denied the existence of such a covenant, could not still do it once the text was published on Nader's Internet site.

29. J. P. Dupuy, *La société en quête de valeurs* [society in search of values], Maxima, p. 69.

30. In the sense of the private dressing room of ladies where they used to play the *précieuses.*

31. Ignacio Ramonet, "Stratégies de la faim" [hunger strategies], *Le Monde diplomatique,* Nov. 1998.

32. Ibid.

33. As reported in *Le Monde diplomatique,* Nov. 1998, p. 6, Catherine Lalumière presented a report to P.M. Jospin, stipulating the serious offense to the State's sovereignty represented by the adoption of the MAI, a defect that escaped the attention of the senior officials of the Treasury Department negotiating the treaty. Jospin took therefore the decision on October 10, 1998, to withdraw France from the talks, thus reconsidering the conditions that he laid down in February of the same year.

34. Bernard Cassen, " 'Le bateau ivre' de la finance" [the Drunken Boat of finance], *Le Monde diplomatique,* Nov. 1998.

35. Recommended on this subject is the reading of Eric J. Hobsbawn's valuable book *L'âge des extrêmes, histoire du court XXe siècle* [the age of extremes: a history of the short 20th century], Complexe, 1994.

I. 5. DISINFORMATION

Glorifying the cult of images—my great, unique and pristine passion.
Charles Baudelaire

Knowing what everyone knows means knowing nothing.
Rémy de Gourmont

He wanted to know everything, but knew nothing.
Gérard de Nerval

The press has succeeded the catechism in ruling the world: after the papal, the paper.
Victor Hugo

Newspaper pubclishers owe a debt to the Devil.
Jean de La Fontaine

Communication, a Genetic Need

Jean-Marie Guéhenno has dubbed our era an imperial age, comparing it with the first such age, the time of the Roman Empire. He pays particular attention to the nature of power that becomes diffuse and flowing and thereby more alienating than before. He describes this chilling age with great sensitivity and remarkable talent:

> The imperial age is an age of mirrors: it is all reflection, a pale world threatened by both precariousness and tedium, a world that must navigate between the storm and flat calm, needing the instability without which no wind will rise, but fearing the unpredictable breaks that threaten unstable periods. This same volatility of a world whose elements are entirely interlinked, and which anything can cause to teeter, lies at the heart of modern angst.[1]

We begin a desperate search for man in a world at once magic and cruel, filled with trouble, anguish, and deceptive calm—the calm before the storm. Might he be that fleeting reflection we think we see in the recesses of a mirror—or has he deserted forever the world he has made and that has made him?

Might globalization really be the emergence of a "new object, the world as such,"[2] a world devoid of the meaning that man's influence on his history used to give it? Might globalization correspond to "the outburst of common and specific problems for all mankind"?[3]

But the idea of humanity has been rejected and perhaps even considered obsolete. What is this world of bronze and glass that makes man a fleeting illusion, a retinal recurrence?

What is this Damocletian era, menacing in its precariousness, ready to disintegrate under the feet of the meager remains of man bereft of his human nature? We live, according to Edgar Morin, in "the complex world."

Complexus means "woven together." Many phenomena intertwine to create this world's complexity. Accordingly, the fabulous development of the means of com-munication ought to be of particular interest to us, since a moment's reflection reveals the decisive role of information in this entanglement.

Communication is at the center of the whirlwind called globalization. It is the eye of the storm. A liquifying agent, communication becomes globalization's beating heart.

In devoting the present chapter to this crucial phenomenon, I shall of course not exhaust the subject. Instead, I will simply underline the central position of com-munication and the dangers arising from this fact, particularly in its aberrations. Because of the central position of communication in the modern world, and its vital role in the life of man of all times, it is important that we focus on these issues.

The impact of communication begins with its mere mention. The word has on its own a magical resonance for the anthropological dimension it expresses. It enjoys an intrinsic value that is virtually incantational: heads turn at the very mention of the word. It is energized by an emotional open-sesame power that both touches our essence and paralyzes us.

Surely communication is the first act we perform in this life. Our protesting cry at birth is not only in response to the pain of our first breath. It is also, and above all, the first message we transmit. We bawl our despair at leaving our watery world, that place of felt-like smoothness where we were created. We express our suffering at coming out into the free air that pierces our lungs and assaults senses accustomed to the cocoon-like atmosphere of the womb. As newborns we cry over our lost paradise, endlessly replaying the story of Adam and Eve.

Communication is as well a mark of the divine mark imprinted in our genes. It makes itself felt as a vital necessity to be in contact with others, to express our feelings to them, inform them of our intentions, announce our decisions. Some researchers have even attributed the "crib death" phenomenon to a lack of com-munication that leads the infant to stop breathing and die.

For the followers of obtuse views, man is a social animal and nothing else. But man is in fact much more than an evolutionary mitochondrion that took advantage of an original soup favorable to the evolution of life. He is God's lieutenant on God's earth, His creature, His order, the fulfillment of His will. It was normal that in a Creation that came out of the Word, the first endowment of God to his lieutenant was a natural device enabling him to capture the message and acquire knowledge.[4]

In the beginning was the Word, in the beginning was speech: *Then He fashioned him* (man) *in due proportion, and breathed into him of His spirit. He gave you* (the faculties of) *hearing, sight and reason. How little grateful you are!*[5]

Speech was essentially granted and taught to us in order for us to express our recognition of God and our gratitude to Him. The faculty of hearing enables us to hear, and perhaps understand, the various Divine Messages intended to guide us in our quest for God, so as to prepare our return to Him.

Instinctive sociability is another divine sign, since communication among ourselves constitutes the human channel of our communicating with God. Communicating is in every sense of the word a sacred duty because of the sacred status of life and the transcendent nature of this action.

Communicating means having the ability and the means necessary to fulfill the original mission of managing our tangible world with spirituality and sense. The Qur'ān relates how the angels submitted to God and recognized their inferiority to Adam when God endowed him with the power of naming.

Is communication still faithful to this noble calling as it is now practiced, in an era where the means outweigh the ends and are guided by vile instincts?

Splits

Severed from divine guidance, any natural gift is destined to become a curse. Having parted from its initial role as the means of communing and sharing, communication has skidded in the eddies of modern times. It has detoured from its normative route and confined itself to its functional value, the sole aspect appreciated by a capsizing modernity. Thus a gift becomes a curse. Nature becomes culture. What is durable becomes ephemeral. Communication becomes disinformation. The truncations of a system of mutilation are more visible in this domain than in any other. Belzebuth, the Prince of Darkness in person, has taken charge of corrupting man's essential genetic need to communicate by altering its nature and hiring out its use.

The devil, alas, is not that easily recognized creature of Western literature, with its scarlet color, barbed tail, goatee and horns. It has the formidable gift of being immaterial and of mingling with the blood of men and running in their veins. It therefore inspires the destructive force generated in hearts that are empty of God, and it ruins, little by little, any great plan. Unable to see the devil's invisible nets, let us speak instead of other, man-made nets that grip the world and whose present situation and the subject of this chapter bring inevitably into the discussion.[6] The communication-facilitating net in question, the Internet, was created in 1969 initially as an effective war weapon in a perspective of violence.

By what evil spell are the means that might have facilitated human communion the same as those used to crush the Other by one's superior power?

How can a means of communication intended to facilitate contact be used especially for purposes of domination?

Communication. Defining the meaning of this Janus-like concept is no easy matter; one of its two faces is extremely beautiful, the other is absolutely hideous. Let us refer to the four aspects of the term as defined by Dominique Wolton, research director at CNRS, the French national center of scientific research, who devoted twenty years of his life to the study of communication:

1. Communication is first the ideal of expression and exchange that underlies Western culture and, consequently, democracy. It presupposes the existence of free and equal individuals, concepts inseparable from that of mod-ernization. We may well recall the terrible battles to establish these concepts that have been waged since the Seventeenth Century.

2. It is also the entire range of mass media that, from the press to radio and television, have within a single century drastically changed the relationship between communication and society.

3. It is as well the whole set of new communication technologies—computer science, telecommunications, audiovisual devices—and their interconnectedness, that, in less than half a century, have modified the conditions of exchange and also of power at the global level.

4. It is lastly the values, symbols, and representations that organize the functioning of the public sphere of mass democracies—and, more generally, of the international community—which allows local communities to enter into relationships with one another and to influence the world.[7]

According to Wolton's detailed definition, communication belongs to the same reference system as democracy and modernity. Between these merely supercifially homogenous aspects, however, a profound imbalance is materializing whose pressure is gradually felt in the modern world. For the sake of academic objectivity, our author admits to being able to analyze the phenomenon only in its conflictual relationship with democracy and the profound confusion it produces on the scene where it is supposed to be in harmony.

The ambivalence that exists between the humanist principle of communication and its functional dimension ends up tearing the concept apart. Its purely technical aspect commands the biggest share, while the smallest is left to the normative sig-nificance. This rift in the principle of communication is essentially due to the tremendous technological boom in this domain. Its normative significance is nevertheless behind the establishment and supremacy of the concept on the world scene.

The first definition of communication here, attuned to humanistic values, first appeared, according to Wolton, around 1160 and had strong religious overtones. Sharing and communion are Christian ideas; modernity admits them, though reluctantly, when needed. The concept of communication was long marked by the flourish of Judeo-Christian humanism. Even today, despite its secularization and the deviation it undergoes through the modernization of moral standards, communication remains very much stamped with the idea of sharing and communion.

The second definition of the concept of communication appeared, according to Wolton, in the sixteenth century as the expression of the swing from the "normative" to the "functional" undergone by the paradigm. This shift in its historical evolution is linked to the idea of transmission and dissemination. Gutenberg's invention breathed new life into this technique of communication. Ever since, the new techniques of exchange that the human genius never ceases to produce have caused a real inflation of the activity of communicating

The concept has become a zombie that harasses us to the innermost recesses of our being. Communicating no longer means communing and sharing, but knowing everything about one another without knowing anything at all. The inflation in this domain is such that "the right not to know" has become part of the claims of the citizen who still preserves a touch of lucidity, or at least attempts to do so. The latent utopia of shared information has become poisoned by this denaturing, especially during the rapid expansion of the techniques meant to serve and facilitate it.

Spells

Communication, originally a magician, has become little more than a wicked witch with diverse evil powers, a Calypso and Circe at once. Calypso captures and imprisons modernity on her virtual and ephemeral island. The Circe of modern times does not change us into swine but, leaving us with our human appearance, acts behind the scenes of our collective consciousness to transform us into spiritless and cynical beings.

Whatever used to lend credit to our humaneness has abandoned us unawares. Under the effect of all-too-modern spells, fairy becomes harpy, and communication comes to mean incommunication and connected solitudes. At a time when huge means are expended to make it clear and complete, our view of one another has never been so blurred, fragmented, and distorted.

Images—Circe's magic wand—have the devastating effect of making us perceive the other only in telegraphic style. Since perception is the very basis of any intuitive knowledge, our apprehension of life and of one another reverts to a primitive view of itself when such a function is sabotaged and led astray.

Circe pursues us beguilingly. The wicked witch drives us back into the obscure recesses of our consciousness, transforming us into new cave men who know no other language beside colorful onomatopoeia. The other is for us no longer our fellow man, but merely the next fleeting image to draw our attention for the duration of a film, a commercial, or a documentary.

"Modernicious" man lives in the perverted illusion of going forward, an impression generated by the proliferation of technology. Walking on the moon makes him forget his duty to moving towards his brother in humanity with open arms and an open heart. By transforming the other into a furtive and fleeting simple image, an illusion, a mirage, a mere reflection, modernity saps a human history once founded on sharing and (friendly or conflictual) exchange. As a result, history has become antihistory in a disastrous march backwards.

Dressed in communication's flashy rags, fearsome Circe has made the free citizen a voyeur, full of ideals but unable to perceive the world except beclouded by vice, boredom, covetousness, and greed—mere dreaming. Wanting to know too much, we end up knowing nothing. The bewitching is complete; the victim of information at any price, at any moment, is doomed to live in a limbo of veracious knowledge.

Communication swept away by technology enshrouds both knowledge and social bonds in a hypercommunicative modern world. Paradoxically—but then, modernity is a nest of paradoxes—the disastrous effect on social bonds is the product of the brutal intimacy with the other that advanced technology offers us, putting us face to face all day long with a flood of beings and objects. Thanks to modern means of com-munication, the dizzying speed of our contact with the other produces an effect that is the opposite of what we expected. The presence of the other becomes too intrusive; it is made in a manner that is too quick and too superficial.

The modern way of filling an anthropological need robs the value of the gesture of all its beauty. Communicating with one another is no longer a conquest in itself exciting and passionate; it becomes, according to our choice, an occasion of toxic addiction to the image, an act so trivial that it no longer arouses any reaction, or a real violation of our privacy. The other is always close at hand. Getting in touch with him has become less a need than an increasingly wearisome game—and sometimes an addiction. We are harassed *ad nauseam* by the distorted image and inopportune presence of the other, which never amounts to establishing any genuine convivial relationship.

Since natural relationships and genuine contact with one another require a certain distance, the proximity enforced by global communication is not well suited to otherness. The excessive familiarity offered by modern means of communication only exacerbates still further the individualism of man who considers himself an evolved animal. "Without an intermediary between them, the more easily visible the other is, the greater the effort needed to tolerate him."[8]

By conjuring away time and destroying distances, Circe plays a mean trick on humanity in its search for convivial interrelationship. She has sowed disenchantment in our hearts, if not the germs of an illness fatal to the human race, then a kind of slowly spreading general autism. We think images unite us, but in fact no rapprochement is made. Each of us remains on his own turf with his clan of happy sensations, fulfilling the genetic quest of communication by means of television, telephone, the Internet, the radio! Each of us lives in a fantasy world atop his impressions. There is nothing to share. We are there, every man for himself—and the media for us all.

The critical sense awakened by the Frankfurt School with regard to the alienation produced by excesses of communication is quickly lulled in the face of fascinating new technologies. The animosity aroused in others by alarmists' arguments about the bad influence of the mass media is anesthetized with each new craze ushered in by new information technologies, and these unleash in rapturous humanity a sort of Babes-in-Toyland zeal.

The illusion consists in believing that these new techniques are able to reconcile rebellious communication with its normative principles. Alas, "techniques have not solved the problems of human communication; they have simply deferred them and driven them back to the edge of screens and keyboards."[9]

The social bond is utterly eroded by what is normally supposed to strengthen it. Driven by new technologies, communication destroys what it is supposed to be regenerating. Cybercafés best illustrate the nonsense to which communication is subjected by advanced technology:

> What can be sadder than a cybercafé where nobody talks, each one being "connected" by remote connection to a lifeless, absent being, however less "restricting" than the physical being sitting at his side.[10]

Under such circumstances, investing a lot in a relationship with others is deemed a heroic deed; to make a real contact is considered as a feat. We are handicapped by our anesthetized senses; today we cannot think of communication, however much we'd love to, without being overcome by a certain vertigo. Reflecting about the other is painful; scrutinizing an event in which he figures becomes a trial of strength, an intellectual torture. The event we think has just started is already at its final stage. Releasing a scattering of other events, it vanishes, leaving us utterly perplexed.

Pursuing a line of thought about communication means risking a venture into an informational fog: the conceptual fog we have emerged from, the present fog of nuance, and a fog of future outcomes. We can only move forward hoping that the good side of our conjectures will prevail over the bad. On a global and historical scale, the experience is still in its infancy. For this reason, we cannot draw final conclusions as to man's future lot in this communicational environment, but we can clearly attest that, from many points of view, the current experience is destabilizing.

A Confiscated Forum

It is not only the social bonds that suffer in the world at Circe's mercy. The other edifice assaulted by that terrible witch is one over which the West waged many a battle to establish and impose as the system of modern and equitable government. That edifice is democracy.

The hypertrophy of communication's functional dimension, to the detriment of its normative function, is aggravated by market logic. Such a tendency considerably modulates the calm atmosphere of well-polished democracies. Relationships between democracy and communications are now more conflictual and amicable.

When mass media burst in upon the sociopolitical field, democracy's purring principles are overturned, driven back to precarious positions. True democrats—not demagogs—denounce the magician's treacheries.

They describe how her evil spell works, how it destabilizes the institutional basis of democracy that was once the protector and guarantor of free communication. Conceived and nourished by democracy, free communication is on its way to becoming its democracy's principal enemy. Easy access to information was meant to crown a long struggle to establish the participation of all citizens in the management of power; under the negative effect of advanced communications, it has become an ordeal democracy itself must surmount.

In the past, the objective was simple: to establish freedom of information; the legitimacy of the press and journalism constituted a fight totally in line with that for democracy, the two going hand in hand through epic, often tragic, struggles. . . . Today, two centuries later, the essential objective has been achieved.[11]

In fact, today when everything seems to be acquired, nothing goes well. At the beginning of the twenty-first century, the merging fields of computer science, television and telecommunications have launched new and greater challenges at the democratic scene. The struggles looming on the post-modern horizon have to do with the hazards of information overdose. The necessity of serving hot information in order to stand out in a field of stiff competition leads to an absolutely inhibitive flood of information: "The dream of live broadcasting is turning into a nightmare."[12]

Journalism, formerly the symbol of freedom of expression and the diastolic organ of democratic protest, has become a symbol of manipulation and takes part in the concept's systolic hemorrhaging. The freedom of expression, once the heart of democracy, no longer circulates the life-fluid of democracy's body but drowns it in its vital flood.

Prolix by professional obligation, the journalist is required to maintain uninterrupted chatter. He is the vestal of the communicational flame. He is the new watchdog[13] of the illusion of communication. The role he is induced to play in this logic of communication and consumption rewards him with a place of distinction; he is at the summit of what Dominique Wolton calls "the infernal triangle," composed of the politician, the journalist and the media.[14] (All three are prisoners of ratings.)

Ratings are a divinity born of the womb of modern communications in order to subject to the absurd the heretofore beneficial relationship between the man in politics and the man of free expression who shapes public opinion. The game between these elements is turning into a comedy.

The journalist no longer pays attention to his role as mediator of democracy; he merely searches the crowd of the showbiz state for the heads that get the most media coverage, and so he secures his survival and escapes unemployment.

As for the politician, he is no longer that wise man to whom we entrust our future and the role of guarantor of rights. He is a fleeting star the least stir aroused by the media can extinguish forever. He can no longer conceive of himself. He undertakes action solely on the basis of the media god, whose wrath he avoids and whose sympathy he seeks. Thus he pays more attention to his public image than to the improvement of his political program. He busies himself seeking the sympathy of the journalist who is more prone to mix with figures that are highly prized by the ratings.

The slow massacre of representation, democracy's sacred principle, is thus established and perpetuated. The circle of the most renowned politicians becomes progressively and increasingly restricted; the others join the masses in their soundproof shells.[15] You either belong to "the broadcasting scene" or you do not exist. The State is a "showbiz state," and the politician applies himself to becoming a "media product" that sells well. The principal function of the politician is thus no longer one of accomplishing his destiny in history of developing or perpetuating the democratic collective consciousness, or of initiating future social action. J. M. Guéhenno asserts the following:

> We might even claim that the principal function of the politician, power-less before the massed confrontation of professional interests, is now one of the professional management of collective perceptions, and thus the creation of continuity: in the imperial age, he claims to be the priest who lasts, though his means are those of the ephemeral.[16]

In his admirable book, *La fin de la démocratie* [The end of democracy], Guéhenno further explains the role of the politician in the global era: "The job of the politician is to play his part as well as possible so as to be always present among the fifty psychodramas that fill the tv screens each year."

Rolling Stone provides an excellent illustration of the "infernal triangle" in which the politician, the journalist, and the media pledge to promote the illusion.

In an interview with former U.S. President Bill Clinton, *Rolling Stone* asked, "What's the biggest laugh you've had since you've been president?" Clinton replied, "The funniest thing happened—in a moment of tension, I guess—was when I was practicing shaking hands with [Yasir] Arafat before I shook hands with [Yitzhak] Rabin. We had an understanding that there would be no Arab embrace." [Laughs]. "Yeah," Rabin said, "OK, I'll shake hands, but no kissing." [Laughs.][17]

The psychodrama produced by the White House itself was a prank whose fall guy could easily be guessed. Millions of viewers were held breathless, in the pure tradition of the thriller. It was agreed, as the magazine explains, that Itzhak Rabin would shake hands with Arafat. Yet the choreography was enlivened for a few seconds by the Israeli prime minister's refusal to shake hands. That Arab viewers broke out in an icy sweat was of no consequence to the smiling President who took a serious moment for all humanity as a mere opportunity, a godsend actually, to increase his popularity and spike the ratings.

Such effects of communication deeply upset the concept of democracy and call the credibility of politics into question. What was once an asset of democracy has become a vice.[18] To deal with the commonweal (*res republica*) in public space was only yesterday the claim around which all the other claims of democracy's champions crystallized.

Equal freedom could not have been confirmed if power management was not confined to private spaces. It is useless to insist on the fundamental role the media played in supporting and facilitating this task. Just recently, for instance, we were calling a miracle the fact that television closes the gap between social strata and enables the fulfillment of the democratic ideal. In the imagination and intention of its initiators, this ideal was to be populated by informed citizens, not by a mass stupefied by the negative effects of the medium. Democracy and the media were soon found to be a barren couple, unable to bear its democratic fruit, the citizen.

The frantic waltz in which democracy and communication are entangled gets further carried away by the economic factor bursting onto the dance floor. The two-step turns into a thousand-step in which we begin to whirl around endlessly and ungracefully. In fact, the dance becomes a game. The Agora becomes a merry-go-round;[19] Circe has struck again.

The issues raised by functional communication are exacerbated by a market logic that distorts the facts and puts the pretensions of a triumphant democracy in an awkward position. What were originally values worth sacrificing ourselves for have become truths that are sacrificed to keep up the appearances of democracy. Image civilization meets the needs of a liberal ideology based on the law of supply and demand.[20] Values are merely commodities, empty concepts that resonate like so many advertising credits.

Man is nothing more than the citizen of a virtual society, living on a notion of democracy and an illusory omniscience. With these he imagines he is taking a full and active role in democratic life. But within this infernal triangle the power of his political nature has already declined considerably. It unravels altogether in the context of an increasingly savage liberalism that imposes its unshakable logic even over domains that had been reserved for the realization of supreme values.

A Muzzled Democracy

We are filled with consternation as we witness the buying up of the media by big finan-cial groups. A French newspaper as prestigious as *La Tribune* was recently brought on the carpet at the request of its majority shareholder, the Louis Vuitton-Moët Hennessys group. The newspaper was severely reprimanded for its objective analysis of the difficulties the very same group had been encountering. The article was hardly subversive.

Under such conditions, where is the freedom of expression? Where is journalism's honor, its defining nature? What of democracy when we witness the progress of market thinking encroaching against freedom of expression?

TF1 is a dependent of Bouygues, M6 of Lyonnaise des eaux, Canal Plus of Vivendi. Karl Zéro, journalist at Canal Plus, related a couple of years ago how he was set three red lines that were not to be crossed in his television news: no soccer, no cinema, no Société Générale des eaux.[21]

It would be futile in one chapter to try to touch on all the deviations hazardous to democracy that are set off by the interaction of the political domain with that of the media in a purely consumerist perspective. The evolution—or devolution—of communications brings about a series of breaks at different levels. Each break deserves a thesis, an extended reflection, in itself.

The art of governing is not the only one that is undermined by the inescapable media coverage in the modern world. "Diplomacy, justice, religion, art, and even scientific research are also performed by press conferences and for the cameras. 'Seen on TV' has become an argument as weighty as *Aristotelis dixit* in the days of old."[22]

The game of globalization is led by communications. It is the expression of a dynamic that is inevitably dragging us towards an unknown destination, a psycho-politico-social upheaval certainly, a new dawn of time. When Wolton enumerates the domains linked by communications, the word "seismic" seems an understatement. Apocalypse would be the right word.

> Communication is a research field that mobilizes no less than ten disciplines: anthropology, linguistics, philosophy, sociology, law, political science, psychology, history, economics, and psycho-sociology. It is not a single discipline but a multidisciplinary subject. This poses formidable problems of translation among disciplines and of overlapping issues.[23]

The overlapping of issues inherent to communications materializes as a cyclonic whirling, in which the wild race to scoop is a powerful dynamo.

Television beats all the records in the deluge of information that fills our minds with its dregs. Max Dorra, Professor of Medicine at Paris V University, attacks television's threat to the culture as "the pernicious prosthesis of all solitudes":

> A biologist went so far as to wonder, in a 1993 English scientific journal, whether the habit of passively watching television's procession of violence and murders, each day and for a long period of time, did not harm certain cerebral structures involved in the fragile mechanism of recollection, and thus contribute to the development of an Alzheimer-type dementia.[24]

One cannot resist an avalanche of questions:

> Who can be sure, indeed, that taking high doses of the rubbish that constitutes 90% of programming will not have an irreversible effect, in the medium and long term, on viewers' consciousness itself?[25]

The question is not even posed for the people of the underdeveloped countries who do not produce the image and who content themselves with greedily consuming the product. They ingurgitate trifles all day long and have no antibody that could diminish the viral effects of excessive media coverage. The widespread illiteracy[26] affecting their youth is a national catastrophe in light of the high percentage this youth represents in the population pyramid.

The scourge is devastating; the stupefying effect already operates in the short term. Their lifeblood already suffers symbolically from Alzheimer's. The youth of the underdeveloped countries, more than that of other countries, are permanently delirious for having been handed, bound and tied, to Circe, the enemy of levelheaded reflection.

Unequal Communication

A sad example of this alienation is illustrated by a girls' high school in Casablanca where the schoolgirls, strangely enough, all began to limp. They were identifying with the heroine of a Brazilian soap opera; she has that handicap now, but it will all turn out well for her in the end as a dream princess. "What desire does this visual drug satisfy, what suffering does it assuage?" we may well wonder with teaching-physician Daniel Bougnoux.[27]

The question allows us to dwell on a crucial point that the media frenzy engulfs and blurs. It is time to regain control of ourselves over the vertigo produced by the media phenomenon, to trace the broad outline of its reality as it stands.

We have the regrettable tendency to eclipse the difference of the relationship we have with communications depending on whether we belong to the center of modernity or come from its peripheral regions. There is suffering—and then there is suffering; there is alienation—and alienation. Everything lies in the degree of receptiveness that we have before the global event. This receptiveness may be greatly conditioned by cartographic—and thus economic and social—latitudes and longitudes. The evident antibody deficiency of our poor school Cinderellas comes from material, intellectual, and moral indigence with which their life as underdeveloped youth is imbued.

Fantasizing has tragic effects for someone who, in addition to having an ill-made and ill-filled head, has an empty stomach. Our teenagers have no shield to ward off the fatal blows of daydreaming, wreaking havoc in a youth that is driven to despair by the present and distressed by the future. The escape into dreams suggested by others through B movies ("Z" would be more apt) is no less fatal than the escape ahead on makeshift small boats.[28]

In their culturally precarious situation, the countries of the South can only be concerned apparently with the worst aspects of communication. In the prevailing discussions of communications, the fact is seldom remembered that in order to communicate, you need the technical and financial infrastructures it requires. The sole medium available to the middle class in the countries of the South is television, the most alienating of the media, and the one that stands at opposite extremes with the communications' normative dimension.

Little consideration is paid to the enormous communications gulf that is widening between the rich countries and the poor. Wherever television has become the opium of the people, communications signifies submission to an audiovisual cultural invasion. If, as it is claimed, communications media enable citizens to be active participants, to which share in this international forum can the Third World aspire, when 80% of its population do not even have a telephone?

This percentage is oddly like another one in connection with the democratic reality of the Greek *agora*. In Athens, slaves, representing 80% of the city's population, were not entitled to partake in political life and opinion. How percentages do resemble each other throughout times and democracies!

If France, a power among powers, considers itself to be underprivileged, without the funds necessary to purchase the hardware adequate for effective communication, and if thus millions of *its* citizens are excluded from the circle of the connected,[29] what can those with no infrastructure hope for?

How to have access to development and be able to enter economic competition when the sole medium that a marginalized humanity has at disposal is mass television? If in the West its (very often idiotic) programs, broadcast by means of dish antennas, assail viewers and stupefy relatively cultivated consciences, they suppress values, stifle cultures, and commit a real genocide in the soul of the countries of the South. Intellectually unarmed in the face of the tragic advance of stupidity that results from widespread illiteracy, minds in these lands are much more easily brainwashed.

The necessities represented by the global market—which flouts every vestige of decency—and the dream generated by its sanitized image of the other (perceived on a screen of lies) basically sap any will to resist, any desire to be different, and any serious attempt to anticipate the future.

This subordination to the superficial image cuts into the flesh and dissolves the last cultural antibodies. Other horrible wounds tear a social fabric already weakened by local economic and political crises.

An Alert

It is a sign of dishonesty to revile without restraint the modern means of communication while the telephone is within our means, the text of our work is born on the screen of our computer, and the Internet enables us to establish relationships of quality. Let us concede to Talleyrand, as Serge Latouche does, that "what is excessive is insignificant." Yet let us borrow other equally sound ideas from Latouche himself:

> I will content myself with pointing out that if I happen sometimes to play the prophet of doom, it is not with the view of contributing to the advent of these misfortunes but rather to attempt to ward them off. Burying one's head in the sand does not seem to me the best solution for limiting probable catastrophes. Alerting public opinion to possible dangers is more the duty of the intellectual than distilling antidepressants on the media.[30]

Latouche thus finds it legitimate to alert public opinion to the probable dangers of the globalization of communications. Like many other wise men, he feels that humanity is menaced by a number of postmodern dangers. It is particularly legitimate, then, to warn those whom the arrogant new world order is about to subjugate forever.

Morin is absolutely correct when he writes, "The global era was born and developed in conquest, enslavement and war. We are still in the global Iron Age and the prehistoric human mind."[31] Since, alas, the global era is a warlike one, he ought to have called it not the Iron Age but rather the Nuclear Age. In his autobiography, *My American Journey,* the notorious General Colin Powell does in fact remind us of this, in maintaining that the use of nuclear weapons was envisaged in the first days of the Gulf War.

At least the Iron Age gave a chance to the defeated. The age of communications gives no such chance to its under-armed, underdeveloped, underinformed, and under-communicating—in a word, subhuman—opponent.

If advanced technology is the sole guarantor that allows us a small place in the sun of human dignity and the means of defending ourselves, who would bet on the security of the regions neglected by modern technology? Along with Latouche, we may well wonder who has the talent to locate the sensitive spots of the suffering down here—that is, in the South:

> Who would bet on Bangladesh, Ethiopia or Burkina Faso? What chance do these states have to enter the technological race, to launch their own telecommunication satellites or build up a successful industry? Whether they adopt a liberal model, a socialist model, or any other conceivable strategy, they have no chance whatever.[32]

Nobody would bet on these regions of the world, nor on any other region of the Third World, since a chasm yawns between them and the superpowers more so in the domain of communications than in any other.

To begin with, what ends does communication serve as seen from the South? When British bombs are dropped on Baghdad with the blessings of the U.S., the answer to this question blazes forth as quick as a Tomahawk: it is to wage wars and subjugate peoples. It is used to trigger "Desert Storms" and playing the "Fox" that has eaten mad cow.[33]

Communication media establish supremacies in minds and consciences before any other place. Jean-Marie Guéhenno says: "In the imperial age, the strong are sufficiently strong as soon as the weak have recognized their place."[34]

The Gulf War demonstrated to the whole world who was the Rambo of Rambos, the Zorro of Zorros, the Supreme Master of the world.

Even as I write these lines, our brothers and sisters in Iraq are on the receiving end of white-hot showers. In the past few years millions of demonstrators have walked the streets of Arab capitals baying at the moon and shouting slogans of pique, painful echoes of the moaning of the victims of globalized, dominating, and alienating communications. Anger is the sole weapon that Uncle Sam, magnanimous and understanding, will allow us. What can shouts do against the supreme weapon?

The face of the Internet is darkened by the black smoke reeking with the scorched flesh of Iraqi victims (and many others) that mingles with the odor of incense burnt in its honor by a communicating humanity. Can we still sing its praises without raising an eyebrow at such the following?

With the Internet, the famous global conscience much advocated by such precursors as Teilhard de Chardin becomes palpable. In cyberspace, the notion of alien does not exist. . . . [W]hat is great about the Internet is the word "sharing." The sharing of information is a long scientific tradition. We have attempted to abolish frontiers.[35]

In the light of the infernos of Baghdad, Palestine, Afghanistan, and elsewhere, we can only be reminded that the Internet was created in 1969 for purely military purposes. The prime concern prompting the creation of the Internet project was to avoid interruptions in communication between the armed forces in the event of atomic war. Since then, despite two cowboy raids, this truth is ignored, and only the beneficial and evident virtues of the Net are praised.

Nonetheless, the first reality of the Net is that it encompasses the world, laying it bare to the inquisitive eyes of the world's richest countries, and facilitates the operation of the punitive forces of a singular Power, with its singular way of thinking and singular oafishness.

Communication As Domination
For forty years, the American pole had found a serious adversary in the Soviet block against which it engaged in a constant trial of strength.

As the "fragmented empire" surrendered willy-nilly, technology became ever more sophisticated, the means grew huge, and the arms that used to counter those of the sworn (and since warded off) enemy began to grow restless—high time to relax for a while and show the world who is now the emperor in an era of computerized modernity.

The configuration of the Iraqi terrain, "which lends itself well like anywhere else to the electronic war,"[36] is ideal for killing many birds with one stone. According to the texts approved by the Security Council, the objectives of American raids on Iraq are four in number. Three are the product of pure demagoguery, replying to the official "fuss" about Kuwait. Only the fourth objective is reliable, namely, the foundation of a new world order of which Mr. Bush Senior claims to be the glorious founding architect.

The Gulf War is the ideal opportunity for testing modern techniques of sophisticated warfare, in which all the dead are on the side of the less modern, the less integrated. What was first done with a computerized simulator that enables the reconstruction of any conceivable battlefield[37] is now put to the test *in vivo*. Rebels are intimidated: "whipping boys" are bombarded. Since there are no longer any lands to be invaded in the Imperial Era, minds are tamed by the image tattooed on them of the invincible country, of a master that commands strict obedience.

Communications technologies are supposedly an electronic scalpel for waging a clean war. Worthy heir of classic butchery instituted by the two world wars, surgical warfare fits acts of heavy surgery.[38] If it is true that certain strikes were meticulously directed, most of the bombs were of the standard type. Napalm is still in use in computerized modernity; nothing has changed in the hideous face of barbarity aside from the cosmetic effects administered by the media event.

Circe, surpassing herself, succeeds in showing us a war without bloodshed and casualties. War is acceptable to the modern public conscience only because it takes place without the human element being directly involved in reports. There lies the principle of clean warfare. The collective conscience remains intact since it is made to believe that advanced new communications technologies enable such amazing feats of guidance precision as that of attacking a land point without a single civilian being hurt. Admiration is deliberately fostered by the clean photographs taken by satellite, and by the co-ordination of various operations made possible by advanced engineering.

If the networks are used for waging war, they are also used for manipulating public opinion and using special effects.

The mass media will become the accomplices of huge networks so as to give meaning to the meaningless and legitimacy to the illegitimate. The Gulf War is a bitter pill that the politician of the new world disorder takes care to coat with all the pleasant flavors you wish. The first choice he will give you is the "necessity" of this surgical operation, guaranteed to be painless.

If we anticipate a little and dissect the metaphor of "surgical warfare," we may suppose that the body undergoing the surgery is obviously the idyllic international community that Mommy America cossets assiduously with the collaboration of her home helpers, the international organizations.

The elements of this international body are not homogeneous and equal, of course. The status of secondary organs is delegated to the countries of the South while the vital organs are evidently located in the North. Killing off a whole nation of the South by imposing an embargo or drowning it under a lashing rain of fire should not be too moving. It is merely the equivalent of an appendectomy, or the cauterizing of an unwanted wart.

High Morality

During the Gulf War, Richard Nixon, "highly moral" between his election and Watergate, gave lessons on deontology and know-how to his valiant counterpart Bush, the founder of the New World Order and the emperor of the two hemispheres:

> If we must go to war, it will not be a war just about oil. It will not be a war about a tyrant's cruelty. It will not be a war about democracy. It will be a war about peace—not just peace in our time, but peace for our children and grandchildren in the years ahead. . . . That is why our commitment in the Gulf is a highly moral enterprise.[39]

All the means of communication were applied to legitimize the indefensible.[40] Far more effective than the press, television is a means for fashioning and pacifying irritated consciences. The lesson drawn from the Vietnam War is that it is highly inadvisable to show images of suffering.

The countries that rule the world now have to face the dilemma of the morbid taste the masses have acquired for necrophiliac television on the one hand, and the need to present a sanitized image of state violence on the other. Another good lesson learned is that blood is okay on camera only when one does not feel direct involvement—and never when children are present or when the enemy is virtually disarmed.

The staff of the press departments belonging to "civilized" countries have served their apprenticeship with the U.S.: there would be no "leaking" of shock images that leave indelible bruises in people's collective memories. The campaigns are immaculate, the troops always impeccable, violence nonexistent. The army is laudable for its valor and chivalry.

This traditional image is courageously defended by interested parties who will not stop for anything to maintain it. Didn't the U.S. Marines go as far as to murder the Spanish journalist Juantxu Rodriguez, a photographer for *El País,* for having taken too much interest in their blunders?[41] The image is no laughing matter.

The solution to the dilemma of information or prevention is found: the impossible is achieved, the war is presented without showing any real image, just a series of substitutes. The viewer is drowned in a flood of archive footage, models, maps, accounts of military experts, debates, phone logs.

The leading lights of warring modernity have passed on the word:

> War itself is the blind spot of the huge device installed precisely for close-up shots. . . . During Israel's 1982 invasion of Southern Lebanon, the United Kingdom's reconquest of the Falklands in 1982, the U.S. occupation of Grenada in 1983, France's incursion in Chad in 1988, and the U.S. invasion of Panama in 1989, none of these countries allowed journalists to follow the events. There are no images of any of these wars except those taken under the control of the armed forces.[42]

Censure has become the rule precisely in this domain. France, for instance, forbids journalists to get too close to the facts; it is left to the staff to invent a war scene in which victims and blood are invisible. Ignacio Ramonet addresses this blacklisting:

> In the Gulf conflict, the practice of censure became explicit rules; referring to an order dated 1914, the French army forbade journalists to be "in contact with fire." The information directors of French television accepted the filming of images from the front to be done by cameramen of the ECPA (School of Army Cinema and Press) and to be supervised, before being aired, by SIRPA (Information and Public Relations Department), run by General Germanos. . . . The Gulf War remains invisible.

Honor is salvaged by concocting a smooth image of the attack. This production resembles movie sequences in which a Hollywood hero delivers telling blows and emerges from the fray quite serene, as if the matter were just a game. The clean image eases the conscience of the era of the "modernicious world."

When our homes are besieged by unverifiable views and forged images, we think we are witnessing the facts. The image is by far the most dangerous weapon possessed by modern communications. It is so oppressive that it adheres to the brain even quicker than to the retina, and it sinks in before we have opened the door of our understanding. The image seeps in, becomes embedded, imposes itself. The policy of "make believe," so dear to Napoleon, sees unprecedented possibilities opening before it in the imperial and modern era.

Overinformation, Disinformation

Summing up, then, we may say that journalism's system of ethics has blown up completely under the pressures of corporate logic. The latter, dangerously linked to an unhealthy political will, conspires in the pretense of a serene new international order—indeed, one that guarantees world security! Serving this objective alliance, mass television must take the mentality of the average citizen-consumer into account in its fictionalizing of the cruel facts. The war as covered on TV must be as visually stunning as the carefully designed package of any consumer good.

As advertising, the news thrusts the citizens of the modern world into the very machinery of the here and now. It makes them forget their own realities, their memory.

Overinformation, disinformation! Propaganda is geared to the instantaneous, the short term. What lasts too long, makes too many remote historical references, no longer moves; well-considered reflection is no longer of interest. In this informational bulimia only the shocking, the rapid and ephemeral image is edible.

Jacques Ellul writes about the relationship of the public with memory:

> The public is only sensitive to the contemporary event; it is the only thing that matters, the only issue in question. Propaganda must thus be linked to what is current; propaganda based on historical factors will go nowhere. We witnessed the failure of Vichy's propaganda against England when he evoked Napoleon and Jeanne d'Arc. . . . [S]uch significant facts so deeply rooted in French consciousness are no longer effective springboards for propaganda.[43]

For this very reason the propaganda for the justice and effectiveness of the Gulf War succeeded.

> The media almost announced that it ended before it had even begun. That also explains the media's adherence to the doctrine of "no war," the fiction of a mere international police operation.[44]

By way of concluding this chapter and the first section of the book, let us say that what provokes such criticism should not be taken as a resentment or rejection of modernity and its tools.

Those who know *islam* by a channel other than the biased media know perfectly that the global dimension cannot frighten the followers of a Message that is meant to be universal. Criticizing modernity does not mean refusing dialog with it—even positive participation in it. God willed that modernity is increasingly inevitable. The manner in which Islam will henceforth have to conceive the world must take account at all costs of this parameter.

The West, for its part, needs to see itself as it appears to the oppressed of the world; it can then adjust a little the image it gives of itself in its officially defended humanist discussions. The modern world is a fact; *islam,* in addition to being a fact, is a hope. If the modern world regains or acquires the ability, the courage, and the wisdom to face the questions it is being asked—if it becomes aware of the landslide that threatens to sap its foundations—it will find in *islam* a means for its edifying that world and safeguarding its humanity.

That is what we will attempt to broach in what follows, after questioning the difficulty the West finds in listening to its "other," Islam.

NOTES

1. Jean-Marie Guéhenno, *La fin de la démocratie* [the end of democracy], Flammarion, 1995, p. 112.

2. Jacques Levy, cited by Edgar Morin and Sami Naïr in *Une politique de civilization* [a policy of civilization], Arléa, Paris, 1997.

3. Morin & Naïr (1997), Foreword.

4. That is, rational knowledge combined with the intuition and faith that lead to the knowledge of the Creator.

5. Qur'ān: S. XXXII. 9.

6. On December 17, 1998, "Rambo" did it again, crushing Iraq with a flood of bombs, and thus flouting the most elementary human rights.

7. Wolton (1997), p. 374.

8. Wolton (1997), p. 57.

9. Ibid.

10. Wolton (1997), p. 131.

11. Wolton (1997), p. 191.

12. Wolton (1997), p. 221.

13. Serge Halimi, *Les nouveaux chiens de garde* [the new watchdogs], Raisons d'agir, 1997. The expression comes from Paul Nizan, who used to speak of certain philosophers as watchdogs.

14. Wolton (1997).

15. Concept introduced by E. Newman to explain the situation of a candidate for a political career who is excluded from his representatives by the media, and who shuts himself up in a soundproof shell without the least chance of being heard.

16. Guéhenno (1995), p. 47.

17. *Rolling Stone,* December 1993, pp. 43–44.

18. In the legal sense of the word.

19. As early as 1937, Mumford saw in the broadcasting networks the means to revive the *agora* of the smallest cities of antique Greece. At the end of the 1960s, he declared the immediate advent of the global village via the cathodic link, as reported by J. W. Carey in the *Journal of Communication,* 1981, vol. 31, no. 3, and by Armand Mattelart in "Nouvelles utopies, grandes inquiètudes" [new utopias, huge concerns], *Le Monde diplomatique,* Nov. 1995, p. 4.

20. American English has coined the term "infomercial" (information + commercial).

21. Halimi (1997).

22. Cf. Daniel Bougnoux, "La Science au risque des médias" [science in danger of the media], in *Le Monde diplomatique* of Sept. 1995, p. 32.

23. Wolton (1997), p. 68.

24. Cf. *Le Monde diplomatique* of June 1996, p. 32.

25. Ibid.

26. Widespread inasmuch as our teaching programs have the assigned role of further benumbing children of school age.

27. Bougnoux (Sept. 1995).

28. Each day, dozens of desperate young Moroccans and Africans attempt to illegally cross the Spanish borders through the Straits of Gibraltar. Dreaming of El Dorado, they most often meet wreckage and death, or they are repatriated in very poor condition.

29. Astard Torrès, in *Mattelart* (Nov. 1995), p. 4.

30. Serge Latouche, *La planète des naufragés, essai sur le sous-développement* [the planet of the shipwrecked: essay on underdevelopment], *La Découverte/essais,* 1993, p. 8.

31. Morin & Naïr (1997), p. 19.

32. Latouche (1993), p. 28.

33. Operation Fox, the second American raid on Iraq, was carried out with the help of the U.K.

34. Guéhenno (1995), p. 99.

35. *Télérama,* special edition (April 1996).

36. Cf. Gilbert Achcar, "Les Nations-Unis au fil des objectifs américains" [the U.N. along the lines of American objectives], *Le Monde diplomatique,* Oct. 1995, p. 8.

37. Cf. Jean Guisnel, "L'Internet, ça sert aussi à faire la guerre" [the Internet also serves to wage war], *Le Monde diplomatique,* May 1996, p. 16.

38. "Surgical strike" is the expression advocated by Henry Kissinger at the beginning of the crisis.

39. The *International Herald Tribune,* Jan. 7, 1991.

40. I apologize to a certain press that will recognize itself and which, I must admit, merits credit for its struggle for objectivity.

41. Cf. Ignacio Ramonet, "La télévision loin des fronts" [television far from the front lines] in *Le Monde diplomatique* of February 1991.

42. Ibid.

43. Jacques Ellul, *Propagandes,* Economica, Paris 1990.

44. Pierre Guislain, "Le spectacle de la propagande" [the propaganda show] in *Le Monde diplomatique* of May 1991, pp. 16–17.

II.
TURBULENT
COLLISIONS

II. 1. SALUTARY CONTACT

More and more, the history of humanity is
becoming a race between education and catastrophe.
Herbert George Wells

So barbarous the atmosphere in which by fate I stand
that my own country seems a foreign land.
Théophile de Viau

Being unable to imagine the Other is one of the constant traits of every
middle-class mythology.
Roland Barthes

To comprehend the Other, you must not commandeer him but rather become his guest.
Louise Massignon

A Lopsided Dialog

In the context of our general development, the balance of power the West maintains with other societies distorts its vision of the other. As the chief engineer of a dangerously lurching megamachine, the West is not about to take anyone else's advice.

A world that conceives of itself as the only civilization worthy of the name and measures the rest of humanity from the heights of its power cannot suddenly and easily regain its modesty and learn wisdom from any other culture.

With all other modes of thinking the West maintains a relationship of dominator vs. the dominated; in such a relationship no conceptual dialectic is conceivable. It allows no discussion of differences except with amnesiacs. The idea of listening to *islam* is not even on the table. Islam has too strong a memory, too mobilizing a history, for it to be anything more than an enemy the moment it attempts to get organized.

It is, of course, entirely in the natural order of things for the West to despise the overtures of those under its sway. It is in the nature of *islam* to invite humanity, however taken with itself, to search for meaning and define its ends. The invitation to renew one's sources in faith and make sense (*dāwa*) will exist as long as there are Muslims, it being the most sacred duty for all who are faithful to the Islamic faith.

As guardians of the Message, they have the sacred duty to inform man about the meaning of his existence and his Ultimate Life.

The social order advocated by *islam* and its conception of power have no meaning except in this context, and have no value except in relation to this end.

Nonetheless, we must be fervent in presenting *islam* to mankind if it is to effect the social harmony it has promoted throughout history. We must invite mankind to *islam* if it is to rescue him from the brink of the abyss and provide the path that will escape ecological catastrophe and the confusion of priorities. If *islam* is to be the remedy for the brutality and violence from which modern societies suffer, we must bring its message to others.

To engage a humanity that wants to hear nothing about life after death, it will be helpful to introduce the teachings and true meaning of *islam* by speaking first of its purely societal and historical dimension.

Violence, violence, and always violence: that is the flagrant reality of the modern world. Words cannot conceal the reality.

The "peace" whose praises international politics sing, this *pax moderna,* is nothing but a balance of terror that might topple over at any moment—while on the fringes of the modern world societies lash out at each other mercilessly and endlessly.

The "security of people" guaranteed by the World's Policeman is merely a euphemism for the security of one people only, namely the United States of America. "Liberalism," that sweet-sounding word, is nothing more than the institutionalized and legitimized law of the jungle.

At the dawn of the Third Millennium, the citizens of the center of this system are no more immune to its dangers than those of the periphery. We need only mention the case of those poor soldiers sent to Iraq who died from a strange disease as a consequence of their exposure to radiation from depleted-uranium bombs their own army ordered them to drop on enemy forces. This indicates that the nuclear threat not only hangs over the heads of modernity's foes—at least, those whom modernity reckons as its foes; the ecological threat is also a universal threat.

In the hearts and deeds of the frustrated citizens of a system that deifies the ego, violence is rampant, even more so in the living-rooms of modernity than in its garrets.

The epitaph an uncurbed modernism prepares for humanity's tomb reads: "Here lies a colossal and unfair civilization: it was near-sighted and violent." But who will be there to write such an epitaph? The modern, atomic apocalypse will leave no survivors.

The imperialism of the system called modernism is global in the economic realm, total in its punishments, dismal in its ignorance.

No one is safe from the hazards on board that are possible at any moment. Passengers who are aware of the dangers know the risks they incur despite their having a place of honor on the drunken boat.[1] Surely the others know—those who live under the illusion that they are running modernity—that it is modernity that is running them, determining the conditions of even the spheres they hold most private.

Surely those who think they are inventing the world must know that it is already destroying them. We have all become more subjects than makers of modernity, prisoners of a system that breaks up under our feet.

Catastrophism or proselytism, it little matters what one calls an invitation to what is essential.

Achilles' Prayer

Michel Serres provides much food for thought about the dominant system in his eloquent image of Achilles. He introduces the allegory of this king's war with a river in spate as one that perfectly expresses our epoch (which is springing leaks everywhere):

> We cannot tell whether Homer, in Canto XXI of the Iliad, intends for this river to symbolize the ever-increasing flow of enraged enemies that assail the hero. Be that as it may, as Achilles continues to fling the numberless corpses of his vanquished and slain adversaries into the stream, its level rises to such an extent that the swollen stream comes menacingly up to his shoulders. Abashed by this new terror he rids himself of bow and saber and, raising to the heavens his now freed hands, he prays. Has he triumphed so completely that his now repugnant victory has turned into defeat? The world—the gods—burst in where rivals once stood.[2]

Pursuing the metaphor further—as concern for the principle of *dâwa* urges us—we may note that a belief in several gods did not rescue Achilles from his swamp nor his barbarity: Achilles still repeats his offences today. The Renaissance, which identified with Hellenism, was precisely the decisive moment when Achilles put his heels into the moving sludge.

Greek philosophy, the initiator of individualism, did not permit man to "gather his heaven and earth."[3] It is, however, written in the book of the days that whatever does not gather man's heaven and earth inevitably engulfs him.

Like Homer's Achilles, surrendering to his gods, the time has perhaps come for the bewildered, modern Achilles to pray. What is meant is not that "pagan prayer"[4] that has led us to our current situation, with our legs in the mire, water up to our chin, threatened with drowning altogether with the next corpse flung into the river of the global village.

In his original style, Serres proposes that the fate of the modern world's masters is irremediably sealed to that of its serfs, as well as to the fate of the environment they are irreparably destroying. The nature of that world creates indestructible, though pernicious, links. "Who can ever say where master and slave fight one another? Our culture," Serres concludes, "detests the world."

What to do then? This is a question that has always preceded revolutions. God alone knows our world needs a real revolution.

To save this world of ours, will it be enough to pray some prayer or other mumbled in a little dark corner or in a church and denied the moment the spotlight is turned on?

Will it do to fold one's hands in a fatalist prayer, with eyes closed to let fate take its course? Certainly not!

It is urgent to come up with another kind of prayer, a prayer that is at once vibrant with the divine, with profound compassion for humankind, with enduring care for one's destiny and that of the world. The prayer that can rescue the modern Achilles is one that, more than a stammering utterance or a glimmer flickering in the depths of the heart, must be a vital force that will gather man's heaven and earth.

To rescue the modern Achilles, there must be a prayer that can effectively raise mountains, dry up the menacing flood; a prayer that can open the way to a better world where a neighbor is not a rival to be eliminated, a foe to be suppressed, an enemy to hate, a voice to win elections, a woman to lust after, or the "next corpse" that is going to make the river overflow.

The prayer that befits the modern Achilles is one addressed to his God, the One Who ceaselessly sends warning signs and shows him the way, the One Whom he has ceaselessly and arrogantly ignored!

Let us cross the Rubicon, the same one into which Achilles, relying entirely on his own forces to subdue the world and nature, is still sinking today.

Islam[5] stands in outline on the other bank, with safety for all humankind.

It is easy to imagine the hue and cry aroused by such a forthright invitation to a faith that is little quoted on the banks of the right-thinking and up-to-date modern world.

A Beneficial Weaning

Not only threatened with drowning in a raging river, the modern Achilles feeds on "earthly food" that produces horrible cravings. Were he to decide to wean himself from such a diet, it would not be easy. Human consciousness is consigned by modern philosophy to black mazes into which filters only the pale glimmer of decaying neon light—the counsel of a few fashionably murky minds.

We have already dwelt[6] on the close links between the prevalent philosophical culture and mass psychology. The thinking of André Gide, for instance, aptly illustrates the general trend of Western consciousness. Fifty years after the writer's death, his thought is still celebrated as immortal and ever relevant. Gide prescribed for modern man the adoration of instinct and the present as the source of his happiness. "Do not distinguish between God and happiness," he solemnly counseled; "place your happiness in the present!"[7]

Gide did not have to exert much effort in persuading his contemporaries to browse blithely on the fields he had prospected for them. His last and best advice, addressed to Nathanael,[8] went unheard, alas. "Cast my book aside!" he cried—too late. The Nathanaels of Darwin's bestial tenet have already chewed their cud.

"Earthly" food; Gide could call a spade a spade. Any conception of humanity that is not born in the bosom of faith as a supreme and sublime truth is the assassin-accomplice of base and debilitating tendencies. Of the man who is prisoner of his ego, the Qur'ān says: *But he inclined to earthly attractions.*[9]

With his hypertrophied head and plugged-up ego, man easily tumbles into the void of the pervading, and usually atheistic, philosophies. He casts himself in without so much as a cry of anguish; you would think it his natural domain, the den of his deepest self. The "vacancy of the absolute" is accepted as inevitable in modern times.

André Comte-Sponsville, along with others, has set for himself the mission of finding palliatives to a morality based on faith.[10] In *La Société en quête de valeurs* [society in search of values], a book dedicated to seeking new points of reference, he develops the art of "unfounded values."[11] The issue, he explains in the book's introduction, is not one of "inventing new values, but new fidelity to the values we have received."

With pity we stroll behind our philosopher through death's corridors, where the fundamental values inherited from Christian humanism await the last rites. Before enumerating alternative proposals in response to the questions of the modern conscience, Comte-Sponsville muses:

> What to do? The first move was of course to search for alternative gods: Nature, particularly in the eighteenth century; Life, especially in the nineteenth century; Science or History in the nineteenth and twentieth centuries. But these alternative gods failed to link the true and the good, what is and What Must Be, the actual and its value, however we define the manner we find satisfying.[12]

He then observes how a morality based on natural principle obviously risks veering into the bestial. It is for him no longer a question of sanctioning what is natural as immoral. That would send us back to angelic pretensions, "confining us to an existence so difficult as to be impossible and a living lie."

Continuing his free fall in the abyss of groundless proposals, Comte-Sponsville assures us that Life seems to him a dangerous deity. Fearing the chaos brought on by a Darwinian logic taken to extremes, he denounces it as well, declaring it unable to make a good god, "since it, too, commits the worst."

Our guide to obscure mazes then tries out Science, History, and many of the other idols exhibited in the gallery of modern literature, as candidates for godhood. Science does not qualify, since it "speaks only in the indicative, never in the imperative." Besides being multiple, it never allows us to make judgments. Nuclear Physics, for instance, does not say "whether nuclear power plants or atom bombs are necessary, or under what circumstances we have the moral right to use them." History would make a bad deity since it induces us to mix genres and fall into finalism. The latter "consists in explaining and judging a process by its end and therefore mistaking results for causes, tendencies for meanings or values."

The author continues to smash idols one after another, and we follow him, momentarily bedazzled by the good measure of his iconoclastic criticism. Unfortunately this wears out over time. Growing weary of the deities passing in review, he concludes that nothingness alone is of sound value: the void to dwell in is now "the vacancy of the absolute." This vacancy is for him the end of both absolute certainties and absolute values.

"It is like a gulf between two crests," he is resigned to admit, "in which each knows his own frailty and that of the other, as well as the gulf between them. . . . [A] great gap has been created, and we must somehow live in it. It's what characterizes our spiritual space."[13]

Overcome, surely, by vertigo, suspended as he is between two crests, he attempts to hang on to the latest gods after avowing helplessness. He seizes Complexity[14] and then loosens his grip saying that if man is more complex than amoeba, that does not "suffice to assure his value, nor to found a morality." In his spiral dive toward the absurd, he grips to the Anthropic Principle, only to abandon it for a hidden one. Then, like a fatal fall, the text ends with a bitter question: "Are morality, values and meaning to be renounced then?"

The answer, though mitigated, is suicidal. Falling into the void must surely disturb sound reason:

> I do not believe anything. . . . With no absolute foundations, there can scarcely exist moral absolutes, values or meaning. Yet being relative does not mean being nothing at all. On the contrary, nothingness might possibly be an acceptable absolute. . . . Today, the stake is one of inhabiting the relativism to which we are destined by the evolution of our knowledge and our beliefs without, however, sinking into nihilism.[15]

We may sincerely wonder how that is possible.

We especially wonder whether such defeatist tendencies can be held by *all* the passengers held hostage on the megamachine that threatens at any moment to crash.

Antidotes

Are we ready to give up and cast ourselves into the void? By reconciling ourselves with God and listening to His Final Message, we could change tack and restore equilibrium to the human epic. Surely that would prove greater wisdom than looking for deities in the void!

To know God as He wishes to be defined to us would shelter us from the attractions of the void for our modern collective consciousness that makes us want it for a habitat. Instead of dwelling in vagueness, as our author-witness of a doubtful and dubious philosophy would encourage us to do, the safest move at a time when everything has sprung a leak would be to climb to the summit.

Individually and collectively, the Qur'ānic Message is our lifeline. The Qur'ān offers access to accessible summits and proposes a favorable balance between matter and soul. It appeals to the Divine that glimmers in the depths of each heart and that is susceptible to be unearthed and cleansed so that man may attain bliss in this life and in the Ultimate Life.

These assertions will surely have annoying stench for certain modern minds and will awaken several demons.

One demon hisses the word "proselytism," which according to the *Petit Larousse* means the "ardent zeal to recruit followers, so as to attempt to impose one's ideas."

The Western-centrist demon in his turn sneers that such an invitation smacks of outrageous pretension. How dare a faith whose followers are almost entirely down-and-out citizens of the South give lessons to a rich and modern world well vaccinated against dogmas and missionary zeal!

The demon of ignorance whispers among his close friends that alarmists are often utopians as well. They're quite mad!

The demon of the thesis of the clash of civilizations sniggers that violence is peculiar to such writing; it is a fundamentalist threat.

May God preserve us from demons of all stripes! You cannot summon a civilization that has the monopoly on terror. The proposal is intended for the individual whose heart is sensitive enough to discern the light of the divine star, the Qur'ānic Message, the last lifeline sent to mankind by its Compassionate God.

In this arena of violence that the planet, turned over to unscrupulous man, has become, the appeal is one of vexation, an entreaty, not a demand. It is a cry of compassion for a humanity destined for the heights, but doomed to the baseness of blind modernism.

Man, who is of divine essence, revels instead in sensations that degrade and brutalize him. The receptacle of the divine is content to be a throw-away cup for the liquor of an aimless life. The creature whose heart is made to reflect the sun of the Spirit confines himself in the twilight of spiritual wanderings.

Islam (in the sense of submission to God) could help him out of the rut. Yet we perfectly understand why modernist conscience is restive to its message, since it regards this *islam* as little more than the contingencies of Muslim history and the deductions of orientalism in the service of colonialism.[16]

A Certain Point of View

The difficulty of the contact between the West and *islam* is essentially caused by the negative regard the former has for the latter; it has multiple causes.

An eventful and "crossed" history with *islam* underlies Western patterns of thought. Orientalist writers have also spared no effort in painting the image of Arabs in the blackest of colors. In so doing they have elicited and perpetuated the extremely negative images that persist in Western collective consciousness. These images have not been rectified by more recent close contact with immigrants; "Arab" has become a synonym for trouble—and thus *islam* itself has been tarnished.

The news favored by media coverage further exacerbates a rejection that is more cultural than natural. In order to scrape off the superficial layer of the dross that mars the image of the Universal Message, we must first dissociate *islam* from Arabhood. This would allow a more objective approach by ridding it of such belittling aspects without paying further tribute to common prejudices.

Islam has certainly an obvious historical link with Arabs, as the Prophet himself (grace and peace be upon him) was an Arab. *Islam* came to transform "scrawny camel drivers," as Arabs are described according to a certain orientalism, into the noble bearers of a Universal Message. That is why no one can deny the indestructible link that *islam* has with Arabhood.

The genetic ancestry of the Prophet is a strong evidence of this close relationship. He is certainly the most noble of Arabs, but the transcendence of the Divine Message is the sole nobility that he recognized. He loved those of his race with a natural love. Yet he did not let discriminatory fondness compromise the universal nature of the Message, nor did he love his non-Arab companions any less than the Arab.

The Prophet (grace and peace be upon him) always underlined a disjunction between Arabhood and *islam*. *Islam* has never been the private historical property of Arabs. As *islam* began to spread among other peoples, the Prophet (grace and peace be upon him) said in a *hadīth* addressing his Companions: "There is no superiority of any Arab over any non-Arab unless by his piety." Nobility and merit are not measured by race, since behavior and faith in God alone count.

The Qur'ān emphasizes this truth: *"The most noble among you in the sight of God is the most pious."* [17]

The relationship between *islam* and Arabhood merits attention only insofar as it raises the good question of what was behind the Arab miracle. What force, what power, what energy dwelt in a handful of camel drivers that had neither the weapons of Byzantium nor the military technique of Persia, to the extent that, within a century after the death of the Prophet (grace and peace be upon him), they spread the Islamic faith throughout most of the world? Arabhood? Surely not. The power,[18] justice and coherence of their Message? No doubt.

In about ten years, *islam* enriched the most ancient cultures that were foundering, and the divine breath of the Qur'ān revived dying civilizations from the Sea of China to the Atlantic, including Greece, Persia, Alexandria and Byzantium. Great decadent empires were saved from chaos in the seventeenth century of the Christian era by the profoundness of a Message that made sense.

Islam again today is able to offer a remedy for the illnesses that afflict the modern world, to provide a cure for a system that has in less than two centuries dug the grave of humankind at a Dantesque scale, and that is within a hairsbreadth of putting an end to its epic.

Islam could—but it is only the religion of the Arabs. And there is an unflattering—indeed disgraceful—image of certain Arabs today that disfigures the face of the Message.

Today's Mesdames Nozière

In his novel *The Bloom of Life*, the late-departed Anatole France wrote:

> Monsieur Dubois asked Madame Nozière which was the most ill-fated day in history. She did not know. "It is," said Monsieur Dubois, "the day

of the Battle of Poitiers when, in 732, Arab science, art, and civilization retreated before the barbarous Franks."

This passage takes on full meaning if science is understood to mean not only the rational sciences that Muslims halted at Poitiers by Charles Martel carried in their saddlebags, but above all the Knowledge of God, Revelation.

The amalgam between *islam* and Arabs is not so fortuitous as the one made by our nice Monsieur Dubois. It is difficult to convince the Mesdames Nozière of today that *islam* is not their unfortunate suburban neighbor who happens to be a hereditary Muslim and who swirls about in the xenophobic intrigues of a foreign land.

How to tell them that *islam* is not represented by that poor immigrant cast up by the moral and material indigence of his home country onto the suburbs of Europe? The black hatred of the deposed Arab ought not eclipse the sparkling of a universal faith.

In the worried France of Le Pen,[19] no pen writes as clearly as Stendhal's: "It is we who were barbaric to the East when we went to disturb it with our Crusades. Therefore, we owe the noblest aspects of our morality to these Crusades and to the Moors of Spain."[20]

Today's Madame Nozière is a low-wage earner in the suburbs, a lady who sees the world projected on modernity's screens as a clash of civilizations; how can she possibly overcome her negative image of Muslims?

How can her eyes be turned towards the essential Message of *islam* that the unpleasant image of some of its present followers conceal?

How is she to be persuaded that *islam* is no one's history, but rather an attitude of humility towards the Creator that needs to be rediscovered so that the sacred flame, of which modern mankind is the dulled and witless vestal, may endure—so that the Ultimate Life may be the best?

How is she to understand that *islam* is not her gap-toothed Zohra or her illiterate Fatima? If Zohra is renounced by her husband, and if Fatima knows nothing of hygiene, it is not because they are *islam*'s perfect representatives, but because the misadventures of their history have cut them off from the teachings of *islam*.

It is certainly not easy to go against a prejudice sustained by all those "poor wretches," all those "well-intentioned people who slam the door in the face"[21] of constructive and real dialog.

On the other side of dialog, you need a very strong character in order to run counter to the media catechism in which Arab and Muslim are synonymous with terrorist and gangster.

Let us then enter into dialog boldly, with open minds and generous hearts! Narrow minds have never made history.

We cannot emphasize enough that anyone really willing to understand *islam* must distinguish it from Arabhood, especially in the present times. The "scrawny camel drivers" that the orientalists loved to belittle bore in themselves the germs of high-mindedness and heroism required of the small number of men who went forth to conquer the hearts of the world. Differentiated entirely from Arabhood, however, *islam* has everything to gain.

Minds that swear only by the ready-to-wear image will find the image of the Arabs extremely disfigured. The culture of the instantaneous does not permit everyone to overcome the direct and contemporary image by which the Arab is always the bad guy. Let us then sacrifice the poor Arab so that *islam* may be reborn. Let us sacrifice him on paper and for the good cause, even if he doesn't deserve it. Let us sacrifice him in order to communicate with simple notions that cannot deal with profundity, with minds that are diverted by the unfortunate reductionism of a harried and harrowing culture.

A Repulsive Image

What respect can you have for *islam* when the inevitable link is made between its Message and these Arabs who are no longer "scrawny" at all, and whose big pendulous bellies are even mushier than their morality?

Islam is equally detestable under the guise of the suburban Arab neighbor who throws her garbage from the window, swearing like a trooper in a guttural language that is worrisome to the ears of the Right.

The current case of the woman who was abruptly and unscrupulously repudiated by the polygamous husband who left her responsible for a herd of children does not encourage dialog with *islam* either.

In his *Arabie Saoudite: La dictature protégé* [Saudi Arabia: a protected dictatorship], Jean-Michel Foulquier exclaims, "O Prophet Muhammad, hurry back! They have gone mad!"[22] He is right to be appalled in examining a system, supposedly representative of *islam,* that wanders farther from it each day, in both content and form. He asks for the Prophet's assistance while believing he had not done his best.

The only way to relieve *islam* of the ugliness of its official representatives is to come back to the teachings of the Prophet (grace and peace be upon him). *Islam,* as instructed by the Messenger, is the very opposite of the barbarity and baseness Foulquier saw.

Foulquier seems to insinuate the same thing, albeit in a surge of irony that calls for the Prophet's return. His book is a harrowing account of what a retrograde practice of *islam* is like: a practice that under the control of oil-sticky power has become a vulgar chronicle of atrocity. He takes us to the recesses of the meanness disguised by the sumptuous garment of Muslim billionaires.

The influence of the dollar heaps opprobrium on a certain Islam and transitively on *islam* in general. It also acts on those who proclaim themselves defenders of human rights.

> The foreign governments whose begging ministers flock there year round could not care less about human rights. Human rights? The riyal now has the final word. Like sand, it buries and hides everything.[23]

Above all, Saudi money spoils the image of *islam,* reducing it to the deformed figures that haunt London casinos, with their fetid breath and generous outlays for unspeakable debauchery. The image of the "scrawny" Arab, though sketched by hostile pens, is by far the preferable: better to be bony and worthy than greasy and abject.

Cellulite certainly serves the Message less than bones. Debauchery disgraces *islam* even more than the specter of famine for which the noble Arab tribes, masters in the art of self-sacrifice, were reproached. We may well wonder what genes the fat Arab, bloated with dollars, champagne, and egoism, could have in common with Hatim Attai,[24] who died before the advent of *islam.* Hatim was renowned in Arab legend for his matchless generosity and altruism.

If there still exist some noble-minded among Arabs like Hatim Attaï (and indeed there are many), the Madame Nozière of today is quite indifferent to them. She would not enquire about the past or present magnanimity of those former coolies, particularly when they have become intrusive neighbors.

It is understandable that anyone uninformed about *islam* should erect an insurmountable psychological wall against the faith of the underdeveloped and barbarous. The molding and disfiguring of the image of a civilization weakened by history's distorted events has become the special field of the modern crusade. The end result is an ignoble figurine that is both simplistic and repulsive: a monstrous gargoyle.

Islam has sometimes the feverish-looking emaciated face of a megalomaniac, the living symbol of immoderation and of harebrained, "spicy," and immature theses. Sometimes it has the sanguinary and cynical look of a neuropath leading his people to death. It can also suffer from the leering look or lustful eye of black-and-white princes with extensive transnational harems. Sometimes it has the sinister look of sullen, semiliterate imams who have hooks for hands and violence for faith.

Islam, in the care of a well-equipped and furious press, will often have the profile of the young terrorist who believes he is practicing *islam* by giving vent to his anger as a pariah against a modernity that is despised for being inaccessible.

The general paranoia cleverly maintained by the simplistic and seductive media, well financed and well directed, will attribute to *islam* every face but its own. Nobody knows it as a faith that once made life on earth agreeable and humane, or as the Last Message sent to mankind by the God of mankind.

Is there still in a postmodern world an obstinate man like Monsieur Dubois who is resolved to go against the current and search beyond the clichés about *islam* that hypnotize other minds and prevent them from going beyond defamation?

Surely there are a few calm and collected minds in the countries of the modern world that can relieve their witless neighbors! Surely there are a few stalwarts who can guide the minds confused by Huntington's charts and defuse their destructive implications!

The Need for Levelheadedness

The chances of finding cool heads and alert hearts in this impetuous and turbulent world are slim. Still, we count on finding them, since man's future depends on it. Those with proven levelheaded reflection must match the rise of singleminded secularism in order for the world to avoid dire predictions. We must find civilized spokesmen who can truly accept difference and are able to recognize in *islam,* if not a saving faith for humanity, at least the culture of a whole humanity.

Michel Jobert risks being ranked among the "friends of cut-throats"[25] in his boldness to speak in clearly positive terms of the universalist dimension of the Qur'ānic Message:

> For the Muslim, the human being is essentially "one," and divided mankind is mankind destined for reconciliation. It is impossible nowadays to remain indifferent to such a conception.[26]

Speaking of *islam*'s modernity, by which he surely means the ability of *islam* to propose solutions to modernity's emptiness, he continues:

> a society of dialog (of "social interaction," as we say today), a conception of time that challenges simplistic linear drawing—so many elements reveal *islam*'s surprising modernity. . . . Meeting the challenges of diversity is consonant with the spirit of the Qur'ān. Does it not say: *We made you into nations and tribes so that you might know each other. Verily the most honored of you in the sight of God is the most righteous of you?*[27]

At a dangerous turning point of history—the axial age we are living in, where proximity to the other is in every conceivable way imposed by globalization—*islam* might remedy society's division into sectors. Excessive communication at all costs urges the citizen of the modern world to natural, though not comforting, reactions within a context of easy violence and extreme inflammability.

While the nature of our changing and globalizing world imposes on us a cruel anonymity by diluting us in a formless mass, it also stimulates individualism and sharpens self-centeredness. Identity becomes a place of refuge, a tool of withdrawal, and an alibi for outright war-mongering.

Exhausted societies are the ideal locus where personal aggressions mount and where inflammable, perhaps even explosive, withdrawal attitudes multiply. Such precarious social links as those created by the fact of watching the same television serve only to delay the conflagration, not to check it.

Islam has already radically cured this illness of decadent societies. Its great unifying power could once again be a remedy. It would be above all the absolute remedy for modern man's spiritual wandering and his ignorance about his Destiny after death. Antidote to the world's fragmentation, remedy to the humanity's balkanization, *islam* awaits to be revived in our hearts and clarified in our minds.

These words will undoubtedly provoke smiles of mockery among those who are comfortably seated in their own self-importance. Many would say, "Sheer utopianism." Utopianism! Jacques Berque so rightly evokes the dynamic function of utopia: "Our forecasts of the future would not be chimerical, but merely utopian, to the extent that utopia is the imaginary projection of history on the march."[28]

More concise, Jacques Monod believes that utopia is perhaps not the unrealizable, but only the unrealized.

Finding Man

Let us move forward in history, let us run faster and farther towards this utopia that is not at all chimerical. Let us say that, freed from the straitjacket in which it is confined in many Muslim societies by certain retrogressive traditions, *islam* would resound favorably in all hearts where the human element prevails over the bestial. As it had already been in humankind's history, *islam* will once again become the guarantor of fundamental human rights. Above all, it will teach man the Truth, the secret of his passage on earth, for "man swarms on the planet feeling useless. Talk of his rights will change nothing when the concept of man disappears."[29]

What is man? What is the other? What can "human rights" mean when claimed by a humanity that considers itself stuck in a meaningless and aimless passage on this planet? What rights—and for which man—when humanity wanes or becomes transformed into a naked beast? Which man are we speaking of: the Northerner living carefree in opulence, or the Southerner who shuffles along in his caravan of woes?

Surely the rights written down in international charters remain a dead letter in a world where words are coined and change meaning from one side to the other, one country to another, one ego to another, from me to the other! "The brave meaning of words," as Merleau-Ponty put it, leads us to wonder if "the right to live" has the same meaning under skies as different as those over Bangladesh and Sweden. Speaking of the right to leisure would be an insult in the "cities of joy"—how numerous they are!—in the world forgotten by modernity or, rather, plundered by modernity. The "Universal Declaration of Human Rights" is a sweet and fluffy daydream which will not stop Realpolitik for one single moment. It is the new opiate of the masses.

You must search for your homeland elsewhere than in the fluctuating and uprooted meanings of modernist culture unless you wish to live in illusion and vague imaginings. What miracle can gather concepts that disintegrate at the least blow of the racist wind, at the least suspicion of economic breeze?

But let us return again to our utopia. Since *islam* has its "geographical dimensions, its population weight, [and] its economic potentialities that make it one of the major components of the international community,"[30] it must strive hard to promote a new conception of balance and, as dictated by its nature, work for the establishment of human dignity in peace and harmony.

In *L'humanisme de l'islam* [Islamic humanism][31] Marcel Boisard becomes the advocate of Muslim law. He presents it as the energetic agent that prompted the awakening of medieval legal consciousness. He asserts that *islam* is "able to bring an essential contribution to the updating of the international law, thanks to its provisions that are protective of human rights."

Father Pierre Lelong, commenting on Broisard's statement, proposes the following:

> In order to be convinced of the validity of such analysis, we as Westerners, Europeans and Christians, must know better the reality of the Qur'ānic message beyond past prejudices and present misunderstandings. In order to comprehend "where *islam* is going," perhaps we need first to ask ourselves if we sufficiently know where it comes from and what it is.[32]

For this reason our continuing reflection will dig through the litter of the inaccurate accusations that overwhelm *islam*. It will denounce deviant practices. It will persist in being politically incorrect, historically unacceptable, and dogmatically unbearable for certain prevalent thinking.

NOTES

1. TN : Cf. I.4, n. 5.

2. François Bourin, *Le contrat naturel* [nature's contract], 1990, p. 14.

3. The phrase is Jacques Berque's.

4. *Prière païenne,* a song by the world-famous Canadian singer Céline Dion; the song is an edifying commentary on modern man's arrogance even at prayer.

5. I use this word not in its sociological or historical sense, but to describe and refer to the faith that brings the creature to submit to its Creator. The word *islam* has etymological ambivalence. It means peace and submission; this is the dimension I allude to when I write *islam*. By "Islam" I refer to the history of Muslims and current socio-political dimensions, as we have emphasized in the beginning of this book.

6. Cf. I. 2. "Philosophical Vertigo."

7. André Gide, *Les nourritures terrestres* [earthly food], Gallimard.

8. Nathanael is the interlocutor in Gide's parable of the same name. In the book, as in all Western literature, the conflict with Christendom's values is latent. The choice of this particular saint (also known as Bartholomew) owes to his having been an apostle of Christ who was flayed alive for his faith.

9. Qur'ān: S. VII. 176.

10. André Comte-Sponville, philosopher and assistant professor at the Université de Paris I, has recently published *Impromptus,* PUF, 1996. *Petit traité des grandes vertus* [a little treatise on great virtues] PUF, 1995. *Valeur et Vérité* [valor and truth], PUF, 1994.

11. André Comte-Sponsville, *La société en quête de valeurs: pour sortir de l'alternative entre scepticisme et dogmatisme* [society in search of values: a way out of the alternative between skepticism and dogmatism], Maxima, Laurent du Mesnil, ed. *Une morale sans fondement* [groundless morality].

12. Comte-Sponsville, *La société,* p. 126.

13. Comte-Sponsville, *La société,* p. 129.

14. Edgar Morin's favorite thesis.

15. Comte-Sponsville, *La société,* p. 130.

16. The chapter that follows treats of orientalism in its own way.

17. Qur'ān, S. XLIX. 13.

18. In no way is power the violence that orientalism and certain crusades seek to ascribe to the image of *islam.*

19. TN: Jean-Marie Le Pen, leader of the extreme right-wing Front National.

20. Cf. Stendhal, *De l'amour* [Love], Garnier-Flammarion, 1965, p. 196.

21. In the words of another contemporary poet, Georges Brasses, describing the gratuitous wickedness of certain morose and conventional minds.

22. Jean-Michel Foulquier, A. Michel, 1995, p. 105.

23. Idem, p. 10.

24. Hatim Attaî is an Arab who died before the advent of *islam.* Across the Arab Peninsula, his generosity was legendary.

25. An epithet hurled at François Burgat for the objectivity with which he has written about Islamism.

26. Michel Jobert, "L'Islam et sa modernité" [Islam and its modernity], *Revue du Tiers-Monde* [Third World Review] no. 92, Oct–Dec 1982, PUF, p. 774.

27. Idem, p. 780.

28. Cf. Jacques Berque, *Une cause jamais perdue* [a cause never lost], A. Michel, p. 269.

29. Idem, p. 299.

30. Idem, in "L'islam à l'horizon 2000" [Islam by the year 2000], 15th century after the hegira.

31. Marcel Boisard, A. Michel, 1980. Boisard is a professor of international law at the University of Geneva.

32. Pierre Lelong, "L'islam et l'Occident" [Islam and the West], in *Revue du Tiers-Monde* (cf. n. 26), p. 750. Lelong is an advisor to the Vatican Secretariat on relations with non-Christian religions.

II.2. AN ENEMY TO OVERTHROW

The jailor is also a captive.
Gérard de Nerval

What shall I do in Rome? I know not how to lie.
Latin poet

Rome! If you complain that you are being betrayed,
Make enemies that I may hate.
Pierre Corneille

Hatred is always more perceptive and more ingenuous than friendship.
Pierre Choderlos de Laclos

A War of Opprobrium

In this chapter we shall be dealing with how the world of modernism relates to the other, that is, with *islam*.

Alongside its universalistic and humanitarian views, the West maintains an age-old warlike stance and a will to dominate which only modernism's enthusiasts fail to perceive. Modern war is nuclear and informational. The nuclear option is left for extreme solutions, while disinformation is directed to the war of attrition.

Having a monopoly on information is a high stake in a competitive and efficient world. Disinformation thus becomes synonymous with disarmament, defeat, and domination. Indeed, disinformation did not need to await the advent of the mass media to be the favorite war machine of an alert adversary. Twenty centuries ago, Sun-Tzu, an expert Chinese strategist, instructed to the Warring Kingdoms how one nation can annihilate another without making use of any material weapon whatsoever.[1] This is what he proposed:

1. Discredit all that is good in the country of the adversary.
2. Ridicule your enemies' traditions.
3. Spread discord and quarrel among the citizens of the hostile country.
4. Set the young against the old.
5. Weaken the will of enemy warriors through sensual songs and music.[2]

Such precepts are so "modern" and so fresh that we wonder if neocolonialism had not taken them literally from the Chinese strategist and preserved them carefully in its bible. Ruse and manipulation take over from open attack. The direct confrontations experienced by colonialism proved to be ineffective methods to subdue the other completely.

More than any other adversary, Islam is seen as a lifelong rebel, a potential enemy and object of total hatred. Crusader Europe's declared rival of old, it remains a potential enemy of the West of today. Though humbled, impoverished, rent, degraded and disarmed, the Muslim world still arouses fears—if not covetousness.

With the media facilitating the task today more than ever, Sun-Tzu's principles work wonders. Never has the image of *islam* been darker and more appalling than in today's media coverage. The sustained volleys of disinformation about *islam* far exceed a reality already sufficiently ill-served by internal crises and age-old rancor. They persist in driving the nail in further and making the portrait even bleaker.

The ingenuity of these strategists of calumny consists in convincing even the children of *islam* to lend a hand and express the most virulent and defamatory views. Bearing the names of *islam* but the hearts of elsewhere, the mercenaries hammer their own identity even harder than the others as they strive to strike the face of their culture wherever the experts suggest.

The greatest defeat, since time immemorial, is that of the spirit. There is no worse capitulation than the one that reduces you to gaze at yourself with the eyes of those who despise all that you represent. There is no worse war than one in which we think we are at peace.

We will close this digression so as to confine in it those mercenaries of thought (all those Salmans and Taslimas who play the martyr[3]), and we will focus our attention instead on modernity's native authors. The latter have at least the advantage of being authentic, an advantage some among us cannot boast of, having lost their cultural identity so completely as to disown you the moment you wear a beard or an Islamic scarf.

At the pace of such a Sun-Tzuesque offensive, Islam finds itself shunted from theory to theory, from suppositions to inferences, from paranoia to schizophrenia, from disavowal to recantation, from myths to illusions.

Between Scylla and Charybdis

So ample and varied is the output of sensational authors regarding Islam that we find two works on the media battlefield as contradictory as Samuel Huntington's *The Clash of Civilization and the Remaking of World Order*[4] and Alexandre del Valle's *Islamisme et États-Unis; une alliance contre l'Europe* [Islamicism and the United States; an alliance against Europe].[5]

The Clash of Civilization promises to become a classic of its kind.[6] Written a few years ago by a leading professor at Harvard and an active member of the John M. Olin Institute for Strategic Studies, the work has become the credo of modern paranoia. The style is academic; the intention is pure, strategic, and allergic to all shades of green.[7] The appalling green of *islam* disgusts the author even more when mixed with the yellow of China. Behind its cool academism hides the latent yet ardent fire of xenophobia and typical American immodesty. Huntington writes:

The West is and will remain for years to come the most powerful civilization. Yet its power relative to that of other civilizations is declining. As the West attempts to assert its values and to protect its interests, non-Western societies confront a choice. Some attempt to emulate the West and to join or to "band-wagon" with the West. Other Confucian and Islamic societies attempt to expand their own economic and military power to resist and to "balance" against the West.[8]

The lack of interest in euphemism and literary tact that characterizes North American literature lays bare a blatant Western centrism. No demagogical or even pedagogical veneer is deemed necessary when you have the capacity for reducing the world to nothing in next to no time. Bored perhaps with writing his own prose, Huntington borrows words from a character in Michael Dibdin's novel, *Dead Lagoon:*

> There can be no true friends without true enemies. Unless we hate what we are not, we cannot love what we are. These are the old truths we are painfully rediscovering after a century and more of sentimental cant. Those who deny them deny their family, their heritage, their culture, their birthright, their very selves! They will not lightly be forgiven.[9]

The "fastest tongue in the West" then adds his own perplexing assessment:

> The unfortunate truth in these old truths cannot be ignored by statesmen and scholars. For peoples seeking identity and reinventing ethnicity, enemies are essential, and the potentially most dangerous enmities occur across the fault lines between the world's major civilizations.[10]

Are these cynical words of a strategist concocting bellicose theories, or a tearful academic yielding to the evidence? Whatever the motive, such thinking is blameful. An accredited advisor of the greatest destructive power had best be prudent and levelheaded. Genocide as a policy is certainly nothing new for Uncle Sam, whose prior record in this area is colossal.[11] When the world each day becomes little more than a racist powder keg, one had best watch one's words. Such views are likely to set the world ablaze at any moment.

With a final apocalypse dreaded at any moment, one had best not tempt fate, especially when it is that of an American citizen. Humankind will either wise up or perish. This is surely the millennium of all dangers; surely it ought to be one of wisdom as well.

But wisdom, alas, does not seem to be the prevailing feature of present-day mankind. Huntington is followed close behind, if you will, by politicians searching for new witches to hunt in order to assure the difficult consensus of heterogeneous masses. On the back cover of Huntington's book, the publishers proudly display what Kissinger thinks of it: "*The Clash of Civilization and the Remaking of World Order* is one of the most important books to have emerged since the end of the Cold War."

Zbigniew Brzezinski, having a complicated name but a simple view of the future, is filled with wonder by this jewel of inductions and deductions: "An intellectual tour de force: bold, imaginative, and provocative. A seminal work that will revolutionize our understanding of international affairs."

These wily old politicians may be in retirement, but there is every indication that others who are in power support such xenophobic philosophies. Besides, in the country of cynical pragmatism, a man like Kissinger would never go into complete retirement.

The first book is an obvious symbol of the uncontrolled paranoia that has seized the West, seeing itself surrounded all sides by Islam, invaded already by it through immigration that is perceived as a fifth column.

Del Valle's book, the other jewel of xenophobia and paranoia, begins inevitably with saber rattling and ends in a bugle call of racism both distinctive and typically French in its academicism: it bears a preface by Pierre-Marie Gallois and a postscript by Jean-Pierre Péroncel-Hugoz. If Mr. Péroncel-Hugoz is a leading academic light in the rejection of the Other, Mr. Gallois is nothing less than a general. Overtaken as he is by persecution mania, it is hardly surprising that the contribution of this senior officer that appears on the back cover of this "geopolitical manual"[12] resembles a clarion call sounding the charge:

> Contemporary events, the perspectives they open, and the place the countries of Islam will take—settling more and more firmly in the world scene thanks to the position they hold on the map and the wealth they possess—make obligatory the study of the pages of Alexandre del Valle.[13]

The editor describes del Valle as having the courage to put the matter bluntly. We may well concede the fact that a goodly amount of (academic) courage is needed to propose such nonsense. According to some of del Valle's whoppers, Madeleine Albright should be a declared pro-Shiite and an accomplice of Islamist activism:

> The Americans and their Gulf allies are thus not ready to accept the total lifting of the embargo. The American Secretary of State, Madelaine Albright, has declared in public and on many occasions that "the total lifting of the embargo on Iraq will virtually be impossible so long as Saddam Hussein is in power." Can we deduce from the statement that Albright wants the victory of the Shiite opposition, or hopes that Iraq will implode under the impact of Kurdish separatism and Islamist activism?[14]

Any laughter prompted by such hallucinations dies in the throat on closer reading of the first page of del Valle's acknowledgments: we may well wonder whether the book was not designed at staff headquarters. The author invokes blessings on his book by mysterious persons who will remain nameless:

I would then like to thank various personalities, among whom some, by virtue of their erudition and courageous actions, have ever been my true masters: General Gallois, General Salvan, and of course, Jean-Marie Péroncel-Hugoz, whose books are authoritative, as well as other senior officers and French or foreign observers whose counsels have been equally precious but whose names, due to their activity, cannot be mentioned.[15]

Such an acknowledgment of indebtedness is extremely intriguing. What are we to expect from a manual written under the benevolence of the presiding military figures, prime academics, and masked figures?

If anyone should worry about this wave of suspicion, it is surely the Muslim societies that possess oil only in theory, live in destitution, and would be incapable of self-defense if a sanguinary Hitler were to set off a new instrument of destruction, a new holocaust.

The dreams of the Far Right must be strewn with corpses, populated with swastikas, furnished with ovens, haunted by sharp and white balaclavas. Its enemies are certainly various and numerous, but Islam is, more than anything else, the one to subject to public obloquy.

Tactics and Manipulation

If the desire may remain pious and uncertain that *islam* as a faith can enrich modernity, Islam as a social body is an inescapable reality for future international policies. Let us hope that insane strategies and xenophobic extravagance give way to intelligent policies that regard the world system as a global one in which the whole humanity is embarked on the same voyage.

May God keep those dark forces where they are: hidden away within small limited circles, curled up in the anonymity of private clubs, hidden behind masks and pseudonyms! May God keep confined among themselves all those with icy hearts—for icy hearts are contagious! Contagious as well is the racist media fever that vilifies all that is Muslim.

Honest journalists, faithful to the sacred principles of their work in denouncing fraud and plotting, have become all too rare among media types. As such, they are commendable and meritorious. These exceptions that prove the rule denounce the manipulation that is prevalent in the milieu that is supposed to inform, but that often misinforms.

In January 1995 Edgar Roskis,[16] in an article as enthralling as many of those published by *Le monde diplomatique*, denounced the duplicity of media images that are always biased and truncated whenever Islam is concerned. In his article, he summarizes how the magicians of modernist communications pull completely fabricated enemies out of their sleeves.

On November 17, 1994, *L'Express* ran a flashy headline that was effective in maintaining hatred of the Other: "Scarf, the plot: how the Islamists are infiltrating us!"

Commenting on the photograph that accompanied the headline, Roskis wrote:

> Ordered by *L'Express* from the ad agency *Sygma,* it presents a young "Muslim" girl—in fact a paid model whose casting was performed in the offices of the weekly. Professionally made-up and dressed in a hijab closer to Dior's "scarf" than to Tati's, the young woman—anything but an "Islamist" high school girl—lends her beautiful face to the argument of the plot. . . . Who noticed it? Who got upset?[17]

If this effect is not really disadvantageous to Islam's image—the face is beautiful, the scarf elegant—it nevertheless proves that the press no longer shrinks from falsehood. Concocting false images and captionless comments has become a must in the domain of the press, the shrewd linking of a real image with a smokescreen in order to influence public opinion in the desired direction. Our author is upset by these comments that turn a neutral image into an appeal to xenophobia:

> The *Dauphiné libéré* of August 3rd ran a front-page lead on some Muslims in a mosque. The photograph, while real enough, bore the title "New Threats" and a caption verging on cynicism: "The North African community (here in prayer in Marseille) dreads being compared to the fundamentalists and fears an outbreak of racism as indirect consequence.[18]

The spirit of the modern reader, pressed by definition, will quickly forge links between the title and the image: the connection between prostration before God and fanaticism is thus quickly telegraphed. What the composition of image and text relays is clear: any practicing Muslim is a potential terrorist, and any mosque is the protective shelter of all dangers.

The overinformed man no longer bothers to go beyond the image, to ferret out what lies behind the statement, to comprehend what motivates an allegation, what prompts a defamation. The advice given by Jacques Berque for the future of a better dialog between Europe and "its Southern bank: Islam" will long remain unheeded.

In "a world to be remade" Berque proposes that the press will have a noble role to play in the flow of philanthropic relationships insofar as it abstains from "depriving the other." Very diplomatic as is his wont, he passes in review the false maneuvers of information that have become classics in the register of a sustained illusion. In the mannered style and tone of kindly reproach as is his wont, Berque writes:

> The martyrs of Timisoara, Fidel Castro's absentee interview, the massacre of Kuwait City's three hundred incubator babies illustrate the prowess of our radio and television in eloquence peppered with barbarisms. Let us keep them as enlightening souvenirs of those beautiful years. Must the increasingly important role of the media and their responsibility keep pace

with the decadence of their language and their lapses credibility? Is disinformation of the public really inevitable? Is there no way to avoid it?[19]

With a friendly prod and a pen dipped in irony, Berque further exhorts the "gentlemen" of the media to honesty:

> Please, TV gentlemen, for the sake of the French language, for the honesty of information and the logic of the word: more Timisoara please, and less malapropism! There is, after all, a Council on Radio and TV—but perhaps it has more serious problems to contend with.

Judging by the repeated offense of radio and television, we wonder if the Council in question has not been created to promote such false images as those official French circulars that do not tolerate difference. The disparagement of *islam* is not only maintained by journalists short on articles or new subjects. It is also part of a general policy aggravated by the sentiment of acculturation prompted by globalization, as we have already indicated. Naming an enemy—and distinguishing yourself from him—becomes a psychosocial necessity in a world that is in a state of decline. Communism once marvelously played that role. Islam is an excellent substitute: it is an enemy that, made-up and wearing dirty rags, perfectly meets the conditions of the perfect foil.

The Cultural Exception

Globalization arouses and exacerbates phobias everywhere that were formerly repressed. The lands of France and Navarre, having always headed the list of the discontented in their acute sense of identity, are particularly prone to the movement to reject the Other—notably Islam. No tempered speech or view will do: rejection is visceral and as tenacious as that village of implacable Gauls that the pens of Goscinny and Uderzo have invented.[20]

The *Astérix* of politics is far more radical than that of the press, except that the Romans are no longer Roman and the boars are no longer boars. The fashion is now: These Muslims are crazy and *Obélix*, the giant Gaul, will now have to pursue little schoolgirls wearing ostentatious and indecent veils.

The Islamist peril is dead-center in the paranoia transmitted by the frenzy journalist to the politician in action or vice versa. The *Circulaire Bayrou* is replete with articles that rely on past hatred to arouse present xenophobia. *Le Point*, that newspaper with a ready pen, titles an article, "France, Islam's elder daughter?":

> It is largely agreed that Arab immigration is a major concern of our domestic and foreign security. . . . Islam neither admits the secularization of power nor that of knowledge.[21]

With the presence of this potential fifth column represented by more than four million Muslims, such messages are received loud and clear by the vigilant *Abraracourcix*. François Bayrou, the great chief of national education, prefaces the pamphlet entitled *Les années lycée* (high school years)[22] with a view to giving pedagogical advice to high school students:

> The *Années lycée* operation is none other than an enthusiastic enterprise. In a time when the young are buried beneath negative messages . . . a certain number of men and women have wanted to show them that the path to success and adventure is still open.[23]

This document, intended to advise high school students in their adventurous progress towards the future, is an "enthusiastic work," according to the statement of the minister. Is the Circular, published in 1994, that prohibits the wearing of the veil an "enthusiastic enterprise" as well?

In the Minister's view, it is certainly one of the gestures meant to save "the young buried beneath negative messages," as he so well writes in his foreword. *Islam* is surely for a secular and right-thinking France one of the most obscurantist and negative messages. The undertaking is so serious that, since then, they have had to look for a mediator (this is no dream!) "in the charge of solving the problems related to the wearing of the Islamic scarf."[24]

The same minister who supported Bayrou's Circular curiously issued a note in November of 1998 stating that he was "alarmed by the refusal of heads of schools to enroll schoolgirls wearing the veil."[25]

"Two cases, one in Flers (Orne) and the other in Grand-Combe, have reopened debate over the Islamic veils in schools."[26]

The debate is not ready to be settled and is likely to last longer since, as Hanifa Chérifi (the mediator between France and those heads wearing the Islamic scarf) states: "Attitudes are becoming tougher on both sides."

Ségolène Royal, Deputy Minister in charge of curricula, who calls for "respecting each one's convictions," seems to preach in the desert of a secularism[27] that betrays its own foundations. Georges Sarre, Chairman of the *Mouvement des citoyens* (Citizen movement), shares "the concerns of the teachers . . . over the possible authorization of the wearing of the scarf within secular schools in the country."[28]

Rigidity begets rigidity just as violence begets violence. The little girls are far from laying down their arms; their accredited interlocutor reports their determination to wear this square of fabric that is for them so symbolic of their identity. When the Republic goes into a rage at the least junior-high-school scarf, you may forget about all political daydreams of a man like de Gaulle, or the reflection of so wise and crafty a man as Berque. We may forget about any future of dialog! French secularism hardens noticeably towards Islam, attaching thus little importance to the cultural exception from this side. The thesis of the "clash of civilizations" advocated by Huntington is approved by Marianne[29] with complete confidence.

Commenting on the recent conflicts related to textile industry that stir France, the Federation of National Education published this brusque communiqué:

> Proselytism constitutes a hindrance to freedom of conscience that is necessary to the development of the critical mind of the young people, and a condition of access to autonomy that is one of the prime missions of the secular education public service.

The text undeniably belongs to the category of the unique thinking enunciated in the very holy Edict of 1787, wherein the Church reluctantly recognizes that there are "non-Catholics" but that "the Catholic religion . . . will continue alone in our kingdom to enjoy public cult."[30] The word "secular" will replace "Catholic" so that the Edict of 1787 will most resemble secularism's edicts of 1994.

Jules Ferry, founding father of the secular school, wanted the new school to help promote a new conception of citizenship far from that defended by the Church. The school was for him a progressive yet certain way to spirit away the faithful of the Church. As he conceived it, it was nonetheless and above all to be a locus of neutrality.

Tariq Ramadan explains:

> In his *Lettre aux instituteurs* [letter to primary school teachers] written in 1883, Jules Ferry stressed on the importance of teaching the elements of a morality that does not shock parents who happen to be Catholics. The secular school is meant to be a neutral and therefore tolerant school.[31]

A passage from this famous letter to primary school teachers stipulates:

> The schoolmaster is constantly to make sure that he does not offend the opinions of any of the children in his care, and the parents that entrust them to him. The schoolmaster is the parents' representative.[32]

Has the role of the school transmuted to such degree ever since, or are we to believe that the Muslim pupil does not merit the liberalities of the secular school, or still that an immigrant parent is not a parent like others?

Secularisms

The secular school no longer merely offends its pupils' opinions, it combats them as well. It not only runs afoul of the parents' convictions, it also shows their offspring the door, making them candidates for social uselessness or vengeful violence.

Yet Jacqueline Costa-Lascoux[33] defines a nice sort of secularism based on two principles: "Freedom of conscience, which compels the State not to interfere anyone's convictions; [and] the equality of all before the law, whatever their religion."[34]

A few pages on, she gives greater emphasis to the latitudinarian aspect of secularism, giving it an aspect of idyllic tolerance. "Emile Littré would insist on the continuous progress of secularism, that is, of State neutrality between religions and tolerance for all creeds."[35]

Is the secular school no longer what it used to be, or is secularism to be secularized? Was Jules Ferry so conciliatory because he had not expected the third age of secularity—where a subjugated and protected culture brandishes its ostentatious signs in the Republic's face? Or is the politician essentially doomed to make decisions for the moment, forever remaining a political schemer? Is this flaw not getting worse in a world which is running out of time? Claude Julien relates the superficiality that directs political decisions that are often deaf to history's beneficial reminders:

> Governments, chiefly because they are little nourished by history and absorbed instead with the present, devote too little time to reflection and forecasting. Obsessed with the short term, they pay only distracted attention to the slow gestation of crises. They become aware of crises only on the point of explosion, when, full of amazement, they discover that they have denied themselves any possibility for at least trying a policy of prevention. Caught unawares they hastily improvise a "crisis management," the results of which are often diametrically opposed to their intended objectives.[36]

France holds perhaps the record in "visual navigation." It is fair to emphasize that Europe is not entirely supportive of the anti-Islamic fever that sets France ablaze. A British journalist cited by Costa-Lascoux states with pleasant humor that in France, "they can still bring down a minister or a government over secularism more easily than cause unrest in the intellectual milieu and the political community over the issue of an Islamic scarf worn by three young girls in a suburban high school."

Great Britain is well placed to poke fun at its neighbor's fits of hysteria. Ignoring the tradition of rivalry between France and Britain, Costa-Lascoux attests to British intelligence regarding difference, volunteering an example of some British schools where young Pakistani girls wear the Islamic scarf without worry. Those in charge are savvy enough to consider the scarf as traditional dress rather than ostentatious symbol. The only limit imposed on this freedom of dress is the obligation to purchase the fabric from the high school uniforms supplier, and thus respect the school colors.

That is what we may call a reasonable and tempered management of difference. Furthermore, these schools would not even think of turning attention to particularities of diet. The obstinate determination of Muslim pupils to eat *halal*[37] is not perceived in England as a challenge to law and order requiring top-level meetings on territorial security. They prepare this kind of menu for pupils just as they would prepare a salt-free diet or a diet for diabetics.

Secular rage is a distinctively French feature. Has secular rage replaced Catholic rage? After all, the darkest page of Catholic intolerance was signed in the same

116

country. Secularism, having become more an antipathy to religiosity than the option of neutrality, would not hesitate to order a new Saint Bartholomew's Day Massacre (secularized, of course).

Having saluted the rare *sang-froid* of the English policy, our respectable Centre National de la Recherche Scientifique (CNRS) research director cannot help making a most ambiguous reflection about this opening that betrays the hard-line brand of French-style secularism:

> Such an attitude certainly favors the manifestation of differences; but it is accompanied by cultural fragmentation and disillusionment that lead, perhaps more surely than secularism does, to a loss of meaning of religious expression.[38]

If democracy is indeed an English invention, the art of the evasive reply is French. Thus, Bayrou's Circular would be an enthusiastic attention intended to safeguard the religious conviction of the little girls and to sharpen their cultural identity by countering it.

Angular policies inevitably provoke a pernicious backfire. The terrible malaise experienced by a youth that is uprooted, whether born in Europe or having taken refuge there, is exacerbated by the feeling of being rejected or cooped up. Every ideological blow advocating violence is likely to recruit the exasperated whipping boys and girls of France.

Contrary to the monstrous caricature that presents the Islamist movement as a destructive trend, the training of young people by responsible Islamist organizations is very beneficial to the suburbs. Young people, given a sense of security and usefulness in an associative framework centered on spirituality (with all due respect to secularism!), become full-fledged citizens determined to serve their host country.

Alain Peyrefitte, a specialist on what ails France,[39] diagnoses the incurable illness of an intolerable desire for assimilation: "France welcomes foreigners of all cultures provided that they accept assimilation and avoid becoming an irritating thorn in France's side."[40]

Up to now immigrants have been tolerated only to the extent that French women decide not to populate their country with pretty blond heads. Immigration is often denounced by the speechifiers of the right as a punishment of the non-prolific French family. As to the famous expression "Multicultural France," it is pleasing to the eye only when a man like Zineddine Zidane is proclaimed the world's number-one soccer player. It becomes a problem for France the moment the dress is something other than the uniform of the French team. The right to be different is particularly not to be confused with the right to visibility. The major problem France finds with Islam is that it is a visible faith.

France's attempt to curb the momentum of its Muslim youth is, unfortunately, a sign of its reluctance to enter the future, for that generation is going to constitute an important piece in the mosaic of the France of tomorrow. Moreover, a country desirous of safeguarding its cultural singularity should make partners, not enemies, of its native population.

The immigrants coming from North Africa could serve as ideal mediators between the two banks of the Mediterranean. At a time when economic factors take first place and the threat of American hegemony looms, it would be good to form a block against the squalls to come. Beyond confessional considerations and any ideological polemics, we are destined for dialog. Glaring at each other from both shores of the Mediterranean Lake will get us nowhere.

To return to our image of a ship as a metaphor of the global world we live in, it is not beside the point to advocate mutual understanding between the passengers in steerage and those in first-class cabins. Shipwreck is a great equalizer: in the face of disaster we are all one.

Will no great Gaul of the caliber of General de Gaulle arise to look beyond the narrow horizons of chauvinistic France? With pedagogical candor and a keen sense of the future, de Gaulle three decades ago spoke these words:

> Look, there is another shore of the Mediterranean, where developing countries have a civilization, a vibrant culture, and a particular sense of humanity and human relationships that we in our industrial societies tend to lose, something we will doubtless be very happy to find again one day in them. Both shores have given rise to great civilizations, and if on both shores we wish to construct an industrial civilization that forgoes the American model, and in which mankind is the end rather than the means, then our cultures must generously open their minds and hearts to one another.[41]

NOTES

1. China during the fifth through second centuries B.C.

2. Precepts drawn from Sun-Tzu's *Art of Warfare* by later commentators; cf. "La désin-formation, arme de guerre" [disinformation as a weapon of war] in *L'Age de l'Homme,* Juillard, 1986, p. 25.

3. TN: The author is alluding to such "deculturated" men and women as Salman Rushdie and Taslima Nasreen.

4. Samuel Huntington, New York: Simon and Schuster, 1996.

5. Alexandre del Valle, *L'Age d'homme,* 1997.

6. TN : The book expands an article of the same name published in the Summer 1993 edition of *Foreign Affairs.*

7. The color green is emblematic of *islam.*

8. Huntington (1996), p. 29.

9. Huntington (1996), p. 20.

10. Idem.

11. As everyone knows, the United States of America was established following one of the greatest genocides in history, in which millions of Indians were exterminated.

12. According to the editor of *L'Age d'homme*.

13. Del Valle (1997), back cover.

14. Del Valle (1997), p. 159.

15. Del Valle (1997), opening pages.

16. Professor of the mechanics of photojournalism at the universities of Paris X (Nanterre) and Paris XIII (Villetaneuse).

17. Edgar Roskis, "Journalisme et vérité: images truquées" [journalism and truth: images involving special effects] in *Le Monde diplomatique* of Jan 1995, p. 32.

18. Ibid.

19. Jacques Berque, "Un monde à refaire" [a world to be remade], *Panoramiques* no. 2, Jan 1994.

20. TN: In 1959, Goscinny and Uderzo, among the most famous French cartoonists and satirists, launched the magazine *Pilote*—Uderzo providing the images and Goscinny the text—which presented the adventures of *Astérix*. It was an unprecedented success in the annals of the French cartoon industry. *Astérix,* a crafty little warrior, is the hero of the adventures; all the most dangerous missions are entrusted to him. He draws his superhuman power from the magic potion of the Druid *Panoramix*. *Obélix,* his very fat and extraordinarily strong sidekick, was endowed with supernatural powers when as a child he fell into the cauldron of the magic potion.

21. From an editorial in *Le Point* of Aug. 28, 1993.

22. Jointly published by his Ministry and Axa Insurance Group.

23. Francois Bayrou, "L'école et l'argent" [school and money], letters to the editor, *Le Monde diplomatique*, July 1994, p. 19.

24. Hanifa Cherifi interviewed by Béatrice Gurrey in *Le Monde* of Jan 10–11, 1999.

25. Ibid.

26. Ibid.

27. TN: *Laïcité,* translated here as "secularism," is a development peculiar to French history. It is closer in meaning to anti-clericalism than to the Anglo-Saxon separation of church and state.

28. Gurrey (1999).

29. TN: Marianne is an allegorical figure representing a woman wearing a *bonnet phrygien* (the conical, red, woolen hat worn by commoners under the Ancien Régime). At the end of the 18th century, the name came to be used to refer to the French Republic, and statutes and busts

began to appear around fifty years later. Every town hall in France has a bust of Marianne on public view, and the image also appears on postage stamps.

30.   Cited by Jean Baubérot in *La Laïcité, quel héritage?* [secularism, what inheritance?], Labor et Fides 1990, and taken up by Tariq Ramadan in *Les musulmans dans la laïcité: responsabilités et droits des musulmans dans les sociétés occidentales* [Muslims under secularism: rights and duties of Muslims in Western societies], Tawhid, 1994, p. 31.

31.   Ramadan (1994), p. 32.

32.   Alain Peyrefitte, *La France en désarroi* [France in disarray], De Fallois, 1992, p. 181.

33.   Research director at CNRS and member of the Haut Conseil de la population [high council on population], Costa-Lascoux is an accredited expert at the Council of Europe and a correspondent of the Commission nationale des droits de l'homme [National human rights commission].

34.   Jacqueline Costa-Lascoux, "Les trois âges de la laïcité" (the three ages of secularism), in *Questions politiques* [political questions series], Hachette, 1996, p. 7.

35.   Idem, p. 10.

36.   Cf. Claude Julien, "Le monde des extrêmes" [the world of extremes] in *Le Monde diplomatique* of March 1995.

37.   Food sanctioned by Islamic law.

38.   Costa-Lascoux (1996), p. 17.

39.   Alain Peyrefitte, *Le mal français* [what ails France], Plon, 1976.

40.   Cf. Peyrefitte (1992), p. 234.

41.   Cf. *Le Monde* of July 20, 1972.

II. 3. REROUTING HISTORY

To bear one's own history, each adds to it a bit of legend.
Marcel Jouhandeau

History is not a science; it is an art. Only through imagination do we make a success of it.
Anatole France

We have made more history than there will be historians to deal with it.
Honoré de Balzac

Posthumous Acknowledgment

This chapter, more than the others, will be interspersed with quotations. In order to make our ideas credible, we shall have to use and abuse references, since the word of the Southerner—and particularly the Muslim—is never good enough.

The task of clearing away prevalent misconceptions requires that we have recourse to witnesses who are more likely to be taken seriously. Our concern to convince our readers of the misunderstanding maintained by exacerbated subjectivity compels us to forgo an argument, however clear and forthright, that relies entirely on its own merits. The serious nature of the subject demands as much.

If we must in the process revise history, it is only because everything that deserves attention in the civilization of the Arabs finds its source in Revelation. Were the matter merely one of writing a history of civilizations that rise and fall in a necessary and natural dialectic logic, the eclipse of the role of *islam* in the course of events would be of little import. Indeed, from that aspect, the eclipse would even be fair.

The problem is that behind the Arab miracle hides *the* Miracle. A divine breath came to praise to the skies a few Bedouins who lived until then in ignorance and in the emptiness of the material and spiritual desert. It is these Arabs, transformed by their faith in God, who would sprinkle all of humankind with the spiritual freshness of which they suddenly became the depositories. The well-sustained and well-orchestrated calumny against Islam and Arabs strives to make the present humankind miss its appointment with God.

Academic tradition has made it its duty to fabricate history in such a manner that no Eastern trait appears under the layers of its false make-up. Western thought diverted history from its original path by making its principal course pass by way of Europe. Such rerouting turns any other event, however major, into some poor relative of universal history. Any historical event that occurs outside the Western framework is merely a blip on the edge of the screen.

The eclipse of Islam in the course of universal history is not the result of benign amnesia; it is an act of sabotage that will have a great impact on man's very essence. Confusing the issue consigns not merely one nation to the fringes of fictitious history; it sentences all mankind to know nothing about its future destiny, the meaning of its present life, and its identity as a creature. The Qur'ānic Message, destined for all mankind, is taken hostage by such a rerouting of history.

Perhaps it is high time that an effective acknowledgment of the role of Islam in saving humanity on the brink of the abyss 1500 years ago lead us to consider it once again as a lifeboat for humanity in peril. Proclaiming her will to pay a debt of gratitude, Sigrid Hunke writes: "Upon the fate of the Arab world, which once before changed the face of the world, perhaps ours will soon largely depend. Beyond what sets us apart, is it not time then to ask ourselves what unites us, what we have in common?"[1]

Precocious enough in 1960, when Hunke's book was published, such a proposition has slowly begun to infiltrate current Western ideological thought. Let us note that the German approach to Islam differs notably from the French, and not only in having arisen earlier in time.

We should, however, make clear what the term "Arab" means for Hunke, so as to avoid misunderstandings with regard to our own approach:

> The present work will refer to the "Arab" and the "Arab civilization" despite the fact that the creators of the latter were not always citizens of that nation. . . . This book will then speak of the Arab civilization just as one speaks of the American civilization. It would no more describe Ar-Rasi or Ibn-Sina (both coming from Persian families that had lived for generations in the Arab countries) as "Persian" than one would describe the former U.S. President, Dwight Eisenhower, as being "German."[2]

The muting of passions in order to take advantage of the lessons of the Arab miracle is certainly not the forte of "Marianne," as Jean-Louis Triaud relates:

> Everything connected with Islam involves in our discussion a passionate dimension. There is a French fear of Islam. Thus the French attitude toward Islam is different from that of the British—the only other superpower involved in the Muslim world. . . . France's revolutionary history and the peculiar secularism contribute, among other factors, to explain this specificity. Gérard Cholvy has suggested this extremely well: "French secular tradition must also be taken into account. It passes over in silence everything pertaining to the religious sphere." And when religion is not silent—as in the case of the conquered and then independent Muslim countries—it is regarded as an intolerable offence against Progress.[3]

With these truths set forth, we can propose that, under the pressure of modern developments, the West tends to admit the deficiencies of its version of history, or rather, the mysteries and the travesty of historical truth. But a faltering attempt in favor of the rehabilitation of Islam in the domain of history is one thing; overcoming the feelings of the hatred it arouses is quite another. It is difficult to find an honorable place for an Islam that has been disparaged in Western collective consciousness by the twin phenomena of rejection and overshadowing.

Still, progress, however minimal, is nonetheless evident. The questions the West is suddenly compelled to pose are already encouraging signs. Jacques Berque subscribes to the idea of rereading the events: "It matters little if Edward Said accuses orientalism of the darkest intentions, so long as the latter is not replaced in deciphering the East."[4]

Let us have a closer look at Berque's statement. "The East" is an exotic and hazy synonym of Islam. On the other hand, the very precise term "deciphering" means that there is a real difficulty, and that the enigma of Islam is complete. It means, as well, that we must counter the current of the orientalist propaganda that describes the West as the bearer of civilization to the barbaric East. It means that we must approach Islam by taking paths other than the beaten track of the thinking that is prevalent in colonizing Europe.

Alain de Libéria states in the pages of *Le Monde Diplomatique:*

> Long forgotten, the influence of the Arab-Muslim thinking on European culture is today the subject of a sort of posthumous acknowledgment that is so keen, it is true, that the projected brilliance comes from a supposedly dead star that comes towards us, shining from afar like remorse or nostalgia.[5]

Our author is not the only one to feel this sudden rush of nostalgia, this appeal from a past that is so present behind the scenes of history, but that has been made to sink into oblivion, deliberately deleted from the records of the modern and informed humanity. He continues:

> When we speak of an "eclipsed heritage," it is essential to know who is assuming that heritage, who recognizes it, and who rejects it. To claim that the West has forgotten its Arabic heritage merely risks being taken as a recasting of an argument no one dares to make up front, but which is prevalent in public opinion on both sides of the Mediterranean, that the Arabs are, have always been, and will always be foreigners in the West.[6]

It would seem that the beginnings of a new reading of history are being launched by an increasing number of authors. The phenomenon is explained in two ways that are not, in any case, antithetical.

The first cause of this sudden questioning may be due to the general malaise felt by a world on the brink of chaos. Survival instinct prompts modern man to look behind him in search of a lifebuoy to cling to and thus avoid the undertow of the void. The disquieting profile of postmodernity compels the pilot civilization of the "megamachine" to cast another glance in history's rearview mirror. The anxious and objective survey of the past makes serious researchers face a wide gap concerning the Arab-Muslim heritage in the internalized outline of history. People begin to wonder what has come of so large a part of its course. And *if* Islam actually had something to reveal?

The second explanation for this sudden infatuation toward Islam and its role in the evolution of humanity may be ascribed to the latent disquiet produced by theses like those of Huntington. Being an Islamophobe is becoming fashionable. The need of knowing the enemy induces the West to look more seriously into historical events. Revisiting the history of Islam is like leaning over the microscope to study the virus that is attacking you.

Islamism is regarded as the sudden manifestation of a germ that has suddenly appeared from the mists of time to reinfect the world, or the recessive and bellicose gene of an indigenous faith that the world thought it had neutralized for ever. Surely it makes sense to search the past in order to detect the possible causes and effects of this fresh outbreak and discern its typical features.

Nostalgia or phobia? Whatever the motive, a "posthumous" acknowledgment is underway. At last it is being discovered that an absence is haunting mankind's memory like a gaping black hole, torturing consciences like some betrayal of the sacred right to know and to teach.

Selective Amnesia

It is being noticed that the culture of overshadowing has been (and will long be) carefully maintained due to a syllabus that suffers from selective amnesia, according to which Islam—that colossal phenomenon of human history—has not taken part in the historical dynamic. But if Islam is an optical illusion, a vague coincidence, if it is not a major element of history, if it is unhistorical, what is History then?

> At the epistemological level, the rejection of Islam from the historical dynamic of Progress took the form, during the composition of disciplines, of a linking of the study of the Arab-Muslim world to orientalism, and, as such, to the realm of the great vanished civilizations. The very status of orientalist discipline postulates a partitioning: between "European civilization" and "unlettered barbarians" stand literate societies whose civilizations are somehow frozen at midpoint. This is the domain of ori-entalism, and it is there that Arab studies have been placed. This casting aside of the "East," well known today, has had, with a few exceptions, the lasting effect of excluding Arab-Muslim studies from the discipline of history. To be sure, French orientalism has produced the works of first-rank scholars: one has only to call to mind Massignon, Berque, Rodinson, Miquel. We will simply note that they do not belong to the "tribe" of professional historians.[7]

It was undoubtedly considered sufficient to confine Islam in a hazy ideological junkyard called the "East" so as to get rid of the bad genie and ward off its seductive power over people. Eclipse and mystification go hand in hand with teacher education, from which Islam is banished.

Erasing Islam from the visual field of the pupil—and then of the student—pertains to a policy that finds an alibi in the impenetrability of the Arabic language. Robert Ilbert presents the excuse of the difficulty:

> The history of the Arab world has so many difficulties that prevent its being fully accepted into university and secondary-school curricula. For the same specialized and complicated reasons, such history requires prior knowledge that is too particular for it to be easily integrated into the curriculum of historical studies. . . . If the branches of history remain reticent, it is largely because primary research on the Arab and Muslim world is increasingly inaccessible to those without a sound basic knowledge.[8]

The alibi is convincing. No oath is needed to believe that a harried civilization that is animated by an active trade in images is not at all inclined to encourage studious and disinterested vocations. It is easily believed that the citizen of the modern world cannot devote a lifetime to defend a serious cause or acquire a genuine knowledge. The culture of the here and now does not permit such perseverance.

Haunted by the concern of an uncertain future in which there will be no room for the philosopher and the philanthropist, the intelligentsia is composed of technocrats with a pointillist view of things. The age of multidisciplinary scholars has been replaced by an era of technicians. In the politics of the North, the direction that knowledge is to take has become motivated by financial efficiency within the framework of frantic globalization.

Statistically, ignorance of Islam is even more alarming. In 1987, Claude Liauzu noted that "in the 109 modernists and contemporanists of the CNRS, only one is specialized in the Muslim world," and that "between 1965 and 1979, 71 doctoral dissertations were defended in the History of the Muslim world—that is, 4.6% per year, less than 10% of the total number of dissertations." Our author concludes: "The sociological and institutional conditions of scientific accumulation and professional reproduction are far from assured."[9]

The conditions in question do not stand a chance of being fulfilled since the real knowledge of Islam requires a measure of sacrifice and a good dose of humility. To master the knowledge of Islam (*a fortiori*, of *islam*) is a vocation that cannot be reduced to a profession. For this reason, orientalism is a discipline left in the care of exceptional vocations. Jean-Louis Triaud states:

> In France, as in the other European countries, the history of Islam is not included in the ordinary stock of knowledge of the professional historian. For want of sufficient knowledge, the latter can only treat of

the Arab-Muslim world from secondary sources. Orientalist "fundamentalism," favoring the knowledge of working languages and a philological approach, and thus transforming the study of the Muslim world into a long initiation procedure, will confirm the historian in the feeling that he cannot have access to the particular keys of a radically different world whose references are unknown to him.[10]

Such lack of interest, whatever its motives, is found at all levels of academic life:

> At the *agrégation*[11] for the five-year period of 1982–86, no question on the written exams concerns the Muslim world; a single essay question on the vicissitudes of European socialism between 1945 and 1960 hardly broaches the subject. . . . As to what lies outside the curriculum, the proportion of questions on the Arab and Muslim world from the Middle Ages to the present ranges from 1.3% to 5.1%. . . . Roll-down maps, we may note, rank the Muslim world first among non-European civilizations during the Middle Ages; in the modern era, it is the Americas; for the contemporary period, it is Asia.[12]

One needn't be a genius to comprehend the reason for such ranking and the secret of such epistemology. Islam is merely an accident of history, fit only to be relegated to the Middle Ages, a period with negative connotations. Disinformation concerning the subject is likely to be the lot of the Westerner for long. His subconscious will still be cluttered up with false ideas.

The overshadowing of the Arab[13] heritage not only blurs the historical landscape, it also erects conceptual barriers that distort our very conception of the world. For instance, the mania to shove all that affects *islam* and its history into an "ideological magma"[14] called the East is established in the morals of Western academic tradition.

An Ideological Magma

"The East" is for most a vague notion lost in the mist of past and weird anecdotes that took place in exotic lands at an indefinable moment, straddling history, literature and fantasy. The most informed perception conceives this East as rigidly set in the eternal Middle Ages. In other words, Islam is a historical aberration, a telescoping of epochs that ought not to have met. Islam is the Middle Ages that do not want to end, an era from the past tacked onto the modern present.

Excursions to the country of anomaly, where past and present merged, produced those delicious *frissons* that were in great demand in the eighteenth century. In the club of great writers, fond of rare sensations and perverse foreignness, talk of the East was a highly prized fashion.

The fascination that such a quasi-virtual East exerted over minds arose precisely from the sensation of intrusion of the past into the present. The fantasies aroused by the mythical East were so strong as to place them out of time, out of logic, verging on dream. As a consequence, those who had not the means to visit these timeless lands had only to invent imaginary trips to be in those climes. Chateaubriand, for instance, unhesitatingly described an East in which he never set foot.

For romantic minds, the East was a country straddling the real and the unreal; you did not have to go there in order to describe it. So completely was it associated with a sort of "realm of the senses" that you could imagine it just by dreaming it. The East was for the West what antimatter is for matter: you only needed to close your eyes to enter it.

When in 1830 France occupied Algeria—that East that is more in the West than certain countries of the West (and that consequently flouts the well-established notions of the Far East)—Victor Hugo dreamed of being a sultan with his own harem. Critics of his day were surprised by his exotic macho daydreams, which led him to justify himself by writing

> The author of this collection is not one of those who recognize the right to question the poet about his fantasies and ask him why he has chosen such a subject, mixed such a color, picked from such a tree, drawn from such a source. . . . Art has no need of restraints, handcuffs, gags; it tells you, "Go!" and releases you in the great garden of poetry where there is no forbidden fruit.[15]

The department of orientalism was first created in response to such ethnic curiosity and the romantic leaps and bounds of a nation that had begun to discover, not without dismay, its destructive technological power. Only later does orientalism yield to political science in the running of the local affairs of colonized countries.

This handover of power is in itself revealing. It was at last decided that the East was no longer that misty land, that anteroom where exoticism and sensual delight combine to stimulate the Muses of poets. The East was suddenly a political fact and, particularly, an economic one, in need of an authority beyond a vague discipline.

Oil first—and later Islamism—will lead to a revision of attitudes. The term "East" will be kept for many reasons. Useful information will be added, not to perpetuate the dream but to create the political illusion. Tactical precision and strategic concerns no longer tally with the uncertain dreamlike frontiers of the ancient East, where poetry and voluptuous imagination used to suit each other so well.

We will henceforth have a Far East, a Middle East, and a Near East. Because of oil, however, there will be no further question of treating all quarters equally. The areas are to be weighed separately. The Arab Maghrib,[16] without enough energy to light Aladdin's lamp, is definitely to be expunged from the Eastern record.

Divide ut regnes—divide and rule.

The conceptual apportionment of the East, far from dispelling the illusion, only makes it more acute. This ranking of Easts according to energy policy beclouds, alas, even more the issue of Western perceptions of Islam and Muslims. One single constant remains constant in this epistemological revolution: Europe is the center of history, the pivot of geography.

Near East? Near whom, near what? Sufficiently near to be reached by tomahawk missiles!

Middle East? Middle in relation to whom?

This semantic, topological and geographical revolution is, alas, not the heart of the problem. The problem has to do with a kind of imperialism that attacks you and pursues you even in the way you perceive space.

Where might the real East and the real West be on a round and revolving earth? Wherever the prevailing way of thinking wants it to be, by Jove!

The Ejection of Islam

Even before such cosmic conjuring tricks had divided up the East according to the whims of the dominant geostrategy, orientalism was presiding over another dismantling. The East, that vague exotic land of romantic lovers intoxicated by heady incense and by voluptuous odalisques with vertebral anomalies,[17] had as well its specialists, in charge of polishing and perpetuating a view of history in which *islam* would be presented as a historical deviation.

Before modern media took over, orientalism had been preparing European consciousness to shape Western perception of the East as a no man's land without a history, a patch of the world of the past that refuses to disappear naturally, and whose beauty can only be equaled with barbarism.

The face of history, messed up by the Arabic eruption, was progressively redesigned by careful cutting and pasting in a face-lift attested by serious scholarship:

> The ejection of Islam from the classic norms of European history was accompanied by a selection of ancestors, a genealogic construction that serves as a founding charter for our culture. Ancient Egypt, Palestine, and Greece . . . were promoted at different epochs to the rank of the noble and legitimate godfathers of Western civilization. Meanwhile, the Arab-Muslim Caliphate, like Byzantium or the Carolingian Empire—one of the coheirs of the Roman Empire and one of the major guardians of the cultural heritage of classic antiquity—was refused filiation and kinship. . . . The Arab-Muslim world is treated like an unworthy relative with whom we want to erase any trace of genealogical links.[18]

Marshal Hodgson, an American author who devoted decades to his research work on Islam, made a conceptual, geographical, and chronological break with the traditional studies. Reintegrating Islam as a major and decisive phenomenon in the evolution of humanity and its access to modernity, this specialist of history ironically asserts:

128

There is a "mainstream" of history, which consists of our own direct antecedents. This includes all West-European history since it became civilized, of course; and, before that time, selected periods from areas to the southeast: Greek history till the time of the Roman empire (but not since—the Byzantines do not count as mainstream); and the Near East till the rise of the Greeks, but not since. . . . The "mainstream" of history, in the traditional image, runs through northwestern Europe in the Dark Ages of the Merovingians—although everyone knows that the Byzantines and the Muslims (and the Indians and the Chinese) were far more civilized then.[19]

He then draws a logical conclusion: "The 'mainstream' of history is simply our own closest historical antecedents."[20]

Several intermediary cutout figures were made before the final edit. Alain de Libéria says that the Greek culture was adopted only as a palliative:

However strange it may seem to those who have passed on to us their view of Europe and "culture," the Greeks of Byzantium did not belong to the West any more than the Arabs of Spain! Worse still, according to Condillac, it is the influx of those undesirable Easterners that prevented the western style, the European style to develop in Italy. Nobody would accept this verdict today. The contribution of Byzantine humanism to the Italian Renaissance is considered decisive. The "Greeks" have since been repatriated in Western consciousness. Why? [Elementary, my dear Watson!] Because we have meanwhile found other "Easterners" to ostracize: the Arabs.[21]

It is the same Condillac who set Petrarch as the father of the Renaissance. Petrarch, to whom is due the initiation of anti-Arab western humanism, has had famous dis-ciples ever since. For him, the Arabs are vulgar brigands of history who captured the Greek heritage in full flow. They stood in the way of the Greek thinking whose heritage passes on to the modern West by right.

An identity based on hating the Arab has been recurrent in the western thinking from then until now. With particularly virulent orientalism, Renan sang the praises of Petrarch, whom he regards as "the first modern man."

The idea of the historical delinquency of the Arab-Muslim civilization was later an ideal ideological basis for legitimizing colonization. E.-F. Gautier and Henri Pirenne echoed the breaking of history perpetrated by the Arabs. If Gautier accuses them of having broken the continuity of North Africa's history, Pirenne holds them responsible for having done the same with Europe's history.

Gautier thus reduces the history of the Maghrib to an incessant struggle between nomads and sedentaries.[22] Jean-Louis Triaud, evoking these clichés, demonstrates that colonization is thus presented as a return of history, a moving history that encounters an interrupted and inhibited history.

The evidence is thus made that the return of history was made possible only by the French conquest: it is the French colonization, the "New Rome in North Africa," that took back the thread of a history broken by the Hilalians.[23]

In light of this particular reading, the history of the Maghrib, for instance, is construed as a confrontation of obscurantist forces in a primitive chaos that had been awaiting the helping hand of history, a formless clay that was awaiting the hand of the artist-artisan:

> Among these preconceptions, there were clichés as tenacious as the primitive chaos of "tribes" and clans, the "dark ages," stereotyped confrontations between Berbers and Arabs, shepherds and sedentaries, mountains and plains, cities and countryside, North and South, partly attributed to (rather than borrowed from) Ibn Khaldūn by such popularizers as Emile-Félix Gautier or Henri Terrasse.[24]

As this chapter comes within the continuous work of clearing a conceptual field saturated with received ideas, we now come to a crucial point of our demonstration. Jean-Louis Triaud situates *islam* in connection with this conception of history:

> As they were perceived, these cyclic phenomena (in the history of the Maghrib) had no profound objective. They were foreign to progress. For want of grasping them as an impossible history, some immaterial essence had therefore to be extracted from them. It was there where Islam came to condense all the countervalues that the occupied society was adjudged to be bearing. Being the quintessence and the central locus of this deposed and decadent civilization, it was the one to be kept under surveillance, struck down and destroyed if need be. The orientalist explanation here came to shed light on the political question: to seek out Islam in order to better dominate the conquered populations. Yet this Islam was lived in a fantasmal manner for two reasons: on the one hand, the memory of the crusades, and on the other, the challenge made to an anticlerical culture. It was the latter that came to structure the underlying notions.[25]

Dubious Documentation

Finicky academism is sent to the devil when Islam is the subject of study. To approach Islam and comprehend its points of reference, the dialectics of history must be flouted. Any approach, whatever its quality, may be used, provided that it helps to furnish the departments of such a fragmented view of history. Concerning a phenomenon that is so insignificant in the official configuration of history, any simple instructor's reading of the case will do. Any blockhead can make a contribution to the understanding of these lands of no historical identity: all it takes is patriotism.

Louis Brunot's *Premiers conseils* is an edifying model of what the arbitrary and politicized approach of *islam* used to be.[26] As indicated on its first page, the manual is a guide for French teachers destined to teach in Maghribi Muslim schools. It is also indicated in the second page that it is "not for sale." After glancing through a few lines of this mysterious and precious book, you soon realize that you are in possession of a guide for amateur ethnologists providing information for the collections of colonial documentation. Colonial intelligence services use all available means.

The foreword leaves no doubt as to the ultimate and secret objective of the teacher's manual:

> While the army subdues the dissidents and protects the submissive and peaceful people, and while the administration assures the material well-being of the adults, the school shapes young minds in preparing a generation that is more advanced and more apt to collaborate with us in the work of progress that France, with typical unselfishness, is accomplishing here.[27]

Still with great "unselfishness," teachers are made to learn how to play the orientalists. The first chapter is entitled "How to use leisure time." This is strange enough for a book supposed to be a guide for teachers, not vacationers! The introduction ends in a joyful and patriotic "And now, let's get down to work!" Then the chapter begins in plain language:

> Do teachers profit as much as they can from their situation in the heart of Muslim society? And particularly, do they teach their experience not only to their colleagues but also to all those numerous people who are interested in things about Morocco and Islam?[28]

The book could as well be entitled "How to make a successful career in Islamology or in the intelligence service." The author continues to encourage those with a potential vocation and advise them to read the teacher's guide, but assures them that there are even better ones:

> Besides these published books, the teacher has at his disposal wonderful talking books that are too seldom consulted: their pupils and their parents. . . . By listening to pupils and their parents, the teacher can conduct very important ethnological studies that savants will welcome with great pleasure. . . . Some will reply that the Arabic or Berber languages are then to be studied. . . . Is it so difficult to learn the dialect of a people whose psychology is less complicated?[29]

The practical guide of obtuse orientalism goes even further in the training of the sorcerer's apprentices. In this jarringly titled chapter, the guide goes so far as to give such precise instructions as the exact format of the files to be used (9 x 12 cm), the manner in which they are to be filed, and much other precise information that aims to facilitate the final sorting of the ideas to be borrowed for a better management of information. Having directed the colonial strategy, these files will go to adorn the shelves of the Department of Orientalism—most certainly!

Why then is Vatin surprised to notice that

> French western science produced only a sketchy and largely unadapted corpus the inadequacies of which its practitioners were themselves late to perceive. How curious is the spectacle of students and researchers who have been taught by the greatest teachers, and have assimilated the best books on the Arab and Islamic world, in general and the Maghribi world in particular, who have acquired clear views of culture, history and religion, and who, coming in a world that is largely incomprehensible to them, have discovered that the weapons supplied to them were quasi-inoperative since they were inapplicable to the living societies they sought to seize.[30]

It is worth indicating that the term "weapons" reveals on its own the handicap of the kind of Western thinking that regards the other merely as a formerly colonized subject, or a possible enemy against whom one must defend himself.

The Other: The Enemy

Claude Liauzu's *Race et civilization, l'Autre dans la culture occidentale, anthologie critique* [race and civilization, the other in Western culture: a critical anthology] presents the inmost depths of the European mind in its relationship with otherness. Commenting on the book, Daniel Hemery informs us that the author deconstructs with rigor and moderation the presuppositions and the mental outlines that, for three centuries, have founded the profound ambivalence of the relationship that the European mind maintains with the Other:

> At the center of this imaginative world, there is that insistence on staring down the Other . . . , to evaluate him and rank him, and to incessantly set up and redo the scale of civilizations. Modern Europe built—with difficulty—its identity only through its relationship with the Other, as the human body of which it was composed was undoubtedly so divided. A view that had a consensual purpose, at once universalistic and racist, inclusive and exclusive, domineering and subduing, but also humanistic.[31]

The natural attitude toward the Other becomes obsessional when Islam is regarded as anti-West. The swing between repulsion and fascination, objectivity and subjectivity, admiration and apprehension will still mark for long the Western approach to the Islamic civilization. Nowadays, the pendulum swings more often into repulsion, subjectivity, and apprehension.

The tendency to "redo the scale of civilizations" is nothing but a sort of euphemism that describes a clear reality and a final ranking: Western civilization stands at the head of all the others, the past and the future. At the heart of the West, there is evidently Europe—forever.

One need only leaf through the literature of this land to become repulsed by the obvious smell of acute navel-gazing. The Other—the native—has no existence of his own worth mentioning: he merits the honor of appearing in famous novels only for his role as a foil, local color—or a gloomy background that serves to bring out the immaculate cleanliness of the white soul.

Ibrahim Warde, examining Edward Said's book, quotes some arguments that capture our attention and commend our approval:

> For Edward Said, "*The Royal Way,* the book of a highly talented European,[32] provides evidence of the incapacity of Western humanist consciousness to call into question the principle of colonial domination." In addition, in [Camus's] *The Stranger* and *The Plague,* books that are read as parables of the human condition, the natives are passive extras absent from the novelistic framework who particularly provide an exotic framework for the angst of the colonists: "Meursault killed an Arab, but the latter is not mentioned by his name and seems to have no past, no father or mother; Arabs die of plague in Oran, but they are equally without names."[33]

Perhaps it is better to be an extra rather than to participate in the intrigue. When a Western pen lingers over the portrait of an Easterner, it is certainly not in his favor. The latter is usually introduced as belonging to a third type. He is some sort of creature between man and beast, more beast than man: a centaur with a human head and a body possessed by the demons of bestiality. In many writings,[34] the Easterner is presented in such a manner that you will only have one wish: that of never coming across him in the corner of a dark street.

In this literature, the Eastern native is an object to be studied or a subhuman lagging behind in the evolution of the human race. Good old Western education, essentially natural since it comes from the best land of the world, gives itself the right to dispense lessons of propriety to all cultures of the world. On this subject, the reader may judge for himself after reading a passage from a randomly selected book—neither the worst nor the most eccentric:

> We are constantly adapting our bodies to an optative behavior that abides by rules where biological, sociological and psychological factors have their role. It is this technique that makes us who we are. For Muslims, the pious man is refused any incognito: even though he is equipped with

a knife and fork, he will somehow manage to get along at our table with only his right hand.[35]

It is obviously more natural to eat with a fork than with your fingers—sufficient reason to civilize the world.

Gustave Le Bon, another gentleman studying local defects, denounces the ill-natured colonized native who refuses to become civilized, balking and rearing up in the face of change. He warns his compatriots who might have qualms about that:

> The sole result of the European education of the Negro as well as of the Arab and the Hindu has been to alter the hereditary qualities of their race without giving them those of the Europeans. They may acquire scraps of European ideas, but they will use them with semicivilized arguments and sentiments. Their judgments waver between contrary ideas and opposite moral principles ... Let us not be deluded by this slight veneer our European education may temporarily cast on a native.[36]

Further our great psychologist Le Bon maintains:

> After much effort, we make what is called an educated native—and immediately he turns against us. Instead of expressing gratitude, he takes revenge against us for the harm that we did to his character, and he uses his imperfectly received education against his master.[37]

Even Westernized novelists who venerate the masters as much as their language merit only downright condescension. Raymond Charles advises them not to cling anymore the way they do to the French language. He regards them as intruders—perhaps even as leeches sticking to a language that denies them. It is a scandal to see a native of Islam having interest in literary niceties:

> On balance, the Arab Renaissance ... still has no Balzac or Shakespeare of its own, despite the impatience of its adherents. ... We may well wonder whether the novel and the theater, inventions of an advanced European culture, are universal modes, and whether the Eastern soul should not rather seek more spontaneous means of expression in poetry.[38]

Reading elsewhere in his book of the "respect" Charles has for Arab poetry, we understand that it is in duly noted reference to the pursuits of their ancestors who had little common sense and a merely superficial affective development.

Being an Easterner means coming form a world that is best suited to nourishing fantasies and producing poetry, since the East is the anti-West.[39] If the West produces modernity, the East produces dreams and nonchalance. If the West produces economic development, the East produces underdevelopment and laziness.

If the West struggles against natural elements to shape history, the East lies down and wallows in unpardonable indolence.

Confiscations

The fatalism of the East is a theme dear to the hearts of many essayists interested in the subject. Yet even in those lands ignored in the mainstream of history there may appear a mind too luminous to be refused or ignored. When this happens, the Western revisionist of history, like a medium at a seance, cannot resist taking over such personalities.

Ibn Khaldūn, the father of modern sociology, this "giant among dwarfs," as the "sworn" friend of Arabs, Jacques Berque, describes him, cannot be abandoned as such to the East. Many gems have been written on the subject! One of the best remains that of Gautier, who wrote in his book *Mœurs et coutumes des musulmans* [manners and customs of the Muslims]

> Muslim civilization is stricken by a strange paralysis of historical sense. . . . In the Middle Ages, the least of our historians makes history the way Monsieur Jourdain[40] made prose; the Saracen with the most astute mind has not the least idea of it.[41]

Let us not underestimate this gentleman; he asked himself a question that everyone ought to ask while reading this passage. As for Ibn Khaldūn? Well, the problem this genius poses to such assertions is settled in a flick of the pen. Gautier reluctantly admits, "This Easterner has a lively mind." He continues, unperturbed: "This goes to say that he has a Western conception of History."[42] He then begins to make dubious speculations in order to give a plausible explanation to his fantasies: "It is to be admitted that perhaps by the detour of Andalusia, a breath of our Western Renaissance had reached the Eastern soul of Ibn Khaldūn."[43]

Examining such nonsense, Yves Lacoste expresses evident irony:

> Let us content ourselves by admitting that a comparison of Ibn Khaldūn and his contemporary Froissard is not to the advantage of the representative of the "Western mind.". . . Why such dogged determination to refuse to admit against the evidence that the Arab civilization had given the impetus to historical knowledge? Why this concern to dissociate Ibn Khaldūn from an Arab world that we have caricatured? Because History, as Paul Valéry says, is a dangerous science.[44]

Other brilliant minds are annexed somehow or other, and their productions are affiliated to Western genius. When it is impossible, for fear of flagrant anachronism, to establish a link between an attractive Arab mind and the beneficial fragrance of the Renaissance, the Arabic name is given Latin resonance. Thus Ibn Sīna becomes Avicenna, Ibn Roshd becomes Averroës, Arrazi becomes Rhases, etc. . . .

One also finds commentaries often enough that stipulate, in utter defiance of chronological precedence, that al-Ghazālī had a Cartesian mind; that Suyūtī, "like" Pico della Mirandola, had defended such and such a principle; that Ibn Khaldūn, "like" Darwin, had spoken of apes. This attitude betrays the obsession that Arab civilization is merely an inveigler of energy and ideas meant to be the exclusive prerogative of the West. Thus Ghazali (1058–1111) is reported to have stolen the idea of methodical doubt from Descartes (1596–1650). Suyūtī is reported to have copied his humanist thinking from Pico della Mirandola, who was born no less than several centuries after him, and heaven knows what else. . . .

While its prestigious figures are confiscated, the East, that unworthy plagiarist, is seized by the collar, shelved in profound discredit and showered with mockery. In his *Islam et capitalisme,* Maxime Rodinson writes:

> There has been discussion of a lack in the Muslim East of the enterpris-ing mind; a listless fatalism has been attributed to medieval Islam that leaves it to God to provide man with the necessary goods of life, should He ever consider it useful to do so. This argument, as we know, is one of the most common in Europe, and it has even acquired the status of estab-lished truth and dogma for the European collective consciousness, well expressed by the Leibzian term *fatum mahometanum.* It was developed in the eighteenth and nineteenth centuries by countless European authors who could rely on the evidence of the spectacle of stagnation manifest in the Ottoman Empire, Morocco and Iran. It is still taken up these days.[45]

This negative image is a necessary hard core against which the West forges his own identity. An anti-Islamic subconscious would serve as raw material and support for an identity that is difficult to establish. Jean-Louis Triaud asserts: "Our European identities are founded on a rejection of Islam that is largely more left unsaid than we may think. The 'Islamic subconscious' weighs heavily on our representation of the world."[46]

In the anti-Islamic subconscious there is certainly a buried feeling of weakness towards this adversary, regarded as possessing a mobilizing and unifying energy that Europe will perhaps never know. It is an anti-identity based on the refusal of Islam, but there still remains in it a possible link in an impossible world. Hating the Other would be a passable social link in a world that finds it hard to find one that is solid and durable. We must use what we have at disposal. A.V. Gennep writes:

> From a practical point of view it is regrettable that the population of Europe is not one in race, language and aspiration; the diverse groups that remain in it seem neither disposed to assimilate mutually, nor capable of merging once and for all within one of these groups.[47]

The most indifferent observer of Islam recognizes that it is a generator of very strong social links. Even in the present time—where it is most torn apart by its domestic divisions and is at its lowest decadence—the quality of social relationships in its realm remains exceptional. Regis Blachère attests to this extremely appreciable distinctive feature: "Today, the notion of community has become like the substance of the Muslim soul; everyone feels this in himself, notwithstanding the social inequalities and even the recent frontiers of touchy nationalisms."[48]

Such federative capacity has always disturbed the will of domination of certain powers. Today more than ever, it is perhaps one of the primordial reasons that incite the evil propaganda waged against Islam. Because of this quality of refusing to die, Islam is presented to the world as the root of all evils.

Islam's Division

The idea that Islam, as a sort of historical squatter, has broken the harmony of the Mediterranean world is an argument highly prized by rough and caustic traditional orientalism. It is even more valued today, when Europe's search of new balances of power is centered on Mediterranean solidarity. The reallocation of roles within the context of globalization passes by unprecedented mutual benefits. The Muslim world, as a whole or in part, would be an excellent partner and a considerable block in restoring the balance of the economic power and counterbalancing the new tsarism that is settling down nowadays. Alas, the psychological heritage is heavy—too heavy.

We have already seen how the Arabs were accused of having interfered between Greek thinking and the Renaissance. Pirenne has decided that those intruders equally disturbed the serene harmony of "the pool." "The Western Mediterranean, having become a Muslim lake, ceases to be the route of trading and the exchange of ideas that it had never ceased to be until then."[49] A few pages earlier he notes that Islam was "the sundering of a phenomenon that has lasted until our day."

Braudel writes unequivocally:

> With respect to the West, Islam is tantamount to the cat versus the dog. We might call it a Counter-West, with all the ambiguities of a profound opposition that is at once rivalry, hostility and borrowing. . . . It is, on its own, the "other" Mediterranean, the Counter-Mediterranean prolonged by the desert.[50]

Regarded as counter-history, counter-Mediterranean, counter-humanity, counter-logic, Islam has never ceased to arouse passionate reactions. Hichem Djaït summarizes what Claude Lévi-Strauss thinks of the break produced by the Muslim faith that has apparently no other ambition than that of annoying the world:

> By its very existence, Islam played the role of the intruder: it split in two a world destined to be united, intervening between Hellenism and the East,

between Christianity and Buddhism. It has islamicized the West, preventing Christianity from being deeply established and from being more itself, which would have procured for it a slow osmosis with Buddhism.[51]

Islam the spoilsport is accused of having caused all the damage in the world. Hichem Djaït formally refutes what the ethnologist with sad "topics" is proposing:

> If Europe, the cape of Asia, has survived and then asserted itself, was it not because it had benefited from a millennium of peace between the end of the Hungarian invasions to the holocaust of the Thirty Years' War? To Islam fell the role of the protective screen against the great surges: Islam absorbed, like a lethal poison, the Mongolian jolt in 1258; Islam subsequently stopped the Timurid wave.[52]

If in this trade-off of ideas Djaït presents Islam as the security force that prevented the backwash of history from overflowing onto a Europe whose shoulders were too frail to face up to it, Pierre Chaunu regards Islam as a vulgar catalyst of history—the only history worth being taken into account, the one that of course puts Europe in the center. Stressing the point that "Henri Pirenne is quite right; the break between Christianity and Islamity is extremely profound,"[53] he goes on to assert, a few pages on,

> Europe's lot is also that harassing presence of Islam, the insurmountable barrier of the Maghrib against which the far-flung outposts and the Turkish upsurge in the Balkans had exhausted themselves. By breaking the Medit-erranean trading circuits and obliging them to turn back from borders of Islam and Christianity, the old rivalry compelled Christianity to swing north, and then east and south on the ocean.[54]

. If Pierre Chaunu has a more positive attitude toward Islam, Pirenne's opinion remains quite present in his speech. The sole historical function that this kind of thinking is willing to accord to Islam is that of wave-break. Let Jean-Louis Triaud notice this on our behalf:

> By breaking the Mediterranean, Islam thus fulfilled the sole historical fun-ction for which it has never received recognition. For the rest, history made a detour toward other skies, leaving the Arab-Muslim and Ottoman world in a timeless, marginalized or motionless situation, in one that is outside the sole time that counts, that of Progress.[55]

Progress, a vague notion currently criticized at home, remains the criterion by which the reliability of an event is measured before it is allowed access to history. Auscultation of the Islamic phenomenon with the stethoscope of progress gives a choice of diagnoses: evident anachronism or reluctant entrance into history. Braudel writes

> Islam entered reluctantly in this hell or purgatory of human beings we call, out of decency, the Third World. Reluctantly, since it had once known a relatively better and undeniable situation.[56]

Decency undoubtedly prevents a certain thinking from getting to the root of the evil of underdevelopment by recalling the plundering of the Third World and the consequences of armed technicity. Chalk these up to the vagaries of history! Yet let us not expect orientalist thinking to be thorough; that is not its assigned role.

Let us continue the ballad with the fortunate people who have engraved the western subconscious.

One of the most original arguments is no doubt the arrival on the scene of evolutionism, according to which Islam is an intermediary (if assuredly significant) stage between primary fetishism and social development. It is a commendable status that serves to refine certain subhuman populations in order to prepare them for access to human dignity.

Alain Quellien, a functionary of the Ministry of Colonies, can explain it to us:

> The propagation of Islam is a step towards civilizing West Africa. The Muslim peoples of these regions are universally recognized as superior in terms of social organization to the peoples that remained animist. . . . We cannot pretend to make them, in one generation or even four or five, climb the rungs of the ladder whose end the old Western world, after hundreds of centuries, still does not see. It should be remembered that nature does not proceed by leaps and bounds, and that it is, if not impossible, at least dangerous for the Black to jump suddenly from his quasi-barbaric state to the very advanced state of our social development. It should be recalled that Islam brings with it a refining power and indisputable moral value.[58]

We are happy to know that from so subjective a source! However, clarification is necessary to make allowances.

Clarification

It is difficult to overcome the optical illusion when the scotoma is inherited from generation to generation. The distortion that is thus perpetrated becomes second nature. It is difficult for a deposed *umma* to find a taker of the idea that it defends of Islam as a principal current of history and a natural state of humanity. Present misfortunes treacherously eclipse the grandeur of a faith that has a universal calling.

It is not a question of arousing bitter nostalgia, but rather of preparing the dialog for an era that will be badly in need of it. In order for *islam* to be recognized as the Universal Message that it is, it will need to be extricated from the rubble of mis-understanding. Its tarnishing by clever hands will have to be made clear: it must be rescued from the heap of anecdotal misconceptions that constitute the sum of the average Westerner's knowledge of *islam*. The image of the Message that once shone on its own must be restored.

To do that, we must perhaps begin by adjusting our angle of vision. Much effort has been expended so far to present *islam* as a barbarism that suddenly appeared on the fringes of history and no longer has a place beneath the sky of modernity. Muslims are regarded as the residue of a history that resists the great modern wash.

We can of course understand that nobody wants to be identified with something that is perceived as a flaw, a rift, or, worse still, a pathological eyesore of history, the transient static in its smooth transmission. For precisely this reason, our concern to validate the historicity of Islam will occupy an entire chapter of this book. For precisely this reason, our words may perhaps be somewhat caustic. For precisely this reason, it has to be pointed out that the angle from which the world is presented to us is not the right one.

The version that we know of history is in fact a provincial version. The real version, the true version, is multidimensional and will turn the modern world's perception of itself upside down. The geographical apportioning of the world in use nowadays participates in this conjuring trick so as to present the world the way European centrism wills it.

For history to be concentrated and lodged in Europe, this region is unhesitatingly made into a continent. Anyone who takes the time to look at the world map with the slightest critical mind will quickly have some questions to ask.

Why is this so? By what criterion is Europe to be considered a continent and not, for instance, India?

The motive is obvious: the principal current of a rerouted history must be given an illusive spacious home in which it does not appear to be confined. Terms are used unscrupulously: Europe thus becomes a continent by the grace of fervent navel-gazing. Hodgson admits:

> Europe is still ranked as one of the "continents" because our cultural ancestors lived there. By making it a "continent," we give it a rank disproportionate to its natural size, as a subordinate part of no larger unit, but in itself one of the major component parts of the world. . . . No wonder then, that despite all our awareness of the distortion of the Mercator projection, and that many better projections are available, it remains the most common form of world map outside geographers' classrooms. It confirms our predispositions. It flatters our egos. . . . Yet what we really want is to face the world as it actually is, not as our Western self-esteem would like to picture it.[58]

That is also the wish of the few iconoclastic thinkers who subscribe to a less subjective view of the world. Awaiting new predispositions, Mercator's projection has still good tunes ahead. Mercator's map reportedly enables a more safe calculation for navigation. Accuracy of calculus and safety of sailors—there's a good excuse!

But how can Greenwich be justified as being the reference meridian? Is it by chance?

Hodgson excites our curiosity as to the fortieth parallel that distorts to excess the proportions of the globe:

> Historically, almost all the great centers of civilization have lain south of the fortieth parallel; all, that is, save Europe. Most of Europe lies north of that parallel. But it is precisely at about the fortieth parallel that the Mercator projection begins to exaggerate areas unconscionably. In consequence, that projection and others like it show Europe on a far larger scale than the Middle East, or India, or China. India does appear to the eye of that projection, as a "country in Asia" on the order of, say, Sweden in Europe. And it is possible to show on such a world map numerous details in Europe, towns and rivers that are famous among us, while India or Indonesia, say, are quickly filled up with only the most essential features—which, indeed, are all we have usually heard of.[59]

Reading Hodgson, we wonder if a pure and simple clarification is alone necessary, or if a real purge to our conception of the world may not be needed in order to set the record straight (which must not necessarily be set according to Greenwich). Why? Because nothing is more difficult to rearrange than deep-seated prejudices and views. Even the boldest thinkers do not dare attack historical falsification head-on lest they suffer the fearsome label of "revisionist."

To question the received historical account qualifies you immediately as a member of the revisionists' club. So we must either abide by a Mercatoresque conception of the world or be labeled as dangerous troublemakers and excluded from the circle of politically correct thinkers. We must either think of history and geography from the point of view of Europe or be regarded as cranks overtaken by events who do not know how to evaluate things in their proper measure.

To be a dupe or not to be! Each line of thought has its price.

Since the real proportions of the globe are entirely distorted by the Mercator projection, the land of Islam finds itself getting the meanest share on the maps of the world. An objective world configuration is to be made normally according to an equal surface projection.[60]

The internalized traditional configuration based on the Mercatorian projection makes it possible to overshadow the fact that, in the sixteenth century, Europe was merely a province in an essentially Muslim world. A visitor from Mars in the sixteenth century would think that the entire earth was Islamic.[61]

Taking advantage of a rerouted history and a falsified geography, the West promotes itself to the center of the perception that ordinary mortals have of the world. What forms the rest of the globe will only have to keel over in the peripheries of conscience. It is a highly skillful manipulation to have succeeded in erasing so many memories forever, and in so short a time: "Contact with the West was peripheral for Islam, no more important or even less important than contact with Eastern Europe, Hindu India, or any other of the various regions with which Muslims were in close contact."[62]

This chapter is not motivated by any wish whatever to get the course of history inverted or time stopped in its course. Historical dialectics is intolerable only for those who are ignorant of the existence of the immutable divine law that governs the universe. Long before Marx used and abused historical dialectics, the Qur'ān informs us that the latter is necessary for the continuation of the human race: *And did not God check one set of people by means of another, the earth would indeed be full of mischief.*[63]

God says in another verse: *Such days* (of varying fortunes) *We give to men and women by turns.*[64]

To lament over the ruins of a vanished civilization is a defeatist and pointless attitude. We can never remind our readers enough that the concerns of this book are to shed light on certain obscure zones cast on Muslim history and to rid of discredit a faith that merits being considered otherwise. The history of Muslims has indeed known deviations that this writing will not only consider contesting, but will also examine in Part Three. The question here is not of stooping to idealizing facts, but of reorienting history.

Jaures put it well: "To remain faithful is to pass on flames, not ashes, from the home of ancestors." To revel in flattering remembrances has never moved the wheel of history forward. An Arab poet said: "The hero is not one who says 'My father was so-and-so,' but who declares, 'Here I am.' "

Islam and Modernity

The prestige that the concept of "modernity" enjoys in many minds leads us in the end of this chapter to examine the role of Islam in the accomplishment of the phenomenon to which it refers. We reach here the peak of the misunderstanding that is crystallizing around history.

If the participation of Islam in the scientific and civilizing progress of humanity is denied, it is namely in order not to share with it the great honor of having engendered the modern phenomenon. The Gordian knot of the war waged on *islam*'s historicity lies in the desire to totally appropriate modernity, considered as the best fate that could befall humankind.

The West claims exclusivity over the genesis of modernity that it considers to be the happy ending of evolving man, the *nirvana* of social progress. If the modern system should turn sour—something not long in happening if ecological destruction continues at its current rate—the West will unhesitatingly wish to share responsibility with few peoples excluded yesterday from history.

It is perhaps within such a perspective that the West deigns at last to grant few rights of historicity to Islam! Maybe when modern man will have noticed tomorrow that the fall is imminent, that the raging *niños* and *niñas* have devastated the earth, that humanity is back to square one, it will then grant modernity's affiliation to Islam.

For the time being, globalization is still for many the positive reference *par excellence*, either because some enjoy it personally, or because many are conditioned to think of it that way. Thus we still see certain local intellectuals who dare you to express an opinion on modernism and call you a blasphemer if you dare to give vent to your misgivings.

The sycophants of modernism heap praise on illusions. The idealization of the modern event is essentially due to its confusion with comfort. Comfort indeed is obsessive; it prevents us from realizing the manifold facets of modernity that are not all so flattering. Those who sing the praises of modernity are the very ones who live on the side dispensing well-being.

What about the opinion of the silent masses who live their daily lives grappling with the reverses of modernity?

How about the destitute, who know only the backside of modernity, or the color of its fangs?

The promise of a rosy future, where comfort will be widespread, is a lure. It is materially impossible to extend to all mankind the living standards of the average Westerner, simply because the earth's resources will not be enough to attain that objective. It is impossible for all six billion human beings (the figure will double to-morrow) to have access to the degree of comfort that unbridled modernism presents as indispensable for the humankind to be modern and upstanding.

Dominique Wolton denigrates this mania to present western modernity as a natural outcome that we will all inevitably reach:

> Evolutionary sociology has always considered modernization as the transformation process of societies that are entering the industrial era, a necessary and indispensable stage to attain economic development, de-mocracy, prosperity. In fact, this sort of sociology has been demolished by criticizing the universality of such processes. The term modernization was chosen to refer to the study of the strategies followed by the developing countries in order to construct a "western-style" modern society.[65]

To think that history is linear is as ridiculous as believing that the earth is flat. Any historical event is born within a context of breaks, contradictions, oppositions, and dominations. History never moves forward in continuity and serenity, but in friction and resistance.

The excessive comfort and ostentatious opulence for some necessarily pre-sup-poses, in the dialectic logic that governs history, destitution for the others. Equilibrium requires equity: the latter is, alas, antithetical to modernity.

Since "Western" comfort is not possible for everyone, what other things might modernity offer? Unbridled violence against the world heritage? Spiritual nothingness? Dialog between a deaf North and a voiceless South? The science that treats the majority of people as guinea pigs or cash cows, or mad cows, or thin cows, or sacred cows?

Let us speak out on the benefits of modernity! Let us speak out on the very modern policy of the rich states that purchase from the poor states the right to treat their people like common laboratory rats, or the right to pollute their atmosphere.

Let us speak out on drug control, this precious service that modernity offers its citizens (those who live in the comfort dispensing side, of course). Let us speak out on a modernity that urges the children of the underdeveloped countries to turn their homelands into garbage sites where the rich (and very modern) countries come to discharge their nuclear and toxic wastes.

Let us speak out on depleted-uranium warheads, on mad cows, on climate change, on school violence. Let us speak out again and again.

Let us speak out until we are breathless! Let us speak in words; let us speak in figures.

When the modern times are recounted to us in figures, it is easier to realize that we are wrestling with perhaps the most tragic period ever experienced by humanity.

Sad indeed is the system that offers earthly paradise to a handful of earthlings, including their dogs, and that subjects to public obloquy the cursed of the earth—those who had the ridiculous idea of not being born on the right side—that is to say, the overwhelming majority of humanity.

Protests

The prestige of modernity is still not widely challenged, but criticism of the system is gradually settling. The West has never been without wise men and women among its children who cast a dubious eye on the advent of the false god of Progress. The Romantic Movement, for instance, was not only a literary trend that advocated escape into the world of the imagination; it was a trend of thinking that ran counter to the harrowing and disenchanting world that nascent modernity had brought. Daniel Boy relates the following:

> In this spirit of romanticism, quality is contrasted with quantity, and also the human element with the material element, and feelings with reason. . . . The revolt against a world of quantification appears periodically in our cultural universe in multiple forms: rejection of "money as king," to take up a word that does not belong to the left, but also the refusal of seeing man put into the equation by the social sciences.[66]

Thinkers, writers and reviewers have incessantly called the notion of progress into question.

Sometimes, the protest has taken a menacing turn as the tone and tension increase. At its height in England in 1811, the Luddite movement fought modern technology with might and main.[67] Their momentum was checked the following year, when the House of Lords instituted the death penalty against them. Thirty Luddites died in their war against the industrializing modernism, twenty-five were tried and hanged, and around sixty were imprisoned.

May of 1968 is one of those periods when refusal reaches a climax. Then calm criticism takes up its course, no doubt benumbed by the universal craze for the comfort that accompanies the modern phenomenon.

To question modernity is still for many a sacrilege, especially when you are listed among the spoil sports of a kind of humanity on its way to progress and comfort. The consciences bribed by a promise of well-being refuse to boo the modern phenomenon even when it behaves the worst.

Modernity, according to Hodgson, is the expression of a violent break in the natural process of humanity's evolution. He situates the "Transformation" (as he likes to call it) in a global context where history is not the hostage of a part of humanity. In the passage that follows, Hodgson reminds us of the studied the hewing of history to which the official line proceeds in order to give the modern event the roots it wishes. He reorients a view he declares to be off-center:

> But this point of view generally rests on the conceptions of world history found in those Western high school texts which trace the whole human story primarily from Babylonia and Egypt, through classical Greece and then Rome, to Medieval Western Europe and thence to the Modern Occident, bringing in other areas only parenthetically and by way of contrast except as they touch Western Europe. . . . Seen in a wider setting, the historical career of the West-Europeans was eccentric but not remarkably outstanding until quite modern times. Above all, it was integral with the whole wider Afro-Eurasian historical life.[68]

The author continues to defend the idea that the modern world, essentially based on the technological boom, is the fruit of a historical accumulation that is proper to the vast geographical area represented by the Afro-Eurasian space:

> There had been a continual accumulation of technique and of knowledge, a continual expansion of the geographical limits of urban, literate society in most parts of the zone of the Afro-Eurasian civilizations for some several millennia. . . . In the Sixteenth Century the West-Europeans still dealt on essentially equal terms with the other peoples of the Afro-Eurasian historical complex. . . . The acceleration within Western Europe was clearly a part of a much wider picture, and cannot soundly be understood except in that wider context.[69]

Modernity is therefore the product of a common Afro-Eurasian history wherein the regional skills of different peoples have combined. It is the outcome of a synergy in which the symbionts are numerous. Islam was the most active historical agent in this symbiosis and had the strongest impact on the Afro-Eurasian region.

Everything happened as if the region had been brooding a phenomenon for many thousands of years, and that the latter hatched contrary to expectation in a particular land called Europe. The "Transformation" represented by modernity was in any case preceded by a notable acceleration of history that stood distinct from the smooth course of the gestation period.

But the irruption of the modern phenomenon precisely in Europe had well-determined causes. A combination of circumstances due to internal conflicts proper to Europe hypertrophied the technical aspect of the "Transformation":

> A key aspect of this Transformation was the institutionalizing of technical innovation. We may conveniently use this as an index of the presence of the Transformation on what may be called its "evolutional" side. . . . More generally, all the technical aspects in a wide range of thought and action were given an unprecedented primacy. All other considerations—esthetic, traditional, supernatural, personal—were relatively muted. . . . This was above all a matter of attitude. Men expected each other to put technical calculations foremost in science—even at the expense of beautiful philo-sophical vision . . . at the expense of personal ties and traditional sanctions. . . . Men learned to expect that wealth would depend more on inventing new machines or finding new markets than on cleverly exploiting old ones.[70]

Europe is then the part of the Afro-Eurasian whole that, by the force of circumstances, recovered ancient and common experience and precipitated their conclusion in a context of profound and Promethean transformation. Modernity, which could have been the ripened fruit of human wisdom, becomes a dangerous tool in the hands of imperialist and mutant Europe. The impact of this sudden trans-formation has been ceaselessly evident ever since. The rest of the world will suffer from this anomaly in bloodshed and disorientation. It will also suffer from it through a terrible time pressure in the face of a transformed West.

NOTES

1. Sigrid Hunke, *Le soleil d'Allah brille sur l'Occident* [the sun of Allah shines on the West], Albin Michel, *Espaces libres,* Paris, 1963.

2. Idem., p. 11.

3. Jean-Louis Triaud, "L'Islam vu par les historiens français" [Islam viewed by French historians], *Esprit,* Nov. 1998, p. 110.

4. Jacques Berque, "Refuser la tentation de l'insularité" [refusing the temptation of insularity] in *Le Monde diplomatique* of March 1991, p. 13.

5. Research Director at the Sorbonne and author of *Penser au Moyen Âge* [medieval thought].

6. Alain de Libéria, "Fracture en Méditerranée: une double amnésie nourrit le discours xénophobe" [a split in the Mediterranean: twofold amnesia nourishes xenophobic discourse], *Le Monde diplomatique,* Sept. 1993, p. 17.

7. Cf. *Esprit* of Nov. 1998, p. 116. The text is taken from a paper given at an international seminar on *l'Explication en histoire: Problème historiographique et problème didactoque* [explaining history: historiographical and didactic problem].

8. Robert Ilibert, "L'histoire du monde arabe et musulman dans l'enseignement" [the history of the Arab and Muslim world in education], *AFEMAM* (French association for the study of the Arab and Muslim world), Issue 2, Dec. 1987, p. 38.

9. Claude Liauzu, "Jalons pour un état des lieux" [landmarks for an inventory of fixtures], *AFEMAM,* Issue 2, Dec. 1987, p. 12.

10. Triaud (1998).

11. TN: *Agrégation* is the highest qualification available for teachers at secondary level. Many university lecturers are also *"agrégés."* Candidates take a series of written papers in which they are expected to demonstrate in-depth knowledge of a single chosen field (mathematics, philosophy, English, etc). The candidates who obtain the best results in the written papers then go on to take the oral examination.

12. Liauzu (1987).

13. The word Arab echoes in my text the meaning given in Hunke (1963).

14. Mohammed Arkoun's felicitous expression.

15. Cf. Victor Hugo in the foreword of *Les Orientales,* Ed. Flammarion, Paris, 1968.

16. TN: North Africa.

17. Ingres's famous *Grande odalisque* (1814) depicts a voluptuous "Oriental Woman" with an oddly elongated back that has three more vertebrae than usual. Why not, since everything is possible in the Orient!

18. Triaud (1998).

19. Marshall G. S. Hodgson, *Rethinking World History: Essays on Europe, Islam, and World History* (texts edited, with an introduction and conclusion, by Edmund Burke III), Cambridge: Cambridge University Press, 1996, p. 6.

20. Ibid.

21. de Libéria (1993).

22. Abdallah Laroui, *L'Histoire du Maghreb, esssai de synthèse* [Overview of the history of the Maghrib], Paris, F. Maspero, 1975, vol. I, p. 203.

23. Triaud (1998), p. 123.

24. Vatin, *Religion et politique au Maghreb: le renversement de perspectives dans l'étude de l'Islam, Islam et politique au Maghreb* [religion and politics in the Maghrib: a change of perspective in the study of Islam, Islam, and politics in the Maghrib], Paris-Aix, *CNRS–CRESM,* 1981, p. 34.

25. Triaud (1998).

26. Louis Brunot, *Premiers conseils,* École du livre, Rabat, 1934.

27. Idem, p. 4.

28. Idem, p. 7.

29. Idem, pp. 8–9.

30. Vatin (1981).

31. Claude Liauzu, Syros, Paris, 1992.

32. TN: André Malraux.

33. Ibrahim Warde, "Du sectarisme et comment le dépasser" [sectarianism and how to overcome it], in the book reviews of *Le Monde diplomatique* of Jan. 1994, p. 29. The book in question is Edward Saïd's *Culture and Imperialism.*

34. Not only novels, but also some essays supposed to be serious documents that aim to better know the other.

35. Raymond Charles, *L'âme musulmane* [the Muslim soul], Flammarion, Paris, 1958, p. 98. The author is a consultant at the Appellate Court of Paris.

36. Gustave Le Bon, *Psychologie politique* [political psychology], cited in Charles (1958), p. 135.

37. Ibid.

38. Idem, p. 129.

39. In Paul Valéry's phrase.

40. TN : Principal character in Molière's *Bourgeois gentilhomme* [the would-be gentleman].

41. *Ibn Khaldoun, naissance de l'histoire passée du Tiers-Monde* [Ibn Khaldūn: the birth of the past history of the Third World), Ed. Maspero, Paris, 1973, p. 103.

42. Ibid.

43. Idem, p. 104.

44. Idem.

45. Maxime Rodinson, Du Seuil, 1966.

46. Triaud (1998); the paper was originally presented at Adam Mickiewicz University, Poznan, Sept. 1995.

47. A. V. Gennep, *Traité comparatif des nationalités* [comparative treatise of nationalities], Payot, 1922, p. 24.

48. Régis Blachère, *Dans les pas de Mahomet* [in the footsteps of Muhammad], cited in Charles (1958), p. 149.

49. Henri Pirenne, *Mahomet et Charlemagne* (Muhammad and Charlemagne), Paris et Bruxelles, 1937, p. 186.

50. Fernand Braudel, *La Méditerranée, L'Espace et l'Histoire* [the Mediterranean: space and history], V. I, Arts et Métiers graphiques, Paris, 1977, p. 143.

51. Hichem Djait, *L'Europe et l'Islam* [Europe and Islam], Paris, Le Seuil, 1978, p. 74.

52. Idem, p. 117.

53. Pierre Chaunu, *Histoire et science sociale, la durée, l'espace et l'homme à l'époque moderne* [history and the social sciences: duration, space and man in the modern era), Sedes, Paris, 1974, p. 204.

54. Idem, p. 241.

55. Triaud (1998).

56. Fernand Braudel, *Grammaire des civilisations* [a grammar of civilizations], Flammarion, Paris, 2nd Edition, 1993, p. 125.

57. Alain Quellien, *La politique musulmane dans l'Afrique occidentale* [Muslim politics in West Africa], Larose, Paris, 1910, pp. 100–28.

58. Hodgson (1996), pp. 4, 5.

59. Idem, p. 5.

60. Hodgson, *L'Islam dans l'histoire mondiale* [Islam in world history], texts gathered, translated from the English and prefaced by Abdesselam Cheddadi, Sindbad, Actes Sud, 1998, p. 294.

61. Hodgson (1998), p. 97.

62. Idem, p. 164.

63. Qur'ān: S. II. 251.

64. Qur'ān: S. III. 140.

65. Wolton (1997), p. 383.

66. Daniel Boy is research director at the CEVIPOF (French Political Life Research Center).

67. From the name of its leader, Ned Ludd.

68. Hodgson (1998), pp. 209–10.

69. Idem, pp. 210–11.

70. Idem, pp. 213–14.

III.
NEW HORIZONS

III. 1. HEAVEN AND EARTH REUNITED

God gave man a face raised towards heaven.
Ovid

Beauteous heaven, veritable heaven, look at me changing!
Paul Valéry

One who gazes at heaven from the bottom of a well will find it small.
Han Yu

Islam, the Long-Awaited Answer

Aside from a few thoughtful thinkers, the citizen of the modernicious and media-driven world does not seem to have a very flattering idea of religion. When it comes to *islam,* the rejection is total and final. For the collective imagination, *islam* amounts at best to the faith of a bellicose and barbaric nation that, in times past, imposed its hegemony on other nations by the power of the sword. Luckily, in 732 the brave Charles Martel prevented those barbarians from crossing the gates of Europe from the West, as did the Khazars from the East.

Thus an event that is far more complicated and far more profound is often broached in a very simplistic manner. Those with a somewhat more intimate knowledge of Islamic history know that the secret of the expansion of this religion does not lie in the physical force of its troopers, but in the greatness of their Message. The sword was only a minor accessory in this conquest.

How could a few hundred Bedouins in less than a century defeat the Persians and the Romans, with their sophisticated armies, and progress still further until their faith reigned over an unparalleled empire?

Hodgson states: "In the sixteenth century of our era, a visitor from Mars might well have supposed that the human world was on the verge of becoming Muslim. He would have based his judgment partly on the strategic and political advantages of the Muslims, but partly also on the vitality of their general culture."[1]

Ignacio Olagüe supports the same idea in a book with a revealing title: *Les Arabes n'ont jamais envahi l'Espagne* [the Arabs never invaded Spain]: "How could a handful of nomads coming forth from the depths of Arabia, have imposed their language and the law of Islam on the fifteen million inhabitants living on the 600,000 square kilometers of the Iberian Peninsula?"[2]

Let us recall that the Iberian Peninsula represented only a small part of the Islamic empire. The question that the author puts is even more pertinent when we take into account the surface area of the land of Islam in general, and the number of all its inhabitants.

If Islam made such dazzling progress, it is because it must have been circulating an extraordinary, vital force. Decadent humanity was awaiting the Message of *islam* just as an arid soil awaits the rain. Humanity was awaiting *islam*, wanted *islam*, hoped for *islam*.

The vital energy that *islam* brought was such that even the civilizations that did not adopt it were touched by the grace of that major event in the history of humanity. The permanent challenge that it represented for them engendered the competitive spirit that would later produce the modern event of globalization, as we indicated in the previous chapter.

Hodgson defends Islam as being a natural and necessary appearance, not an insane eruption in history:

> There prevailed in the middle of the first millennium C.E. a radically different temper from that of the age in which Hellenism had spread. Everywhere now the idea of a universal religion as commanding the allegiance of a population was taken for granted. It was into this cultural setting that Islam erupted, claiming to be the culmination of universal religion. . . . [H]is community made itself master of the whole region from Nile to Oxus. In doing so, it did not enter essentially alien territory. When Islam was announced there, the new doctrine did not seem strange, and indeed increasing numbers found it quite a logical further step in their own religious development.[3]

Islam was therefore a return to those eternal and universal values that are well established in the depths of human nature, and which the vicissitudes of history and the vagaries of life fail to suppress in man. *Fitra* is the Qur'ānic term that signifies an indelible nature proper to the essence of the creature; for man, it is a sort of spiritual genetic code. *Fitra* is "a natural aspiration for transcendence."[4] Only hearts that are truly unnatural and locked shut are not concerned by this aspiration. All of us, therefore, have a kind of compass which, when not too much damaged, is able to detect the truth of God's uniqueness.

One of the major principles of the teaching of the Prophet (grace and peace be upon him), *al amru bil maruf, wa nahiyu 'ani lmunkar*, could be translated literally as "Exhorting to do what is known, and persuading to avoid what is unknown."[5] What *islam* proposed espoused and met profound verities. Its proposition perfectly filled the void of expectation. The ground was propitious to heaven's Ultimate Message to earth, since man was suffering from all the evils that a decadent society inevitably engenders: despotism, slavery, blatant inequality, indigence of the masses, luxury and debauchery among the affluent, widespread prostitution.

By reawakening man's true nature (his *fitra*), *islam* not only liberated him from his baseness and the disabling weight of his instincts; it liberated him altogether. In addition to being the verbal recognition of God and His Prophet, the testimony of the Islamic faith—"There is no god but God"—is a declaration of war on the arbitrary. In his dialog with the supreme commander of the armies of Persia, Rib'iy bnu Āmir[6] eloquently summed up the true objective of what the orientalists call the "Arab conquests," which are in reality an unprecedented Movement of Liberation:

> "What is it you wish?" the Persian commander inquired. [Rib'iy replied,] "God has ordered us to divulge His Message, to struggle in order to liberate men from the adoration of men and facilitate for them the adoration of God, to release them from the injustice of religions and offer them the equality of *islam,* and to emancipate them from the hardship of this life and propose to them the prosperity here below and in the Ultimate Life."

Indeed, the Message was perceived as such by the peoples.

The Christians persecuted as heretics by the Roman Church saw in *islam* a liberator, and were as numerous to embrace *islam* as the skeptics or the pagans. The Monophysite Christian and the Nestorian, for instance, also felt close to this faith which, in addition to offering a privileged relationship with God, excused them from the too subtle contortions of Catholic theology.

Even the official Church saw the nascent faith as a sort of Christian heresy. Saint John of Damascus considered *islam* as such. The idea recurs anew in the fourteenth century. Without considering the defects of his reasoning, Dante, in Canto 28, presents our Prophet Muhammad (grace and peace be upon him) not as a pagan, but as a heretic.

Islam then prevailed very quickly in the hearts and the souls, and was adopted rapidly and without great difficulty by half the people of the planet, if not more. Jacques Neirynck[7] states that the fear that the West has of *islam* today comes exactly from the image, given by the hostile and well-prepared speeches still present in the collective Western subconscious, of a faith that succeeded in converting a great part of the peoples to *islam* without having to wage war:

> In a caricatured view of history, the expansion is often presented as the result of a martial conquest made of massacres, pillaging, and forced conversions. This is part of the traditional image of a conquering and violent *islam*, but the image does not hold water. How is it possible to imagine that a few Bedouin tribes and a few towns of the Arab peninsula could succeed in conquering half of the ancient Roman Empire against the sentiment of their populations? . . . Christian minorities, by the way, survived throughout the whole of the Middle East and Egypt, which proves that conversion was not systematically imposed. Thus there remains an enigma: why did the Christians in their contact with *islam* easily change religion?[8]

Further on, the author indirectly answers the question by saying that the Prophet Muhammad (grace and peace be upon him) was certainly "a conqueror," but not in military terms. The great victory of *islam* is due to qualities other than swordsmanship.[9] *Islam,* the continuation of the other monotheistic religions, came in fact to offer a most appealing horizontal relationship with one's fellow creatures in addition to the vertical relationship with God.

These two dimensions, vertical and horizontal, are indissociable in *islam*. Never have heaven and earth been joined as they were with the advent of the Messenger (grace and peace be upon him). If Christians easily embraced *islam,* it is because they dreadfully missed that relationship. Not only did their heaven refute their earth, but they were also terribly divided between a Father who lives vaguely in it, a Son who paid for all humanity, and a holy, yet very vague, Spirit. Furthermore, the Christians who embraced *islam* did not lose Jesus (peace be upon him), but found him again in more human traits, even closer to their hearts.

The simplicity of the Qur'ānic Message, appealing to spirituality without insulting rationality or disparaging social interaction, quickly conquered hearts. The kingdom of Heaven was, thanks to *islam,* within the reach of all, however humble they might be, no matter what social class they might come from. The Qur'ān presents a God of Mercy and offers with Him a proximity never tasted by man before *islam: I am closer to him* (man) *than his jugular vein,*[10] God says in the Qur'ān.

Anyone reading this verse with an alert heart is overcome by vertigo. Certain Muslim mystics were so overcome by vertigo that even the barriers between the creature and the Creator appeared open to them. Hallaj, mystic of the third century A.H., could not help luxuriating in such a sense of inebriety. He declared, "There is no one but God beneath my dress."

The converts were not all like Hallaj, but the proximity with God was comforting for the peoples who had been kept from the affairs of heaven by prelates of all kind. The Prayer is a daily ritual whereby the creature may enter into dialog with its Creator without the need of any intermediary or translator. God is no more that theological entity confined in the hazy heavens, where only the initiates can find their way. If heaven is a very present notion in the entire Qur'ān, in no way is it that habitat of a distant abstraction called God. It is the symbol of height, transcendence, mystery.

Islam proposes a spiritual alchemy that transforms the spiritual delinquent of yesterday into a cosmic being capable of dominating the worlds, provided that the pact with God is concluded.

Islam, an Egalitarian and Contractual Community

In addition to filling a spiritual gap, *islam* brought about a previously unknown egalitarianism. From the profound fusion between the transcendental dimension and the sense of community sprang a society whose major concern is equity and equality before the law. Encouraging the gradual abolition of slavery, the Prophet (grace and peace be upon him) taught his disciples that "People are equal as the teeth of a comb." This principle of equality was long to govern all the relations of Muslims.

The *sharia* (Islamic Law) is not that primer of tortures presented in a certain simplistic thinking. It is the very quintessence of that egalitarian spirit and its expression in equitable social rules. Far from being a penal code and a catalog of punishments, it establishes a contractual spirit hitherto unknown by humanity. The political domain is the first to be subject to this spirit inspired by the teaching of the Prophet (grace and peace be upon him).

Hodgson asserts that the fascination of *islam* for the peoples can be partly explained by the incredible culture of equity and contractual justice that encompasses even the political domain:

> [The *sharia*] was highly egalitarian—we might well call it contractualistic. A very wide range of relations were left to contracts between responsible individuals, including, in theory, the entire gamut of politics. In principle, no one was properly a ruler until he had been accepted in covenant by the representatives of the Muslim community. . . . Even the marriage law, in which ascribed status played a relatively large role, reflected this egalitarian contractualism.[11]

For the Western and Westernized public, the *sharia* is, alas, likened to the acute schizophrenia that prevails beneath the skies of Arabia, Black Africa and elsewhere. For many uninformed readers, it amounts to hands cut off indiscriminately, to bodies beheaded in a blood bath before the eyes of a frenzied crowd. According to such evil propaganda, *sharia* is a chronicle of barbarity that regards its subjects as a matter for stoning, beheading, mutilating, and persecution.

Were this the case, the millions of men and women who throughout the ages have embraced *islam* with attested ease and fervor would all be incurable masochists. People are too intelligent to embrace in unanimity a faith that brings them only misfortune and mutilation. To become Muslim is in itself a responsible and contractual act. It is in all conscience that the Muslim accepted—and still accepts—fulfilling his pledges to God.

Let there be no compulsion in embracing the faith,[12] the Qur'ān says. Islamic Law is in reality a contract of adherence to which the believer subscribes with full knowledge of the facts upon embracing *islam.* The books of Muslim history abound in accounts of the dialogs that preceded conversions, in which the candidate is informed of his duties and obligations. In view of the number of the converts, these can scarcely have been so coercive as some would have us believe.

Thanks to the great talent for communicating inherited from the Arab traditions and passed on orally from generation to generation, information about the new faith was concise and exhaustive. The Arabs' famous *balāgha* enabled their high-level performance as far as persuasion and communication are concerned. The verb *ballagha,* derivative of *balāgha,* means to inform, to convey and communicate a message in a precise and faithful fashion.

The messages borne by the victorious Arabs were not only oral. The acts and behavior of the Muslim soldiers in the lands converted to *islam* were more eloquent, more convincing than any speech. Mass conversions took place namely because the bearers of the Message circulated a positive and attractive image, a phenomenon unprecedented in the history of military conquests.[13] Their levelheadedness and their wisdom inspired the peoples with confidence. They convinced by the nobility of their acts, and their exemplary behavior persuaded people of the credibility of their speech.

The peoples who embraced *islam* did so because they had a most positive first contact with the *sharia,* the Islamic Law that is now demonized. The first thing they learnt from the Law was the great clemency of the victors towards the vanquished, their great tolerance towards the human element and the great respect for nature—attitudes that are dictated by clear *hadiths.* Let us again allow an objective pen to assure us of the particularity of those men whose way of life was the *sharia.* In his *Histoire des musulmans d'Espagne* (history of the Muslims of Spain), the Orientalist Dozy writes:

> The Arab conquest was good for Spain: it produced an important social revolution; it eliminated a large part of the evils under which the country had been groaning for centuries. . . . The Arabs ruled in the following method: the taxes were absolutely reduced in comparison with previous governments. From the rich, the Arabs took lands that had been divided into immense feudal domains cultivated by serfs and discontented slaves, and distributed them equally among those who worked the land. Filled with enthusiasm, the new owners cultivated the land and obtained better harvests. Trade was liberated from the limitations and the heavy taxes that overwhelmed it and developed notably. . . . All these measures produced a state of widespread well-being that was behind the good reception given in the beginning of the Arab domination.[14]

Sigrid Hunke joins her voice to the voices of those who dare to read history without taking the beaten track established by the exclusive thinking. Speaking of the Arab miracle, she says:

> But what is absolutely astounding in all that—never seen since the time of Cyrus, the founder of the Persian Empire—is the fact that the victors did not indulge in any destruction. . . . There hardly exists a nation that has behaved with so much clemency and humaneness towards its adversaries and "infidels." It is thanks to this attitude, to a great extent indeed, that the Arabs were able to influence and penetrate so deeply and for such a long term the peoples they subjected to their domination.[15]

Islam came to advocate *rifk* (gentleness) in a world of violence, equity in a world of injustice. *Islam* came to reunite heaven and earth, to reconcile life and death. *Islam* came to make sense and propose transcendence as the spiritual daily bread of everyone. Each trivial gesture, each established word projects the Muslim as present with his faith inside the sacred that is no longer reserved for the privileged few. Furthermore, what the spreaders of the Appeal brought in their saddlebags was a sense of community, inseparable from the personal relationship with God, that produced on the social plane a symbiosis appreciated by a certain humanity hitherto cruelly torn apart by various forms of selfcenteredness.

Would not the exceptional power of the social fusion that *islam* offers, recognized even by its enemies, be a conceivable antidote against postmodernity, in which the return of tribalism promises to be violent? *Islam* could once again offer disoriented humanity the possibility of constructing a society of confidence in which a brother would not turn on his brother. Advice for the lovers of privileged social ties:

> Islam was far the most widespread of the great religions. Moreover, despite its wide extension, it did not lose its social cohesion; a Muslim was accepted as fellow-citizen everywhere from Morocco to China, as Ibn Battuta's travels demonstrate.[16]

The reality of *islam*'s expansion is then very different from the bloody myths and the black legends in circulation. *Islam* has never been imposed on people and has always been welcomed by them, wholeheartedly and felicitously. It is important to note that people often converted their sovereigns to *islam*. Thus, the Mongols of Iran and Transoxania adopted the religion of their subjects.

The wars waged by the Muslims were not ordinary crusades conducted to impose their faith on the peoples by the sword. *Jihad* was not a war of religion. It was a war waged on the despots who refused the faith of their people and saw it as a threat for the stability of their régimes based on the arbitrary and the exploitation of others. To some extent *jihad* was a struggle to "democratize" societies. The attraction of *islam* was anyway such that it spread without having to use the sword.

Sharī'a, an Intelligent and Flexible Practice

It is by obedience to the recommendations of the Islamic Law that the Arabs, armed missionaries, were so clement and so tolerant. Islamic Law is a judicious combination of a corpus of rights to be claimed and obligations aiming specifically to guarantee those rights. Nowadays, the innumerable rights recommended by *sharia* are evoked only in camera among seasoned orientalists; in public, however, they zoom in on its penalties, presenting Islamic Law as an irrational machine that unscrupulously crushes the human flesh.

A few years after the death of the Prophet (grace and peace be upon him), Omar Ibn al Khattab (second caliph) ordered not to cut the hand of the thief who came from a region where famine was prevalent. Thanks to this flexibility, *fuqahā*'s (doctors of jurisprudence) will comprehend that *sharia* is not a rigid practice but a set of regulations obeying rational standards, that *sharia* is at the service of man rather than a sentry that hunts down his least weakness, as some fixed interpretations may lead one to think.

The rules of Islamic Law are always to be situated in the general context of the education dispensed by the Prophet. That educating system, which was to prompt a veritable upheaval in mentalities, had the mosque as its epicenter. The mosque was the beating heart of the nascent Islamic society. Its first role was to maintain the remembrance of God, and to celebrate the sermons and the gathering of Friday Prayer that are so many reminders of faith.

Prayer at the mosque enables the faithful to supply themselves at a place of enriching spiritual energies.

Because he is as weak as any other human being, the believer naturally tends towards forgetfulness, narcissism, and egotism. *Islam* offers him different stations devoted to God's recollection and meditation with a view to giving him the occasion and the company that enable him to renew his faith constantly.

The daily cycle of this renewal is the prayer that is performed five times a day. The weekly cycle is the Friday Prayer. Ramadan, month of fasting and intense spirituality, is the annual station. Pilgrimage is an experience recommended and compulsory at least once in the lifetime of each Muslim. Thus, the life of the Muslim is a continuous succession of ebbs and flows.

Ebb: a regenerating return to the inner world, to the lands of one's profound essence, to the serenity of one moment at the furthermost bounds of eternity.

Flow: involvement in the external world, action of the man as a body, of the physical man, of the social man in a movement of physical struggle with the heavy tasks of the material world.

These different pauses in the shade of the absolute regenerate the spiritual dimension and thus maintain the Muslim in remembrance of man's supreme responsibility of being God's lieutenant on earth and the maker of his own history. It is in this general atmosphere of spiritual support and communitarian moral mutual aid that *sharia* took all its sense and achieved its objectives. It then represented the safeguard for a community that elected greatness and promotion of virtue.

This, then, is the role of the Islamic Law, not that of distributing punishment at all costs. It is very revealing that the Prophet Muhammad (grace and peace be upon him) sometimes used to turn his head and pretend not to hear the adulteress who came to confess her crime. It is important to point out that it was the culprit who came to claim his punishment for fear of God, or for love of Him. Besides, the sentences concerning the crime of adultery were almost entirely executed against believers who were insistent about receiving their punishment here below.

The crime of adultery, in particular, may be taken as witness of the discretion that characterizes the application of the Law. Adultery is almost impossible to prove if the Qur'ān is followed to the letter. The Qur'ānic text sets out as an imperative condition to have four witnesses who have attended the crime until a deciding stage that leaves no doubt about the wrong deed. In fact, the description of the witness is to be almost clinical or is worth nothing.

Moreover, if three witnesses are involved without a fourth witness, they will be sentenced to flagellation even though they tell the truth. The one who participates in this misadventure is adjudged for the rest of his life as prohibited from bearing testimony in any domain whatever; he is a liar for life in the community and unworthy of confidence.

These drastic conditions, intended to protect the culprit, prove that punishment is above all a sign that enables us to measure the ugliness of the act, reprehensible in the sight of God. With all these facts in mind, we may understand that punishment is of a deterrent nature, and that only the one who provocatively flouts the moral code and excessively violates the social code comes to the stage of being stoned. In a very sensible society, such a code stands in stark contrast with depravation and pathological permissiveness.

The cases reported in the lifetime of the Prophet (grace and peace be upon him) speak for themselves. Those concerning the stoning sentence do not exceed a dozen and are all cases in which the culprits came forward, motivated by a profound faith and willing at all costs to expiate their fault before death, preferring the Ultimate Life to this life.

Their affair is a matter of an alert conscience, a heart full of the real life: the certitude of God. Possessing a compassionate nature, the Prophet (grace and peace be upon him) used to ask the penitents several times, trying to allege that the act did not perhaps go to a stage that deserves punishment, dissuading them from pursuing their deposition, and urging them to reconsider their statement. It is they who insisted, they who testified without any need for a trial to be set up.

Islam created moral responsibility, the reverent fear of God, before setting up courts. *Sharī‘a* could not have progressed otherwise, nor could it have been accepted and recognized as a rule of life by peoples of such varied mores. It could not have been harmoniously combined with customs as different as of those who constituted the whole *umma*[17] had it not enjoyed utmost flexibility.

From the determination to safeguard such flexibility sprang a science that examines the essential goals of *sharia,* and that determines the rules of adapting Islamic Law to any circumstance. This is known as *ijtihād.* From a range of attitudes of the Prophet and his close Companions, lessons were drawn to deduce that rigidity and *sharia* are poles apart.

The first Qur'ānic and Prophetic teaching on which was based *ijtihād* comes from the very principle of the uniqueness of the Creation. The Muslim soon learnt that physical and psychological laws emanated from the same Creator, and that the duty of the faithful was to fathom them in order to find the right balance between the Book of Revelation and the Book of Creation. The awareness of the uniqueness of Creation prompted an extraordinary general theory-based approach of things whose aim was to make the practice of *islam* possible anywhere and for anyone. Did not the Prophet (grace and peace be upon him) tell Muad Ibn Jabal, the Companion whom he was to send to teach *islam* to the newly converted of Yemen, to rely on his logical reasoning and on rationality? Let us listen to wisdom and mercy conversing:

> "Which rules will you follow to manage their controversies?"
>
> "The Qur'ān," the Companion replied.
>
> The Prophet went on: "And if you do not find an answer in the Qur'ān?"
>
> "I will base my judgment on the *sunna*[18] of the Prophet of God," Muad replied.
>
> The Messenger (grace and peace be upon him) enquired: "And if you should find nothing [that solves the problems of the host society]?"
>
> "I will use my own reasoning," the Companion concluded.
>
> The Prophet then expressed his joy: "Praise be to God, Who has guided the Prophet's envoy to what the Prophet appreciates."

The *hadīth* is edifying on several accounts. Like many other *hadīths,* it is the tangible proof that the Prophet teaches his disciples that the mind is a gift of God that is to be put on the back burner only when the Qur'ānic text leaves no doubt. The Companions assimilated this principle very well, and so did many imams and thinkers of the following generations. For that reason, the dynamic of the Appeal and the propagation of the faith progressed apace with that of *ijtihād.*

Such furthermost flexibility of *sharia* enabled the mass adoption of *islam* by peoples as different from each other as, for instance, the Persians and the North Africans, the Mongols and the Black peoples of Africa. Had it not been the malleability of the texts and the role of logical reasoning, it would have been impossible for *islam* to embrace all that geographic area and to befit that immense diversity of peoples.

Ijtihād was adjudged by the Great Companions to be an integral part of the Islamic faith. Their rightly guided practice in this domain leaves us stunned, we the Muslims in the present Muslim world who have become narrow-minded. Such a rightly guided Imam as Omar Ibn al Khattab could express opinions very different from one another according to the region for which he legislated. When people remarked that what he said one day was different from what he said the day before, he replied that yesterday belonged to another epoch, and that the circumstances in which he expressed the second opinion were different from the ones in which he expressed the first.

The Pedagogy of Mercy

Let us not imagine that such practice is similar to that which has adapted the Bible to modern times by erasing certain precepts and adding what comes to mind. There can be no similarity, since the attitude of the Companions was based on a reverent fear of God and on the imitation of the acts of the Prophet (grace and peace be upon him). In reality, such flexibility finds its origin in the very sources of Islamic Law: the Qur'ān and the *sunna.*

162

The Qur'ān is composed of 6,632 verses. Among these thousands of verses, only 250 (approximately 3%) come within the domain of legislation. This small percentage is not a gap, but a voluntary omission on God's part, an omission that imports a great meaning. It expresses the divine will not to block practices, but to leave the faithful the opportunity to use their neurons, that other gift He gave us.

This corresponds to the spirit of mercy proper to *islam,* emanating from a compassionate God, as the Qur'ān informs us. It also suits the universal destination of the Message. The Qur'ān leaves the task of providing further information to the human nature of the Prophet (grace and peace be upon him), the Divine Gift to all mankind. As the Qur'ān informs us, the Prophet (grace and peace be upon him) is the manifestation of Mercy: *We sent you not but as a mercy for all creatures.*[19]

The Prophet (grace and peace be upon him) supported this verse, saying: *I am the Granted Mercy.*

This personified mercy endorsed such malleability by proclaiming, and often reminding his Companions, that he was only a human being like others. The Qur'ān informs us: *Say (O Prophet): I am but a man like yourselves. The inspiration has come to me that your God is One God.*[20] In the same sense, Muhammad (grace and peace be upon him) said, "I am but the son of a poor woman who lived in Mecca and who fed on dried meat."[21]

The teaching of God's Envoy (grace and peace be upon him) established a major break with the classic perception of the sacred. By acting as he did, and by divine exhortation, the sacred is no more prisoner of some few dogmas limited in time or space, or the private property of some privileged few of "heaven." The sacred, thanks to Muhammad (grace and peace be upon him), is within the reach of every Muslim whose action is guided by the intention of doing Good. Better still, *islam* is the sole faith that gives to man the right to err:

> "Whoever makes an effort of interpretation (*ijtihād*) and comes to a correct decision will be recompensed twice (by God). He who makes an effort of interpretation and comes to an incorrect decision will have only one recompense."[22]

Such pedagogical method thus left a large space for the resourcefulness of the Muslims. The Prophet (grace and peace be upon him) had confidence in their spiritual capacity to preserve the spirit of the Message. History proved him right. *Islam* is still alive in the hearts of hundreds of millions of persons notwithstanding the devastating misfortunes that have befallen the *umma*.

The Companions, who were the closest guardians and disciples of the Messenger (grace and peace be upon him), soon managed to find the happy medium. Thanks to their intuition and to the light of faith in their hearts, they knew how to estimate the status of the Prophet at its true value. His human part was not antithetical with his sacred stature—quite the opposite. That is why the love of the Companions for our Prophet (grace and peace be upon him) was unparalleled.

They knew that the Qur'ān, while reminding on many occasions that Muhammad (grace and peace be upon him) is a human being (which is much to the credit of this Messenger made of goodness and compassion), orders every Muslim to respect to the letter the prescriptions of the Prophet: *So take what the Messenger assigns to you, and refrain from what he prohibits you.*[23]

Obedience to the Prophet (grace and peace be upon him) was quickly perceived (because explicitly specified by the Qur'ān) as a *sine qua non* of faith. Muhammad (grace and peace be upon him) facilitated for them this obedience by educating his disciples in a spirit of consultation and participation in the accomplishment of the common work. His human nature itself is a mercy and a positive thing for his *umma*, as it is a pedagogical pretext that aims to keep the mind in a state of alert. If the Qur'ān orders the Companions to follow the orders of the Prophet (grace and peace be upon him), it informs his disciples, on the other hand, that he has a private domain and that he leaves them the right to reflection in the other domains.

The most striking event reported in *Sīra,* the biography of the Prophet (grace and peace be upon him), reminds us emphatically that his was an essentially pedagogical dimension. This is the event known as the "grafting of the date palms." When the Prophet expressed a dubious opinion of grafting, his Medina supporters, the *ansar,*[24] abstained from performing this technical operation even though it would have afforded them a better yield. The negative result obtained became an occasion of a precious lesson. Etched in the memory of the disciples, the event established in their minds the fact that the Message is a collection of general rules that grants human reasoning a large space for maneuvering.

"I am but a human being," the Supreme Teacher (grace and peace be upon him) assured them. "When I instruct you in something pertaining to worship, do it; but when I give you my personal opinion, remember that I am a man like you. You are better informed than I am in the affairs of your world."[25]

Another anecdote supports this attitude. During the preparations for a campaign, the Prophet (grace and peace be upon him) had commanded the Muslim troops to organize in a certain manner. One of the Companions, knowing well the teachings of the Prophet (grace and peace be upon him), asked him then whether the decision emanated from a divine inspiration, or if it were an opinion based on the Prophet's personal experience. The Messenger replied that it was not an inspiration but a human choice. Renowned as an expert strategist, the Companion proposed other tactics, to whose adoption Muhammad (grace and peace be upon him) found no objection.

In the light of these few revealing anecdotes, we may advance unhesitatingly that certain fixed opinions are far from the spirit of *islam* and of his Messenger. The *hadīth* in which the Prophet urges Muad to base his judgment on rational thinking to teach *islam,* and thus respond to the expectations and questions of the newly converted peoples, denies the idea that "everything is there" in the Qur'ān that enables to perform the technical management of society.

The argument that the Qur'ān is a "political program" is a harebrained thesis that runs counter to the teachings of the Prophet (grace and peace be upon him). The Qur'ān certainly contains all the guiding principles of a moralized society, but it passes over in silence certain things that are as many blanks left to *ijtihād*, to the effort of interpretation.

The *sunna* came to complete the Qur'ān by instituting a model of practice. It came to perfect the broad lines that protect from deviations, and set up safeguards preventing man from overstepping the limits established by God and preserving his essence. *Islam* is a contract of confidence with God, and its few rubrics are accepted as clauses of a contract of submission with a Creator Who knows more than we do about our nature.

The Prophet (grace and peace be upon him) proceeded by the Grace of God to mediate between the divine and the human, between heaven and earth, between the transcendental and the natural. His essence of goodness and compassion is a buffer that enables the requirements of transcendence to be tempered into a practice within the reach of man's weakness. All that he endorsed was in accordance with the divine direction, since he himself is a gift of God, a divine outstretched hand personified in a human body, and with a human heart.

The Qur'ān says: *But no, by thy Lord, they can have no* (real) *faith until they make thee judge in all disputes between them, and find in their souls no resistance against thy decisions, but accept them with the fullest convictions.*[26]

Many Muslims find this verse restrictive; it is, rather, the guarantor of an attitude that is moderate, tempered, and accessible. It is a profound misunderstanding of the *sunna* and its beneficial effects for the community to interpret it in a prohibitory sense. The related facts concerning the life of the Prophet (grace and peace be upon him) belie this impression; it arises whenever precepts emanating from superficial interpretations are confused with the teachings of the Prophet (grace and peace be upon him).

The specialists of the *Sīra* report that the Prophet often reminded his overzealous Companions of their human nature. On several occasions, he had to remind them that *islam* did not recommend self-flagellation or restrict their natural penchants. The Messenger (grace and peace be upon him) informed us that *islam* did not prohibit man from being at ease in his humanity, but that it merely channeled his primary instincts in order to domesticate them gently.

To certain Companions who did not know how to temper their spiritual ardor, who did not sleep in order to perform supererogatory prayers, who fasted every day and refused any sexual life, he said: "I sleep and I wake up (to pray); I fast and I eat, and I marry women. Whoever acts otherwise will not be one of mine."[27] His entire teaching is actually a reminder of the practice of the happy medium, not an incitement to extremism as certain current Muslims, illiterate where faith is concerned, may alas understand.

The moderate nature of this teaching is called *yusr,* from which comes the term *taysīr.* The translation of Arabic words being always difficult, three or four words must combine to render the right meaning of the word. *Yussr* means at once easiness, feasibility, adequation, accessibility. *Tayssîr* is the act of making things practical, accessible, and easy to do. *Sharī'a* has always had the rule of *taysîr* as basic principle.

Aisha, spouse and soulmate of the Prophet, and an abiding source of edifying information about the life of the Messenger and his pedagogical method, said: "Each time the Prophet had to choose between two options, he chose the most accessible so long as it was not a flagrant contravention of God's recommendations."[28]

The Sacred Duty of Ijtihād

The Companions who lived close to the Prophet (grace and peace be upon him) preserved for us the spirit of gentleness and compassion, the *yusr* that had become like a second nature for them. Later, when the political gusts threatened the perpetuity of the Message, an effort to safeguard this spirit began. The deviations of power, which we will examine later in this book, increased the fear of the Muslims for the purity of the Islamic Way that teaches *yusr* and intelligence. An intense effervescence of reflections began very soon. Its aim was to lay down normative rules and institute a sophisticated methodology based on a rational reading of the Message in order to meet the obligation of preserving its spirit.

Strictly speaking, the science of *ijtihād* took its full sense only with ash-Shafi'ī[29] (God bless him) although the effective contribution of some imams before him is highly commendable. A number of *ulemas* (scholars of *islam*) had already laid down a body of precepts that help to achieve better comprehension of Qur'ānic Law. The diversity, proliferation, and harmonious coexistence of the juridical schools are another proof of the utmost malleability of Islamic Law and its absolutely extraordinary power of adaptation.

Thus we had Abu Hanifa in Kūfa, Mālik in Medina, and many other sage masters. Since the aim of this book is to refute certain received ideas that pass *islam* off as unspeakable obscurantism—and not to compose an academic treatise—we will not go into detail about an experience that is rich in precise facts and in high-performance rational procedures. We will content ourselves to call to mind some broad lines of this epic of knowledge.

The schools of thought represented then a very wide range of the reading of the Islamic Law. Two major trends, however, can be drawn as claiming to represent either of the traditions of these two companions: Abdullah ibn Omar, who opted to refuse any personal interpretation even in the absence of an explicit text, and Abdullah ibn Abbas, who, on the contrary, often had recourse to personal opinion and anticipation.

We will see later that the loss of momentum of *islam*'s wonderful dynamic took place concurrent to the progressive abandonment of *ijtihād*. Extremely tempered, the subsequent thinking would only bear the ashes of the intense source of the Qur'ānic Message for want of having in itself the ardor and the willpower to safeguard its flame. By abandoning the virtues instructed by the great masters of *ijtihād*, we have cut ourselves off from the very essence of our faith. The flowing source offered by God to humanity by means of His Message has dried up in some minds.

The cancellation of *ijtihād* under the influence of despotism made of the Islamic Law what it appears to be today in the eyes of the non-informed observers, and gave the occasion to the "well-intentioned" analysts to denounce archaism and nonsense. Through considering the free fall of our thinking ever since it abandoned *ijtihād,* we can only prove any criticism to be right, however bitter it may be. The community gradually sank into the dark nights of *taqlid.*[30]

There were soon no more exegetes of such scope as the great imams of the first centuries of our history. Had it not been Sufism and its great masters, the flame would have gone out forever.

The atrophied way of thinking gave rise to incredible and wild imaginings in the domain of jurisprudence. Coming within the tradition of absolute plagiarism, certain books of *fiqh*[31] make the informed reader of the *sunna* utterly perplexed. *Taqlid* successfully instituted an imbroglio of rules in which only warped minds can find their way. By reading certain jurisprudential books dating back to this long period of stagnation (1258–1870), we wonder what relationship there is between those unordinary details and the Islamic Law at the time of the Prophet (grace and peace upon him). The Law was clarity itself, civility itself, tolerance itself, greatness itself, malleability itself—in a word, *yusr.*

Once the mind was put on the back burner, the parrot became the mascot of the team of the doctors of the Law, unwillingly subjugated to serve the regime in power. The practice emanating from their decisions (*fatwās*) weighed heavily in the balance of the factors that prompted the decline of the Muslim societies. Blind *taqlid* is high treason perpetrated against the Qur'ānic spirit and the teachings of the Messenger (grace and peace upon him). It is also high treason with respect to those giants of *islam* who instituted the rules of *ijtihād,* or who put it into practice from the day following the death of God's Messenger (grace and peace upon him). The latter had no intention whatever of creating dogmas, but rather of providing their contemporaries and future generations with methodological tools so that the source would not run dry, and so that the Message might remain accessible to all mankind.

Their profound comprehension of Revelation made them think of Creation as a constant evolution, that the world is new each day. The majority of them trained the students who attended their circle while linking them always to the sources—the Qur'ān and the *sunna*—aware that these two sources are the generators of sense and life. They sought to establish rules that enable the *umma* to read in the Book of Creation and to adapt to Destiny, a work of God just as the Qur'ān is the Revelation of God. Mulay 'Abd al-Qādir al-Jīlānī, the great scholar of *islam* and figurehead recognized as reference by the *fuqahā'*[32] as well as by Sufis, the Saint of the saints in the eyes of the *umma,* said: "Destiny is obscurity (in the sense of enigma); go forth into it with the torch of the Book and the *sunna.*"

The rightly guided imams of the first centuries had as a matter of fact the major concern not to create dogmas. They all expressed this clearly, and resorted to the two essential sources (the Qur'ān and the *sunna*) as safeguards against deviations.

For Imam Mālik, a good disciple of the Message, we find this famous warning in the Muslim milieus: "Every opinion [expressed by a scholar of *islam*] is susceptible of being accepted or rejected. Only the opinion of the one who lies in this grave counts." Mālik was seated beside the tomb of the Prophet (grace and peace upon him).

Abu Hanifa, the other figurehead of the effort of adaptation, said: "If I have expressed an opinion that contradicts the Book of God or the *hadīth*s of the Messenger, reject my opinion."[33]

Ibn Hanbal, reputed to have a rigorous reading of the Message, said: "Do not blindly follow my opinions, or those of Mālik, ash-Shafi'ī, al-Awza'ī or ath-Thawrī. Draw [your opinion] from where they took their own."[34]

Alas, exactly the opposite happened. Fratricidal confrontations soon broke out between the disciples of those different schools. They would tear the Muslim world apart—and still do. Rather than being a source of richness, difference soon became a cause of fighting or cold war. The fratricidal struggle was to the advantage of an imposed Central Power that fanned the embers of discord to better play the role of the supreme guarantor.

Suffering from total stagnation at the level of the effort of reflection, the Muslim world would make the opinions of these great masters a cause of fixation and intolerance. Muslims to this day remain reliant on the thinking of those who incessantly reminded them of the relative nature of their teaching. We are still adopting practices directed to the jurisprudential law instituted by these venerable imams instead of being directed to the Qur'ān and the *sunna,* which are ever a source of constant appeal to reason and adaptability. Instead of drawing lessons from their aforementioned recommendations, we have immortalized the relative part of their brilliant work. We kept ruminating over their theses that perfectly met the needs of their time and the inhibitory conditions of the Power of those days with which they were compelled to compromise.

The Rise and Demise of Ijtihād

The absurdity of blind *taqlīd* appears clearer when the notion of *ijtihād* is well assimilated. Tariq Ramadan defines *ijtihād* as being the "effort performed by a jurist either to derive a law or a prescription from less explicit scriptuary sources, or to formulate a detailed juridical opinion in the absence of reference texts,"[35] Michel Jobert proposes a further detailed definition of *ijtihād* that renders it a continuation of Revelation:

> Revelation is thus not a moment in history. It is continued in our efforts to find "the right path," and to make our own progress intelligible. This effort is *ijtihād*. It is to be performed in uncertainty and humility. Because its success has no guarantees, its validity is assured. Contingency is our challenge. We must in no way yield to it: it is our duty to resolve it.[36]

Jobert's reflection is interesting insofar as it brings up the subtle relationship of the Muslim with contingency. *Ijtihād* is a means for gathering the heaven and earth of the Muslim. Thanks to this effort, heaven is joined to earth and the absolute is wedded to contingency.

Contingency in the light of the Islamic teaching is called *fitna*. This word comes from the verb *fatana,* which literally means to put a noble metal in the furnace to rid it of dross. In its general sense, *fitna* refers to a period of unrest and instability. The real sense to draw first from Revelation, and then from history, is that life on earth is a perpetual *fitna*—that is to say, an ordeal, a daily trial.

Life on earth is a permanent adaptation and a continuous struggle to remain on the right path. The earth turns, and night and day conspire to prevent man from having a moment of respite. The day dispatches him to the night, the night releases him to the next day. Life is a stormy sea. Revelation is a lighthouse to which we have recourse so as to avoid ending up on a reef. Life is an incessant struggle to safeguard our spiritual energy and our humanity, and to win each day a battle against moments of meaninglessness.

Ijtihād is precisely that unremitting effort of reorientation and readaptation: a safe navigation on the waves of our passage in this life on earth. It is a constant mobilization whose aim is not to lose sight of the Light of the Message, not to give oneself up to the absurd of contingency, not to forget God.

Such effort, intending to overcome the vagaries of history and to avoid sinking completely into contingency, springs in fact from the stirrings occasioned by the latter. It is important to point out that it is the fear of the Muslims to find themselves cut off from their sources that produced this extraordinary science of adaptation. In the Prophet's lifetime, the Companions made *ijtihād* without having to indicate its bases. They made it naturally either by imitating the Prophet or under his supervision, or by intuitive and profound comprehension of Islamic Law, internalized thanks to their frequent contact with the Messenger (grace and peace upon him). *Ijtihād* was part of their education and their approach of the faith. They did not have to be reminded of it. Let us recall in this regard the dialog between Muhammad (grace and peace upon him) and Muad. The Prophet was testing his disciple to ascertain that the effort of reflection was a teaching assimilated like that of confidence in God, submission to God in the domain where the mind cannot—and will never be able to—reach or delimit.

Only later would *ijtihād* be structured and become the subject of a methodology. Because they were confronted to constantly new situations engendered by the expansion of *islam* and the changing nature of power, the *ulemas* found themselves forced to establish a science of *ijtihād*. At the time of Imam Mālik (717–801),—that is, one century after the death of the Prophet (grace and peace upon him),—*ijtihād* was more of a practice than an art with well-established rules. In his excellent book, Tariq Ramadan states:

For such first scholars as Abu Hanifa, al-Awza'ī and Mālik, the distinction between the different sciences was not very clear. The famous compilation of the latter's *al-Muwatta'* (the beaten track) is still a mixture of decisions and opinions of the Companions and their disciples. Historical circumstances . . . were to considerably modify the scholars' way of thinking and presenting the results of their researches.[37]

Our Islamologist cites four symptomatic events that had awakened in the *ulemas* the desire to safeguard the faith. They thus established intelligible rules to enable them to found a basis for the practice of *ijtihād*. The symptoms commence with the reign of Muawiya, the Companion[38] of the Prophet (grace and peace upon him) who usurped power based on popular sovereignty and consultation. Democratic[39] in its origins, power then became despotic and hereditary. The warning signs of the threats to the Islamic faith can be summed up in these four:

1. The introduction of new practices in the affairs of state.
2. The dispersal of the *ulemas,* and the high risk of losing important pieces of information because of a tradition more oral than written.
3. The appearance of a manifest determination to instigate doubt within the community through the circulation of false *hadīths*.
4. The appearance of conflicts that seriously divided the community and reached the stage of confrontation in the name of different convictions.

With his customary moderation, Tariq Ramadan reveals these historical circumstances as being all equal, and perfectly relativizes the break at the level of power. In fact, it is more just to consider the break at this level a decisive one. The change in the nature of power had the sole positive effect of stimulating the spirit of general approach that acts as instinct of self-preservation. But the distortion of power, despite its initially beneficial effect, ended up getting the better of this same spirit of innovation in a slow movement of withdrawal.

NOTES

1. Hodgson (1996), p. 97.

2. Ignacio Olaguë, Flammarion, Paris, 1969, p. 280.

3. Hodgson (1996), pp. 23, 105.

4. Tariq Ramadan's phrase. *Fitra* may also be translated as "character, natural disposition, instinct, nature."

5. Jacques Berque literally translates the Islamic adage as "the ordering of Good and the pursuit of Evil."

6. A fighter in the Muslim ranks during the war waged on the Sassanian empire, he was part of the three-man delegation in charge of conducting talks with the chiefs of the opposing army. The historical accounts emphasize the contrast between the simplicity of the emissary and the splendor of the tent wherein he was received. Rustam ordered him to lay down his arms. Very proud, Rib'iy refused, reminding him that the initiative of talks came from them, not from the Muslim troops.

7. Researcher, teacher, and journalist, Neirynck is the author of numerous books, among which is *Le Manuscrit du Saint-Sépulcre* [the manuscript of the Holy Sepulcher].

8. Jacques Neirynck and Tariq Ramadan, *Peut-on vivre avec l'Islam?* [can we live with Islam?], Favre, 1999, p. 29.

9. TN : For corroborative argumentation, cf. Sir Thomas Arnold's *The Spreading of Islam in the World: A History of Peaceful Preaching*, Goodword Books 2001, New Delhi (first published in London, 1896).

10. Qur'ān: S. L. 16.

11. Hodgson (1996), pp. 115–16.

12. Qur'ān: S. II. 256.

13. I use the word "conquests" unwillingly, as I cannot find an equivalent in French of the word *futūhāt*, meaning literally "openings." Their military maneuvers aimed to open the lands to *islam* and to guarantee the freedom of the peoples to embrace it, not to conquer lands in the traditional acception of the concept.

14. Reinhart Dozy, *Histoire des musulmans d'Espagne jusqu'à la conquête de l'Andalousie par les Almoravides 711–1110* [history of the Muslims of Spain up to the Almoravid conquest of Andalusia], Leiden (1861), 1932, v. II, p. 43.

15. Hunke (1963), p. 213.

16. Hunke (1963), p. 183.

17. *Umma* means the Muslim community.

18. The *sunna* is the corpus of the teachings of the Prophet (grace and peace be upon him).

19. Qur'ān: S. XXI. 107.

20. Qur'ān: S. XVIII. 110.

21. Related by Al-Hākim and Tabarani.

22. *Hadith* reported by Bukhārī and Abū Dāwūd.

23. Qur'ān: S. LIX. 7.

24. From the verb *nassara,* meaning to back, to support.

25. *Hadith* reported by Muslim and others.

26. Qur'ān: S. IV. 65.

27. Reported by Bukhārī.

28. Reported by Bukhārī and Muslim.

29. Ash-Shafiʿī was born in Arabia in 767 A.H. and died in Cairo in 820. According to the *Encyclopedia Universalis*, "This theologian played a great part in the formation of Muslim legislation. He traveled across the Arab East, studying in the great centers of jurisprudence and taking particular interest in the Malekite and Hanafite doctrines. Maintaining his independence from the various masters he met and the schools he attended, he had the great merit of creating a new synthesis of the different aspects of Muslim jurisprudence. Starting from ideas with which Muslims were familiar, he was able to restructure these aspects in a coherent manner. . . . It was in Cairo that he gathered his theories in his book *Rissala* [the letter], which has often made him regarded as the father of Muslim Law."

30. *Taqlid* means the blind and uncritical imitation of predecessors in the field of law, without making an effort of adaptation.

31. In fact the word *fiqh,* which Jacques Berque translates as "case law," refers in the exact sense of the word to deep knowledge of the matters of *islam. Taqlid,* or the folly of copying from former scholars without any effort of adaptation whatsoever, takes it completely away from its original and noble sense and perfectly meets Jacques Berque's definition.

32. *Fuqaha*s or doctors in case law.

33. Tariq Ramadan, *Etre musulman européen: étude des sources islamiques à la lumière du context européen* [on being a European Muslim: a study of Islamic sources in light of the European context], Tawhid, Lyon, 1999, p. 105.

34. Idem.

35. Ramadan (1999), p. 430.

36. Jobert (1982).

37. Ramadan (1999), pp. 74–75.

38. He was admittedly a Companion of the Prophet (grace and peace be upon him). Still it must be reminded that he belongs to the category of the last-minute Muslims: those who embraced *islam* after the peaceful, yet resounding, victory of the Muslim troops over those of *quraysh* in the conquest of Mecca.

39. I use this word in its purest etymological sense—that is to say, the "people in power." In fact, the system of *shūrā* is as different from that of democracy as the history of Europe is from that of the Muslim world.

III. 2. A NOT SO SIMPLE PAST

It is history's enemies who eventually make it.
Eugène Ionesco

Let us assemble our facts and get a few ideas.
Comte de Buffon

Like vitriol and sugar, vice and virtue are products.
Hippolyte Taine

Thoroughbreds are tied up in stables
While carefree mules scamper.
Darham, Moroccan artist

Awakening the Memory

In our quest of the purity of the Message, it is essential to recall the bitter reality of the Muslim countries. We are used to summing up such decay in a single word: fatalism. "Too bad for them! Their religion has made incorrigible quietists of them." So say observers with firmly entrenched prejudices, whenever it strikes them to wonder about the decay of Muslim countries. But reality is not as simple as such labels.

In Islamic countries a current of thought adopts an equally cursory reading, ascribing all our setbacks and trials to the West, which colonized us and waged war on us. According to this line, we are decadent because that's what the other side wants—period.

Of course it is inconceivable to deal with our present domestic crises without taking into account our status as vanquished with respect to a powerful and victorious West. It is in our blood; witness the attitude of our elite, trained to perpetuate Western cultural domination. In our colonial reality, Western civilization is undoubtedly the pale neon lighting that dazzles us and guides our hybrid politics and our derivative literature.

Colonization is not in fact over yet, since its effects, far from having been absorbed, are still ongoing. We are sill experiencing the ebb of a corrosive reality, of a historical event that is not easily overcome. The pages of history are not so easily turned as those in textbooks. In reality, they are too heavy to turn and next to impossible to get through.

While appearing to be free and sovereign, the decolonized countries are no more determined to sever the umbilical cord than the former colonial powers are prepared to loosen their grip just like that. A link is thus perpetuated by a loyal elite, a creation that enables the nostalgic power to depart the better to stay on, a dull yet efficient and often perverse clone. What had served as umbilicus connecting the culture of the civilized race in order to invigorate and maintain the domination has become the diseased appendix that now aggravates the illness of a body whose entire vital functions have begun to fail.

Afflicted with such pundits, what chance do our Islamic societies have of standing one day among free and sovereign nations truly free and sovereign? With such myopic officials ruling us at sight, what chance do we have to emerge from the underdevelopment and economic stagnation behind our subservience and humiliation?

In the context of overwhelming globalization, the centripetal force sucking everything into its infernal whirlwind, it makes all the more sense to blame our ills on the West. The phrase "global village" has a downhome flavor; its bucolic accents tickle our imagination and flatter our humanism. But the reality behind the traditional image is very different.

It is easy enough to understand why the West stands at the center of the cur-rent worldview. Still, the complexity of the realities must not cause us to teeter into the kind of acute paranoia such facts might inspire. Nothing is more convenient—nor more crippling—than blaming one's own faults on someone else. Explaining all our tragedies in terms of domination is an easy solution that only perpetuates our withdrawing from exerting any effort of our own. Such a path leads to despair.

It is urgent to reexamine our history, to reconsider our deplorable lot by first examining crises that are home-grown. The domination to which the Muslim world is subject is due to a combination of circumstances in which the deciding element is not the overwhelming power of another civilization but the decay of Islam.

Reawakening Islam will necessarily entail serious self-criticism. For it to advance, the myths stored up in our memories, myths more seriously distorted within than without, will have to be expunged. Scrutinizing history with objective eyes is a beneficial exercise that will help shake up lethargic minds and overcome their pathological nostalgia. Our damaged memories and diluted identities are in need of an asceticism rigorous enough to recover the vitality afforded by a faith that is supposed to be universal but has become little more than a safe-conduct used by certain politicians who vehemently protest that "We are all Muslims!"

Curing an amnesia sustained by our deviant regimes remains a difficult challenge to overcome. Passing on the torch of a convalescent memory will perhaps help get us back on our feet again. Really understanding matters will help us out of the debris. It will render us useful to the rest of humanity, to whom we will re-offer *islam* as a balm for bruised hearts, as the beneficial wind that brings rain to barren soils.

The mercy residing in the Message could at last hinder the wind of insanity that has our world in its grip. The world, forgetful of everything, of humankind itself, might then stop its furious processional that carries us away, powerless, to an unknown destination. It would then turn to the rhythm of tolerance, of love of neighbor, of right guidance. It might then turn again in the right direction and at the right speed.

The path leading to this wise and human world will long continue to be ignored since its defenders are stuck in their own political, ideological, and economic impasses. Between contradiction and abdication, the official bearers of the Message no longer represent it honorably. Who but a few eccentrics short on sensual exoticism would care to belong to the faith of the emirs of oil? Which woman only slightly informed about *islam* would not be horrified by the so-called Muslim practice of the Taliban, who pretend to represent "true" *islam*?

In the chapter devoted to the media, I emphasized repeatedly that the image given of *islam* is not to be trusted. That does not prevent us from believing that an *umma* that cannot defend itself or its image deserves what it gets. To comprehend exactly what has happened to it, our community must go further upstream in our history.

Retrospective: The Prophet and Power

The events that followed the death of the last of the Prophets have marked the Muslim community to this day. The political upheaval that took place a few years after the death of the Messenger (grace and peace upon him) continues to reverberate in the bases of our present societies.

The Prophet (grace and peace upon him) died on June 8, 632 of the Christian era, shortly after the Pilgrimage of Farewell, during which he gave his last counsels to the community of the faithful. His ultimate prescriptions came to crown a long path that established a system of *shūrā* (consultation). The Prophet (grace and peace upon him) instituted a new world order by going against the models of power known until then. The community was sovereign, and consultation was its mode of government under the auspices of Islamic Law.

This Law is based on few main principles including faith in God, the achievement of equity on earth and continuous *ijtihād*[1] in order to deal with contingencies in the absolute without ever failing to remember that God is the source of both.

As no man is a prophet in his own country, the Messenger (grace and peace upon him) was harshly oppressed by his own tribe, the Quraysh,[2] after they despaired of converting his supreme mission in an additional manifestation of their own grandeur.

Believing that this scion of the most illustrious family of Qurayshi nobility was enamored of power, and looking askance at the way he vilified the pagan gods of their community, his prestigious tribe proposed crowning him king. To this the Messenger's uncompromising reply took the form of a metaphor: "By God," he said, "even if they were to put the sun in my right hand and the moon in my left so as to make me renounce my mission, I would not."

The Qur'ānic Message shook the foundations of the proud mercantile town of Mecca, as well as the rest of Arabia, whose tribes lived by raiding, privilege, and slavery. Feeling threatened, and having already tried unremitting harassment and then persecution, the Qurayshis opted for more radical means, making an attempt on his life.

For all that, Muhammad (grace and peace upon him) never ceased to proclaim what God had charged him with informing His creatures: the Oneness of the Creator. He continued to teach men the meaning of their lives and what awaited them after death. That in itself would not have annoyed the tribes so much had *islam* not spread abroad such revolutionary concepts as equity, the equality of men before God, and the organization of a community around the principles chosen of their own accord by its members.

Spirituality for *islam* has always gone hand in hand with the struggle for human rights. A society based on laws that secured the rights of everyone was being born under the stupefied eyes of the Arabs, who could not manage to organize themselves in a community and who, over incredible trifles, would not hesitate to wage tribal wars over generations.

Islam means submission to God, and therefore to the rules of His Creation. The essential mission of the Prophet (grace and peace upon him) is to teach us how to manage such submission in the best possible conditions, not always easy to assume in a hostile and treacherous world strewn with pitfalls. As *islam* advocates a state of perfect harmony with natural laws, whether those proper to the essence of being human or those having to do with human societies, the idea of the Islamic state was indeed present from the beginning for the Messenger (grace and peace upon him).

As human societies require the organization of power, the holy Prophet then had to occupy himself with organizing the nascent Islamic society in order to establish the Message on a stable political basis. For this reason and while continuing the Appeal, he secretly met in the environs of Mecca with some elements of the Khazraji tribe living in Medina (or Yathrib, as the city was then known[3]), who willingly embraced *islam*. The latter received the new Message through the sustained efforts of the Prophet (grace and peace upon him). Notwithstanding the trouble he encountered, he continued to propagate his teaching at the very center of Mecca during the periods of pilgrimage.[4]

During those well-determined periods, when Mecca teemed with foreigners, one might see few stealthy figures in the darkness edging their way onto the Mountain of Minan. Those few Muslims coming from Yathrib met in secrecy with the Messenger. Their objective was to deepen their knowledge of the faith as well as to draw up plans and think of the methods to follow so that *islam* might safely take root in the town they came from.

The second year the Yathribites met with the Prophet, there were eleven of them who took the solemn oath, vowing to commit themselves to the belief in the Oneness of the Creator, not to fornicate out of wedlock, not to steal, not to kill their children,[5] and not to disobey him when he ordered them to do good. One may notice the social dimensions of that oath, as well as the gentle progressiveness that distinguishes the pedagogical method of the Prophet (grace and peace upon him). For those taking the oath, it was not a matter of doing (obligation), but of refraining from doing (abstention). The commitment thus would not seem too difficult. As such, it was the first Islamic pact—the first *al-bay'a*[6]—and the first social contract founded on faith and the free will.

A Society of Confidence

During the third year the number of the faithful had increased in Medine, and the number of visitors to Mecca from amont them had increased, too. Among the seventy-three visitors there were now two women, the famous Nussayba[7] and Asmā' bintu 'Amr. These also took the oath, just as the male visitors had done. In so doing they asserted and illustrated another basic rule of *islam,* namely the full and complete citizenship of women. The Prophet of *islam* (grace and peace upon him) always recognized women as full-fledged partners in the nascent society.

This time the oath was enriched with other elements, stressing the obligation to defend the nascent faith by combating all those who sought to exterminate it. In his biography of the Prophet called the *Sīra,* a primary source on the subject, Ibn Hisham reports:

> The Prophet (grace and peace upon him) proceeded to the last pact of allegiance that took place in the *Aqaba,* committing interested parties to combat "the red and the black."[8] He personally committed himself to certain things, laid down conditions for the others concerning his God and promised them Paradise if they did not break the pact.

The principle of *jihād* was born, and it is certainly not what some pretend it to be. *Jihad* is resistance exclusively. Considering the small number of the Muslims who swore allegiance to the Prophet (grace and peace upon him), it was impossible for such an oath to have focused on the offensive. Furthermore, on no account can *jihād* be likened to the acts of torture to which victims are subjected, or to the reprehensible act of planting bombs that kill innocent civilians, children, and women.

If the Prophet (grace and peace upon him) rejected the power offered by the mother of the towns, as the Arabs used to call Mecca,[9] it was just because power for the sake of power held no interest for him. Kingship was not a model anything like the spirit of equity that he represented. He prepared the embryonic society and taught it to view power differently. The link he forged with them as their spiritual and temporal leader (imāma [the function of being a leader]) is based on the principle of the mutually binding contract. In the beginning, he worked towards persuasion, and then proposed the pact that set down conditions binding both the ruler and the citizens.

He might very well have adopted a totally different process by first strengthening his power as a king. That would certainly have facilitated his sacred mission, since it is much easier for a king to impose his views, especially in Arabia, where epic style and prestige were highly prized. The Prophet (grace and peace be upon him) did not do so, simply because he was a paragon of virtue whom God encourages the faithful to follow and imitate; he was *al-musharri'.* This word may be literally translated as "Tracer of the Path." But he was no empire builder. He is a Messenger of Mercy who came to establish the best possible laws for managing a world of men, made for man, the microcosm of the cosmos, the creature whom God honored with His

Breath. In this he is guided by God, Who tells him in His Revelation: *Let there be no compulsion in embracing faith.*[10]

No doubt for this reason, Muhammad (grace and peace upon him) instituted the first Constitution in the history of mankind, once Medina accepted him as undisputed leader. Orientalism does not dwell too long on this political act, passing over it as if it were an insignificant event. This exceptional historical document deserves, however, careful consideration and meditation on the open-mindedness from which it emanates.

The Constitution clearly expresses great concern for the respect of man and for intelligent social management. In it our "Tracer of the Path" teaches us how political rule must consolidate the social body. The political pact came to reinforce the nascent links between the community of Medina, the *ansār,* or supporters,[11] and the few faithful who emigrated with the Prophet and came to take up residence in Yathrib (the *muhajirīn* or immigrants). As soon as he came to Medina, the Prophet began to establish bilateral fraternal relationships between supporters and immigrants. These took the form of a voluntary pact in which each host undertook to share everything with his destitute and rootless immigrant brother.

From the very first day, the Envoy of God (grace and peace upon him) created the mosque, a wider space of solidarity enabling the realization of large-scale social and spiritual osmosis. The mosque soon became a place of worship but also of reflection, discussion, and solidarity: a place where at least five times a day the actors of a nascent society mingled—nascent in their humanity, nascent in the development of human values that *islam* teaches.

Was it for all that an angelic society without clashes, misunderstandings, and disputes? Far from it! The two social groups that formed the community were very different. It will be noticed in the *Sīra,* for instance, that certain immigrant companions did not at all appreciate the relative emancipation of the female *ansār.* They complained about the contagion that put Meccan women on the defensive vis-à-vis their husbands.

We may easily imagine that the disputes submitted to the Prophet (grace and peace upon him) must have been more numerous than we might think. Yet all such controversy occurred within a protecting womb that avoided their degenerating into social hatred or class divisions: the womb of faith in God and in the Last Life, and of love in Him. This utterly new method of participation could only strengthen those sacred links reinforced by generosity and self-sacrifice. These were virtues the grateful immigrants could not lose sight of.

The love felt for the Prophet of God was a propitious spiritual lubricant that helped to harmonize the parts of an inevitably heterogeneous society. The wisdom of the Prophet was not content with this solidarity based on voluntary donation. He did not rest until he wrote down in black and white the text that was to govern the embryonic society.

Legislative effort was all the more necessary since the moral corpus required a legal framework and a social consensus that went beyond the community of the faithful: Medina was not one hundred per cent Muslim. Jewish tribes and few Christians lived there as well. Normalization had to take place through codifying social links with the People of the Book, those toward whom the Qur'ān incessantly recommends the Prophet (grace and peace upon him) and the faithful depositories of the Last Message to be well disposed.

The Constitution of Medina would be the expression of a truly unique tolerance, especially in a world that knew as a model of government only the yoke exerted by dictators of all sorts. The extreme originality of the procedure adopted by our Prophet (grace and peace upon him) proves the divine inspiration of which he is the subject, and the mercy of which he is the envoy.

The Constitution of Medina

This subsection is devoted to the Constitution of Medina, but we must first emphasize certain essential ideas that take us back to the heart of our subject, and to the innermost recesses of the country we are visiting here: the country of our undertow as Muslims. I have stressed that the only way for our fractured *umma* to get out of its rut and revive its civilizing mission is to wage a large-scale battle on ignorance.

The most devastating ignorance is doubtless that of one's history. The lack of knowledge about oneself and one's history is even more caustic when it is maintained by a world order in which national and international tsarism combines to perpetuate the moral and physical massacre of the nations. Perhaps one day people will speak of the mental holocaust the Muslim peoples have lived through. Perhaps some *mea culpa* will be proclaimed one day in the future when the conscience of humanity is awakened. While awaiting such an uncertainty, Muslims can only rely on themselves.

Our track record exudes odors of disaster, and our *umma* is abased to the lowest of positions; it is destitute, indigent, underdeveloped, manipulated, distracted, disoriented, and deceived more by its own people than by any other adversary. The illiteracy of its peoples, the egotistic—even psychedelic—rashness of its rulers keep it in a constant state of moral poverty, of unbearable poverty altogether.

While recovery no longer seems possible, the beginnings of an awakening are taking shape. Within the Muslim world a common frame of mind is gradually developing that questions our history and aims to correct it. History itself is being questioned, not only by intellectuals but also by certain *ulemas* [religious scholars]. Among such questioners of history is the Yemeni Zayd bnu 'Ali al-Wazīr, upon whom we shall call in presenting the Constitution of Medina.

In his imposing work *al-Fardiya*,[12] Lwazīr denounces the fatal deviation that the *umma* underwent in the transfer of power from the *shūrā* to the *Fardiya,* literally "the power of the individual":

> The first thing we learn from the text [of the Constitution] is that the *umma* governs itself through institutions that differ from the models of power known until then that were based on despotism and absolutism.

. . . The Constitution emphasizes the fact that the *umma* governs itself by means of communitarian institutions. . . . It mentions four relational frameworks: Muslims among themselves, Muslims and Jews, Muslims and pagans, and finally a much broader framework we may describe as one of general structures.

Framework One: Muslims

1. "The faithful and the Muslims who belong to Quraysh and Yathrib, those who join them, and those who have fought on their side will be considered part of the particular *umma*." The article thus abolishes any tribal link and bases the social link on faith in God.

2. "The Qurayshis are free to adopt laws ratified among themselves before the advent of *islam* provided that they meet the norms that guarantee equity among the faithful." It is also mentioned that "each tribe is free to keep its own laws so long as they are respectful of the spirit of equity." This article emphasizes the principle known these days by the name of decentralization. Each group has the right to manage itself as it sees fit providing that it does not thwart the principles stipulated by the Constitution.

3. "The faithful are of equal merit and the most socially privileged must defend the weakest; the members of the society governed by the Constitution owe each other special solidarity and are united in war and peace by ties of blood which are of equal value."

4. "Any person having accepted this document and believing in God and in the Last Judgment must not support or host anyone who would violate the laws stipulated therein. Whoever acts in this way will call down upon him divine malediction and wrath on the Day of Judgment, will not be allowed to make transactions with the rest of the believers, and his testimony will not be accredited by the community."

The document thus sets up safeguards for a nascent society against the corruption of the social body.

Framework Two: Jews

1. The document entitles Jews to be among the Muslims as constituent elements of the *umma*. The principle of citizenship was thus instituted.

2. The text recognizes and guarantees Jews the right of freedom of worship as well as the right of property. "Muslims have their religion and the Jews have their own," the Constitution states. Thus the right of freedom of worship and the protection of minorities were established.

3. The Jews adhered to the principle underlined in the Constitution which stated that "if any unexpected event or dispute likely to be an offence against the security of the social body should arise among those adhering to the principles of this document, it is the Messenger of God who will take a decision." Thus (as Louis Gardet says) "the minority recognized the principles of the *umma* and received in turn well-defined rights and committed itself to equally clear duties."

4. The principle of decentralization is spelled out, giving Jews the same right to manage themselves as that provided for in favor of Muslims. "The Jews have the right to self-financing; the Muslims as well."

5. The text commits Muslims and Jews to mutual self-defense. "They must stand together and fight anyone who threatens their collective security. They will loyally dispense mutual counsel to each other, will maintain relations based on the spirit of good and far from the spirit of evil, will not do harm to their allies and will defend their cause should they be victims of attacks." Thus the equality of citizens before the law was achieved, as well as the duties incumbent upon them.

6. The Jews are to "participate financially in the war effort as long as the latter may last." This principle enlightens us about the meaning of the *jizya*,[13] which is paid by those among the Jews who do not wish to fight in the ranks of the Muslims. Those who fight in the ranks of the Muslim army are not only exempted from the *jizya* but are entitled to a sum paid by the *Bayt al-Māl* (Treasury Department). *Jizya* is therefore not an act of humiliation for the Jewish or Christian minority, but a token of consideration shown for the Jewish citizen who refuses to wage war on his coreligionists. . . . If the Jew has no objections to taking part in the fight, he is to be exempted from the protection tax (the *jizya*).

Everything was perfectly fine between the Muslims and the Jewish minority of Medina until the day the latter allied themselves to Quraysh against the Muslim community. By thus infringing on the constitutional principles they had accepted in the beginning, the Jews forced the Prophet to banish them from Medina as political renegades.

7. This specifies that "the Jews who are dependent on us are entitled to our protection and have a guarantee that they will not suffer from injustice and discrimination."

Thus, thanks to this pact, Muslims are obliged to defend Jews who have joined the *umma* just as they would defend their own coreligionists.

Framework Three: Pagans

1. The pact assures *Banī Aws Manāt* the right to form a particular community while enjoying the rights it stipulates provided that they respect its obligations. This tribe was not Muslim, but would embrace *islam* later, after *Al Khandaq*.[14] It was considered part of the *umma* even before its members converted to *islam*. Indeed, among the fighters in the Battle of Uhud was a pagan called Qazmān bnu Khārith.

Framework Four: General Principles

1. "A believer cannot be killed to avenge the death of an unbeliever."[15] Nascent Islam thus protects the life of its community including that of its minorities, the Jews, the Christians and the pagans who swore allegiance to the Prophet, against the *Kuffar* (wrongly called unbelievers) who fought against God and His Messenger. The notion of unbelief (*kufr*) is therefore made clear by the text. It does not have the meaning assigned to it nowadays (the fact of not believing in God and His Last Messenger); otherwise, the Prophet would not have given them the rights and obligations the way he did. He would not have either sentenced to death a Muslim who might kill a person of the "People of the Book."

Ali, the Commander of the Faithful (God bless him), the very symbol of the fairness of Islam, sentenced to death a Muslim for the killing of a *dhimmī*.[16] He also deemed that the compensation to be paid for a *dhimmī* killed by accident must be exactly the same as that paid to the relatives of a Muslim. . . . On another occasion, he sentenced to death a Muslim guilty of murdering a Jew. Even when the Jew's relatives renounced their complaint, Ali (God bless him) did not agree to remit the sentence until he had ascertained that the relatives had not been the victims of any pressures or threats."[17]

The Community and Power

When the Prophet (grace and peace be upon him) died, he left behind a community established on the principles of social justice and intense spirituality, a responsible and educated community in complete support of the communitarian values of participation and freedom. He crowned his support for the principle of *shūrā* (consultation) by his ultimate silence as to his successor, leaving the community free to choose its rulers.

The sacred text of the Qur'ān and particularly the *sunna*, which includes all the deeds and gestures of God's Envoy (grace and peace be upon him), are a source of directives from which general principles are drawn. The first principle is indisputably that of taking into consideration the Last Life and the connection that is always to be established between our actions, whether they pertain to the intimate, private, social, or political domain, and our *post mortem* future. Social justice becomes not a political or humanitarian conviction, but a sacred duty and a spiritual ascent.

Another principle to be derived from the reading of original *islam* is that social and political responsibility is on no account the matter of one individual. According to the sense of our Islamic teaching, power is always a matter of the entire community. It is with a sorrow unto death that we witness throughout our history how the usurpers of power have manipulated the meaning of Qur'ānic verses in order to prove what cannot be proved and to legitimize the indefensible.

All Muslims, for instance, learn by heart, having heard it often in the key speeches at Friday prayer, that obedience to the imam is emphasized in the Qur'ān. But the verse they always invoke should give them second thoughts, for in it God orders us thus: *Oh you who believe! Obey God, and obey the Apostle, and those charged with authority among you.*[18]

The verse orders us to obey "those" (plural) who hold power "among" you; on no account doest it instruct us to obey "the one" who holds power "over" you. The despots of all stripes who have successively subjugated us prefer to read the verse vertically. According to the school of deceptive despotism, the verse alludes to the group of individuals who have held absolute power throughout history.

The community, still imbued with the spirit of the teaching of the Messenger and its immediate history after his death, relates quite the opposite. Educated in the meaning of *shūrā* from the days of the Messenger, the Muslims of Medina met after his death in a place called *Saqīfat banī Sā'ida* to discuss their future even before interring his most holy body.

Lwazīr, like many Muslim authors and thinkers throughout the ages,[19] repudiates the "power of the individual" and emphasizes that what happened at the *Saqīfa* is the greatest evidence that nothing had been decided by the Prophet (grace and peace be upon him) before his death. It was his clear will to let a suitable person be chosen at a suitable time by an adult and well-directed community.

Let us once again cite Lwazīr to describe what occurred on that day despite the great sorrow that dwelt in the hearts of the Muslims and the tears that blurred their eyes:

> On the day of the *Saqīfa,* the *umma* began to practice its system and organize its particular administration. It elected its caliph after a long and heated debate. The dialog, the debate, and the error[20] that ensued from it indisputably prove that the election of the caliph was the work of the Companions who made an effort of reflection (*ijtihād*) to give shape to the principle of *shūrā*. Had the procedure of *shūrā* been decided by divine decree, there would have been no deliberation, and there would not have been the *fitna* that nearly sundered the *umma,* had God not prevented that from taking place, as Omar stated when recalling the debate later. If the choice were a divine order, Omar certainly would not have dared to describe it as such. It is undeniable that the election of Abu Bakr on the day of *Saqīfat banī Sā'ida* took place at the end of a debate, not in response to a (sacred) text.[21]

The author is alluding to the sacred nature (in the sense of untouchable) that the organization of power will have later due to an erroneous interpretation of the events of *Saqīfa*. The Umayyads[22] would carefully maintain this justification of power in order to legitimate their own.

Lwazīr further defends the idea that the *umma*, sure of its right to reflection recommended by the Qur'ān and the practice of the Messenger, chose Abu Bakr as "caliph" but preferred to see Omar as *Amīr al-Mūminīn* [commander of the faithful]. These different and varied titles are not empty words for the Arab people, who consider the use of words as perilous and effective as that of swords. They are tangible evidence of the vivacity of a nation and of malleability inherited from the teaching of the Messenger.

None of the four Companions, who respected to the very end the principle of *shūrā*, applied it in the same manner. Abu Bakr proposed Omar as a candidate. The latter was chosen not for that reason, but because he was a very good candidate. Abu Bakr (God bless him) presented Omar just as a Muslim giving counsel to his community would do. Omar was praised for his strong character and his exemplary probity. Accepting him as *Amīr al-Mūminīn*, the *umma* was not mistaken. Omar's uprightness remains inimitable in the entire history of humankind.

He was a paragon not only of virtue but also of intelligence and uprightness. When he was stabbed, he had time before he died to propose another model of election by nominating six candidates.

This variety of models proves that these leaders are justly called Rightly Guided Caliphs[23] since they knew that the truth is to be sought in reflection and in adapting political realities to the spirit of fairness that is intimately linked to contractual practice. If the latter is undertaken within the context of faith and is endorsed by the community, it must advance the spirit of the Message.

The school that trained the caliphs also taught them to grant others (as they had to themselves) the right to be mistaken. They did not imprison the community in a legal straitjacket; instead they set an example of the attitude we are to have toward an ever-changing world. In this regard, the attitude of Ali (God bless him), the fourth and last Caliph, was perhaps the most instructive. After the assassination of Othman, the previous Caliph, Ali was approached as his successor. But when he was told that he would have to swear an oath to follow to the letter the principles taught by the Prophet and his two successors, he refused, saying that he could undertake to respect only what the Messenger had taught, not what Abu Bakr and Omar had recommended. It was not out of self-centeredness, individualism, or contempt for the opinions of his predecessors and brothers in God that Ali did this. Ali was far-sighted; he was right; he understood. Ali was par excellence the pupil of the school of *shūrā* and *ijtihād*.

Can there be any better proof of the obligation for reflection and continuous adaptation to an evolving world than the response of Ali, cousin, son-in-law, and favorite disciple of the Prophet, husband of Fatima (the Messenger's particularly cherished daughter), and, after Khadija (the Prophet's first spouse) the first Muslim?

To undertake to repeat exactly what his predecessors had done would have effectively confined the community in archaism and illogicality. When we recall that Ali's concern to preserve the right to reflection came just few years after the death of the Prophet (grace and peace be upon him), we can only cry bitterly over the lot of our poor *umma*, gorged on *fatwās* issued in the fourth century after Hegira.[24]

Power in the Service of the Message

Convinced to the very end of the principles of *shūrā,* the Companions (elected to be caliphs) perpetuated their convictions in speeches that still resonate in our wounded memories like the nostalgic sounds of bygone days. In their first official speeches they expressed eternal principles, steadfast jewels whose light has been abruptly and totally eclipsed by our eventful history.

The first act of Abu Bakr (God bless him), when the community elected him as Successor of the Prophet, was to remind in a public speech of the essence and the sense of power:

> You have charged me with running your affairs, but I am not the best of you. If I go in the right direction, support me. If I take a wrong path, redirect me. . . . The weakest among you will count most for me until I restore to him his due. The strongest among you will be worth nothing in my sight until I get him to agree to fulfill his obligations. . . . Obey me so long as I obey God and His Messenger. If I do not, you are absolved from obedience to me.

Each word of this exhortation is worth its weight in gold. In a few sentences Abu Bakr (God bless him) defined the concept of power in *islam.* In this brief and apparently insignificant speech resides the philosophy of *shūrā.* Its core ideas contain very modern political inflections. The first idea that emerges is that the person of the ruler—the caliph in this case—is not sacred as such, but owes his sacred status to the sole fact that he has been elected by the community. That is his first and last merit, his sole legitimacy. It is the community that is sacred, not the person of the elected imam. This is the famous principle of popular sovereignty.

We have seen that Abu Bakr invited the community to dismiss him if he failed to obey the fundamental principles on which his nomination was based. Here indeed we have one of the essential elements of a constitutional system. The social bond that links the Muslim nation, or the community of the faithful, is neither the race, the tribe, customs, nor territory. It is rather the recognition of God as Sole Sovereign and of our brotherhood in Him. This faith that creates freedom is the basic foundation of what is to be any Islamic Constitution.

Translating these great principles of faith to daily life and adapting them to the changing nature of the world created by God remains the task of *ijtihād:* tireless *ijtihād,* sensible and intelligent *ijtihād,* as it must ever be since it entails a constant effort to adapt the Qur'ānic text to the social context.

An informed disciple of the Prophet, Abu Bakr (God bless him) established the system of the community's sovereignty which delegates power to the caliph. The idea is clear that power emanates from a mutually binding contract based on obedience to the great principles of *islam:* faith in God and in His Prophet, and the establishment of justice on earth. The practice of such power is in no way relinquished to the arbitrariness of the caliph, but remains the everyone's duty. The community neither resigns during the delegation nor during the exercise of power. It is a partner, not a helpless spectator.

This dimension of power for Abu Bakr is equally manifest in his attitude with the army, whose men were for him not mere underlings but full actors in the ongoing history. After a general communication, Abu Bakr addressed a special communication to the Muslim army. He did not address his counsels to the Chief of the Army, Usāma bnu Zayd, but gave them to all the soldiers. His speech concerned a body, not the chief of the army who was then going to give his orders to his subordinates. To this end, the Rightly Guided Caliph appealed to the conscience of each of the soldiers. In his speech he appealed to the Muslim as much as to the serviceman, creating very novel ethics of war that would long be a source of sacred obligation for the Islamic military action.

Abu Bakr said:

1. Do not break alliances.
2. Do not betray one another.
3. Do not be violent for the sake of violence.
4. Do not mutilate your adversaries.
5. Do not touch their children, their elders, or their women.
6. Do not touch their palm trees; do not burn them; do not cut down any fruit tree.
7. Do not cut the throat of their goats, heifers, or camels unless for food.
8. You will find some people who have devoted themselves to monastic life; do not touch them; let them pursue the life they have chosen.[25]

That is the code of honor of the Muslim *mujāhid* (resister) and the expression of the great principle of mercy inherent to the faith on which the ruler and the citizen agree.

Omar, the successor of Abu Bakr, endorsed and developed such political conscience based on the spirit of the Message. A good disciple of the Prophet, Omar knew that the recognition of God's supreme might implied that of man's weakness in view of his nature as sinner. Omar (God bless him) began his mandate by publicly criticizing himself. In all the history of power, no such sincere speech can be found that attaches so little importance to the one who is supposed to be the leader. Always true to form, Omar reproves pompous speech with these words: "God! I am weak, make me strong. I am brutish, make me gentle. I am miserly, make me generous."[26]

Many of those elected at the head of their country ought to learn humility from the school of Omar. He further exclaimed:

> I am a divine trial for you just as you are one for me after my Companion (the Prophet). Among your affairs, whatever I am able to manage by myself I will leave to no one else to take care of. The affairs I am unable to manage directly by myself I will delegate to trustworthy and sincere persons. If they successfully carry out their mission I will recompense them, but I will severely punish them if they fail to fulfill their duty.[27]

And Omar kept his word. His faithfulness to God and to His Messenger (grace and peace upon him) made him a statesman who worked for the well-being of all, for social justice, and for the prosperity of the community. One need only dwell on one example among hundreds reported on his mandate to draw conclusions that are useful for the foundation of a revolutionary philosophy of power. To join the school of Omar in this field would be entirely to our advantage, we the Muslims who are still searching for our path and cannot find it. Let us then discover the politician of great stature that Omar (God bless him) was by contemplating the following:

> Some representatives of the people of Kūfa [presently a province of Iraq] came to complain to Omar about Sa'd bni abī Waqās [appointed governor of Kūfa]. Omar then told them, "What is to be done with the people of Kūfa? If I appoint a pious man, they criticize him for his incompetence, and if I appoint a strong man, they criticize him for his impiety!" Mughīra bnu Shu'ba then made a proposal to Omar, "Prince of the Believers! As for the pious incompetent, his piety is to his advantage [in his relationship with God] but his incompetence is a disadvantage to you [as guarantor of the State]. As for the agent who is gifted [in the management of the commonweal] but who lives in impiety, his competence serves you [as guarantor of the State] and his impiety is his affair with God. Omar then said: "You are right, and you are that [competent but impious] man. Take charge of their affairs."[28]

Such was Omar, and thus was born the notion of technocracy and competence used for the purely technical management of the commonweal. This exchange of views between the supreme chief and the citizen adviser, as well as the practice that resulted from it, may seem unbearable to certain upholders—and detractors—of *islam* and *shūrā*.

The upholders will feel destabilized before Omar's malleability and open-mindedness, characteristics that are proper to any Companion in frequent contact with the Messenger. We too can only be surprised by such an attitude, since most of us have been worn down like pebbles by a thousand-year flow of the stupefying jurisprudence that assassinated *shūrā* at the very dawn of Islam and has since deadened our reasoning. Successive regimes have stunted our consciences, limiting our ability to think how God's world might be adapted to God's Message, and vice versa.

Detractors will be even more upset with Omar's advice, since it does not correspond to the subconscious image—an image engraved in their minds by blind-eyed and incompetent orientalism—of a history of intolerance, exclusion, barbarity and foolishness. The fact remains: Omar was a giant of the intelligent management of power who did everything to enable it to serve the Message and guarantee the objectives (*maqāsid*) of the Islamic Law (Qur'ān and *sunna*). The objectives or *maqāsid* are five in number:

1. The preservation of faith.
2. The preservation of life.
3. The preservation of the wealth [of the *umma*].
4. The preservation of the mind.
5. The preservation of issue.

Worthy guarantor of the Message and its *maqāsid*, a man of faith and intuition, Omar (God bless him) was as well the precursor of the separation of powers. Taha Hussein attests:

> The charge to establish a system of justice among the people he gave not only to governors; he sent judges to stand as guarantors of God's Law, judges who were subject to no other influence than that of the Qur'ān and the *sunna* (the path and practice) of the Messenger. If they could not find a precise answer in the Book and the *sunna*, they acted according to their own discretion (*ijtihād*) by attempting to take into account the principle of fairness as fully as they could. The judges were in no way inferior to the governors, but were appointed by Omar himself. Once appointed, they were answerable to no one other than God, Whom they had to obey by drawing inspiration from His Message and the directives of His Prophet.[29]

In his famous *Ahkam sultania* (rules of kinship) Mawardi reports the following encounter:

> Someone came to Omar to complain that Ali [an appointed judge] had taken a particular decision in a certain affair. Omar replied, "If I were the judge, I would have decided differently." The plaintiff retorted, "What then prevents you, as Commander of the Faithful, from refuting Ali's judgment?" Omar replied, "If the Qur'ān and the *sunna* were clear about this affair, I would have done so. But Ali's decision was based on reflection, and his reflection is worth the same as mine."

Such was Omar! How can one not admire the greatness of the education of the Prophet (grace and peace be upon him) that produced such men as him? Ali (God bless him) was in turn called to power and proved the complete success of this pedagogy. A great among the greats, he ruled in those darkest periods of the Great Ordeal, attempting to get things back on an even keel and restore the spirit of justice that had been betrayed when the Umayyads seized the institutions of state at the time of Othman (God bless him).

The first and striking characteristic of Imam Ali's experience with power was his refusal of it. His election by the community of Medina had been the result of unanimous and spontaneous choice. Ali (God bless him) was the right man for the job and, as the great strength of his faith and character were known to all, it was natural that they should think of him in such difficult times. He alone, they believed, could save a nascent Islam suffering from the great political and economic instability generated during Othman's reign. Only after repeated entreaties from everyone did he reluctantly, and inwardly grieving, accept the office of the Commander of the Faithful. He set aside his distaste for power for the good of all, in whose eyes he was the highly skilled seaman appointed by the *umma,* with hearts filled with confidence and hope, to attempt a rescue operation.

The Great Ordeal

In the memory of the *umma,* the eventful times in which Ali was besought to take the situation in hand have been called *al fitna al kubra* [the great ordeal]. The period has come to be a torment to our collective consciousness; we are branded by it. *Al kubra* is in fact a superlative: the Great Ordeal has been our greatest ordeal, our greatest pain, our greatest grief. With pain and woe we look back on the misfortune of seeing the harmony of the Companions rent apart. We witness the Clash of Titans: Absolute vs. Contingency. It is written that spirit and matter cannot be joined except by superhuman effort. It is in this context that jihād has true meaning; it is the effort of joining nearly irreconcilable poles.

Ali (God bless him) tried to get things back on an even keel. He was savagely assassinated in February of 661, less than four years after his nomination. With him ended an era in which power served the Message; after him began the era in which power enslaved the Message. When Ali took the office of the caliphate, he faced a delicate situation in which explosive economic and socio-political facts had become entangled. He inherited an accumulation of events that, albeit confined to a relatively short period of time, were nonetheless complicated and difficult to manage.

The evil was essentially the result of the spectacular expansion of Muslim society in record time. Overnight the *umma* found itself thrust from the state of a restricted community—living in consonance and emotional stability centered on the person of the Prophet (grace and peace be upon him)—to an empire with incredible wealth in material sources and human elements.

The story of Omar and Abū Hurayra reported by Ibn Khaldūn in his *Prolegomena* reveals to what extent the events were new for our Companions. Abdelhadi Gafouri[30] relates the events with commentary:

The territorial expansion forced the State to organize its finances. For this purpose, 'Omar bnu al-Khatāb created the *Bayt al-Māl*. This caliph was thus the first to have created a treasury department. The history of its creation is interesting and deserves to be related. It reveals, on the one hand, the Muslims' lack of experience as far as financial matters are concerned, and, on the other, the influence foreign countries exerted over their economic and financial legislation. Abū Hurayra, having just come from Baghdad, informed the Caliph that he had brought with him 500,000 dirhams. Omar found the sum was exaggerated or even unimaginable, and asked Abū Hurayra if he knew what he was talking of and particularly if he knew the value he had brought. The Caliph then mounted the platform and declared, "I have received a lot of money; do you want to have your share in weight or in number?" It was then that Walid Ibn Mughira stood up and said, "Commander of the Faithful! In other countries, I have seen foreigners keeping registers and having a treasury department." Omar then replied, "We will then keep registers."[31]

In the same context of daily, indeed hourly *ijtihād,* Omar also believed it was more appropriate to break with what Abu Bakr had decided in the domain of managing public moneys. The latter had distributed the revenues equally between all the Muslims. Omar thought that merit and seniority in *jihād* had to be taken into account. By so doing, Omar's objective was clear; in any case he did not hide it. A man with a full and strong nature imbued with uprightness and faith, Omar was not used to hiding anything. "I will be careful," he said, "not to put on an equal footing those who fought with the Messenger of God and those who fought against him."[32]

Omar was alluding to those who had become Muslims during the conquest of Mecca. These had fallen in with the camp of *islam* after having fiercely fought it. Upon witnessing the Muslims' unbeatable power and prestige as victors, they professed their faith—some sincerely, others merely following the crowd. The first Muslims, though compelled to accept them into the community as full members,[33] did not welcome them in their hearts with the same warmth as that reserved for the converts who had chosen *islam* of their own accord.-The turncoat converts were always held in suspicion. It was clear that the Companions and the first Caliphs tried to prevent their accession to power, fearing certainly political deviation and the lust for power that even a reverential fear of God may not temper.

This was the framework within which Omar had acted, believing it was the most appropriate attitude to adopt. His apprehension, shared by the greatest Companions, turned out to be well founded, since the Umayyads, who were to seize power a few years later, were part of the class of last-minute converts the community called "Muslims of the Victory." Omar, the just ruler, had inadvertently begun a process that was to serve the ambitions of those people much more than it would harm them. The experience had an unfortunate aspect that enabled a few who were already affluent to increase their wealth. The financial policy of Omar (God bless him) gave rise to a privileged class that distinguished itself from the ordinary Muslims. The difference would become flagrant after Omar's death.

An rightly guided and perspicacious man, Omar soon realized that he had taken a false path. In his political program of the following year, he announced that he would revert to the original resolution of Abu Bakr (God bless him). He did not have the time to correct his error: he was brutally assassinated. The measure, though highly equitable in itself and initially accepted by the community as fair, was to awaken demons that had not been completely defeated in certain Arab minds. Since the first Muslims were inevitably Qurayshis, tribal privilege soon became confused with social merit.

The Umayyads took thorough advantage of this ambiguity and developed it so as to legitimate their own seizure of power. They worked stealthily to establish the idea that power falls rightfully to the Qurayshis to whom they belonged.

This plausible confusion between merit and tribalism explains the will of Abu Bakr to put a stop to the ambitions of last-minute Qurayshi Muslims by granting exclusive electoral right to the *muhajirīn*.[34] The irony of fate turned that decision into a Trojan horse for these late Muslims with hegemonic ambitions. In his book titled *Othman,* Taha Hussein writes:

> Abu Bakr was anxious that power should come to the *muhajirīn* so long as there were among them people who were able to conduct their mission successfully. The Qurayshi would transfigure this wish by working for their own interests, as dictated by their tribal instincts, and transgressing the standards of *islam* by ignoring the extremely important principle of the equality of Muslims.[35]

Slowly but surely, the Muslims who had come late to the faith progressed towards the conquest of power, using a process of elimination in the figurative as well as literal sense. They defended the idea that the Prophet's family were natural heirs. Taking this logic to disastrous extremes, they unhesitatingly persecuted or assassinated the grandsons of the Prophet (grace and peace be upon him) in order to remain the Messenger's sole closest relatives. At the same time, they deviated completely in their financial policy already in the days of Othman, elected after Omar (God bless them both). Only the idea of the caliph's absolute freedom as regards recompense was kept; those of equity and merit were ignored. Little by little, the clever Umayyads used and abused Othman's excessive kindness to draw on the treasury department as they saw fit.

Omar's assassination was part of the sure progress of the will of power that dwelt in the Umayyads, and it was present long before Mu'āwiya had made his coup. The Ummayad conquest of power had clearly begun earlier. They had hatched their conspiracy on three fronts: 1. access to key positions; 2. amassing great wealth; and 3. launching an ideological attack on the system of *shūrā*.

Through the person of Othman (God bless him), they tilted the notion of power towards a model closer to monarchy than what the first two caliphs had promoted and defended. The subtle nature of their strategy consisted in playing on the symbolic figure of Othman, a Companion with a stature recognized in the history of Muslims. Alas, they acted so slyly that in the end anger prevailed over any other consideration. The flagrant iniquity of their regime completely destroyed the esteem and respect due to the Companions. Othman was assassinated after a sordid history of forgery in which they involved him.

An ordeal, a Great Ordeal, and the beginning of the tragedy that still tears us apart. Henri Laoust says so rightly: "[Othman's] murder was to open one of the most formidable splits in the history of Islam."[36]

Ali and Pandora's Box

History is never as simple and straightforward as we may think. The death of Othman produced an emotional, political and social tidal wave that may be explained by many facts.

One explanation is the sacred dimension attached to the person of the senior Companions like Othman (God bless him), which meant that notwithstanding all the errors perpetrated in his name, the community still takes such unfailing status into account.

Another explanation is certainly found in the assiduous work of the Umayyads. They knew how to choose their followers and how to conduct publicity campaigns, positive for their allies and negative for their enemies. Mu'āwiya was a real genius renowned for his political savvy. In addition to his being a Companion, the prestige of his status as a learned Qurayshi notable of noble birth was a bonus.

As the Muslim empire became immense and without the means of a modern communicating world, the peoples were much more conditioned by their governors than by the distant central power personified by the Caliph. The populations were then much more dependent on these governors than the central power of the caliphate. Aware of this fact, the Umayyads had established a network of senior officials who were somehow or other supportive of their cause.

When we add to this the fact that power had produced a system of privileges which the beneficiary class had no desire to renounce, we can understand how Imam Ali (God bless him) had inherited a wide-open Pandora's Box.

His experience with power was all the more painful since he opposed with a policy of virtue his fearsome and determined adversaries' policy of ruse and Machiavelism, a policy of equity against one of nepotism.

Ali began a series of reforms that dealt strong blows to the carefully organized network of the Umayyads, and the angry response this provoked was quick and efficient. Our Companion's misadventure with power ought to constitute an open book from which any theorist of the Islamic power to come (God willing!) ought to draw edifying lessons.

Ali's probity required that he go straight to the point, but he failed to notice that the social order was deeply unsettled and that the balance of power had become precarious. Was the new Caliph's head-on reform too daring? Perhaps, since Ali took stringent and harsh measures in his attempt to right the situation as quickly as possible. His philosophy of power, based on everyone's participation and the establishment of a system that restricted the power of the rulers, deserves our dwelling on it for some time. We will content ourselves here with enumerating the principal measures that aroused the anger of the system at that time and provoked the Umayyad's counter-offensive that ended again in murder.

1. Notwithstanding the counsel of Mughīra bnu Shu'ba, Ali ousted the governors (*wulāt*) appointed by the previous caliph. He could not risk keeping such overly influential figures who had acquired a taste of power often in total ignorance of the interests of the people. Ali was aware that not even their nomination by Othman (God bless him) would assure him their fidelity. As their ambition grew enormous, they unhesitatingly took part in the affair of Othman's assassination.

Ali (God bless him) refused to adopt the ambiguous attitudes proper to sly politicking. Was he right? Was he wrong? Intelligent as he was, had he simply underestimated the extent of corruption? However this may be, his gesture shows admirable courage and uprightness. Gafouri informs us on this matter:

> Everyone knew that many governors had been behind the rebellion fomented against Othman and his assassination. In addition to the repression they exerted on the Muslims, Ali reckoned that they were greedy, stupid and ignorant of politics and the basis of government. Mughīra bnu Shu'ba had advised the Imam to confirm these governors in their positions. Ali refused to follow his advice which, had he done so, might perhaps have minimized these governors' opposition to his policy.[37]

Ali further provoked the angry response of the system by not appointing Qurayshis in place of the governors of the time, thus breaking the elitism that was setting in and was about to set a precedent.

2. The nomination of these non-Qurayshi governors was in keeping with the principle of the immutable right in *islam* that had been set aside by the system of the time, the principle that all Muslim citizens are equal before God and the Law.

He thus lifted the political discrimination exerted over the *ansār* by choosing from among them governors of the distant regions. He concretely opposed the tribal tendency that *islam* had sought to erase.

The event that perhaps had most awakened the vengeful demons in his adversaries was the creation of the *Dīwān al-Mazālim,* a term that might be translated as Complaint Department. Annexed to the caliphate, this department was responsible for receiving citizens' complaints. In particular it was intended to conduct investigations on the too rapidly amassed fortunes engendered by the abuse of power, so that these might be returned to the Treasury Department. The measure was especially disliked by his enemies.

Abdul Hadi Gafouri relates an incident that reveals the bad habits that had set in and which Ali had sought to combat.

> The most striking, and no doubt the most moving, example that best illustrates Ali's weakness before his unscrupulous enemies is given by this scene that occurred between the Imam and his brother 'Aqīl. The latter, old, blind and poor to boot, came to ask his brother, who had become Caliph, to give him money from the *Bayt al-Māl*. Ali replied, "You are not entitled to this money. But wait until I get mine, and I will give you some of it." The reply angered 'Aqīl, and he joined the ranks of Mu'āwiya.[38]

The Umayyads, who, according to Zayd ibn Ali Lwazīr, had long before begun to hatch their plot,[39] hastened to take action. Perfect manipulators abetted by their experience of power, they played on the emotional tensions produced by Othman's assassination, on the natural antipathies, and on the influence they acquired through the occupation of key positions. Combining ruse and subtlety, they corrupted influential persons and successfully destabilized Ali's caliphate barely six months after his accession to power.

The Battle of the Camel (December 9, 656) marks the first upheavals indirectly fomented by the Umayyads. Aisha (widow of the Prophet), Talha, and Zubayr rose up, crying out for vengeance against the assassins of Othman. The rebellion was suppressed. Talha and Zubayr were killed in the battle and Aisha was escorted back to Medina, full of remorse. She had remembered too late a premonitory warning of the Prophet, who had foretold such political error.

The End of the Caliphate

The infernal process had already been started. Mu'āwiya would challenge Ali to another battle (*Siffīn*), always putting forward the sacredness of Othman's blood and the illegitimacy of the regime that, according to the Umayyad version, was involved in these murders. Having joined the Syrian army, Mu'āwiya had recourse to the principle of arbitration when he felt the situation had become critical and the victory compromised. This principle set forth by the Qur'ān concerns "two factions of believers waging war against each other." Henri Laoust sets out the event as follows:

> The legitimacy of this arbitration is admitted by Sunnism as well as by Shiism. What is added is that it was a trick masterminded by the shrewd Amr bnu al Ass who was then in the ranks of the Syrian army which Mu'āwiya had joined and saw in that last-minute stratagem the way to sow discord in the opposing ranks. At first distrustful, Ali eventually accepted. Contrary to the opinion of the supporters of all-out war, he followed the advice of a member of his entourage who was secretly supportive of the Umayyad cause. Breaking once again the community's unity, this conflict did take place without arousing intense reprobation.

Without mutual consultation, a number of Companions decided to stay out of the struggle, declaring that they were ready to fight infidels but refused to engage in fratricidal struggles. These first *mu'tazilas,* as they were called, became the protagonists of neutrality and abstentionism (*imsāk*), which many Sunni doctors would later advocate as the sole attitude in conformity with the Qur'ān and the *sunna* in any civil war (*fitna*). Resorting to arbitration, the initiative taken by Mu'āwiya, thus met a widely shared desire to see peace reborn in the community, not by means of weapons but by a peaceful procedure.[40]

A detailed development of the event would be long and tedious. Let us say that the arbitration, entrusted to Abū Mūsā al-Ash'arī on Ali's side and to Amr Ibn Al Ass on Mu'āwiya's side, was favorable to the Umayyads.

Abu Mussa is the very model of the good-natured Companion, reveling in a purity of faith no worldly pleasure rigidifies. A just man among the just, at the service of the just, with no experience beyond his blind love of the Prophet (grace and peace be upon him) and the Companions, he had as adversary the fearsome Amr Ibn Al Ass. Already before the advent of *islam,* the latter had gained the reputation of being a resourceful individual. He used subtlety and had no difficulty in duping the upright Abu Mussa.

Was Abu Mussa naïve to such a degree, or had he chosen Ali's path of sincerity? Ali rightly said that if he wanted to use cunning, he would need no one to show him how. His conscience as a Muslim required him to be upright and honest. This choice was also that of Omar (God bless him), who said, "I am not a sly person, and a sly person would not fool me."

Many questions arise, many mysteries still remain; the Islamic world has everything to gain by elucidating them, on the condition of doing so dispassionately. If our passions cannot be defeated, if they are irrepressible, then we had better let sleeping dogs lie. But the wound was not a slight one, and our injuries will not be quickly healed despite the passing of so many centuries.

It would therefore be illusive to attempt to clear the tangles of our complicated history's landscape in one chapter or two, or a hundred. We will continually be bombarded with crucial questions. Yet it is perhaps the nature of life itself and the essence of history to ask ourselves questions.

Was it politically fatal that cunning should prevail over fairness? However that may be, Mu'āwiya finally succeeded in stirring up ill-feeling in his opponent's supporters by playing admirably on their passions and arousing the anger caused by the violent death of Othman. Ibn Al Ass, Mu'āwiya's champion during the arbitration, obtained legitimacy for him. When Abu Mussa recognized Mu'āwiya's argument, Ali was deposed.

Great schism was on the way. The Kharidjite School, whose representatives still exist as a minority in the Muslim world, will never forgive Ali for having accepted the principle of arbitration. They withdrew their allegiance (*al-bay'a*) to Ali and criticized him violently. They even waged war on him during the famous Battle of Nahrawan.

The mention of the Kharidjite revolt at the end of this chapter enables us to dwell nostalgically on a last glimmer of the greatness of the just Ali (God bless him). A man of *shūrā*, Imam Ali was the first to respect the principle of freedom of expression. Notwithstanding the advice of his political entourage, at no point did he attack the freedom of the Kharidjites, who criticized him in public. Ali Lwazīr tells us about the matter:

> His attitude towards the Kharidjites is the most noble expression of his commitment to the path of political freedom; he did not deprive them of their rights to enjoy the public economic advantages of the time, nor to pray in the public mosques; he accepted their testimony in the courts. About them he made this statement, which is an expression of his deep conviction, "If they keep quiet, we will leave them at peace; if they talk, we will have talks with them; if their action goes against the public good, we will fight against them." This statement also guarantees the important right to remain silent. Ali is the forerunner on the subject. . . . Nobody before him had guaranteed this right as had the Imam. He might have extorted from them, under duress, precious pieces of information and thus avoided to fall into many of their traps.[41]

Ali followed his convictions to the end, even if that should cost him his life—which is what actually happened. Such are the great men, the men of principle and *shūrā*. Ali Lwazīr goes on to speak of this Great Companion, a just man to the end of his path, to the end of his life:

> Imam Ali defended the absolute freedom of expression. Some Kharidjites joined him in the mosque and had talks with him like the one reported here. [Kharith bnu Rashīd said,] "By God, I won't obey you and I won't pray behind you!"[42] "You fool," Ali replied, "you would disobey God, deny your pact, and harm no one but yourself. Why are you doing this?" "Because you accepted arbitration, you flinched at the critical moment, yielding to the will of those who have harmed themselves.[43] For this I give you no credit and I find you ridiculous; I am angry with you." Ali used no repressive measures against him. He invited him to a public debate to make him see reality and to attempt to win him over. Kharit accepted, saying that he would come back the next day, and Ali let him go freely.[44]

Does such a spirit of equality lead to the despotism of a single person, as Montesquieu states in *De l'esprit des Lois* [the spirit of the law]?

In the case at hand, it is certain that the sense Ali (God bless him) had of equality and freedom was extremely favorable to the rise of Muʿāwiya, that is, to the despotism of a single person. Was the option for absolute freedom too precocious for a period not yet cured of barbarity? Had Ali promoted a system whose time had not come yet?

Long before liberal democracy, the system of *shūrā* as practiced by Ali rested on transparency and on respecting the opinion of others. In his propaganda against Ali, Muʿāwiya criticized that system as aberrant. He prided himself on having had the last word since Ali (God bless him) did not know how to keep secrets and was too open, whereas he, Muʿāwiya, favored dissimulation in the exercise of power.

The Umayyads, it is true, had the last word. Their principal argument was the sword, their word was violence, and they wielded terror and manipulation with outstanding dexterity. Imperturbable and full of arrogance, the Umayyad machine was advancing towards power. Ali would eventually be assassinated; Hassan, his son, would be poisoned; Hussayn would be massacred as well as Abdullah ibn Zubayr and hundreds of the Companions among those who had learned the Qurʾān by heart, and any rebellious will that would move or rise up against such particularly pernicious despotism. It was the end of the beginning and the beginning of the end.

NOTES

1. The effort of reflection that enables us to adapt the general recommendations of the Qurʾān and the prescriptions of the Prophet to specific events of social, political, or economic life.

2. The name of the most prestigious Arab branch to which the Prophet belonged. The Qurayshi had the distinguished honor of being the official keepers of the *Kaaba,* the sacred edifice inherited from the monotheism Abraham had taught.

3. The city that welcomed the Prophet (grace and peace be upon him) after his flight from Mecca. He took up residence there until his death. After the coming of the Messenger, Yathrib was *al Madina* (Medina), the City or the Luminous City, as it is known to this day.

4. I call to the attention of the uninformed reader the fact that pilgrimage to Mecca had existed long before *islam.* The Arabs, who had indirectly been under the influence of ancestral monotheism, believed in one Almighty God, Whom they called *Allah,* and in a horde of less prestigious gods. It was clear for them that their ancestor Abraham had constructed this cubic edifice, the Kaaba, at the command of that great God. They came then to pay homage twice a year to Allah, and in the meantime to some three hundred other deities, taking advantage of the occasion to conduct business.

5. Concern about the status of woman is already present with our Prophet, inasmuch as this clause concerns mainly the little girls who were interred by their fathers in obedience to a barbaric custom. Boys never met with this fate.

6. Mutual binding contract.

7. Nussayba is a key figure among the most illustrious of the female Companions. Many women later accompanied the army of Medina, providing assistance in the nursing team. Yet Nussayba was part of the fighting troops, as she wondrously wielded her sword. The Prophet praised her in a particular *hadīth* in which he thanked her for having wholeheartedly defended

him in a battle. She ended her life with one arm missing, enjoying high esteem from the entire Muslim community, notably from Omar (God bless him).

8. Literary expression of classical Arabic meaning "without distinction of race."

9. From the dawn of time Mecca was considered the heart of Arabia and the mother of towns. The offer made by his town would have entailed that the other towns be dependent upon it in their commercial and religious activities. His grandfather had already been recognized as a veteran by all the Arab tribes.

10. Qur'ān: S. II. 256.

11. Literally, *ansār* is the plural of *nasīr,* meaning "the defender." The *ansār* are the supporters of the Prophet and the Islamic faith.

12. Zayd bnu 'Ali al-Wazīr, *al-Fardiya* [the power of the individual], *markaz at-turāth wa'l-buhūth hyamami* [Yemeni Heritage and Research Centre], 2000.

13. I take the liberty to add this indication that does not exist in the text in order to translate the word *jizya*. This word refers to the tribute that the People of the Book (Jews and Christians) pay in the land of Islam and that is interpreted by the orientalist thinking as an awful racial discrimination instituted by *islam*.

14. *Ghazwat al Khandaq,* the Battle of the Trench.

15. Once again, I interrupt the author to indicate that a corpus of laws governing social relations had been instituted that prescribed capital punishment in the case of first-degree murder and cash compensation in the event of second-degree murder. It should be noted that the text takes into consideration a most critical period in which a community attempts to settle itself within a hostile and cruel milieu. Under no circumstances must this article, indeed even the Constitution, be taken as an immutable text like the Qur'ān. There is no question of transposing it to what we live under today and saying that a believer may kill a non-believer with impunity. Further, the Qur'ān says, *To kill one single human being amounts to killing all mankind.* We ought to draw inspiration from the spirit of the laws that constituted the text and that are inspired by a great sense of justice, tolerance, realism, and intelligence.

16. Here is another word that has been elaborated to demonstrate the injustice of the Islamic system, insulting thereby the Arabic language, which sees only respect and dignity in the word. Among the Arabs, to have somebody in one's *dimma (dhimmī)* means to have him under one's protection but also to be responsible to the highest degree for his well-being, since he is regarded as a guest of honor. It is a serious attack on the honor of the Arab to fail in his duty vis-à-vis his guest, and an utter dishonor if he cannot protect him and dispense the best available treatment.

17. Lwazīr (2000), p. 52. My translation [into French].

18. Qur'ān: S. IV. 59.

19. Such criticism is in fact recurrent in the history of the Muslims. It was regularly developed by a few *ulemas* (scholars) whom the regime in power eventually assassinated. Yet such an attitude remains an exception and is diluted in the main current of the Doctors of Law, who preferred to compromise with such deviation rather than to expose Islam to division. It is now evident that their precautions were useless. The *umma* was in any case divided by

the deviations of a deviant regime that was supposed to defend the unity of the Muslim community. Among those opposed to despotism who defended the idea of the legitimacy of the power of the community (or the people) are, for instance, Arrazi (jurist and thinker, 1149–1209), Naisabūri, and, later in the nineteenth century, Muhammad Abdu (one of the fathers of the Islamic reawakening of the nineteenth century), to mention only a few among the less virulent.

20. It is important to stress that our author is Shiite. The Zaydites, to whom he belongs, are however less hostile to the Companions of the Prophet (grace and peace be upon him) than other hard-line Shiite branches. I disagree with the fact that he considered the election of Abu Bakr (God bless him) an error. Nonetheless, it is high time we overcame the mutual resentment between Shiites and Sunnis by learning mutual esteem, understanding, and tolerance. Many reproaches made by Lwazīr and other Shiites concerning our political deviations are justified.

21. Lwazīr (2000), p. 114.

22. TN : First major dynasty in medieval Islamic history, which established itself in Damascus after the death of Ali (God bless him), the last of the Rightly Guided Caliphs. The Umayyads ruled a growing empire from 41 A.H. (A.D. 661) until 132 A.H. (A.D. 750). Their dynastic name is derived from the grandfather of Abu Sufiyan, Mu'āwiya's father, whose name was Umayya bin Abd Shams. They were ultimately overthrown by the Abbassids. (Cf. Ian Richard Netton, *A Popular Dictionary of Islam,* 1997, Billing & Sons Ltd., Worcester).

23. TN: The title of Rightly Guided Caliphs is exclusively applied to the first four successors of the Prophet (grace and peace be upon him), namely Abu Bakr, Omar, Othman, and Ali (God bless them all). They are called rightly guided because they were elected and accepted by the community through the process of *shūrā,* however various may have been its forms in their election. In contrast, the rulers who followed them arbitrarily called themselves "caliphs" with a view to maintaining the illusion that they had been elected by the community. Just as the Prophet (grace and peace be upon him) named his four successors as Rightly Guided Caliphs in one of his premonitory *hadīths,* he stigmatized them as kings, with all the pejorative connotations that this term bears. In Islam, the title king refers to one who has usurped power without yielding to the principle of *shūrā,* whose most deciding agent is the free will of the community.

24. I do not wish to be misunderstood as calling into question immutable texts that cannot be subject to revision. I only wish to underline that such divine orders pertaining to social organization are, on one hand, very few and, on the other, subject to conditions that guarantee their practice within a strict framework of equity. I wish also to underline that our venerated imams had established rules of research of methodological rigor that are still valid. Therefore no iconoclastic desire or complex of cultural inferiority ought to direct our criticism.

25. Ibn al Attir, reported in Lwazīr (2000), p. 146.

26. *Akhbār 'Omar* [News of Omar], Dar Alfikr, Beirut, 1989, p. 59. My translation [into French].

27. Idem, p. 60.

28. Idem, p. 141.

29. Taha Hussein, *Ashaykhan* [the two Elders], p. 193, cited in Lwazīr (2000), p. 151.

30. Sorbonne Ph.D. in Economics, Iraqi graduate, and specialist in the analysis of the Islamic conception of economy.

31. Abdul Hâdi Gafouri, *Islam et économie : réflexion sur les principes fondamentaux de l'économie islamique* [Islam and economy: reflection on the basic principles of Islamic economy], Al Bouraq, 2000, p. 62.

32. Abu Yūsuf, *Al ahkam assultaniya,* cited in Gafouri (2000), p. 64.

33. There is a teaching of the Prophet (grace and peace be upon him) that underlines the attitude to be adopted towards those who utter the profession of faith: "There is no god but God and Muhammad is the Messenger of God." While war was at its height, a Companion thrust his sword into an enemy who, seeing he was defeated, uttered the expression. He knew that a Muslim must not kill another Muslim. The Companion justified himself before the Prophet, who was angry with his action, saying that the warrior did not believe what he said and that he uttered the profession of faith (*shahāda*) only to escape death. The Prophet (grace and peace be upon him) told him then the famous *hadīth*: "Have you opened his heart?"

34. Those among the Qurayshis who took part in the expansion of faith from the very beginning, and who had to quit their town for fear of persecution.

35. Lwazīr (2000), p. 144.

36. Henri Laoust, *Les schismes dans l'islam* [schisms in Islam], Payot, Paris, 1977, p. 9.

37. Gafouri (2000), p. 82.

38. Gafouri (2000), p. 81.

39. The author judges it would have been impossible to stage a *coup d'état* on the scale of the one perpetrated by Muʿāwiya had there not been beforehand an infrastructure that facilitated it. He refuses to consider the seizure of power by Muʿāwiya as a personal strategy of the latter. The entire book is concerned with a powerful Umayyad lobby.

40. Laoust (1977), p. 12.

41. Lwazīr (2000), p. 220.

42. To obey the chosen ruler and accept him as imam of prayer is part of the rights enjoyed by the ruler over the citizens when they accept the *al-bayʿa* (the political contract) = allegiance.

43. A common expression referring to those who disobeyed God and who deserve hell.

44. Lwazīr (2000), p. 221.

III. 3. IN THE LAND OF OUR BACKWASH

Whenever the savages of Louisiana want fruit, they cut the tree at its foot and pick the fruit.
There is despotic government for you!
Montesquieu

Times like our own are the sewers of history.
Victor Hugo

History, Stephen said, is the nightmare from which I am trying to awake.
James Joyce

O my country, country of noble and beauteous people!
You were once a vast sea; they have made brooklets of you.
Darham, Moroccan artist

A Very Heavy Heritage

Such is the conjuncture of circumstances that leads up to spectacular turning points in history. These cardinal moments, these tumbling instants, these axial points in the progress of history suck you in and knock you off balance in a movement no one can stop, no one can avoid. The axial period in Muslim history is rightly described as *al-fitna al-kubrā*, which can be translated literally as "the greatest ordeal."

As our critical sense has been anesthetized by centuries of despotic practice, we Muslims no longer grasp the disastrous and decisive effects of this crucial period. Our current illiteracy does not help matters. Our minds have been glossed over by the erosion—or rather, the corrosion—exerted on us by our political systems that stand in stark contrast with *shūrā*. We have been tamed so as to have no opinion. The more the centuries passed and our community grew in number, the more its spirit of initiative and creativity shrank away.

The more the times advanced, the more we have submitted to the political logic of a system in which one is everyone, and everyone is but one serving the vices and (very rarely) the virtues of those self-defined demigods who successively came to power to deaden our minds. Decadence inevitably awaited the chance to trip us up—and humanity as well, since we were supposed to pass on to humankind the Great Message that gives meaning to life and death, to the passage of mankind on this planet. We have failed in our role. The entire earth suffers from it, even the biosphere that energetically protests and reacts.

Our habitual minimizing of the deviation that took place at the level of power has proved the complete success of the *Fardiya* (power of one person) inaugurated by the Umayyads. Having long germinated in our side-tracked minds, this mystifying ideology has completely prevailed, since it has become an insurmountable taboo to call into question the current political regimes of our day, the exclusive preserve of one man or a few people. In the long run we have accepted being the docile subjects of tyranny without feeling the least moral ill-being.

It is true that the most efficient weapon in the hands of any usurping system is systematic terror. The machine is now so well oiled that the Muslim world is no longer even in need of fierce doorkeepers at the pay of its despots to set it on the "right" path, the path of unconditional submission to the ones holding power. Eventually, we totally internalized sacred obedience to a system of divine right. We now practice self-censorship without the tyrant having to call us to order. Dictatorship does not even have to use its huge means; we are all candidates to mediocracy, ready to cooperate in a fashion more despotic than the despot.

Such deviant power assassinated *shūrā*. A few years after Ali, there was no more room for the dynamic initiated by the Rightly Guided Caliphs at the epoch when the participation of the citizen was the rule, when the freedom of expression was in place. There remained on the scene of Islam only such torturers as Zyad Ibn Abih, al-Hajjāj, Ibn Hubeyra and other sadists serving a very ambitious regime, resolute and with no other principle than that of enduring. With thousands of skeletons in its closet, absolutism endured, biting into the flesh of the community, leaving indelible marks in the depths of the popular soul, and wreaking havoc.[1] *Al-mulk al-ʿād* [mordacious monarchy] was announced by the Prophet in one of his premonitory *hadīths*.

Thus the community passed from massacre to massacre, from abdication to remission, from torture to treason. So great was the psychological upheaval that even today in the 21st century we still feel its intensity in our flesh. In the depths of the hearts there exists an eternal funeral oration: "Hussayn! Hussayn! Hussayn!" the Shiites still sing today in tears. "Hussayn! Hussayn! Hussayn!" the hearts of the Sunnis echo, as they know full well the immense love of the Messenger (grace and peace be upon him) for this grandson given him by his daughter Fātima az-Zahrā' (God bless her).

The recognized biographers of the community report the touching image of the father, the grandfather—the Prophet (grace and peace be upon him)—full of goodness for his grandchildren. They report how quietly he continued his prayer with his granddaughter, Umāma, who was playing and climbing on his shoulders while he was prostrate. He kept her perched on his holy shoulders.

They also report that God's Messenger (grace and peace be upon him) loved to kiss Hussayn and Hassan and to clasp them in his arms, to his very holy chest. The Companions noticed the gleam of love in his eyes when he watched them playing and moving in front of him.

The Sunnis, not only the Shiites, know that the recommendations of the Prophet are very clear concerning *Āl al-Bayt*, his descendents.[2] *Say* (to the faithful), *no reward do I ask of you* (for my revelations) *except the love of my relatives* (and descendents), the Qur'ān says.[3]

For this reason, the assassination of the Prophet's grandsons has left indelible marks in the hearts and collective memory of the *umma*. Bloody *Karbala* remains alive in each Muslim conscience, in letters of fire, in pain and in bitterness. Unspeakable Ordeal! Great Ordeal!

In 680, having just withdrawn from Mecca, Hussayn headed for Kūfa after he had refused to swear allegiance to Yazid, whom his father Mu'āwiya had imposed on the community. He had supporters and sympathizers in the Iraqi city, and he decided to go to them with all his family and some friends in order to lead the uprising against this regime that enjoyed no legitimacy.

On October 10, 680, after having vainly conducted a week of bargaining with the commander of the Umayyad troops that hurried to stand in his way, Hussayn, the grandson of the Messenger (grace and peace be upon him), was massacred and fell as martyr to the great cause.

Many of those who pretended to support him retracted. Their excuse is perpetuated in the records of human high treason: "Our hearts are with you, but our swords are in the service of Yazid," they said.

Their swords mercilessly pierced the body of our beloved Hussayn, the grandson of the Messenger, the son of Fātima az-Zahrā' and Ali. His striking physical resemblance to his highly venerated grandfather did not prevent his enemies from bringing back on the point of a spear, like a vulgar hunting trophy, his severed head. The women of Hussayn's family, the beautiful Hashemites, were brought back with their heads uncovered.[4] In their torn hearts lay the endless pain of having lost all the males of their family. They experienced the immense humiliation of seeing the eyes of slave traders gazing lustfully at them. They could not imagine for a moment who they really were.

Divisions

The funeral procession still haunts our history, having eternally fixed the atrocity of that day in our imagination.

This major event was behind Islam's great schisms. It is this crucial moment that has triggered every kind of extremism. A veritable madness seized certain segments of the community. As *islam* is a comprehensive system that intricately links the political domain to the other domains, these political upheavals inevitably became theological upheavals.

There has been an extraordinary embroidery of theological opinions around a political event around which positions might have been limited. But as times of unrest are always favorable to opportunists who love to fish in troubled waters, currents of thinking developed, ranging from the most sensible to the most harebrained. If in this wave of replicated revolts some were justifiable and sensible, many others were the expression of inordinate emotional reaction. The latter gave rise, for instance, to such extremist groups as Murjism, the al-Azāriqa, the Zanādiqas, and many other forms of extremism, one begetting another, one rising in answer to the other.

It is not the object of this chapter to list these diffractions, so much the more that the manipulation of attitudes concerning them for political ends is certain. The particular matter at hand here is to emphasize that this period has played a decisive role in the configuration of current concepts and attitudes that in turn determine the Muslim thinking.

The Great Ordeal! The painful, heartbreaking Ordeal! Two trends would emerge in this implosion that occurred in the face of the deviation of power, namely Shiism and Sunniism.[5]

The Sunnis are in the habit of drawing a discreet veil over this period, abstaining from discussing it other than with tortuous verbosity.

Conditioned by the laudable enough concern to remain neutral about what happened between the Companions of the Prophet (grace and peace be upon him) for his sake, certain Sunnis have chosen a sort of silence that verges on foolishness and plays into the hands of unscrupulous despotism.[6]

Muslim ethics is essentially based on respect: self-respect, respect of the other, respect of the environment, and particularly respect of our Prophet (grace and peace be upon him), his Companions, and those who have preceded us in the Path of God. This reverence for the ancients testifies to the union of hearts throughout the ages, combined with what we now feel across borders with all Muslims. Our faith is indestructible with this spiritual fusion. There resides the heart of our Muslim ethics.

The question that the Sunnis ought to ask themselves is this: where do ethics stop and politics begin?

The Shiites, on the other hand, adopt an attitude opposite to that of the Sunnis, excluding all the Companions from the spiritual circle that joins the last generations with the first in a mystic alchemy. They recognize no ancestry to the Companions save Ali and a limited number of the friends of the Prophet (grace and peace be upon him), thus depriving themselves of so many sources of spiritual light that emanates from those holy men.

The very strong emotion aroused by the assassination of Ali, particularly beloved by the Prophet (and by the Sunnis as well), and his two sons, the grandsons of the Messenger, has turned the logic of love into one of hatred. They hate Yazid, the son of Mu'āwiya, and they retrospectively curse all those who preceded him in power, even when it comes to such giants as Omar and Abu Bakr. Disconsolate from the tragedy of *Karbala,* the Shiites express their grief by indiscriminate rejection of all the Companions, of whom, in their opinion, very few may be excused.

We must say that the emotional shock was so intense that the intervening centuries have failed to alleviate the pain. The Shiites, who beat their chests with grief in their religious feasts, mourn the one we all mourn: Hussayn, the illustrious descendant of our Prophet (grace and peace be upon him). Among them are those who still punish themselves, after all these centuries, by mortifying themselves in blood and tears for having failed to defend him.

Shiite mysticism is one of anger, anger vented against all the Companions, and it regards the family of the Envoy (grace and peace be upon him) as sacred and sometimes as divine. It is again here the expression of that spiritual fusion of the *umma* that challenges the temporal dimension. Yet the sentiment of hatred for the Companions, inherent to the Shiite faith, spoils the purity of their love for the restricted family of the Prophet. Against what the Sunnis regard as sacred (the Caliphate, which ought to have been a temporal function like any other), the Shiites erect the spiritual power of the Imams, whom they regard as sacred. During all these past centuries they have set the power of spiritual suggestion against the power of the sword.

That is where we are still now. To think that one day a complete synthesis might be made between Sunniism and Shiism is a facile fiction, since our wounds are of the kind that leave big scars. Yet an attempt to come closer by taking advantage of the strong points on either side remains possible to a large extent. Sunniism has a treasure to offer: that unconditional love of the Companions; Shiism offers a capital of dissidence that might breathe new life into the purring spirit of the Sunni masses. It is certainly not by mere accident that Hezbollah belongs to Shiism, and that the Iranian revolution is Shiite.

If Sunniism goes hand in hand with capitulation before despotism, Shiism is first and foremost the incubation of a devastating anger. A third path must now be sought. Meanwhile we continue to suffer, today more than ever, the burden of our very heavy historical heritage.

The Mark of Pharaoh

We can only truly understand the cause of our current decline if we go further back in our history. We will only find ourselves if we admit that the accursed mark of Pharaoh has inevitably corrupted the entire system. So long as power was in the service of the Message, we made great strides in our history. When the process was reversed—when despots began to use the Message for personal ends, deviations began.

The germs of our deviance were already astir in the days of Mu'āwiya. They were already lived in the sumptuous palaces of Hārūn ar-Rashīd; they were coiling in the folds of his gold-embroidered caftans and circulating in the magical corridors of his well-supplied harem. There is, alas, not the slightest trace of that in the official accounts of the history set down in the inner circles by hands at worst filled with dinars, at best trembling with fear, naturally in complete support of the regime's line.

Without entirely subscribing to the thinking of the contemporary Moroccan author Abdellah Laroui, we may acknowledge to his credit that he has well defined the role of the chronicler. No historian existed in our cultural heritage, at least until Ibn Khaldūn. The chronicler, according to Laroui, reports a flat image of the facts:

> The attitude of the chronicler towards the events is always the same. And it is from these *akhbār,* these pieces of news, that a synthesis is almost mechanically effected, according to the whims of a patron, in a dynastic history, a biographical collection, the history of a generation or a nation or a cultural era, or again a local, tribal or family history, or finally a geographical index. We have here a virtually perfect illustration of what is humorously called the "cut and paste" method.[7]

It is true that when you read history in the records of the great chroniclers like Tabarī, for instance, you feel a certain annoyance before this monotonous delivery of accounts that are not linked by any main theme or historical framework. Fragmented chronicles for a fragmented history!

We thus inherit an accumulation of impersonal accounts of unequal importance yet presented on the same scale of value. In the same detached style, for instance, we are informed that Sukayna, daughter of Hussayn, had very beautiful hair and that her father's head was slit by Yazid Ibn Muʿāwiya. Such unflappability, as we might call it, in the face of events produces an uninteresting and impersonal history, wanting in the power of events. So flat and blurred are its accounts that the fleeting periods of time it attempts to capture seem easily interchangeable. Laroui expresses the sensation this way:

> In the notes of many erudite studies, Baladuri, Yāqūt, Ibn Khalliqan, Ibn Hajar, Suyūtī and so on are put together as though no necessity justified such an association, as if all these chroniclers were of equal distance with regard to their subject. Not even chronology is taken into account; Ibn Hajar is often quoted before Tabarī . . . to such extent that history appears, no matter the level of synthesis, like the mere accumulation of accounts of singular events.[8]

All these facts—fear, corruption, the disorganized mind of the chroniclers—recommend that the perception we have of our history ought to be gathered around a methodical analysis that is likely to give us a meaning, stimulating thus in ourselves a need to find our way back again. The best way to regain the summit is to know the paths of descent.

A methodical repositioning that places power at the center of history will enable us to understand our past and present suffering. It will certainly be to our advantage to see again more seriously what our Prophet (grace and peace be upon him) said in this regard: "The knots of *islam* will come undone one by one. Each time one comes apart, people will cling to the other: the first knot to be untied will be power; the last will be the prayer."[9]

This statement has the advantage of being clear as to the decisive role of power in an Islamic system. Power is the major junction. When its nature is changed or usurped, it rends apart the social fabric at all the vital levels. "Rending apart" befits the metaphor used by the Prophet (grace and peace be upon him), who alludes to the knots that hold the dress. *Islam* is a dress for the *umma,* which is compared in another *hadīth* to a body. The Prophet (grace and peace be upon him) says: "In their affinity, mutual love and solidarity, the faithful may be compared to a body that reacts with fever and insomnia when one of its members is suffering."[10]

This sacred solidarity is one of the last knots to be severely tested by the domino effect produced by corrupted power. The system of inequalities engendered by despotic regimes eventually lacerates the body of the *umma.* To our spiritual impoverishment, occasioned by our progressive estrangement from the altruistic and humanistic teachings recommended by *islam,* is added our material indigence. Both work to compromise the sense of community.

In the state of decline of our history, the elite currently in power aggravate our illnesses by individualism and practice the policy of *après moi le déluge!*

If we wish to save the body—let alone its tattered dress—from disappearing, from being dissolved in the corrosive acid of heedlessness to God, of nonsense and blind imitation, indeed, from a final holocaust altogether, it is urgent that we revise, understand, and react!

The Impossible Example

Ali Lwazir explains that among the other factors that enabled despotism to establish its authority and subjugate people throughout all these centuries is an excessive idealization of the epoch of the Rightly Guided Caliphs. In a section entitled "The Impossible Example," he writes:

> The first representations of the Rightly Guided Caliphs endowed them with consciences freed from worldly burdens that soared in the air, surpassing in practice all the standards established for managing power. Thus the achievements of that period were transformed into models radiant with light that hovers over reality, inaccessible and intangible. Rendering them unique created the feeling that it was impossible to relive their example, thus sustaining a reality beyond attainable standards. We can readily understand how such representations created a mentality that regarded the era of the Rightly Guided Caliphs as an ideal that cannot be reproduced, an inaccessible model. It was logical, then, to seek a model that *was* accessible. The alternative within reach was obviously the system of the Umayyads and the other forms of power that followed.[11]

Our love of the Companions of the Prophet (grace and peace be upon him) led us to regard them as infallible supermen whose faith and practice of justice cannot be imitated. We are inclined to see in each of their decisions a sacred action, a divine inspiration that is inaccessible to ordinary mortals. Loving and revering the holy Companions of the Prophet (grace and peace be upon him) is admittedly part of our faith; yet to regard their deeds and gestures as sacred—to the extent of forgetting that they are human—has done a great disservice to the progress we ought to have made.

Such idealizing runs counter to the teaching of the Prophet (grace and peace be upon him). It has contributed to encouraging tyrants and normalizing a political reality which acknowledges the rule of one over everyone else. Accepting what does not conform to the Prophet's teaching has legitimized the aberrations of "the power of the individual." The Ummayads were keen to exploit this argument. They hastened to pose an "accessible form" against the "impossible model" of the first holy caliphs.

As no one could govern with the virtues of the Rightly Guided Caliphs, any prince could rule with the means of power at hand, namely violence and guile.

The weakness inherent in this representation of things is appreciable. The first error is that the role of the Prophet (grace and peace be upon him) in our judgment is not given the importance it merits. His advent as Messenger, and his presence within the community his Message perpetuates are the sole, the first and the last credit it has. As a consequence, no Companion nor any other member of the *umma* may aspire to saintliness except to the extent that he remains close to the home of mercy, the teaching of the Prophet (grace and peace be upon him).

The other consequence, related to the fact that the spiritual power of the Prophet (grace and peace be upon him) does not end with his death, is that each member of his *umma* is capable of attaining spiritual purity so long as he wholeheartedly and sincerely observes his path. It is even evident that the absence of physical contact with our beloved Prophet favors privileged relationships. That is attested by the *hadīth* that announces the coming one day of the Brothers of the Messenger, those who would believe in him without having met him.

Moreover, the idyllic view of the era of the Rightly Guided Caliphs owes to a misinterpretation of the nature of the society created and desired by the Prophet (grace and peace be upon him). His teaching includes a legacy of a spirit of group solidarity. The spiritual heritage he left to his Companions is a shared heritage, a force that can be effective only to the extent that unity takes precedence over disunity. At the level of government—and particularly here—the caliphate is in no way to be the expression of individualism but rather one of a communitarian choice animated by a communitarian conscience.

A Revealing Barometer

The gravity of our political deviations can be measured by several indices. The status of women bears eloquent testimony to the deviation of the nature of power and its repercussions on the social aspect of our life as Muslims. The status of women is traditionally recognized as a powerful barometer of the decadence or civility of civilizations.

As an identifiable point of the reference, the period of the Abbasids stands more prominently in our diverted and manipulated memory than that of the Prophet (grace and peace be upon him). The reign of Hārūn ar-Rashīd flatters our feeling of membership and fires up our collective imagination. Evocation of this epoch is always associated with the Thousand and One Nights. It is synonymous with splendor, jewels, and especially with beautiful slaves and palace intrigue. In the curricula of Muslim countries the reign of this sovereign is unanimously presented as the zenith of Islam.

This approach to our Muslim past is doubly misleading: (1) we gauge the history of *islam* by purely material values while relegating spiritual values to a dark corner and regarding the spiritual quest as a matter of vocation or eccentricity; and (2) we normalize our intellectual and emotional relationships with a system whose nature and legitimacy ought to be called into question.

This myth further undermines our moth-eaten memory. To cite but one example of the numerous repercussions of this official view ingrained in our Muslim subconscious, we will touch on the status of women, thus opting for an indirect approach so as to broach a subject that concerns an entire *umma* in which the first victim of its decline is woman.

In the history of declining civilizations, women are always the scapegoat. Our Muslim societies are no exception to this rule. It will be to our advantage to develop our history heuristically; to do so we must consider the upheavals experienced by women in the land of Islam as being intimately dependent on the conception of power and its involution from *shūrā* to autocracy.

The Prophet (grace and peace be upon him) came to rescue the Arab woman from the limbo of history so as to make her a full and responsible human being, ready to assume the heavy responsibility incumbent upon those who make sense of life.[12] The system that came to replace *shūrā* made it its duty to erase the outlines of a nascent society wherein the woman is man's equal in "the ordering of Good and the pursuit of Evil."[13] It encouraged an enslaving mentality that considers woman a common if beautiful commodity of speculation.

The goodwill of the princes who usurped power as from Mu'āwiya went against the Qur'ānic teachings that recommend the progressive abolition of slavery. The mark of Pharaoh in this domain is most profound, as the first victim of this degeneration from the top is surely woman.

The *jāhiliya*[14] that the Prophet (grace and peace be upon him) came to remedy was characterized by a state of deep ignorance and perdition of the godless. Ignorance as such—both of sense and of essence—has always had as a corollary social violence and the law of the strongest. *Islam* came to create a new balance and to promote new values by censuring despotism, whether political or chauvinistic in practice. The link between these two expressions of ignorance is so strong that it engenders a perfectly clear dynamic of cause and effect; the liberation of woman from the yoke of tradition can be considered only in the sense of a global struggle that aims to eradicate archaic and authoritarian political systems.

It is easy to subscribe to this argument once we examine the historical relationship between the deterioration of the status of the Muslim woman and that of power. But let us first examine the pre-Islamic period. We note at first that, with few exceptions, all the peoples of the earth had adopted the same attitude with regard to woman, an attitude of distrust and suspicion, attraction and repulsion similar to the attitude toward the dark forces of nature.

These sentiments were expressed in different ways, but the watchword was always the reification of the woman. For the Arabs of the *jāhiliya,* this reification was a bit less abject than that of the Romans or the Greeks. Yet it was no less cruel. They were so jealous of their women, whom they regarded as properties, that they would not hesitate to bury them alive. The newborn girl child was at the mercy of the *paterfamilias,* who held the power of life and death over her. Among certain tribes, he sometimes even buried her for fear of dishonor, should he deem that necessary, without the least reproach or worry—quite the opposite. Many settled and rich tribes who could do without the woman's social work used to bury her symbolically when they did not inter her physically. The practice of *khidr* was widespread in Arabia. *khidr* is the word that describes the bearing and the house of the woman who never goes out of her household.

The example of Khadija (God bless her), a free and independent woman, the first spouse of the Prophet and the first support to his cause, was not commonplace in the Qurayshi nobility to which she belonged. It is certainly not by pure coincidence, however, that she was elected by God to be on the path of the future Messenger (grace and peace be upon him). Non-believers might call this a coincidence, an accident not representative of the image of the woman advocated by *islam*. A predestination, we would reply, that serves as proof that the woman that *islam* wishes is far from being the thing of "caliphs" and men, but an active actor in the progress of history.

It is equally revealing that the Muslim community of that time declared the year of the death of Khadija (God bless her) a "Year of Sadness." This was uncommon in a society that Omar (God bless him) recognized as deeply misogynist: "Before *islam*," he said, "we used to attach little importance to women." The same Omar who before his conversion to *islam* buried his daughter, the same Omar who admitted the chauvinistic nature of his society and from whom women used to hide behind the back of the Prophet (grace and peace be upon him), is the Omar who during his mandate appointed a woman to head the financial administration of a large city.

This change is the result of the education the community received from the Prophet. Successfully and progressively, the Messenger of *islam* rescued men from the prison of their vices, their habits, their ill-fated customs. Left to their own devices, their natural instincts would have engendered and unleashed destructive forces in governing a society where the weakest had no place, and where the law of the strongest was the sole valid rule. The weakest could only submit or escape an unenviable lot by means of tortuous paths of hatred, treachery, ill-will, and guile.

Jahiliya also describes a society where distrust and violence are exacerbated by want and need, a society where men live by submitting women to their physical might, where tribe crushes tribe, where man fights man, where barbarity prevails. Muhammad (grace and peace be upon him) came to guide the Companions and the Muslims with the might of love, to free them from the vicious circle of violence and self-centeredness. Yet he behaved towards them with the care of the teacher who is concerned about making progress without brutal ruptures or traumatic shock-treatment.

As our Prophet (grace and peace be upon him) was fully aware that the Arabs were captious regarding the status of women, his gentleness was even more in evidence in that highly sensitive area than elsewhere. By ordering the Companions to allow women to go to the mosque, he posed a veritable moral dilemma for the Muslims. The concern to obey the Prophet (grace and peace be upon him) and his teaching prompted a dynamic of woman's liberation and promotion from the state of a thing to that of an active citizen.

When we consider that the mosque was the very heart of the nascent community—the locus of meeting and social life as well as its place of worship—we realize the scope of this apparently trivial commendation. The Prophet (grace and peace be upon him) was inviting women to enter, by the main gate, into a social field hitherto exclusively reserved for men.

Before this, women did not exist in this field, since social life frequently consisted of waging war and engaging in trade—which amounted to the same thing, considering the state of insecurity endured by the desert caravans, where raids were common. The Message of Peace with God and with the Other made woman a partner of man in this society of growing confidence.

Instigating the presence of women in the mosque was first of all proof of their equality before God, Who received them in His House the same way as men. Women were not only securing public space and times that had been exclusively male preroga-tives; they were also entering the sacred space as God's guests. What further annoyed certain Companions about these three acquisitions was no doubt the fact that the dawn and night prayers (*Fajr* and *'Isha'*) were performed at times where it was unthinkable to allow women out in a society particularly touchy in matters of honor.[15]

The community then lived in constant transformation; it was becoming accustomed to obeying the counsels of the Prophet as matters of Islamic Law, since *He says nothing that does not come from God.*[16]

Liberated, Responsible Women

The Message fashioned a generation of women among whom Aisha (God bless her) is the symbol par excellence, a generation of responsible and free women. *Islam* educated magnificent women who knew their rights as well as their obligations, and who perfectly understood their roles in establishing that society of confidence. With admirable force, they took hold of God's gift to them of their humanity, at last recognized, and their dignity.

We thus had such figureheads as Um Haram. This great lady of Islam, were we to cite her alone, did not content herself with entering the public arena as a full believer responsible, just like any other Muslim, man or woman, for the life of the community. She even requested the Prophet (grace and peace be upon him) to beseech God so that she might die with a group to whom he predicted martyrdom in distant lands. The Messenger (grace and peace be upon him) found it natural to answer her request. Dozens of examples of female disciples of the Prophet[17] can be mentioned.

It is also interesting to note that if Paradise was expressly promised by God's Envoy (grace and peace be upon him) to ten men of his entourage, it was promised to twenty women. If we know what such promise represents in the eyes of a society that defines itself above all as being turned towards the Ultimate Life, the status of the woman takes all the more significance.

Aisha, this personification of *islam* par excellence, left (and will eternally leave) an indelible mark on our memory. If the Companions vowed her particular respect, it was no doubt because the Prophet (grace and peace be upon him) vouchsafed her singular love. Yet that was not the sole reason for their admiration. Aisha had exceptional personality and intelligence. With legendary precociousness she had been initiated by her father into the Arab genealogy and was ranked among the scholars of Arabic language and literature. A great number of *hadīths* were memorized and transmitted by her to the Companions, who readily came to consult her about the most delicate theological questions.

Since the family is a determining factor in the development of personality, we understand how privileged Aisha's relationship with her parents was. Her birth within one of the rare Muslim families completely supportive of *islam* enabled her to grow up in an atmosphere where woman was no longer the plaything of the sexist and chauvinistic man. Abu Bakr, her venerated father (God bless him), was reputed for his gentle nature, very close to the *fitra,* and for his absolute confidence in the first statements of the Prophet (grace and peace be upon him). Surely he was *as-Siddīq*—a kind of superlative that may be translated "extremely confident." Indeed, he was the Companion par excellence, recognized as such in the Qur'ān account of his accompanying the Messenger during his flight from Mecca.

Assiddîk, confident in the teachings of Muhammad (grace and peace be upon him), unhesitatingly repudiated forever the typically Arab view of the daughter as a curse. The love he had for his daughter Aisha was touching.

It is reported that one day, as Aisha kept him company, he spoke of 'Omar bnu al-Khatāb, saying, "There is no one on earth I love more than Omar." As Aisha had doubtless gestured disapproval, he corrected himself exclaiming, "What have I said?" Keen as was her wont, Aisha hastened to repeat his statement. He quickly corrected himself to prove the love he felt for her. "I meant to say, more agreeable to me than Omar, my children, closest to my heart."[18]

This kindness of a father for his daughter is striking proof of saintliness in an Arabia of rough and steely ways often fatal to women. Abu Bakr was the worthy disciple of the Prophet (grace and peace be upon him) who used to manifest in public his great love for his daughters, notably Fatima (God bless her). He would stand up to offer her his seat, approach her all smiles, and kiss her on the hand or forehead.

In those days the Prophet was inaugurating a new era for woman, the era of the Message that denounces the inequitable practices suffered by the oppressed of the system, be they slaves or women. We are told in the Qur'ān: *When news is brought to one of them, of* (the birth of) *a female child, his face darkens, and he is filled with inward grief! With shame does he hide himself from his people, because of the bad news he has had! Shall he retain it on* (sufferance and) *contempt, or bury it in the dust? Ah! what an evil* (choice) *they decide on!*[19]

Another verse, mentioning the Day of the Last Judgment, says: *When the female* (infant), *buried alive, is questioned—for what crime she was killed* . . . (Then) *shall each soul know what it has put forward.*[20]

212

Thus owing to the Qur'ān and the practical teaching of the Prophet (grace and peace be upon him) in his *sunna,* the community gradually developed a new concept of the role of woman by regarding her as the equal of man in the sight of God and His Messenger (grace and peace be upon him). The specificity of her status distinguished her only to the extent that her function in the family and society assigns to her duties that differ from those of the man; this in no way presupposes a difference in essence or dignity.

The momentum initiated by the women of the Prophet's lifetime would continue into the advent of the Caliphate. History portrays levelheaded, kindhearted women taking over from the generation of the *sahābiyāt* (female companions). Among second-generation women, *tābi'iyāt,*[21] stand countless women of outstanding personality competing with men in the realm of knowledge and active participants in the life of the community. The history of the Muslims is studded with the luminous names of women who in their wake left generations of women to come a glimmer of hope and evident proof of the esteem *islam* has for them: Aisha bint Talha, Fātima bint Sirīn, Sukayna bint al-Hussayn, Rābi'a al-'Adawiya, and many others. These perfect women took active part in the life of their community; they have made their mark on the history of the liberation of woman initiated by the Prophet (grace and peace be upon him), a liberation that reconciled her with God, her faith and her role as builder of the future.

A Cruel Relapse

The destiny of woman that had been promoted by the Prophet (grace and peace be upon him) ended, alas, with the advent of despotism embodied in Mu'āwiya. The respect we owe the Companions surely allows us to judge him sharply. But criticism is not necessarily synonymous with hatred; our Muslim perception of the world makes us see each past and ended action with a certain fatalism. Free will affects the here and now; as for the future we may only speak of destiny.

The last specimens of the adult and responsible woman were moreover decidedly eloquent in their criticism of Mu'āwiya. But the decline and retreat of the Muslim woman had begun. Before long, the brutal loss of her vital momentum would bear out the warning of the Prophet (grace and peace be upon him), who on his deathbed said by way of recommendation and premonition, "Be mindful of the ordeal of women."

Not totally cured of its old natural penchants, the community would soon make a chauvinistic interpretation of this recommendation, oblivious of the fact that Muhammad (grace and peace be upon him) could not possibly have exhorted anything so contrary to what he had defended all his life. This *hadīth* may simply be listed among those through which the Messenger informed the Muslims of the ordeals that awaited them, going to the far end of his mission as *bashīr* and *nadhīr.*[22] If Muslims have so misinterpreted the Messenger's recommendations and warnings, it is because they have forgotten the very essence of the Qur'ānic Message, and they suffer from a fragmented view of their faith. It is precisely the profound dimension of *islam* our misogynous exegetes so desperately lack. When this dimension *is* taken into account, we have in our heritage such scholars as al-Ghazālī (Algazel), who reconsidered the status of woman with relatively[23] benevolent eyes. Today, we have Qaradawi in Egypt, Kubayssi in Iraq.

The status of woman was not only fashioned very far from this deeper meaning. It underwent the passions of the princes who perpetuated disastrous traditions and instituted practices at extreme odds with the Qur'ānic Message. How sound are these words of Zakia Daoud, supporting the idea that the history of the status of the Muslim woman is essentially political:

> In the three cases of authoritarian regimes that used the situation of women to further strengthen and perpetuate their own existence, it was the women who paid for their mistakes. It is in the soft underbelly of the inner seraglios that the tyrants' extravagant behaviors are proved true, and where the slow composition and recomposition of the social processes is best measured. The problems thus faced today are part of the dispute between civil societies and the regimes in power.[24]

Wallowing in the luxury of a corrupted and corrupting power, the princes superbly ignored the teachings of the Qur'ān that had been revealed precisely to release man from his shackles in the literal and figurative sense. Their *futūhāt*[25] went to their heads. The great flood of beautiful female prisoners of war reawakened the universal instincts to possess women. *Islam* recommended keeping the prisoners of war for a certain time within the Muslims families with a view to making them appreciate *de visu* what the life of a Muslim is about, and what it offers in terms of psychological balance and answers to anxieties. The objective was to initiate them into a lifestyle based on striking a balance between the spiritual and the temporal, between transcendence and daily life, and then to set them free to return home as informed missionaries of *islam*.

Detention became the rule, as it enabled these princes to take advantage of a kind of feminity that was refused to the free Arab women: the symbol of scared and misdirected dignity. The morals of the court rubbed off onto Muslim society, especially in cities that had long struggled within a hyperchauvinist Arab aristocracy.

It is true that the status of woman varied from country to country, from rural to urban conditions, and from region to region. But the prevailing culture, reaching back to the *khudūr* of history,[26] was one of woman-as-object. Ibn Khaldūn's adage, "societies embrace the faith of their kings," aptly applies to the status of woman. As a kind of what he calls *dīn al-inqiyād* (imitated faith), the whole society, somehow or other under the influence of this unconscious imitation, was imbued with a misogynistic culture that reproduced *jahilian* traditions while imagining itself on the path of *islam*.

Lapses

Semantics is useful here in witnessing a deviation that flowed outwards from the inner circles of society to its broad periphery. The concept of the *wali,* mistakenly translated as "guardian (of a minor)," may serve to demonstrate an etymological lapse that reflects comparable lapses of faith, system, and society. This later, perverted notion of *wali* rightly makes the hair of more than one feminist in the land of Islam stand on end, but they might be reconciled by its original sense, derived from a root meaning of supportive proximity. In the Qur'ānic verse that identifies God as the "*wali* of the believers," the sense of the term is surely not one of "guardian" but one of "support."

Another verse further reveals this meaning: *The believers, men and women, are protectors,*[27] *one of another.*[28] It is ridiculous to translate the phrase as "mutual guardians."

The principle of the *wali* was adopted by the majority of the imams in the first sense of "support" or "supportive friend." They regarded it as a means to protect the woman, not to bully her, diminish her, nor make her an eternal minor under supervision. Marriage used to lie within a logic of social links involving the two families. It was not merely a binary union. We may, however, upbraid Muslim jurisprudence for having failed to keep a *hadīth* as important as that of the *wali.* The Messenger (grace and peace be upon him) ordered: "Do take into account the opinion of mothers in the marriage of their daughters."[29] The main interested person remains certainly the daughter who gets married. Islam just wants to reinforce its social relations and institute a dynamic to which partake all the members of the two families. We equally begin to wonder why in practice we have wandered so far from this framework that makes the family a protecting nest, not a cruel jail for the woman, mother and daughter alike.

Why then has the concept developed this way? The semantic lapse from *wali* as support to *wali* as guardian is not an innocent one. It accompanied the political and social lapse that saw the revival of a most merciless patriarchal tradition. History is certainly not linear but really made of twists and turns. Back to spiritual square one, the Arab-Muslim world abandoned the integration of woman into its social life and returned to its pathological jealousy of females. The privileged class, making decisions for everybody, decided to cloister the woman once again.

Originally meant to protect the woman—by providing a male counterbalance in a set of relations where the psychological dimension must not be overlooked—and to be a moral support in case of dispute between the two parties of the marriage treaty, the *wali* became, by this return to *jāhiliya,* her torturer, her guardian. His guardianship, combining with that of an equally chauvinistic husband, brought about an objective alliance between the males across history and across their different status.

Between males, whether *wali* or husband, the complicity that developed was reinforced by an increasingly difficult economic situation. Considered by the males of her own family as one more mouth to feed, the woman is virtually sold to her husband. The *wali,* meant to be a refuge, is rarely concerned with the suffering of his ward. He prefers not to see anything as long as the "mouth to feed" is where she belongs. In this legal, historical, and economic imbroglio, the entire fair sex is liable to falling prey to male violence, an expression of violence that descends from the very top of the social ladder and lurks in the depths of hearts where faith has wilted.[30]

The circle of violence, physical and moral, slowly closes around women, the traditional victims of decadent societies. The pressure issuing from a corrupt and violent regime finds domestic expression in a deep deviation from the spousal relationship which, according to the Qur'ān, is to be one of tenderness and mercy.

A Moroccan proverb, doubtless with equivalents in the other Muslim countries because of their common history, says: "People humiliate me and I humiliate 'wisha,[31] my little woman."

Such is the *fitna* of the woman alluded to by the Prophet (grace and peace be upon him). It is the ordeal of the woman we failed to protect, or whom we eventually stifle while trying to protect her.

Confronted with the stir of the Great Ordeal, our imams of the first periods of *islam* promulgated the principle of *saddu ath-tharī'a*[32] just as a country in a state of war declares the state of emergency. Undoubtedly, they were really concerned about the fate of the *umma*. Thoughtful and certainly brave, they were seeking a solution to a real crisis. But the state of emergency has become a permanent state. The rights granted to the woman by the Prophet (grace and peace be upon him) were consigned to the scrap heap of history, a history that continues to slide now worse than ever. Depriving women of their rights in the name of a state of emergency that became normal was to shake the structures of the Muslim community.

Women are the wombs of the society in the literal and in the figurative sense (even truer in the figurative sense than in the literal). Their mirror, so to speak, is society. When they are beaten, marginalized, humiliated, deprived of their rights, despised, and illiterate, their lot inevitably rubs off on their environment. They cannot pass on the torch of faith, courage, the fighting spirit, and intelligence. They can no longer be the guarantors of a balanced family that produces a healthy society full of promise.

A society that treated its women that way deserved to be colonized, which came about like a slap of destiny. So long as there was no differing civilization that might function as a mirror and suggest a way of life in stark contrast to the established reality, the fatalist mentality could reproduce itself infinitely across the centuries. Woman underwent such marginalization as naturally as she breathed the air. She did not even suffer from it. She accepted being cloistered by a community that had reverted to its original misogyny, which she herself joins at the age of menopause so as to become even more ferocious toward her own sex.

There is no worse torturer of the woman than the woman as mother-in-law and ignorant of God. Having reached the sole honorable status (that of mother) which a society of *fitna* grants to her fellow women, she ignobly abuses the status. This mother infantilized her male child and eventually stifled him through showering on him the excessive tenderness she should normally have shared with her husband. Ignorance, frustration, and the idealization of the future husband, on whom the mother transfers all her suffering and pins all her hopes of being respectable, create an intolerable situation for the poor spouse. The latter will then have to suffer from the conceits of the spoilt son and the cantankerous character of the mother-in-law who will express the aversion she feels for her own image of the woman by the systematic humiliation of her daughter-in-law.

Even intrigue has a social color. From the bottom up, save the exception that proves the rule, the atmosphere in the home is one of mistrust; nothing is spared so as to give vent to suppressed angers and frustrations.[33] If, thanks to affluence, palace intrigues among women are relatively fluid and muted, in the cottages they are quick to tear each other's hair out. The ill-fated services of the *fqihs*,[34] well equipped with disgusting potions to which the unfortunate spouses have recourse, often go as far as poisoning. Were we to disinter the mothers-in-law and the husbands of long ago (and today as well, by the way) and to conduct serious examination on the causes of their death, we would certainly be greatly surprised.

Such is what they have managed to do to our societies and our families once they severed from us the lively sources of our faith. It is not because woman is ill-tempered that she is cantankerous, or that she resorts to unscrupulous procedures. The superficial woman, the superstitious woman, the crafty woman, the lying woman, the woman who indulges in sorcery, all are purely the product of a chauvinistic society that failed to realize the *fitna* of its women. Responsibility ought not to be cast on the woman but rather on our wandering, all of us, from the vital teachings of our Prophet (grace and peace be upon him), from the spirit of the Message.

NOTES

1. The Muslim chronicle relates that one of the champions of the Umayyad cause was struck by a pebble thrown by one of the faithful while he was delivering the Friday sermon (which, then as now, consisted in praising the "caliph"). He closed the doors of the mosque and cut off the fingers of all those who had come to pray.

2. Literally "People of the House." Salman, the converted Persian who became a Companion particularly appreciated by the Prophet, was declared a member of *al Lbayt*.

3. Qur'ān: S. XLII. 23.

4. This was an insufferable affront, an act of aggression towards a Muslim woman as serious as rape. Souha Béchara, celebrated author of *Résistante* [resisting woman] and a Muslim woman who does not wear the veil, stated this fact in a Swiss program in which she was asked what was the worst suffering of the Palestinian women tortured in the Israeli prisons.

5. Lwazīr (2000) supports a highly interesting argument that accuses the despotic regimes of having invented these two notions by manipulating the interpretation of history. The link between Sunniism and the four imams generally considered to be its founding fathers is the pure fabrication of the Abbassid regime, which had taken over manipulation and demagoguery from the Umayyads. The reality was more complicated; the relationship between the Sunni

and the Shiite imams was much more intimate than they wished it to be known. Imam Abu Hanifa (God bless him), for instance, supported Imam Zayd and militated all his life—even at the cost of it—in favor of the descendents of Ali and the Prophet.

6. I wish to emphasize that Shiism is a vast philosophy of history and of *islam* that merits much more attention. Such designation applies to a range of very varied attitudes. Beyond the major branch of the imāmates of Iran, Pakistan, Lebanon, and an important diaspora, Shiism is a loose conglomeration that ranges from the Ismaeli sect with its quasi-pagan practices to the Zaydi doctrine (very close to Sunniism) and even includes a group that does not recognize the Prophet as Messenger and accuses him of having usurped this role from Ali.

7. Abdellah Laroui, *Islam et histoire* [Islam and history], Éd. Bibliothèque Albin Michel in *Idées* 1999, p. 42.

8. Laroui (1999), p. 42.

9. *Hadith* reported by Imam Ahmad and Tabarani as related by Abu Umāma Bahili.

10. *Hadith* reported by Bukhārī and Muslim as related by Numan bnu Bashîr.

11. Lwazīr (2000), p. 29.

12. I write this knowing of the circulation in the Islamic countries of ready-made ideas concerning putting the woman under guardianship and her eternal status as minor. The polemic surrounding the topic is volatile; the problem cannot be discussed in depth in a single work. Women live among the interstices of a particular history that is made of breaks and lapses. During an unstable course of events against which the jurisprudential schools struggled they have lost their rights—but this is not the subject of this book. I shall defer a study of the complicated issue of the woman in *islam* until, God willing, I can devote a prospective book exclusively to it.

13. *L'ordonnance du Bien et le pourchas du Mal,* in Jacques Berque's phrase, renders the divine order addressed to the Muslims to "order Good and combat Evil."

14. *Jahiliya* is the state of ignorance and, inevitably, of violence that characterizes impious societies. It is commonly translated as "the pre-Islamic period."

15. *Qays,* a bashful lover of the pre-Islamic era, was for life refused by his tribe permission to marry his lady friend for having dared to mention her in his poems.

16. Qur'ān: S. LIII. 3.

17. Arabic distinguishes between male (*sahâbi*) and female (*sahâbiya*) Companion or disciple of the Prophet (grace and peace be upon him).

18. *Akhbâr Omar* (1989).

19. Qur'ān: S. XVI. 58.

20. Qur'ān: S. LXXXI. 8–9, 14.

21. *Tabiî* and *tabiya* refer respectively to the man and woman belonging to the second generation of *islam*.

22. *Bashîr* and *nadhîr,* lit. "one who gives glad tidings" and "one who informs of punishment in the Life to come and warns of deviations in the present life."

23. I say "relatively" since nobody easily escapes the prevailing social environment: tradition weighs equally heavy for even the most open-minded *mujtahidîn*.

24. Zakia Daoud, *Féminisme et politique au Maghreb; sept décennies de lutte* [feminism and politics in North Africa: seven decades of struggle], EDDIF, Casablanca, 1996, p. 8.

25. Translated as conquests by incomprehension, or by eclipse of the Islamic phenomenon. Cf. II.3., "Rerouting History."

26. *Khudūr* or "curtains" refers to life retirement, the antecedent of the harem.

27. *Awliya* is the plural of *wali*.

28. Qur'ān: S. IX. 71.

29. TN: Reported by Abu Dāwad in his Suman.

30. In addition to the destabilizing of cultural relationships occasioned by globalization, the context of underdevelopment and unemployment aggravates the status of the woman today more than ever.

31. The term *'wisha,* diminutive of Aisha, may be affectionate, but it often expresses lack of consideration and respect.

32. Arabic phrase for a state of emergency, when certain recognized rights or practices are put on the back burner for such compelling reasons as, for instance, safeguarding the unity of the community.

332. I know very well that there are many exceptions. Certain Muslim peoples whose traditions are not chauvinistic and certain families who have remained close to the sources do not correspond to this black image; but the exceptions prove the rule. To proclaim that the woman in the land of Islam has always been well treated amounts to burying one's head in the sand or adopting cant.

34. This is another, very revealing semantic lapse. *Fqih* means an erudite person, a scholar of *islam*.

III. 4. THE MESSAGE, THE COMPASS

A society without religion is like a ship without a compass.
Napoleon I

Anything incomprehensible may nonetheless be true.
Blaise Pascal

Secrets that are especially malicious hide in the light.
Jean Giono

Parallel Worlds

Have you heard about the man who mistook his wife for his hat? This is not a joke; it is the very serious story of a patient whose case was related in a special report published in *Le Monde*.[1] In one of the articles in this report, Eric Fottorino writes:

> One of the most disturbing cases related by Sachs is the story of the music teacher who actually mistook his wife for a hat. At the end of a consultation, the neurologist writes, "He took his wife's head and attempted to lift it to his own and put it on. . . . His wife regarded him as if it were a matter of habit." In reality, the teacher's visual area was so damaged that he was unable to recognize faces for what they were. He no longer had any sense of perspective, but lost (or found) himself again in details: he spotted Churchill by his cigar, Einstein by his hair and mustache, his own brother by his typically square chin.[2]

Le Monde's special report on the human brain holds many other surprises in store for us concerning the precariousness of our neurons. Aside from a few gratuitous Darwinian remarks, the descriptions it contains are very unsettling. Other alarming pathological cases are examined, such as the case of the woman who lost the faculty to see in three dimensions and for whom movement no longer meant anything. She saw objects perfectly well, but did not understand that they could move: "She also had difficulty pouring tea because she could not see the level rise in the cup. In the same way, she could not easily cross the road as she did not see cars moving."

Harrowing on several counts as well is the case of that lady who lost her sense of personality, was no longer able to feel her body, and who lived with the terrible impression of being disembodied.

In the report we also read the dreadful story of the hemiplegic who complained "to have awakened to find in his bed someone's amputated leg. When he pushed it away, it followed him and is now attached to him . . . after losing awareness of his paralytic limb, he incessantly called it an 'imitation or facsimile.'"

Disturbing is the case of those numerous patients who can see colors only in half of their visual field. Their disease bears the name "hemiachromatopsia" ("hemi" meaning half). Those who suffer from achromatopsia (colorless vision) are plunged in a complete monochromatic world: "The patient sees life in gray, without the means of finding a trace of green or red in his flights of fancy. His dreams also take place in dreadful greyness."

The most striking example in this range of neurological horror remains, surely, the case of patients who have lost any memory of their left side. For them the left part of the world simply does not exist. For instance, a man with this condition will shave his right cheek but forget his left, or he will slip on his right sleeve and leave the other trailing since it does not exist in his mind.

Outrageous, disturbing, these terrible diseases could be obvious signs for one who seeks the truth of his being. God says in the Qur'ān: *Soon We will show them our Signs in the* (furthest) *regions* (of the earth), *and in their own souls, until it becomes manifest to them that this is the Truth.*[3]

The various examples of blindness, due to a weakness of the brain, ought to remind us that not only is the human brain very vulnerable, it also is unable to perceive all truths. Thus our perception always remains relative and dependent on a chemical equilibrium or disequilibrium. In short, it is only what is consistent with the law of majority that we call truth, reason, or standard.

If all human beings were color-blind or suffered from achromatopsia, there would have to be prophets to speak to them of colors. If all the human beings perceived only their right side, there would have to be prophets to teach them that they have a left side.

In his immortal book, *L'homme cet inconnu* [Man the unknown], Alexis Carrel, treating science in an original way, proves the existence of parallel worlds. One need only have recourse to a device that can detect infrared rays to plunge into an absolutely strange world.

Is it not a spark of the sacred that advanced technology enables us to see? Is it not the glimpse of the divine that the microscope or telescope enables us to detect? Surely these are the "signs" the Qur'ān speaks of, the "horizons" cited in the verse. The horizon of the infinitesimal causes us as much vertigo as the infinitely great. Einstein made for us a breach into a parallel world that has disclosed many others. Quantum Physics widens this breach and engages us in an unaccustomed world in which all certainties disintegrate, notwithstanding their being well established on rational equations.

The Nobel Prize winning physicist Niels Bohr[4] had a significant answer to the enigmas that plagued researchers in his field. Jean Guitton relates, "When anyone came to expound a new idea for solving the mysteries of the quantum theory, he would jokingly say, 'Your theory is insane, but not enough to be true.'"[5]

The quantum theory was able to be developed precisely because it abandoned the beaten track of the rigid mind fixed on infallible Cartesianism. It is an attempt to designate what is imperceptible. The renowned astrophysicians Igor and Grichka Bogdanov disclose a world that belongs as much to hallucination as to equation, a world that produced the sort of vertigo we feel when confronted by the convolutions of the human brain related at the beginning of this chapter.

Grichka tries to explain to lay persons like us something that, we must admit, requires an open mind:

> The success of quantum theory lies in the fact of its being developed aside from, and most often against, ordinary thinking. That is why there is something "insane" in this theory, something previously beyond science. Without being clearly aware of it, it is our representation of the world that is at stake and begins irreversibly to topple. . . . Let us take a flower; if I decide to put it out of my sight in another room, it continues to exist all the same. At least this is what ordinary experience allows me to take for granted. Yet quantum theory says quite another thing: it maintains that if we were to observe this flower with sufficient fineness, that is, at the level of the atom, its profound reality and existence are intimately linked to the way we observe it.[6]

The chapter is titled *L'esprit dans la matière* [mind in matter]. The incredible discoveries which this explored matter provides seem to make some scientists, despite their very superior IQs, lose their minds. The experiment of what physicists call the Planck[7] wall is most amazing. Grichka gives an idea of the limits of human understanding:

> Physicists haven't the slightest idea of what might explain the appearance of the universe. They can go as far back as 10^{-43} second but not beyond. They then collide with the famous Planck wall, so named because the illustrious German physicist had been the first to indicate that science was incapable of explaining the behavior of atoms in conditions where the force of gravity has become extreme. . . . Beyond the Planck wall lies total mystery. . . . It is also the extreme limit of our knowledge, the end of our trip towards the origins. Behind this wall still lurks an unthinkable reality, something we will perhaps never be able to comprehend, a secret that not even physicists imagine revealing someday.[8]

Even though they were to disclose it, a certain frame of mind would marshall against such research. This is the mentality that awards its savants Nobel Prizes the way Oscars or Césars[9] are given to good actors, but it never allows such doubts to filter into the curricula. Classical teaching programs prefer to limit themselves to straightforward traditional thinking rather than trusting the wild imaginings of relatively insane savants.

It is safer to content oneself with sound and pretty good physics (which, after all, enabled us to "mess up" the planet and conquer the moon) rather than divulge the theses of a cosmic physics that blurs the borderline between the perceptible and the imperceptible, between the real and the unreal, between science and religion, between spirit and matter. They offer as an excuse the surmise that certain physicists are out of their depth.

Igor Bogdanov attests:

> Some among them have indeed attempted to cast a glance at the other side of the Wall. . . . One day I met with one of these physicists. He maintained that in his youth his work had enabled him to go as far back as the time of Planck and to cast a furtive glimpse at the other side of the Wall. For fear that he might be encouraged to talk about it, he whispered that he had perceived a vertiginous reality: the structure itself of space disappeared into a gravitational cone so intense that time fell back from the future to the past to reverberate at the bottom of the cone in a myriad of instants equal to eternity. . . . One had the strange sensation that the old savant talked of that as if of a kind of metaphysical hallucination that had struck him for all time.[10]

Once pushed to the extreme, the investigation shatters the boundaries of reality. We discover that the present is past, the future is present, and that time and space merge together. A good mocking blow to the operating part of our brain![11]

Besides, there is no need to search for parallel worlds elsewhere as they exist in ourselves. Pascal said so elegantly: "I have my fogs and my fine weather inside myself." More than winters or summers within ourselves, there exist infinities as well. Beneath our cranium moves a "mental galaxy, a constellation of 100 billion neurons united by thousands of billions of microspaces."[12] There are even as many parallel worlds as human beings. Speaking of the world of dreams, Heraclitus said, "For those who are awake there is a single, common universe, whereas in sleep each person turns aside into his own private universe."[13]

Vertigo at the prospect of the infinitesimal: the field of genes is even more outrageous than that of neurons. Vertigo when we scan the sky. What distinguishes our investigation into these dimensions is that no sooner do we think we hold the truth than it slips right through our fingers and leaves us utterly perplexed.

God says in his Ultimate Message, the Qur'ān:

> *Blessed be He Who holds Power and Who is Almighty. He Who created Death and Life, that He may try* (and know) *which of you is best in deed ; and He is the Exalted in Might, Most Forgiving—He Who created the seven heavens one above another: no discrepancy will you see in the creation of the Most Gracious. So turn your view again: do you see any flaw? Again turn your view a second time: it will come back to you humiliated and frustrated.*[14]

The "second time" in question might mean the two poles of plus infinity and minus infinity. It might also mean one look with the naked eye and another with an appropriate instrument. The further observation is continued, the more it leads to humility and submission to the Creator of the universe, of life, and of everything.

All these investigations and this determination to advance in modern science tend towards discovering the secret of life. Each step we take in this domain makes us, however, more disoriented than informed about the mystery of this life. The word *islam* means both submission to God and peace with oneself, with the world, and with others. It means the capacity to listen to the Qur'ānic Message, alone capable of guiding us and revealing to us the meaning of our earthly sojourn. Revelation is our compass in the stormy sea of our knowledge—eternally relative, eternally precarious, eternally renewable.

In no way are we proposing that reason be cast aside, or that the Qur'ānic Message combats it. The history of the relationship of Muslims and the "exact" sciences proves the opposite.[15] The rational mind is merely returned to its proper place, just as the master of a house sends his pet dog back to its kennel. While it is clear that the dog is a member of the household, there is a world of difference (not a parallel world this time) between the pet and the lord of the manor.

The Qur'ān and the Bible

We now come to an important stage of this book which aims to lift, one by one, the opaque veils that hide the purity of the Qur'ānic Message.

Any conscience must react *a priori* somehow or other to this Sacred Text. Those who have a ray of light deep down their hearts feel liberated upon reading its inspiring verses. For some, the Qur'ānic Message has a spiritual effect just like a soothing breeze that would disperse the clouds and reach the heart to vitalize it. Others do not know this happiness, either because the necessary sensor for receiving its light does not exist in their hearts, or because the clouds have a cumulonimbus density from which the wind draws only hail and lightning. Not all hearts bear the seeds of Spring.

All the same, there remains a third category of people who are predisposed to receive the Message but are befuddled by the hodgepodge of harmful notions we have already dealt with. It is for these people that we have covered all this distance, from the first page to this one. There remain only a few patches of fog to come through before we reach our destination and present the Message in its original light.

Let us begin by clarifying an ambiguity which leads to misunderstanding and which is occasioned by the tactlessness that even well-intentioned children of Islam fail to observe. The majority of those who know Islam only through the news of the day believe that the Qur'ān comes from a vague and exotic deity called Allah. For them, Allah is the Arab equivalent of the Great Manitou.

Communicating in languages other than Arabic, certain Muslims are regrettably accustomed to maintaining this false idea by not translating the name *Allah* as God. Speeches in foreign languages that hammer out this word—and other expressions incomprehensible to non-Arabic speakers—sustain the notion of Allah as a particular exotic deity.

The fact of suggesting to the new converts to change their original names for Arabic ones also maintains the idea that Allah—this Arab deity—accepts only Arabic names for those who join the ranks of the *umma*. In so doing, such enthusiastic advisers believe they are emulating the Prophet (grace and peace be upon him). If in fact the Messenger changed the names of some among those who had embraced *islam,* it is because their names had pagan meanings such as "sun worshipper." He also changed certain shameful names which some parents had chosen for their children for fear of envious or malicious looks, and which certainly created complexes for those who bore them. For example, he named "Beautiful" a woman whose name had been "Stubborn."

The Messenger (grace and peace be upon him) did not systematically change foreign names for Arabic ones. *Islam* grants the right to keep the name our parents gave us if only to maintain a good relationship with them. In fact it is an obligation for Muslims to maintain that privileged relationship with their parents, even when they are pagans or unbelievers, and especially so if they are upright and pious. Many young converts sever all ties with their parents over the stupid question of Arabic first names, without taking time to engage them in dialog. The obstinacy with which the enthusiastic new convert renounces the name his parents chose for him, usually with great love, deeply injures their sensibilities. Blocked from the outset, they refuse to learn any more about the religion that has confiscated their son and makes him a foreigner with a strange name.

For those whom the awkward behavior of neophytes has misled concerning the depths of the Islamic faith, let us emphasize that the Qur'ān is not the Sacred Book of the Arabs alone. It is of course in the Arabic language, yet it is for all humankind, since it is intended to extend and broaden the discourse of the Bible itself.

Allah is no exotic deity created by Muhammad (grace and peace be upon him). *Allah* is the Arabic word for God. Allah is thus the equivalent of Elohim, Yahweh, Jehovah, Lord, the God of the Universe. He is the One Who saved Noah (peace be upon him) from the Flood, the One Who befriended Abraham (peace be upon him), the One Who spoke to Moses (peace be upon him), the One Who tested Mary (peace be upon her) and Who granted her the miraculous birth of Jesus, the One Who answered the prayer of Zachariah (peace be upon him) and gave him a son when he despaired of ever having one.

God says in His ultimate Message, the Qur'ān:

We revealed the Torah, wherein there is guidance and light. To it refer the Prophets who submitted to God, in order to judge the affairs of the Jews, as well as the rabbis and the scholars of the Torah to whom was entrusted the protection of a part of God's Book, and they are witness thereto: therefore fear not men, but fear Me, and sell not My Signs for a miserable price. Those who fail to judge by what God had revealed are truly unbelievers.[16]

As to the Day of the Gathering of the Prophets (the Day of the Last Judgment):

Then will God say: O Jesus, son of Mary, recount My favor to you and to your mother. Behold! I granted you as support the Sacred Breath, so that you did speak to the people in childhood and in maturity. I taught you the Book and Wisdom, the Torah and the Gospel. By My leave you created out of clay the figure of a bird and then you breathed into it. By My leave it became a bird. And by My leave you healed those born blind, and lepers. Then you brought forth the dead by My leave. I did protect you from the Children of Israel when you did bring them these signs. Those amongst them who did not believe said: 'This is nothing but evident magic.' "[17]

And addressing the Muslims:

Say: We believe in God, in what was revealed to us as well as what was revealed to Abraham, Ishmael, Isaac, Jacob, and the Tribes, and that which was given to Moses and to Jesus, and to the Prophets from their Lord. We make no difference between one and another of them, and we submit ourselves to God.[18]

There is then no doubt: the Qur'ān is in the direct tradition of the previous Revelations, and many of its chapters assert this fact. Why then this Qur'ān, if the Torah (Pentateuch) is recognized as being a message of God and the Gospels are the source of great wisdom?

Therein lies the whole question. The Qur'ān replies by describing its own verses as being Purified Texts. On many occasions, the Qur'ānic Message alludes to the manipulation to which the Torah and the Gospel were subjected. Note that the Gospel is always referred to in the singular. Might this mean that only one among the Gospels has remained close to the original teachings of Jesus (peace be upon him)?

It is no longer a secret that the Bible has been pieced together from many sources. No one disputes the fact that it is not, strictly speaking, composed of revealed texts.[19] While it is sure that certain principles transmitted by these Scriptures are authentic to the teachings of Moses and Jesus, many have been knowingly or unwittingly altered.

The Qur'ān denounces the fraud which consisted in deliberately concealing one part of the texts. The Pentateuch is the first to be called into question.

God says in the Qur'ān: *Say: Who sent down the Book which Moses brought as a light and guidance to mankind? You did write it on (separate) sheets. You indeed divulged one part thereof, but you concealed the largest part. Who taught you what you and your ancestors knew not?*[20]

Other verses seem to speak more generally, as reproach is addressed to the "People of the Book," a Qur'ānic expression referring to the Jews as well as to Christians: *People of the Book! Why do you clothe truth with falsehood? Why do you conceal the truth while you have knowledge?*[21]

Or again: *Some among them pretend to read the Book by affecting its style, so that you might think it is part of the Book while it is not. They say that this is from God but that is not true. They tell lies against God while they well know it.*[22]

Indeed, contrary to what the Church has throughout the centuries let it be understood, the Bible does not have God as its source. The secular spirit that invaded the West has had the positive role of unveiling these facts. Confronted by a modern world that is determined to communicate, the Church can no longer guard its jealously kept secrets. The Church now recognizes the contradictions and deficiencies in the Scriptures. In our time the sacred is inevitably filtered by rationality, and this has exposed the Bible for what it is.

Until the Middle Ages, the Jewish Tradition was taken for the work of Moses (peace be upon him). Abenezra contested this certitude in the twelfth century, but his protest remained futile and solitary.

In the sixteenth century Carlsdadt noted that Moses could not have written the account of his own death in Deuteronomy [34:5–12].

Like a woolen garment from which the first strands come unraveled, many contradictions were found, little by little, starting with the Old Testament and ending with the New. This led to calling the entire Bible into question.

In his Critical History of the Old Testament of 1678, Richard Simon underscored the chronological paradoxes, repetitions, confusion of stories, and, particularly, stylistic differences that indicate that the Scriptures are indeed "scriptures," and that the plural befits them. Jean Astruc, physician of Louis XV (1753), in his *Conjectures sur les Mémoires originaux dont il paraît que Moyse s'est servi pour composer le livre de la Genèse* [conjectures on the original writings which it appears Moses used to compose the Book of Genesis], made public the argument about the multiplicity of sources that literally blow up the Pentateuch.[23]

In a case of one thing leading to another, the continual scholarship of the nineteenth century revealed four sources of the Pentateuch.

According to this research, the Pentateuch is composed of (1) A document, called Yahwist, written in the country of Judah and dating back to the ninth century B.C.; (2) A more recent Elohist document presumably written in Israel; (3) the text of Deuteronomy, composed between the eighth and seventh centuries B.C.; and (4) a Priestly Code dating back to the period of exile in the sixth century B.C. Thus in the course of the nineteenth century it was proved that the Pentateuch was not dictated by Moses under the influence of divine inspiration, but a book concocted over three centuries. In the twentieth century, the number of partitions was discovered to be even greater than previously believed. In 1941, for example, A. Lods discovered three sources for the Yahwist document, four for the Elohist, six for Deuteronomy, and nine for the Priestly Code "not including additions spread out among eight different authors. . . . Many of the constitutions or laws contained in the Pentateuch had parallels outside the Bible that go back much further than the dates ascribed to the documents themselves. . . . Many of the stories of the Pentateuch presuppose a milieu different from—and older than—the one from which these documents were supposed to have come."[24]

Maurice Bucaille, who remains a fervent Christian notwithstanding his bitter criticism, attests:

> Thus the Pentateuch is shown to be formed from various traditions brought together more or less skillfully by its authors. The latter sometimes juxtaposed their compilations and sometimes adapted the stories for the sake of synthesis. They allowed improbabilities and disagreements to appear in the texts, however, which has led modern man to the objective study of the sources. As far as textual criticism is concerned, the Pentateuch provides what is probably the most obvious example of adaptations made by the hand of man. These were made at different times in the history of the Jewish people, taken from oral traditions and texts handed down from preceding generations.[25]

Not only has the Hebraic tradition of the Bible, which Christians share with Jews, been called into question. The New Testament was also soon put in the hot seat. It is as heterogeneous as the Old Testament, being progressively (from 50 to 150 of the Christian era) composed of 27 books, including (1) the four Gospels; (2) the Acts of the Apostles, (3) thirteen letters by the Apostle Paul, (4) an anonymous work titled "Epistle to the Hebrews," (5) seven letters claimed to be "catholic," and (6) the Book of the Apocalypse of John.

Adding to these 27 books the 22 sources of the Old Testament, the Bible is then composed of 49 pieces.

The linguistic adventure undergone by the Scriptures does not help matters. The multiplicity of sources and the linguistic aberrations could only lead to the erosion of its contents. Mohammed Kassab, Algerian university teacher and researcher, notes:

> Let us recall that the Old Testament had been written in the Hebraic Language with few passages in Aramaic. Then a first Greek translation was done in the third century before the Christian era under the aegis of King Ptolemy. At his accession, the New Testament was also entirely written in this language, from Aramean and Hebrew sources. By the end of the second century, there existed a Hebraic version of the Jewish Bible and a Greek version of the Christian Bible. Between the years 390–405, the Christian Bible was again translated into Latin by Saint Jerome and emerged from the seventh century on as the official version of the Catholic Bible (Vulgate) recognized as authentic at the Council of Trent.[26]

1973, the Reverend Father Roguet deemed it useful to publish a book entitled *Initiation à l'Evangile*[27] [initiation to the Gospel] in order to answer all the questions about the Holy Book that had begun to torment Christians. Before its publication he had conducted a column in a Catholic weekly in which he learned to face up to the urgent doubts that had come to surround the texts. These were disconcerting enough to warrant serious study.

As times have changed, the propagation and spread of culture enabled immediate access to the whole Biblical text. Unlike their Protestant neighbors, Catholics were not used to reading the Scriptures in their entirety. They were soon very surprised at their inherent incoherence. Bucaille relates his own experience on this subject:

> Books of religious instruction only contained extracts; the *in extenso* text hardly circulated at all. At a Roman Catholic school I had copies of the works of Virgil and Plato, but I did not have the New Testament. . . . [I]t was only much later on that I realised why they had not set us translations of the holy writings of Christianity. The latter could have led us to ask our teachers questions they would have found it difficult to answer.[28]

The confusion before the New Testament is generated by the patchwork effect already proved true with the Old. Attempting at first to reassure the faithful by introductions that explained the inexplicable and that claimed to be convincing, the Church eventually opted for the exegetical revolution implemented at the time of Pius XII (deceased in 1958).

In his book titled *Foi en la résurrection, Résurrection de la foi* [faith in the Resurrection, the Resurrection of faith], Reverend Father Kannengiesser speaks of the change of perspective made by the new methods of exegesis. The faithful are exhorted not to take literally the events reported in the Bible, but to consider them as "writings suited to an occasion" or again "combat writings."[29]

Slowly but surely the veil is lifted. There will soon be no question of taking the Gospels as eyewitness accounts of the Companions of Jesus (peace be upon him). The era of Saint Justin (100–165), who described them as "The Memoirs of the Apostles," is in the past. The infighting between the Apostles must be taken into account, as we know now that they grouped themselves into factions. Furthermore, the late date of the birth of the first gospel writings (140 A.D.) is a justification for casting doubt on the veracity of the accounts. These are so many facts which indicate that the texts of the Gospels are far from being consistent and reliable. From eyewitnesses, their authors passed to the status of mere spokespersons of an oral tradition. In his book *The Christology of the New Testament*,[30] O. Culmann writes on this subject:

> The evangelists strung them together, each in his own way according to his own character and theological preoccupations. They linked up the narrations and sayings handed down by the prevailing tradition. The grouping of Jesus' sayings and likewise the sequence of narratives is made by the use of fairly vague linking phrases such as "after this," "when he had," etc.—in other words, the "framework" of the Synoptic Gospels[31] is of purely literary order and is not based on history.[32]

230

In 1962 the Second Vatican Council, in its dogmatic constitution on Revelation, condemned the Old Testament "as containing material that is imperfect and obsolete" but still gave an immaculate image of the Gospels and their authenticity. Today, dozens of exegetes acknowledge the invalidity of such discrimination. When closely examined, each Gospel betrays the personality of its author, the particularity of his character, his personal career, and his approach of the teaching of the Messiah (peace be upon him).

The Gospel of Matthew, a converted Jew, is a sort of prolongation of the Old Testament with only a few reservations. According to him, Jesus accomplished the destiny of Israel. This Gospel expresses a tradition of the Judeo-Christian community but "was trying to break away from Judaism while at the same time preserving the continuity of the Old Testament. The main preoccupations and the general tenor of this Gospel point toward a strained situation."[33]

Thanks to secular suspicion and modern curiosity, Matthew is no longer that customs officer employed at the tollgate or customs house at Capharnaum who kept company with Christ, but a foreigner who took inspiration from the Gospel of Mark—himself suspected of not being an Apostle but a mere disciple of Peter. The eminent theologian teaching at the Catholic Institute of Paris, the Reverend Father Kannen-giesser, stresses that this Gospel, much more than the others, is larded with absolutely improbable accounts and that it is the worthy precursor of the scenario of "Jesus Christ Superstar," the American movie about Jesus which takes extreme measures.

The Gospel of Mark is the shortest. Its writing is situated in the year 70 A.D. Father Roguet describes its author as being a mediocre evangelist, remarkable for the awkwardness of his style and setting little store by chronology. His writing, like Matthew's, is characterized by a total absence of credibility. Furthermore, if the entire work is recognized as being canonical, the Ecumenical Translation explicitly indicates that the final section of his book is a late addition.

The third part of the Gospels, that is the Gospel of Luke, is according to Cullman the work of a real novelist. The author cannot be regarded as direct witness of the teachings of Jesus, as he announces in his "Prolog to Theophilus" that he is going to base his judgment on the testimony of alleged eyewitnesses.

Contrary to Matthew, who was a Jew, Luke was a converted pagan and man of letters, and contrary to Mark, his style is literary, meticulous, and highly readable. He lays emphasis on the good relationship of the Messiah with those same Samaritans who Matthew said were shunned and ignored by Jesus—a fact that is entirely strange about the Messiah (peace be upon him).

These are not the only differences between the Gospel of Matthew and that of Luke. Their genealogies of Jesus are so different as to be contradictory. Luke equally contradicts himself according to whether he talks of the Ascension in the Acts of the Apostles, of which he is the recognized author (and which form an integral part of the New Testament), or in his Gospel.

We come at last to the Gospel of John, which the experts do not rank in the same category with the first three Gospels. Everything leads us to believe that the argument of eyewitness testimony is probable. The writing of the text dates back to 60 A.D., and does not therefore rule out the probability of the Apostle having indeed kept company with Jesus at a very young age and having written his memories at a later age. For the exegetes, the fact remains that the writing is so special that Father Roguet, in his *Initiation*, detects in it "a different world."

More inclined to meditation than narrative style, might this book, this other world, be that Gospel of which the Qur'ān speaks? Or does the Qur'ān allude to the common spirit that the synoptic gospels share with the Gospel of John?

However that may be, John's work is appreciably different from the others. He does he mention, for instance, the institution of the Eucharist nor does he mention the Ascension. He is also—and particularly—the only one to speak of a mysterious "Paraclete," a mystery to which we shall return in greater depth.

These dissensions induce Christians themselves to overcome the myth of the irreproachable Gospels drawing their source exclusively from the divine. Let us hear in this connection Maurice Bucaille, who, divided between the tender faith and an objective spirit, states:

> The historical nature of the Gospels is beyond question. Through descriptions referring to Jesus however, these documents provide us above all with information about the character of their authors, the spokesmen for the tradition of the early Christian communities to which they belonged. . . . This leads us to compare the Gospels with the narrative poems found in Medieval literature. A vivid comparison could be made with the *Chanson de Roland,* the most well-known of all poems of this kind, which relates a real event in a fictitious light. . . . The same holds for the Gospels: Matthew's phantasms, the flat contradictions between the Gospels, the improbabilities, the incompatibilities with modern scientific data, the successive distortions of the text—all these things add up to the fact that the Gospels contain chapters and passages that are the sole product of the human imagination. These flaws do not however cast doubt on the existence of Jesus's mission: the doubt is solely confined to the course it took.[34]

The same author has quite a different assertion concerning the Qur'ān. In his introduction to the part concerning the Qur'ānic Message, he says:

> The ideas in this study are to be developed from a purely scientific point of view. They will lead to the conclusion that it is inconceivable for a human being living in the seventh century A.D. to have expressed assertions in the Qur'ān on highly varied subjects that do not belong to his period and for them to be in keeping with what was to be revealed only centuries later. For me, there can be no human explanation for the Qur'ān.[35]

Or again: "Such statements in the Qur'ān concerning the Creation, made nearly fourteen centuries ago, obviously do not lend themselves to a human explanation."[36]

And again: "I consider that the existence in the Qur'ān of the verse referring to these concepts can have no human explanation on account of the period in which they were formulated."[37]

The Qur'ān as Purified Leaves

While not systematically denying the former Scriptures, the Qur'ānic Message informs us that its verses are purified leaves: *Verily, this is a reminder! Therefore let those who so will, keep it in remembrance. (It is) set down in pages held in honor, exalted* (in dignity)*, and purified in the hands of noble and virtuous messengers.*[38]

The word "messengers" refers to the Archangel Gabriel and the virtuous scribes who applied themselves to setting down in writing the Qur'ān during the lifetime of the Prophet (grace and peace be upon him). When this Sūra was revealed, there were already in Mecca forty-two copies of the Qur'ān out of the total one hundred and fourteen copies. For this reason the Qur'ānic Message, unlike the other Scriptures, is not a reminiscence of individuals more or less informed, more or less in contact with the historical realities. Inspired, the Prophet Muhammad (grace and peace be upon him) ordered his disciples to put it down in writing as it was revealed.

Different means were used to serve this task: parchment, leather, wooden tablets, the shoulder blades of camels, soft stones, etc. The memories of the faithful were surely fixed by most sacred means. The Prophet (grace and peace be upon him) recommended to the faithful to learn the Qur'ān by heart, reciting its verses during their prayers. The *ḥāfizūn* (those who know the whole of the Qur'ān by heart) were very numerous in the nascent community and have never ceased to be so ever since. Even to this day in the *umma,* hundreds of thousands of Muslims know by heart the Qur'ānic text and hundreds of thousands prepare to learn it *in extenso.*

This twofold method of preserving the text, by writing and by memory, proved to be precious. A short time after the death, in 632, of the Prophet (grace and peace be upon him), Abu Bakr, the first Caliph of Islam, put Zayd bnu Thābit, former scribe of Muhammad (grace and peace be upon him), in the charge of preparing one copy. On the initiative of Omar, the second Caliph, Zayd consulted not only the entire documentation he could collect in Medina, but he called to witness the *ḥāfizūn* as well as copies of the Book gathered on various objects and belonging to ordinary people. Thus a meticulously prepared edition was obtained. Historical sources inform us that after he ascertained the authenticity of each text, Caliph Omar made a single volume of the text (*Mushaf*), which he preserved and passed on to his daughter Hafsa, the Prophet's widow.

Concerned to the highest degree about the purity of the Qur'ānic text, the Messenger (grace and peace be upon him) had even advised the Companions not to write down his sayings on the same tools as those of the Qur'ān, as they were not part of pure Revelation. He recommended this so as to avoid a possible confusion between the Qur'ān and the *hadīths*. Since the Qur'ānic Message had denounced as a vile crime the manipulation of the former sacred texts, the Companions were meticulous on this subject.

The rapid expansion of *islam,* which we have mentioned on many occasions in this book, would give further impetus to the effort of preservation at the time of Caliph Othman (third Caliph). Urged by the duty of remitting the Sacred Text to the four quarters of the Muslim empire, Othman put a commission of experts in the charge of an ultimate recension and last revision. The commission would consult Muslims who knew the whole Qur'ānic Message, using a rigorous method that enabled it to avert the slightest doubt concerning the veracity of the document.

According to Professor Hamidullah, there still exist in Tashkent and Istanbul copies dating back to the era of Othman. Aside from a few possible printing errors, the most ancient pieces known nowadays in the Islamic world are identical; the same can be said about the pieces kept in Europe (at the Bibliothèque Nationale de Paris where there are fragments dating back, according to experts, to the eighth and ninth centuries A.D., i.e. the second and third centuries A.H.). Save some very minor variations that change nothing in the general meaning of the verses, the known ancient texts (which are numerous) all agree.

The minor differences discovered here and there relate to the diacritical marks that can make the verb in Arabic read in the active or in the passive voice. Context soon reestablishes the meaning for the trained reader of Arabic. A certain mystic approach even regards such variations as the divine will to propose several readings in one. For this interpretation, the bivalence allowed by the precariousness of the Arabic language[39] exactly expresses the connection between the divine and the human, between the profane and the sacred. It also expresses a continuous repositioning between the reverent fear of God (*alkhauf*) and the hope in His mercy (*ar-rajā'*), a balance that is the very foundation of the Islamic faith.

For instance, *mukhlasūn* ("those who are faithful to God") becomes *mukhlasūn* ("those whom God makes faithful") if we move a diacritic mark. This perfectly joins what a Qur'ānic verse states: *You will not except as God wills.*[40] Such bivalence is in fact an integral part of the miracle of the Qur'ān. The mirror effect between the passive and the active ought to arouse the modesty of the Muslim who attributes his action to the divine will. As the Qur'ān states, "*It was not you who threw* (the arrow at the target) *when you threw it, but it is God Who did it.*[41]

Major Demarcations

Islam's profession of faith is: "There is no god but God and Muhammad is the Messenger of God." We are thus required to dwell in this comparative approach to the notion of God, and to wonder whether the Gospels have not alluded to the advent of a final Messenger.

What we learn about God in the Scriptures is for the Muslim mind extremely blasphemous. The Qur'ānic Message condemns such a particularly execrable image of the Creator which appears in the Old Testament and which would not befit even the vilest of creatures. God, according to this holy book, is an obnoxious entity. Forgetful, He will use the rainbow as a reminder of His commitments towards humankind. He is indecisive and capricious. In the Book of Genesis we read:

> Yahweh regretted having made man on the earth, and his heart grieved. "I will rid the earth's face of man, my own creation," Yahweh said, "and of animals also, reptiles too, and the birds of heaven; for I regret having made them."[42]

God also serves as cicerone, as marker or beacon, as roadsign, so to speak: a sort of Disney's Blue Genie in Aladdin's serials! We read further:

> Yahweh went before them, by day in the form of a pillar of cloud to show them the way, and by night in the form of a pillar of fire to give them light: thus they could continue their march by day and by night.[43]

The Book of Exodus goes further in such delirium. In it we learn that God is capricious and greedy. He demanded a tent to live with the Israelites, a well-filled table with luxurious crockery, plates, pitchers, bowls, wine, and bread.[44] He appreciates the smell of smoke emitted by the flesh of sacrificial animals.[45] To thwart His decisions, a few cabalistic signs suffice. By using these signs, He was compelled to postpone the death of Moses. He was defeated by Jacob, who came out victorious after a night of fighting with Him though seriously injured in his hip. This victory earned Jacob the name of "Israel" (the one who defeated God); his people will no more eat the muscle of leg of animals as a sign of honor for his tendon severed during the battle.[46]

In the Book of Ezechiel, we find a fantastic description of the meeting of this Prophet with his Creator. It is under the guise of a chimera—appearing in an explosion of lightening, flames, floating torches—that God chose to appear before him. To all such insane ravings, the Qur'ān replies: *Glory to the Lord of heavens and earth, the Lord of the Throne. He transcends all that they invent.*[47]

God makes Himself known in the Qur'ānic verses as God of Mercy and Compassion. He informs us about His Attributes and His Names. The Qur'ān refutes pathological anthropomorphism which accompanies the description of the Lord of the worlds in the Old Testament. He also informs us that He is close to His human creatures even if their senses cannot apprehend Him: *No vision can grasp Him, but His grasp is above all comprehension, yet He is gentle, and acquainted with all things.*[48]

However if the Qur'ān asserts His proximity, it denies any idea of intimacy and denounces the falsification of God's image in the Gospel more than any other.

The multiplicity of the sources of the Scriptures itself enables us, curiously enough, to find in certain passages of the Bible itself testimonies which also accuse such falsification. The Book of Jeremiah refers to the anger of God against false prophets who clothe their sayings with God's own and lead the people astray,[49] or again those forgers who transcribe the law and contort its meaning and false prophets who make worthless predictions and misleading fabrications.[50]

God equally informed the Prophet Malachi of the wrongdoings of the priests:

> The lips of the priest ought to safeguard knowledge; his mouth is where instruction should be sought, since he is the messenger of Yahweh Sabaoth. But you, you have strayed from the way; you have caused many to stumble by your teaching. You have destroyed the covenant of Levi, says Yahweh Sabaoth.[51]

In this regard, Mohammed Kassab writes:

> Those who finalized the layout of the New Testament could not fail to notice the tendency of the doctors of faith to change the nature of the foundations of the religion, nor could they fail to know that one of the objectives of the Prophets, beside the propagation of faith, was to condemn the priests for their propensity to wander from the Divine Message.[52]

Perhaps the most serious deviation which these priests perpetrated was that of eclipsing the advent of a Prophet who will come after the Messiah (peace be upon him). The Qur'ān informs us:

> *Jesus, the son of Mary, said: "O Children of Israel! I am verily the Messenger of God, (sent) to you, confirming the Torah (which came) before me, and giving Glad Tidings of a Messenger to come after me, whose name will be Ahmad.*[53]

Ahmad means in the Arabic language "the most worthy of praise," the most perfect personification of the divine will, of the Holy Spirit, the accomplished finish of the divine tendency to Mercy. Markedly different from the others, as we have been informed, the Gospel of John clearly speaks of a "Paraclete" who will come after Jesus. The acts of falsification and the uncertainties of translation made of this famous "Paraclete" a Holy Spirit belonging to an imperceptible world. John reports the words of Jesus concerning this mysterious entity as follows:

> But the Advocate [Paraclete], the Holy Spirit, whom the Father will send in my name, will teach you everything and remind you of all I have said to you. . . . [H]e will be my witness. . . . [N]ow I am going to the One who sent me. Not one of you has asked, "Where are you going?" Yet you are sad at heart because I have told you this. Still, I must tell you the truth: it is for your own good that I am going, because unless I go, the Advocate will not come to you; but if I do go, I will send him to you. And when

he comes, he will show the world how wrong it was, about sin, and about who was in the right, and about judgment. . . . I still have many things to say to you but they would be too much for you now. But when the Spirit of truth comes he will lead you to the complete truth, since he will not be speaking as from himself but will say only what he has learned; and he will tell you of the things to come. He will glorify me, since all he tells you will be taken from what is mine. Everything the Father has is mine; that is why I said: All he tells you will be taken from what is mine.[54]

Let us look into the meaning of the word "Paraclete," a derivative of the Greek *paraklêtos*, which means in that language "defender," "advocate," or more generally "someone called upon for help." Given the eventful linguistic path of the Gospels, Mohammed Kassab maintains that certain commentators have contested the word *Paraklêtos* and put forward that it is a distortion of *periklitos*, which means "praiseworthy." Others attest to the original word being *periklutos*, that is, "glorious."

No matter what the vicissitudes of the concept, it perfectly refers to the Prophet Muhammad (grace and peace be upon him). Among the attributes that we give to our holy Prophet is *ash-shâfî*, which exactly and simultaneously means, " The one called on for help," "the advocate who pleads with God." *Ahmad*, as we have seen, is the other given name of the Prophet in addition to *Mahmûd*, which both mean at complementary degrees "the praiseworthy one." If Paraclete means glorious, Muhammad (grace and peace be upon him) is the sole Prophet to whom glory on earth was granted. As to the translation of "Paraclete" by Holy Spirit, it cannot be rejected, since Muhammad (grace and peace be upon him), just like Jesus, is the Breath of God.

It is an illusion to believe in the advent of a Holy Spirit as a pure spirit. The text of John is only confusing if taken in this far-fetched sense.[55] Let us again hear Muhammad Kassab:

"for he will not speak on his own authority, but whatever he hears he will speak" etc. The capacity to listen, to hear, to talk is part of the constitution of a being provided with organic functions incompatible with a spirit who is, by definition, an incorporeal entity. Hence the conclusion that the notion of Spirit was introduced afterwards. Scholars additionally emphasize that there is a relationship between the assertion of the Gospel, which precisely indicates that the Paraclete will not speak on his own initiative, that he will report what he has heard, and the position of the Qur'ān according to which *"He (the Prophet Muhammad) does not speak under the influence of his inspiration but does only divulge the revelations which are transmitted to him"* (Qur'ān: 53. 3–5).[56]

The Messiah, the Qur'ān and the Bible

The passage of the Gospel of John evoking the "Paraclete" is disquieting for an informed Muslim. Reading the text obviously raises several questions. Why does Jesus (peace be upon him) speak of going and order his disciples not to ask questions? Was the Messiah (peace be upon him) preparing them for his Ascension, which for Muslims took place without Jesus dying?

The Qur'ān says:

> *We punished them* (the children of Israel) *for their infidelity* (to Jesus) *and because they uttered against Mary a grave false charge and for having said, "We killed Jesus the Messiah, the son of Mary, the Messenger of God." But they killed him not, nor crucified him, but so it was made to appear to them. And those who then differed in his death remained full of doubts thereof. They have no absolute certitude thereabout, but only conjecture. For a surety, they killed him not—God raised him up unto Himself; and God is Powerful and Wise.*[57]

The episodes of the New Testament that relate the history of the crucifixion perplex anyone who attempts to approach it. In the Gospel of Matthew[58] we are informed that a plot was hatched against Jesus (peace be upon him) who (advised by God) informed his twelve disciples that he would be betrayed by one of them. We are also informed that Judas Iscariot was that traitor and that he did not hesitate to sell the Messiah (peace be upon him) for a measly thirty silver coins given by the Chief Priests. We are also advised that the famous Kiss of Judas occurred at night. The traitor had to point out Jesus (peace be upon him) to those who wanted to arrest him, but did not know him, by kissing him on his forehead. Lurking in the dark, they awaited that sign.

What follows is mysterious yet significant for the Muslim mind. Judas went the following day to return the coins and proclaim that innocent blood would be shed. Why? The official version describes it as an act of repentance. But we might very well suppose that Judas, realizing at daybreak that he had been mistaken, thought fit to return the money before he was discovered and accused of treason.

Still more puzzling is the sequence where Jesus (peace be upon him) told Peter that the latter would betray him three times before cockcrow. The latter replied to the Messiah (peace be upon him): "Even if I have to die with you, I will never disown you."

We then learn that all the disciples fled the next day (the day of the trial) save Peter, who went to the public place. We are told that three times when he was recognized and accused of being among the disciples, he replied: "I do not know the man."

Why would have Peter risked attending the trial? We might easily believe that he came to keep his promise to die with the Messiah (peace be upon him). Knowing Jesus (peace be upon him) very well, he knew that the man was not his Master and he continually repeated his assertion.

The other indication in the Gospel which could reinforce our argument of the double is the attitude of the so-called Jesus during the trial. As the Gospel relates, he only spoke in snatches and had only this sentence in his mouth when he was being questioned: "Yes, it is as *you* say." How could Jesus (peace be upon him), whose good speech is the basis of teaching, opt for silence at such critical moment? Was he afraid of death? That would be unworthy of a Prophet. The attitude is extremely perplexing if we know that the whole town was present and that it was the ideal moment to plead the cause of the faith in God. Even militants of little stature do not miss the occasion to speak in courts—the ideal place for propaganda—especially when the penalty is capital punishment.

The rest of the story related by the Scriptures is even more bizarre. Deceased on Friday, Jesus was reportedly put in a tomb cut out of the rock. The three holy women who came the next Sunday to embalm the corpse noticed it had disappeared. Then Jesus appeared to them, alive indeed, and stayed among his disciples for forty days, eating and drinking, before the Ascension took place.

Why would the miracle of Jesus' resurrection not be worth the miracle of his substitution for a mysterious double? The Qur'ān says nothing about the nature of the double. Was he a man of the neighborhood who resembled, to the extent of being taken for, the Prophet Jesus (peace be upon him) and about whom even Judas was mistaken in the dark? Was it an optical illusion?

Islam teaches us to be modest before any mystery which stands no chance of being solved, and to say, "God alone knows." For believers, the miracle is a testimony of God's might. The Qur'ān informs us that fire became innocuous for Abraham (peace be upon him), who was condemned to the stake for having smashed the idols, that the rod of Moses became a giant snake which countered the magic of Pharaoh's sorcerers, and that Salomon had the power to use winds and djinns.

Muslims believe in the Ascension of Jesus and await his return on earth with as much hope and love as the Christians have for him, if not more so. Yet they refute the idea of his death and crucifixion.[59] Jesus is not the Son of God, but His Word and a Prophet to whom He granted many miracles—from his birth without a father to his elevation into heaven. It is true that the course of life of Jesus (peace be upon him), very particular in the history of the Prophets as well as his miraculous gifts, may seriously mislead and confuse those who take him for a deity.

The story of Jesus is, in fact, the expression of the Divine Will to break all the laws of Nature, an indication that God is not prisoner of the laws which He established. What ought to have emphasized the Sovereignty of the Creator gave rise to the deification of the creature. Subjugated by the immensity of the Miracle, the Christian consciousness could not see the forest for the trees. Is the idea of the Father and the Son the consequence of such bedazzlement, or is it rather the result of linguistic treason?

Is "father" the reduced translation of a word that is richer and subtler than that of a parent? We will see in a passage to come how difficult it often is to translate certain sacred notions into a language that does not have the necessary aptitude to transmit them. Some people well trained in Catholic theological contortions would say it is trivial to associate the word Father with that of parent, and that it is a question of a notion much more profound and philosophical. Ordinary Christian mortals cannot have access to this conception that is, after all, confusing. For them, Jesus is the child of God just as they are the children of their parents who gave them birth. More than the Son of God, He is for them the Savior whereas His Father is not very conciliatory towards their race. Certain convinced Christians speak of the inordinate dimension taken by the status of son. Michel Lelong, Catholic priest and consultant of the Office for Non-Christian Affairs at the Vatican, states:

> If Christ were to come back among us today, perhaps he would tell Christians to talk less about him and more about the One whom he called "His Father." . . . In certain Christian congregations we are witnessing a marked tendency to take away the sacred aura surrounding God, which leads to speaking more of man than of God, and of Jesus Christ rather than "the One Who sent him." There is a real problem in that, because if we attentively examine the Catholic—and perhaps even more the Protestant—publications, we find in them a propensity to speak of Jesus Christ much more than of God, and sometimes without even mentioning God by name.[60]

Jesus (peace be upon him) must certainly have mentioned the Mercy of God toward His Creatures by comparing it with that of a father for his children. Aramaic had perhaps the linguistic possibility to express that in one word. The popular reminiscence which inspired the writers of the New Testament and the translation of words full of fineness into languages less inclined to conciseness made of it a story of father and son. Certain *hadīths* could be equally understood in this sense had it not been the great vigilance of the exegetes who, in mastery of the Arabic Language, knew its nuances and subtleties.

The Qur'ānic Message, which informs us that Jesus is an exception to all the rules of nature and denies the story of crucifixion, orders us on the other hand not to engage in theological disputations with the "People of the Book" (Jews and Christians). It exhorts us to talk to them and argue with them in ways that are best. *And argue with them in ways that are best,*[61] the Qur'ān says. "Ways that are best" for man and also for that on which we agree the best, that which brings us together and does not bring us into conflict.

What brings us together, beyond our complicated histories and our differences, are indisputably the humanist values, love for the neighbor, self-sacrifice, the work for equity, respect for mankind, the meaning of life.

The Language of the Qur'ān

Now that we have distinguished the Qur'ān from the earlier Scriptures, let us dwell for a while on the language of the Message.

Jacques Berque's particular and passionate experience with the Arabic language will serve us well here. The magic of his witty eloquence takes us back to another magic—as, when illusions confronted the truth of the Miracle, the illusory snakes of the Pharaoh's sorcerers led to the rod of Moses. Berque, who with consummate artistry has juggled with the language of the Arabs, writes the following in the preface of his translation of the Qur'ān:

> The Qur'ān cannot be prefaced. In these few words I will merely describe the conditions under which the present work was achieved. It will have taken me sixteen years, a dozen of preparation and five more during which it was virtually my sole concern.

Superficial study of Arabic has led many orientalists to pedantry and superficial judgment; yet a thorough study leads to modesty. Jacques Berque was unquestionably among the few daring Arabists of great moral fiber. Those who took him for an unconditional friend of the Arabs confused his reverence for the beauty and enduring character of a language with the love of a nation. Berque knew how to value the majesty of the Qur'ānic word at its true worth. The attentive reader may note on the cover that the work is an *essai de traduction,* an attempt at a translation. Such humility is highly significant from an expert of the Arabic language who is as well an original interpreter of the language of Molière.

Jacques Berque is above all an excellent witness to the argument we are setting forth here, since his testimony is not that of a sympathizer, as many might believe, but rather one of an objective adversary and confirmed esthete. In all his writings it is easy to read between the lines to discover bitter criticism in what seems to be praise, and accusation in what seems to be a plea. The opponent remains very correct and respectable; resentment does not prevent him from keeping the modicum of objectivity required of a top-flight academic.

In a wry and ironic style, the noble observer of Arabic taken for its friend explains the greatness of a language whose indestructibility is frightening, and whose trans-cendence is irritating:

> A century ago, despite the state of decline of the culture—clinging stubbornly in *Qarawiyīn, az-Zaytūna, Al-Azhar,* and *Nejdef* to the drone of glosses and commentaries—and while the state of monuments, economies and hearts lay in ruins, one thing remained intact that might "restore all the rest": the classical language. Its linguistic reserve is the Qur'ān. . . . Through its religious dignity, its esthetic enchantment, and its major role in education, the Qur'ānic text transmits the great language like embers that rekindle the flame.[62]

Wavering treacherously between compliment and murderous innuendo, the remark of our "friend" is nonetheless right. Decadent Islam regards the Qur'ān as a text—for some it is part of cultural archives—not a source of life. According to Berque, we have in our genes a verbal profusion that aggravates our economic underdevelopment. Our verbalism is an inflation of virtue. He expresses this argument in a style that is not wanting in originality or verbosity, as is the case with his entire work:

> Here are people who feed on a language. . . . Yet the verbal profusion by which the modern world has attempted to balance technology's devastating breakthroughs has been even more magnified by the Arabs, with their formidable powers of archetype.[63]

Tracing the contribution of the Arabs to this modern and industrialized world, he ascribes our congenital inaptitude for producing industry to our linguistic compensation or vice versa: the problem is there anyway, he claims. In fact, the grudge this wizard of the French language bears Arabic is flagrant. He finds it too rich for his taste, too subtle, too sacred, too resistant.

Linguistic chauvinism plays tricks here, but even so, the tribute is certain. Speaking of the Muslim grammarians who, for the sake of preserving the Qur'ānic language, decoded the classical language in order to master it, Berque advances not without a note of pique, perhaps even of rancor:

> Coming out of their hands like a perfect whole, carefully rationalized, normalized, and endowed with its incredible divine and human resonance, transformed into a jewel case as valuable as—or perhaps more valuable than—a collection of objects, and concealing the phases of its formation under synchronic inventories, the Arabic language escapes history inasmuch as it defiantly towers above it. If the Qur'ānic message raised it to such a high degree of incantatory power, the work of the grammarians made it a system of fearsome richness. One lexicographer estimates the number of its roots[64] at 19,000—another at some 21,000—each capable of producing more than a hundred or so words by the mechanism of derivation *ishtiqāq*. Organized according to precise structures and a rigorous logic, this richness was already manifest in the days of our Charlemagne.[65]

Let us appreciate Berque's scintillating style, which conceals less glittering intentions. The author reminds us of those drab brunettes who feel distaste for the evanescence of a platinum blonde. Even so, it is he who admits the arbitrariness of the signifier Ferdinand de Saussure noted in European languages. The signifiers denoting similar concepts are not logically linked, as Berque explains:

Unlike the case of European languages, Arabic words are very often obvious derivatives of a root. *maktūb, maktab, kātib, kitāb,* for instance, are all constructed from the single root *ktb* (to write) whereas French, referring to the same objects, resorts to five words having no link with one another: *écrit* (writing), *bureau* (desk), *bibliothèque* (library), *secrétaire* (secretary), *livre* (book). All five French words are "arbitrary"; the Arabic words are joined by a logical transparency, to a root which is alone arbitrary. . . . [W]hereas European languages solidify the word and fix it in a precise connection with the thing in such a way that the root no longer shows through, and the word becomes in turn a thing "signifying" something, the classical Arabic word clings to its origins. It draws its substance from its linguistic lineage.[66]

Jacques Berque does not perhaps have a feeling of friendship, strictly speaking. Yet he is certainly living out the pangs of passion. Fascinated, overwhelmed, perplexed and piqued, he wavers between two sentiments, two ripostes: to raise his fist or admit his powerlessness. On the one hand he issues against this imperturbable sphinx language, this "haughty paradigm," the challenge of modernity and its linguistic tools; on the other, he bows in humility before the nobility of Arabic: With all the bitterness of passion, he writes: "I really wish Arabic, today, might be able, both legitimately and effectively, to express all the concepts and objects of modernity."[67]

He'd love to, but he does not acknowledge that Arabic has the ability to achieve such an honorable distinction. Even though Arabic will one day come to terms with modernity and internalize it, thanks to its richness and malleability, Berque, like the schoolmaster who crowns the class dullard with a dunce's cap, sends Arabic to an eternal corner, judging it too prone to transcendence to embrace the concepts of modernity.

Does the real "referent" not remain elsewhere? No doubt it is due to the weakness not of the idiom, but of its objective context. It does not matter. [Arabic] triumphs in what is oratorical rather than in the utterance. Its homeland is what is general. No wonder it disregards all the borders of time and place! Therein lies its strength, providing common refuge to all who speak it, from the Senegal to the Indus, with an exalting hospitality whose warmth can be felt by the foreigner who begins to learn it![68]

We do not know what is the nature of the warmth that motivated certain translators of the Qur'ānic Message. Is it as intense as Jacques Berque's? Does it, as with him, emanate from a desire to push colonial research to the extreme,[69] to enter the unknown lands of the native's language that he regards as a rock, as a force whose capacity to resist was unsuspected?

Whatever the motivation of the translators, translation itself is but another veil, pernicious and dangerous, that masks the profundity of the Message as much as the beauty of the text. If Jacques Berque saw fit to betray his own anxiety before the language he tried to translate and which he described as a "rock," others seem to have got down to work without such scruples.

The Qur'ān and Translation

Translations of the Qur'ānic Message by Westerners conditioned by Christian religious literature are often cavalier, as is the imagination that accompanied them. Moreover, the end of certitude that we have seen above[70] is concomitant with the end of vocations. If we bear in mind that the Arabic language has begun to lack experts at home, we cannot upbraid the West for having failed to produce enthusiasts of Arabic even as late as Jacques Berque, even half-convinced, even with negative passion.

The translation of the Qur'ān, however, presupposes a particular vocation, indeed even a passion and a sound training in the Arabic language, since the principal Miracle manifested by the mission of the Prophet (grace and peace be upon him) is the power and the beauty of the Message.

The Arabic word for the miracle of the Qur'ān is *i'jaz*, which literally means (here is, by the way, an example of the richness of the Arabic language) something no one else can do. The Arabs, those virtuosos of language, those verbal goldsmiths, those wizards of speech, acknowledged their incapacity to take up the linguistic challenge the Qur'ān thrust upon them. The worst enemies of *islam* admitted defeat. Muslims know by heart the passage of the *sira*[71] that relates the day the *qurayshis* commissioned one of them, known for his particular expertise in the subject, to make his report. What was this Qur'ān whose recital alone often sufficed to revolutionize the life of their close relations, their slaves, and the status of their women? Was it a poem so beauteous that it bewitched its audience? Was it a set of magical formulas and powerful incantations? The emissary came back with his head bowed, swearing to his fellows that it was neither poetry nor magic, but a language that is marvelous, impregnable, and transcendent.

In the pre-Islamic period, the Arabs adulated the art of words to the extent of making it a deity and adoring its power. The proof is that on the walls of the *Ka'ba*,[72] the best texts of Arab poetry or *muāllaqāt* (exhibited poems) used to be consecrated by being hung there as an acknowledgment of their excellence where polished style is concerned. All the pilgrims knew the texts by heart, swooned at their subtleties, and reveled in their fluidity.

The Arabs divided themselves into two categories: they were either poets or those who drank deeply from their words as a kind of nectar needed to sustain their inspired and epic nature. Any Arab was stirred, naturally and intensely, to the greatness of words, to the beauty of verbs, to the magic of names. The veneration of the language made of the poet a sort of god who came to swell the ranks of the bevy of worshipped idols. Arousing his wrath was feared like the plague, even more than that of the innumerable deities represented by the statutes. The satires of the poets were fatal to one's honor and face—two basic notions of Arab society. They almost preferred to face the sharp sword rather than the murderous word that forever assassinates dignity and stains prestige.

The art of poetry, well mastered and practiced like a religion, pushed in the extreme sensibility to the sentence, to the turn of phrase, to the power of the image, to the magic of what is recounted. If the Qur'ānic Message had not surpassed all these expectations, if it had not quenched (and even more) this thirst for language, we certainly would not have heard of *islam.*

Islam means submission. This nation of poets, knights of language as well as the sword, submitted to the matchless majesty of the Qur'ānic text. The Message was not poetry; it was by far more sublime. Its strange beauty penetrated the ears of a sensitive people, producing a strange alchemy of the soul; it reached the essence of their being and touched the divine chord that dwells inside every man: his *fitra.*

Are we saying that the Qur'ān is reserved for the Arabs, genetically inclined to poetry? That is not the case. There are several ways to be stirred by the Qur'ānic Text, notably through the heart. Who does not know the stories of those converts who, not knowing a single word of Arabic, reacted all the same by reading the Qur'ān in English or in Danish or in other languages? There are certain privileged persons (spiritually speaking) who perceive the Light of the Message in any language, for whom text awakens the harmonious notes of the faith in a state of dormancy in the dusty furrows of their hearts, just as the needle of the phonograph awakens music in the grooves of a record.

In this regard, the testimony of Cat Stevens[73] is particularly moving. Stevens did not need to become a confirmed Arabic-speaker to capture the truth of the Message. After all these years since his embrace of *islam,* the former singing star still movingly speaks about the reversal he experienced upon reading the *Sūra* of Joseph (*Yūsuf*) in his mother tongue.

Returning to the problem of translation, our criticism is leveled at those who placidly broach the text, armed simply with their primary (or perhaps primitive) knowledge of Arabic and with their defects as Arabists. The result is a mechanical translation that is not even academic and that misleads the average reader, who does not have a sensor of Light like that of Cat Stevens.

The translated Text often becomes insipid to the point of affectation. When, in addition, the conscience and subconscious of the translator are conditioned by the Christian literature ridiculed by a society in revolt against any idea of religion, the outcome is truly disappointing for anyone acquainted with the Message.

Admittedly, the value of the Qur'ān does not reside exclusively in the literary beauty of the text. Yet if God chose this language to send His Message to human-kind, it is because this language has specific virtues: it is the sole language capable of circulating the notions of the sacred in all their fullness. Each word is a phonetic reverberation of the sacred; each syllable is on its own a kind of euphony, indeed even each letter. Certain *Sūras* begin, by the way, by a sequence of independent let-ters which, etymologically, mean nothing but whose vibration is perceived by the

Arab ear as a celestial note. The written transcription of Arabic itself is on its own a continuous inspiration for the Muslim mystics who know how to read divine signs therein. Let alone the rhymes that, alas, are missed in the translations.

Let us take, for instance, the word *muddathir*. Fluid and light in Arabic, this word becomes an oafish and ridiculous phrase when translated into French (since that is the language used to write this book). It is a word that refers to a man who drapes himself in his garment. God thus calls His prophet (grace and peace be upon him), coming back home afflicted and trembling from his first experience of Revelation, to wrap himself up in a warm garment. Berque's erudition and dexterity do not suffice to exempt him from borrowing several words from his language to translate *muddathir*: "He sleeps under a cloak," he says.[74] Why cloak? We will never know.

Régis Blachère, less cavalier but more sensitive to the cold, translates: "The one covered with a coat."[75] Why coat? That we will never know either. Each translates under the influence of his imagination, his attraction, and his fantasy.

Very numerous indeed are the examples which come close to the meaning, but which deface the text and force it to become a pale reflection of itself. An Arab Muslim does not find the majesty of his Qur'ān when he reads even the best translations. Like a withered flower, like a child prematurely grown old, like a certain freshness that has vanished: the translated Qur'ān gives rise to all these impressions.

No language is worth that which charmed the nation of poets (the Arabs) by the majesty of its words and the elegance of its turns of phrase. It is known that the translation of a text is inevitably a betrayal.[76] As for the translation of the Qur'ān, it is an absolute betrayal especially when it is the product of orientalism. The Light of the Qur'ān is however so condensed that enough will remain thereof in the translated texts for those who have a seed in the depths of their heart. Spiritual photosynthesis is always possible—even with a weakened beam of the Message.

NOTES

1. "Voyage au bout du cerveau" [journey to the end of the brain], five-part special report in *Le Monde* of February 3–7, 1998.

2. Eric Fottorino, "Naufrages et boussoles" [shipwrecks and compasses], *Le Monde*, Feb. 1998.

3. Qur'ān: S. XLI. 53.

4. Niels Bohr: Danish physicist (1856–1962) who elaborated a theory of the atom's structure by integrating Rutherford's planetary model and Planck's quantum of action. He established the "Principle of Complementarity": a quantum object may, according to the experimental conditions, be described either in terms of waves or in terms of particles. He won the Nobel Prize in 1922.

5. Guitton, Jean, & Grichka and Igor Bogdanov, *Dieu et la science* [God and Science], Grasset et Fasquelle, 1991, p. 130.

6. Ibid.

7. Max Planck (1858–1947), winner of the Nobel Prize for Physics (1918).

8. Guitton (1991), p. 48.

9. TN : French film award.

10. Idem, p. 49.

11. It is scientifically proven that only one part of our human brain is operating.

12. *Le Monde*'s special report (1998).

13. TN: Heraclitus, *Fragments;* Text and Translation, with a Commentary by T. M. Robinson. Toronto, Buffalo, London: University of Toronto Press, 1987. Fragment 89, p. 55.

14. Qur'ān: S. LXVII, VV. 1–4.

15. The following chapter will (God willing) take up the relationship of *islam* with the exact sciences.

16. Qur'ān: S. V. 44.

17. Qur'ān: S. V. 110.

18. Qur'ān: S. II. 136.

19. TN: No one, that is, among the informed. There is, however, a large fundamentalist Christian population, particularly in the United States, whose reverence for the Bible leads them to believe quite the opposite—even regarding (English) translations.

20. Qur'ān: S. VI. 91.

21. Qur'ān: S. III. 71.

22. Qur'ān: S. III. 78.

23. Maurice Bucaille, *The Bible, the Qur'ān and Science: The Holy Scriptures examined in the light of Modern Knowledge*, translated from the French by Alastair D. Pannell and the author, Ed. Seghers, Paris, 1976, p. 31.

24. Bucaille (1976), p. 31.

25. Bucaille (1976), pp. 31-32.

26. Muhammad Kassab, *Gloire à Dieu ou les milles vérités scientifiques du Coran* [glory to God, or the 1000 scientific truths of the Qur'ān], Ed. Salam et Ed. Sarri, Algiers, 1990, v. I, p. 105.

27. Ed. du Seuil.

28. Bucaille (1976), p. 61.

29. Maurice Bucaille, whom I frequently cite and who gave me material for this passage, seems to be a happy follower of such malleable approach of the Scriptures.

30. Oscar Cullman, *The Christology of the New Testament*, London, SCM, 1959.

31. The three gospels of Mark, Matthew, and Luke.

32. Cited in Bucaille (1976), p. 70.

33. Bucaille (1976), p. 73.

34. Bucaille (1976), p. 116.

35. Bucaille (1976), p. 130.

36. Bucaille (1976), p. 152.

37. Bucaille (1976), p. 196.

38. Qur'ān: S. LXXX. 11–16.

39. TN: Like most semitic writing systems, Arabic is consonant-based, indicating merely the presence of the long vowels (ā, ī, ū); many consonants are written with the same graphic symbols distinguished by diacritical marks. Editions of the Qur'ān from the earliest period have been scrupulously marked to show vowel qualities, consonant gemination, etc.

40. Qur'ān: S. LXXVI. 30.

41. Qur'ān: S. VIII. 17.

42. Genesis 6:6–7. The citations from the Bible are in the version of *The Jerusalem Bible,* New York, Doubleday 1966.

43. Exodus 13:21.

44. Exodus 25:23–30.

45. Exodus 29:16–18.

46. Cf. Genesis 32:23–33.

47. Qur'ān: S. XLIII. 82.

48. Qur'ān: S. VI. 103.

49. Cf. Jeremiah 2:3–30.

50. Jeremiah 2: 8–9.

51. Malachi 2:7–9

52. Kassab (1990), p. 57.

53. Qur'ān: S. LXI. 6.

54. John 14:26; 15:26b; 16:5–8, 12–15.

55. TN: Kassab's following assertion is totally sustained by Bucaille, who rightly observes that "according to the rules of logic therefore, one is brought to see in John's Paraclete a human being like Jesus, possessing the faculties of hearing and speech formally implied in John's Greek text. Jesus predicts therefore that God will later send a human being to Earth to take up the role defined by John, i.e. to be a prophet who hears God's word and repeats his message to man. This is the logical interpretation of John's texts arrived at if one attributes to the words their proper meaning. The presence of the term 'Holy Spirit' in today's text could easily have come from a later addition made quite deliberately. It may have been intended to change the original meaning which predicted the advent of a prophet subsequent to Jesus and was therefore in contradiction with the teachings of the Christian churches at the time of their formation; these teachings maintained that Jesus was the last of the prophets." Op. cit., p. 113.

56. Op. cit., p. 55.

57. Qur'ān: S. IV. 156–158.

58. I cite Matthew notwithstanding the criticism addressed above to his work. The Prophet (grace and peace be upon him) ordered the Companions (and therefore all the Muslims) who asked him if they had to believe the accounts of the "People of the Book": "We don't believe and we don't belie." That would mean that in the Scriptures there is both wheat and chaff. Besides, I am citing what was related only to make a comparative study with what the Qur'ān reveals to us, not to certify or reject.

59. TN: The eminent Muslim scholar Ahmed Deedat has provided well-documented evidence that crucifixion was rather "crucifiction."

60. Lelong (1982), pp. 181–182.

61. Qur'ān: S. XVI. 125.

62. Jacques Berque, *Les Arabes*, Sindbad, Paris, 1979, p. 44.

63. Berque (1979), p. 45.

64. TN: The underlying structure of consonant roots (or radicals) that characterizes the semitic languages has been systematically developed to a comprehensive extent in Arabic, chiefly by the classical grammarians noted by Berque here. Most of these radicals are made of three consonants (cf. the typical discussion of *ktb* in the next citation from Berque's work); derivatives are regularly formed by means of gemination and affixes, as well as patterns of vocalization.

65. Berque (1979), p. 46.

66. Berque (1979), p. 48.

67. Berque (1979), p. 49.

68. Berque (1979), p. 50.

69. Berque was a superintendent who for many long years under the colonial administration of Morocco held the office of civil controller in the *Imintanūt* region—precisely in the *saksawa* tribe that had been the subject of his doctoral dissertation.

70. Part II: 3, "Rerouting History."

71. The account of the life of the Prophet.

72. Edifice considered as sacred long before the advent of *islam,* as we have explained III.2.

73. Cat Stevens: famous British star singer of the 1970s who embraced *islam* and became known as Yussuf Islam.

74. Berque (1979), S. 74.

75. Régis Blachère, *Le Coran: traduction* [the Qur'ān, a translation], Ed. G. P. Maisonneuve et Larose, 1966, S. LXXIV.

76. The Latin verb *tradere* is the source of both *traduire* (translate) and *trahir* (betray). The Italians have the wise adage, *Traduttore, tradittore* (translator, betrayer) to which I fully subscribe where translations of the Qur'ān are concerned.

III. 5. THE MESSAGE AND KNOWLEDGE

You are no doubt close enough to be told with
a loudspeaker: "Islam does not condemn reason—so come closer!"
Mohammed Chafik[1]

Science was the twin of religion; it should never have ceased to be so.
Maurice Bucaille

An accumulation of facts is no more science than a heap of rocks is a house.
Henri Poincaré

We cannot entirely know a science until we know its history.
Auguste Comte

Of all the social sciences, the science of man is the worthiest of man.
Nicolas Malebranche

The Sacred Duty of Knowing

One day, a father received a letter from his hospitalized son; it deserves our attention:

> Dear father . . . , I am in the Orthopedic Ward, next to the operating room. To find me, cross the main entrance and walk along the south gallery. That's where the assistant physicians and students examine the arriving patients. Those who don't need to be hospitalized are given a prescription which they can have filled next door in the hospital's dispensary. Once they examined me I was registered and brought before the head doctor. Afterwards, a male nurse took me to the men's department, had me bathe, and gave me clean hospital clothing.[2]

This letter, which might have appeared in a script of the serial *ER,* was written a thousand years ago in the land of Islam, as Sigrid Hunke reports. The institution described by the patient was one of hundreds of hospitals which the Arab-Muslim civilization boasted of at that time.

The author asserts a page later that "on its own, the city of Cordoba boasted fifty hospitals in the middle of the fifth century." The rest of the patient's letter to his father tells a great deal about the high degree of humanist awareness widespread in the land of Islam at that epoch:

On the left-hand side you pass the library and the big amphitheater where the head doctor gives lectures to the students. . . . Walk alongside the Department of Internal Diseases and the Department of Surgery. . . . If you hear some music or singing through a partition, enter the room. I might already be in the livingroom reserved for the convalescents where they amuse themselves with music and books. . . . You should know that I have absolutely no desire to leave. Everything is so bright and clean here! The beds are soft, the sheets are white damask, and the blankets as smooth as velvet. Each room has running water and is heated whenever the nights turn cold. . . .[3]

Berque could not put it as well. It is certainly the Message's great incantatory power that was able to exorcize the demons of obscurantism that dominated humanity in that epoch. It is the selfsame power that made a nation of humanists out of a nation of poets and turned a nation of dreamers into one of observers and sages.

While Europe, imbued with superstition defended by the Holy Church's dogma, reveled in the expectation of miracles that never came, the miracle of the Qur'ānic Message developed the sense of observation—the first stage of discovery and scientific deduction.

Thanks to the Teaching of the Prophet (grace and peace be upon him) which guided them in this direction, Muslims endeavored to decode the Book of Creation—the perceptible world—since the Holy Book (the Qur'ān) explicitly ordered them to do so. Indeed, the word *qur'ān* literally means "reading par excellence." The first verse revealed[4] to the Messenger commanded him—and those who believe in him—to read!

"Read!" was the first word the Archangel Gabriel addressed to the Messenger (grace and peace be upon him). Terrorized and afflicted by the view of the supernatural, Muhammad replied: "I do not know how to read." After he commanded him three times to read, he revealed to him the very first verses, magnificent and rhymed (in Arabic, of course): *Read in the Name of your God, the Creator, Who created man from a hanging substance.*[5] *Read in the Name of your Lord, the Generous par excellence, Who taught by the pen, Who taught man what he did not know.*[6]

Thanks to the Message and teaching of the Prophet (grace and peace be upon him), Muslims learned that the knowledge of God was tantamount to beholding His Creation. To endeavor to decipher in the tangible world the signs of God and His laws is above all else an act of adoration. The fact of being God's lieutenant on earth implies knowledge of this earth, the world, its laws, its mysteries.

Tawhīd, the notion of God's Oneness, excludes duality in the conception of man, life, and death. There is no god but God: the profession of the Muslim faith is also the implicit way to acknowledge the harmony of the Creation. As it is written: *Have they found for themselves* (the unbelievers) *deities capable of raising the dead? If there were* (in heaven and earth) *other deities beside God, there would be confusion in both* (heaven and earth).[7]

Another *Sūra* calls for meditation and discloses the notion of balance:

> *The Most Gracious, Who taught the Qur'ān, Who created man, has taught him to express himself clearly. The sun and the moon follow courses* (exactly) *computed. Herbs and trees bow in adoration. The firmament He raised on high, and He has set up the Balance* (*mīzān*, in Arabic). *Transgress not* (due) *balance. Establish the balance equitably.*[8]

Typical of the Arabic word, with its multidimensional meaning, *mīzān* means simultaneously an instrument of weight, the weight itself, and balance. The just weight that does not wrong the partner in whatever domain is implicitly recommended, as well as the exact computation which enables us to achieve knowledge of the natural balances.

Oneness of God, oneness of the Creation: the exact sciences take root in certain Qur'ānic verses. The Qur'ān invites the sight to observation, arouses the mind, and opens horizons in a questioning as full of challenges as of encouragement. The following verse opens our eyes on two worlds: that of belief in the invisible (the djinns as well as that of boundless ambition where knowledge is concerned: *O you assembly of Djinns and Humans! If you can pass beyond the zones of the heavens and the earth, then pass! Only by virtue of power can you pass.*[9]

Admittedly, the power of the djinns[10] does not obey the same standards as our own. Their mention is made to remind us of the limits of our senses and our knowledge. It defies the mind that we ought to use, not abuse. The power which the exact sciences grant to man has enabled him to escape the earth's attraction. Yet the heavens are still to be conquered as to the world of the djinns; it will always remind us of our limits.

The cosmos is so vast. The power of man in the conquest of the heavens will certainly go far if, meanwhile, he does not destroy his original home, earth. The power of human science is admittedly imposing these days, but true power is God's, since He has the power of assuming the original balance, by which the apple always fall on the ground, the earth always turns in the same direction, and the elliptical convolutions of our planet about the sun depend on a rigorously maintained balance.

Who then holds Power, of which God willingly grants a minuscule share to man by making the cosmic laws constant? Only a minute repositioning in the distance of the planet earth in relation to the sun is sufficient for all our scientific acquisitions to be called into question and for our life on earth to be seriously turned upside down—unless we leave its orbit to lose ourselves in a hostile cosmos.

The encouragement to learn and explore contained in the Qur'ānic Message soon saw the springing up of specific and inimitable scientific vocations in the land of Islam. We are light years from the attitude the Church engendered among its followers. The faithful in the Christian countries of those days were to have, in principle, no curiosity and no ambition to comprehend the mystery of being! It was blasphemous to seek to penetrate the secrets of the Creation.

The attitudes of the Muslim and Christian worlds of that time were poles apart. Faith was not synonymous with fatalism: a true love of knowledge developed concurrently with submission to God. Every Muslim had the sacred duty to learn to read and write. Because of that, the Muslim world became in less than a century a world cultivated to a degree never before attained in the history of humankind save by the modern Western world.

Let us point out, however, that if between the Muslim world of those days and the Western world of today the literacy rate and degree of love of research and culture is comparable, the philosophies that underlie the two branches of culture are as antagonistic as matter and antimatter, know-how and know-why. If culture, as established in the "modernicious" Western world, is an effective way to escape the sacred (which, let us not forget, was defended by a rigid and inquisitorial Church), it was in the land of Islam a window looking out by means of reason onto the sacred. In the Muslim world, people used to study with a view to attaining spiritual perfection. God deserves that we glorify Him more by having access to the knowledge of the natural laws which He instituted (the famous laws of balance).

Thus the mosque was a locus for adoration, for genuflexion, for meditation— but also a place for understanding the perceptible world. With unceasing amazement, Hunke relates the role of the mosque in the fifth century of the Christian era (that is, the third century of the Muslim era). She supports the idea that there is no dichotomy between faith and science in the land of Islam, that each perfects and sustains the other, and that they have always been close friends. Thus it is from the sacred space of the mosque that science was launched. She says, filled with wonder:

> Each mosque has its library. . . . Beneath the arches of the mosque, the student always has the chance to listen to the lectures of visiting eminent teachers who often come from the furthermost regions of the Arab empire. They are scholars who, on their way to Mecca, pass by one of the centers of intellectual life, or explorers who, as historians, geographers, botanists, collectors of Islamic tradition or the ancient literary heritage, cover the whole country from the coasts of the Atlantic to the Caspian Sea.[11]

This sudden feverish thirst for knowledge that accompanied the spread of the Qur'ānic Message is at least unexpected, since it came from a nation with no previous history in the subject. The Muslim world inherited the knowledge of the other civilizations, particularly of the Greeks,[12] improved it, focused its development on man, and made him its chief propagator for the rest of humankind. By objective parameters, other civilizations might have been thought better inclined toward promoting the sciences. There was no indication of such a direction in the culture of those tribes of camel-drivers, who were surely great poets and courageous nomads, full of wisdom and generosity, but nothing more. Hunke inquires:

Thus neither Byzantium nor Syria or Persia (though the crossroads of the Eastern civilizations) succeeded the Ancients. This role fell to a nation which came suddenly from the desert and which was indisputably able to win straightaway world predominance in the cultural domain—a position they maintained for eight centuries, longer than the Greeks themselves. To what elements does this nation owe to have been able to make such an achievement? And what was the conjunction of the historical, social and spiritual constellation that enabled the attainment of the Arab miracle?[13]

The explanation of the Arab miracle comes from this *islam* that came to join man's heaven and earth, awakened and encouraged his mind, reclassified his priorities, developed his humanism, gave meaning to his life, and cured him of his divisions. The war of the gods that had haunted minds and numbed actions would no longer have room in the head of Muslims. Sure of God's Oneness and confident in Him, sure that the material world is anything but pure accident, sure then of his mission and his duty, the Muslim is prepared to run the world under the best possible conditions.

The simplicity of the precepts of *islam* and the malleability of their application enabled diverse peoples to embrace it without difficulty. The contribution of these peoples to the field of knowledge enriched the scientific heritage of the *umma*. Knowledge being the support of faith, the land of Islam became everywhere a nursery of science and culture.

Read in the Name of Your God, the Creator

The Prophet (grace and peace be upon him) informed the Muslims: "On the Day of the Last Judgment God will inflict a harness of fire on anyone who acquires knowledge and fails to teach it."

It is by loyalty to this teaching that the greatest names of the Arab-Muslim science have always had a pedagogical concern. They have often (if not always) collected their theses in writing with a view to sharing and teaching their knowledge. As a result of such thinking, there soon was an absolutely extraordinary proliferation of schools.

It is appropriate to emphasize here again the extreme difference between the practices in the land of Islam and those in Christian lands. In the year 800 the Synod of Tours found itself forced to order priests to preach in the local language, since no one could still understand sermons in Latin. Their incomprehensibility owed to a strategy of exclusion that enabled the clergy to maintain their monopoly on knowledge. In the land of Islam any newly converted region spontaneously created schools in which all could have access to the Qur'ānic Message without having to seek the help of a cleric. The sciences which issued from these schools were merely a natural corollary of the Knowledge which the Revelation circulated that informs us of the meaning of life on earth and our destiny in the Ultimate Life.

As the elimination of illiteracy is a religious duty, thousands of young pupils, boys and girls, entered onto that arena of learning that would later send them on to higher schools. Let us leave Sigrid Hunke again relate the apotheosis of knowledge in a chapter fittingly and nicely titled *Les glaives de l'esprit* [swords of the mind]:

> Children of all backgrounds attend the grade schools for an extremely modest sum. Better still, as the State pays its teachers, the latter must educate indigents free of charge. In many other regions, and particularly in Spain, state education is free. In addition to the eighty public schools already existing in Cordoba in 965, al-Hakam II established seven new ones reserved for the children of the poor. . . . Even among the Bedouins we find traveling students educating children. Where might one find a hole in this dense network covering the whole nations of *islam*? Indeed, the education of the Arabs is not confined to the elementary level. . . . Thus in all the big towns, new higher schools came into being. The students live upstairs . . . . The kitchens, staff cooperative and the bathrooms are in the basement. On the first floor, classrooms and reading rooms adjoin one another. Here ambitious Arab youths become initiated into the Qur'ān, the traditions, grammar, philology, rhetoric, literature, history, ethnology, geography, logic, mathematics, and astronomy.[14]

The Qur'ānic Message had aroused this thirst of knowledge which also materialized in an incomparable love of books and reading.

In the year 1000 of the Christian era, Ibn al-Nadim published his ten-volume *Kitāb al-Fihrist,*[15] a catalogue of books in Arabic containing only their titles and a biographical note about each author. Had he made an inventory of everything? Apparently not, in view of the great creativity, the constant new thirst of knowledge, the daily and sacred duty of passing knowledge lest one resemble a beast whose harness will come from Hell.[16] In Cairo, 2,200,000 volumes[17] required the care of several hundred librarians in Cairo. Alexandria had twenty times as many manuscripts.

As of 891, Baghdad boasted more than one hundred public libraries. Even a small town like Nadjaf (Iraq) had forty thousand volumes. Hospitals made it their duty to acquire recent publications so that the students of medicine could remain informed about the latest scientific news.

Like their princes, the people venerated books whatever the human experience they related or explained. The Muslim considered himself the natural heir of all that the human mind had produced. Thus Hārūn ar-Rashīd, victor of Ammūriya (Amorium) and Ankara, demanded nothing from his opponents beyond the delivery of all the ancient Greek manuscripts. His son, al-Māmūn, required as war compensation from the Byzantine Emperor Michel III all the ancient philosophical books in his possession which had not been yet translated into Arabic. Nassirdin Tussi, who does not have the stature of these two great princes, had nonetheless a collection of 400,000 volumes. Ibn Sīna (Avicenna) found himself invited at the age of eighteen by the Sultan of Bocchara, whom he had treated, to choose some books among those of a library so rare that it stunned the man of science. Al Assas, Fatimid Prince, had some 1,600,000 books. His son added to them another set of manuscripts—the total number of books occupied no less than 18 rooms of the palace. When he died in 963, the Vizier al Muhallabi left 117,000 volumes—not an exceptional figure among members of that affluent community.

Yet this book fever was not a fad of the rich alone. If the quantity of volumes was a token of wealth, each Muslim family, modest though it might be, had its small library. Like some of the essentials of life, books became the friends of the Muslim to whom the Qur'ānic Message opened to the world and urged to acquire knowledge about himself and the other.

Knowledge: A Form of Worship
The Muslim civilization is reputed to have been outstanding in all the branches of the exact sciences, but particularly in astronomy. Let us refer again to Sigrid Hunke for want of having at hand a profusion of sources relating without negative waves the actions of the Muslims of yesteryear and of today. The German author recounts the anecdote of two brilliant Arab astronomers questioned by some theologians while they were fully engaged in discussion over the evolution of planets:

> "At what fountain do your minds find refreshment?" One of them replied, "We are reading the commentary of a verse from the Qur'ān: *Do they not look at the sky above them? How We have made it.*"[18] Indeed, [Hunke continues], astronomy has a deep religious significance for the Muslim. ... Thus according to one of the greatest Arab astronomers, al-Batānī,[19] astronomy comes "soon after all each individual must know about the commandments of the religion, because it is through this science that man obtains the evidence of God's unity and the knowledge of the prodigious greatness, sublime wisdom, power, and perfection of His work."[20]

We are on a different planet from that of Descartes, who writes in his "Discourse on Method" that science is a matter of becoming the "masters and owners of nature." The approach of science in the modern world is performed in a spirit of revolt against God (that of the Church), violence inflicted on nature, and capitalism—indeed even colonial conquest, since it has to do with possessing and appropriating nature. *Islam* loved sciences for the sake of meditation. Science for the Muslim savant was an active contemplation. Whereas the western science is recalcitrant, Islamic science follows the movement of the natural laws while never failing to remember that it is in the service of man, the whole man, and all men.

In contrast to the overall and balanced view which motivated the Arab science, philosophy, which enabled the blossoming of Europe and then of the West, declared war on God as well as on man. The technological spark of the West did not fly out by a desire for perfection, but by the rage of an "unchained" Prometheus, whose foaming lips and lustful red eyes boded little good. Suspicions have widely proved true ever since. "To put Prometheus back in chains," in Albert Jacquard's expression, is becoming urgent.

The fundamental difference between these two philosophies of science explains the sudden gap that plunged the Muslim world into decline. The technological explosion in Europe (in the logic of determination, power, and appropriation) caught unawares the Muslims who persisted in their humanist conception of science. With wisdom unable to withstand the rifle, alas, colonialism was able to promote another view of things. The prevailing model would no longer be one of man in touch with the world to better worship God and establish a relationship of respect and harmony with nature, which he is responsible for safeguarding. The ideal would henceforth be one of the aggressive and arrogant man fighting against the forces of nature, mechanically consuming all the pleasures provided by a world he violates and desecrates.

As mentioned in the previous chapters, the handicap experienced by the Muslim world in the face of modernity is undoubtedly due to endogenous crises centered on Power. Yet this is not the only explanation of our progressive abdication of excellence in the sciences. That Muslims have not pursued their researches in the direction of development understood by modernity is due to their refusal of its principle, not to genetic incompetence. Islamic science has always refused to separate itself from faith, and therefore from humanism. Making sense has always been the motto of the Muslim savants.

Man and his destiny are the major concern of all the lights of the science of the Arabs. As man's destiny is not confined to life on earth, science is not only and exclusively in the service of man's physical well-being. It regards that physical and social well-being as the requisite condition for the spiritual exercises beneficial for his Ultimate Life. The result of this *Weltanschauung* produced universally recognized spectacular scientific breakthroughs. There was not that caesura between ethics and knowledge, between life and death, which engendered the aberrations of the armed and hedonistic world.

The mystic dance of the whirling dervishes is an excellent symbol of the link between heaven and earth that the man submitted to God maintains. Turning in the direction of the cosmos, present with the absolute and absent from himself, the dancer holds out one hand upward and the other downward. The right hand seems to receive an invisible flux while the other seems to dispense it. To bend to what is transcendent, to what is Spiritual, to become its Conductor (in the electrical sense of the word), and to pour it out in the perceptible world in a pure form—as love, charity, goodness, serenity, faith—but also in a concrete form of medicine, astronomy, dietetics, and practical inventions.

The circle closes slowly, and the waltz is even more beautiful when the heart provides its vital power. The concrete secures the transcendental, the transcendental sustains the concrete, and the spiritual ascension is accomplished—that of man who prays, that of the community that invents the means of mutual assistance for the defense of the weak and the oppressed, and for the recovery and the propagation of the good. I do not mention dervishes, whirling or no, with the idea of recommending them as models, since a dance, however mystical, will not solve our multiple crises. We take the symbol to illustrate an idea, and then pass on.

Such is Islamic science, such are the savants of *islam*. Enamored of the Absolute, they organize the contingent. Prisoners of contingency, they submit to its rules and adjust it so that the sacred may find an abode in every act. In the language of the Message, the tangible world they explored was called, in distinction from the covert world (*al-ghayb*), the world of *shahāda*. *Shahāda* is a rich and polyvalent concept, like many Arabic concepts, meaning both "observation" and "witness."

"Do not bear false witness," the Prophet (grace and peace be upon him) said. This *hadīth* concerning the criminal field is also applicable in the field of scientific testimony. Respect for probity as regards testimony, observation, and precision were sacred tasks for the savant who had also the duty of informing the others.

If astronomy had attained such an unrivalled position at the time of our first savants, it was due to the desire of contemplating the divine work as well as the concern for the essential necessity of accurately defining the hours of prayer and those of fasting (the month of Ramadan). If Ibn Qaraqa dreamt of building huge instruments, it was certainly in order to taste the mystic inebriation with which the view of the overwhelming greatness of the sky provides the Muslim, but it was also to perfect the measures of time.

Scientific ambition knew no bounds. If science in the modern Western context estranges man from the field of the sacred and immunizes him against faith, in *islam* it admits him further into the circle of the sacred while holding rationality in high esteem. Alain is not Muslim when he says: "To think is to deny what one believes." The giants of Arabic science, those men of genius, would rather say, "To think is to support and demonstrate what one believes." In *islam* such reflection is pure worship. Does not the Prophet (grace and peace be upon him) say that "an hour of reflection is worth more than a night of prayers"?[21]

Concerning reflection and observation, the horizons of ambition were admittedly open to the infinitely possible since God is "capable of everything" (*alā kulli shay' in quadir*). The Muslim savant is called to the effective contemplation of God's omnipotence since he is submitted to Him, and since His Lord commands him to be rational in his relationship with the tangible world. Beyond the tangible world, faith takes over, since God informs the Muslim savant that his mind is limited and that there exists another world—parallel perhaps, transcendental surely—where his mind is inoperative.

The Savants: Creatures of Islam

Sure in his mind and armed with his faith, the Muslim apprehends the world in an unparalleled surge of curiosity and creativity and with an extraordinarily developed experimental concern.

In the year 1100 (5th century of the Muslim era), Ibn Qaraqa, who had built in Cairo a huge armillary sphere of five meters in diameter, wished to make a bigger one as "the bigger the instruments, the higher the precision of their work," he said. The alidade soon came to offset the inadequacies of the armillary sphere.

Al-Khawārizmī had already cited 43 uses for the astrolabe, the instrument of measure whose main purpose enables the accurate calculation of the time of prayer, as well as locating Mecca, to which every Muslim is required to turn for prayer.

Jabir bnu Aflah invented the azimuthal quadrant which already contained some elements of modern theodolite. Geodesy[22] was well advanced at a time when the Christian world had no need of it whatsoever, as the matter was settled: the earth was flat and at the center of the universe.

Thabit Ibn Kurrah moved in the ellipses of scientific knowledge as naturally as the planets which he studied.

Al Hashani calculated the relationship between a circle and its diameter (the famous pi).

Olung Bek, prince and astronomer, reckoned the solar year to within 14 seconds of the present calculation.

Thanks to the incentive of the Qur'ānic Message, the Muslim saw with new eyes the macrocosm represented by space, knowing that it is governed by immutable divine laws. He sought to penetrate its secret, thus obeying the divine command given him as God's vicar on earth. His attention as a believer was also directed to his body, not in a narcissistic or hedonistic interest, but because his body is the sup-port of his soul and is a gift from God. Indeed the Prophet (grace and peace be upon him) taught respect for this body, whether alive or dead. He said, "Fight dis-eases, since for each disease there is a remedy." The Muslim savant, brilliant in this field as well, excelled in the quest of remedies.

Ibn Baytar (pharmacologist, physician and teaching specialist) expounded his methodology, writing in an exceptionally ordered spirit to demonstrate the impor-tance of the experimental approach, and to express his perennial concern to teach the least bit of acquired knowledge:

1. Draw up a complete synoptic table of simple remedies and their directions for use.

2. From the theories of ancient and modern authors, report only those whose accuracy my personal observations and experiments have enabled me to prove, and set aside everything whose veracity I could not check or which proved to be in conflict with reality.

3. Avoid repetitions save in such cases where they are necessary for the clarity of the description.

4. Use alphabetical order to enable the student quickly to find what he is searching for.

5. Call attention to each of the remedies which have hitherto been either incorrectly used or incorrectly described by the ancient or mod-ern physicians who have based their judgment exclusively on academic knowledge.

6. Wherever possible, give in each language the names of the various drugs along with their accurate spelling and pronunciation, duly verified by myself during my travels.[23]

Ibn Baytar was neither the most brilliant nor the most competent with respect to the transmission of knowledge. Many Arab physicians left indelible marks in the history of medicine development. Yet it is not the intention nor within the means of this chapter to name all of them. Let us remember but one illustrious sage—and by his Arabic illustrious name, Ibn Sīna, rather than the Latinized form Avicenna. This universal and encyclopedic genius (980–1037), whose theses are referenced everywhere,[24] published the most studied books in the entire history of medicine. The editions of his *Commentaries* are countless. His *Canon of Medicine* was the basic book in the universities of the Western Renaissance. His clear classification of diseases, his systematic description of the symptoms, his methods of diagnosis of pleurisy, pneumonia, the abscess of the liver, and peritonitis made him the undisputed master in those fields for eight centuries and more.

Dixit Arabus ("the Arab said") was an established expression in the universities of the Renaissance West, an expression meaning that the knowledge was sure, the diagnosis accurate, the remedy efficient, the symptoms had been recorded. The "Arab" in question was none other than Avicenna.

Let us remember another giant among many others in the field of medicine: ar-Rāzī (865–925), whose *Continens* [compendium] had gained widespread acceptance for at least ten centuries. His *Treatise on Smallpox and Measles* was published more than forty times between 1498 and 1866.

Ibn al-Haytham (rather than Alhazen), the brilliant astronomer, was also a physician specializing in eye surgery. This peerless ophthalmologist gave the first anatomic description of the eye and discovered the laws of vision which referred him to optics and experiments based on the darkroom principle, unjustly attributed to Leonardo da Vinci.

Al Mawsili cured cataract by suctioning crystalline with a hollow needle: a technique not successfully practiced in the West until 1846, by Doctor Blanchet.

Abu al Kassim (d. 1013) discovered the secret of hemophilia, practiced ligation of arteries,[25] taught the art of fine suturing with cat intestine (the present catgut), invented an absolutely revolutionary collection of surgical tools required by ophthalmologists as well as stomatologists. He was several centuries ahead of Percival Pott (1713–88) in his study of spinal tuberculosis (Pott's disease).

Long before Michel Servet[26] and Harvey,[27] Ibn Nafis discovered the lesser blood circulation.

Malpighi, the Italian physician who studied capillaries in 1660, was three centuries behind Ibn Kuff.

Jenner (1749–1823), thought to have invented smallpox vaccination, was ten centuries behind the Muslim physicians.

Ibn Zuhr (Avenzoar, 1090–1160) practiced tracheotomy on a goat to examine its consequences. Ibn, Ibn: always Arab-Muslim names that had long been shining in the firmament of scientific glory.

Perfect and Inquiring Minds

Such welling up of knowledge and discovery was extraordinary—but even more extraordinary was the world of the Muslim savant who breathed harmony by reflecting the oneness of Creation. For him there was no epistemological break between the world of the stars, the seas, mankind, medicine, esthetics, and poetry. Everything was the work of God, and everything brought the Muslim man back to his Creator.

Ibn Haytam (Alhazen) studied the luminous phenomenon of stars; this took him back to optics and then to the ophthalmic medicine. He excelled in all three fields.

Ibn Badja (Avempace) exercised his talents in medicine, astronomy, mathematics, botany, music and poetry.[28]

Omar Khayyam, known in the current world chiefly as a poet, was especially an encyclopedist to whom are attributed some 14 scientific treatises and books,[29] among which one treats of the value of Euclid's postulates and another a demonstration of the problems of algebra.

Ibn Rushd (Averroës) was not only philosopher, but physician and jurist in particular.

Al Kindi[30] was the author of 270 books on astronomy, meteorology, optics, and pharmacology, etc.

The real miracle that accompanied the Message was manifest by that unparalleled birth of those brilliant and comprehensive minds. The eyes of the heart opened up to the Book of God and the eyes of the head to the Book of Creation. Those curious eyes—curious about the entire man, his environment, his being, and his appearance—incessantly scrutinized the horizons to discover the laws of the universe, the laws of balance.

Ibn Butlān was interested in the influence on human nature of climate, as well as food, the emotions, movement or inactivity, sleep.

Al Bayruni, a light among the lights of astronomy, excelled in all disciplines. He was at once mathematician, astronomer, botanist, geographer, historian, linguist, and physician.

Avicenna, one of the undisputed masters in the field of medicine, was a brilliant geologist and topographer. What he wrote in 1000 A.D. is evidence of experimental awareness of the already sophisticated world; his writings are replete, not with "perhaps" or "I think," but "I saw, I observed, I noticed," as for example:

> The formation of mountains may be explained by two different phenomena. Either it is due to the folding of the earth's crust, which can be produced by a violent earthquake, or to the action of water tracing new paths and hollowing out valleys. The strata are of different kinds, some soft, others hard; wind and water erode the first. Water is the main cause

of such effects. The existence of such effects, the existence of fossils of aquatic animals on many mountains, furnishes evidence of such a cause. . . . In my youth, I saw on the bank of the Oxus river deposits of alluvium which the locals used to wash their heads with. Some twenty-three years later I noticed the same alluvium had been transformed into soft stones.[31]

Such curiosity about Creation, such thirst for observation (as noted in Avicenne's report) were widely shared throughout the Muslim world. As a consequence, peerless works by travelers and discoverers were to appear. Avidity for knowledge in *islam* went on a par with the trust in God. The quest of knowledge urged many scouts to distant lands; a host of masters of the instructive tale, matchless navigators, and ambitious geographers, embarked upon long trips. Henri Miquel, speaking of Makdisi and Ibn Hawqal, describes them as "experts of tracks and footpaths."[32]

Four hundred years before Marco Polo, interest in geography saw extraordinary expansion in the land of *islam*. Ya'qūbī (d. 897) published in 889 *Kitab al-Buldān*[33] [the book of countries]. If all local government officers of these days took Ya'qūbī as a model, the world would not be what it is. The *Encyclopedia Universalis* attests:

Ya'qūbī was a local government officer. His travels, particularly his notes taken on the spot, bring geography closer to reality. In Armenia, Khurasan, India, Egypt and North Africa, Ya'qūbī, by his own account and as evidenced by his book, made inquiries of crowds of people. He thus combined his academic knowledge with the concerns of concrete observation and specific annotation (*i'yān*), two notions would come to carve a decisive place in geography.[34]

Yāqūt (1179–1229), encyclopedic in his breadth, divided his time between erudition and traveling in order to establish his geographical encyclopedia on observations checked with his own eyes. Of his imposing works remain a book on Arab genealogy, a work on toponyms that normalized the names of various places, and two dictionaries, one of literature, the other—in ten volumes—of geography.

In 903 Ibn Rusteh composed his encyclopedia titled *Kitāb al-A'lāq an-Nafīsa* [the book of costly finery],[35] of which only the seventh volume is extant. Treating of geography, this part of his book initiates a synthetic method which moves from fragmentary facts to general and united knowledge, a method anticipating the genius of Ibn Khaldūn.

Balkhi, Istakhri and, somewhat later, Ibn Hawqal were all great travelers. In addition to originality of their style, they came to mark their discipline with the seal of realism and scientific accuracy. Ibn Hawqal, who traveled to every corner of the globe, left an atlas[36] commented with a most agreeable literary style.

Makdissi (d. 1000) left his native Palestine to verify and increase his knowledge on site. He produced books that take the descriptive genre to a level and originality never previously attained.

One of the most brilliant in the field is certainly al-Idrīsī (twelfth century), the noble descendant of the Prophet (through Mulay Idriss, founder of the Idrissid dynasty of Morocco). Born in Ceuta, he went to Spain and then settled in Sicily. There he put his genius at the service of the Norman kings. His book on the entertainment of the world traveler[37] is known by the name of the Book of Roger (the second king of that name), who commissioned the book from him.

Idrissi inherited the precision of Khawarizmi's calculations, as well as the method developed by Ibn Hawqal; he was himself a disciple of Balkhi and Makdissi. André Miquel summarizes this approach in the following words:

> The description of the world could no longer be, as it was for Khawarizmi, a simple listing of figures, longitudes, or latitudes: instead, [Idrissi's] project would realize the geography sketched out, mentally as well as in practice, by Ibn Hawqal and Makdissi. In other words, it would be comprehensive, encompassing the activities of mankind, as well as their natural environment. By returning to the traditional sources, but according to a schematic rigorously developed over the course of the history of the discipline, Idrissi's geography appears as both an overview of the entire world and the very description of that world.[38]

By dint of his conscientiousness and the scope of his work, Idrissi surpassed Ptolemy, publishing some 70 geographical maps.

However conscientious and committed Idrissi may have been, he is but one name among many in the roster of the eminent savants of *islam,* whose passion for travel and meticulous description was widely developed throughout the Muslim world. Conceiving knowledge as indivisible, and the world as the witness of God's Oneness, this wholeness of spirit produced excellent geographers who were at once perspicacious historians, chroniclers, and ethnologists. In addition to the hospitality which the Muslim found everywhere among his coreligionists, the religious duty of visiting Mecca facilitated the birth of these vocations. The land of *islam* thus witnessed an outpouring of travelers who gleaned pieces of information that, directly or indirectly, and to a greater or lesser extent, enriched the scientific and literary patrimony.

A branch of literature bearing witness to this habit of *rihla* (travel) thus saw the light of day. Since pilgrimage was a religious obligation, even as the transmission of the slightest knowledge was an act of faith, transcribing, keeping notes, and producing commentaries of voyages became second nature among many Muslims. Gharnati and Ibn Jubayr were the first precursors of this genre, which would find echoes as late as the eighteenth century with the Moroccan Zayani as well as Abdari and Ayashi.

The master of the genre remains indisputably Ibn Battūta, who in 1325 merely set out for a walk in the city where he was born and returned home 24 years later for a respite before packing up his bags yet again and heading out toward new horizons.

From Morocco he traveled to Constantinople, and then to the High Nile (Eastern Africa), the Indies, and China. He returned by way of Nigerian Sudan.

Precursory Minds

Ibn Khaldūn (1332–1406) gave the greatest titles of glory to the constructive curiosity which took sociological investigation very far in the land of *islam*. He had found a new approach based on traveling and observation, as well as on an analytical spirit and global approach. Thus he became the father of modern sociology and of an innovative conception of history.[39]

Yves Lacoste writes: "As Hitti attests in his *Récits de l'histoire des arabes* [historical accounts of the Arabs], Ibn Khaldūn was the greatest philosopher and historian *islam* has ever produced, and one of the greatest of all time."[40]

G. Marçais has characterized Ibn Khaldūn's book as "one of the most substantial and most interesting books the human mind has ever produced."[41]

In *A Study of History*, Toynbee supports their assertions: "Ibn Khaldūn conceived and formulated a philosophy of history which is probably the greatest work ever made by any mind, at anytime and in any country."[42]

Ibn Khaldūn is even greater than all these descriptions. Yves Lacoste, despite his evident negative undercurrent, makes assertions that speak volumes about the precocity of the genius of Ibn Khaldūn, whose keen intelligence and innovative method had no immediate heirs. His book is still of great help to a serious study of the causes of underdevelopment:

> Discovering the thinking of Ibn Khaldūn is not a matter of giving one-self a change of scenery in Middle Ages orientalism or escaping into the distant past of some exotic land. . . . To study the work of Ibn Khaldūn is not to turn one's back to our times, but to further the analysis of the deep causes of our most serious current problems. . . . Writing in the fourteenth century, Ibn Khaldūn's scientific analysis of the economic, social, and political conditions of medieval North Africa lays bare a number of fundamental historical problems.[43]

André Miquel also accords him a few lines in his *L'Islam et sa civilization* [Islam and its civilization]:

> It is to the famous *Muqaddima,* the book's prolegomenon, written in "imperial conciseness," that Ibn Khaldūn owes most of his glory. Given the whole of Arabic literature, he is not the first to ponder the phenomenon of human society and its evolution. But he had the genius for systematizing his reflections, thus deriving a corpus of laws that govern, according to him, the rise and fall of empires.[44]

These are Islam's children! Their contemplative eyes surveyed hills and dales and beyond. The seas were also no secret for them.

I now cite a specialist in the hatred and exclusion of Arabs and *islam,* Daniel Boorstin. This gentleman, author of *The Discoverers* (a veritable "masterpiece" where dishonesty and historical rerouting are concerned), cannot precisely find a way to erase the influence of the Arabs in this field. Untruthfulness would surely have been too flagrant. The absolutely exceptional role of Ibn Majid cannot be disregarded. The Arabophobe author thus concedes one paragraph to the role of the Muslim world whose title, "Why not the Arabs?," is at least dubious.

In an 800-page collection devoted to discoverers, he grants the Arabs six pages. His testimony is nonetheless significant. From the very first lines, begrudgingly and already regretting the writing of these few pages, he embarks on the argument that it was a pure accident of history that the Arabs had become good seamen. We will choose one of his better bits and leave him the venom that fills his mouth. The author, at his best, devotes his genius to a love of war and territorial expansion. Well and good; a bellicose mind apprehends the world only through the categories of his understanding:

> But in the Mediterranean, empires were repeatedly won and lost on the water. There the ship was the sword of empire builders. . . . That was where Arab maritime prowess developed freely. The brilliant embodiment of that prowess, Ibn Majid, son and grandson of eminent Arab navigators, who called himself "The Lion of the Sea in Fury," achieved fame as the man who knew most about navigation in the dreaded Red Sea and in the Indian Ocean. He became a Muslim patron saint of seamen, in whose memory orthodox mariners would recite the first chapter of the Qur'ān, the Fātiha, before venturing out on dangerous waters. Author of thirty-eight works in prose and poetry, he covered every maritime topic of his day. Most useful to Arab navigators was his *Kitāb al-Fawā'id,* or Nautical Directory (1490), a compendium of everything then known of nautical science, which included information to guide seamen through the Red Sea and the Indian Ocean. Even today, for some areas, his work is said to be unequaled.[45]

We may note in passing that Ibn Majid's knowledge is isolated as some Arab lore concerning Arab sailors exclusively. We also note that Ibn Majid's adventures are confined to the Red Sea and the Indian Sea. All this is done to spare the reader the bad idea of regarding Ibn Majid as the initiator of Vasco da Gama, who, by the magic of the author's dexterity (how clumsy, in fact), came across Ibn Majid by "astonishing coincidence." Let us listen to this beautifully and extremely vague testimony:

> Divine providence must have been watching over Vasco da Gama on his first voyage. By an astonishing coincidence, when on reaching Malindi he

finally secured a competent and trustworthy Arab pilot to steer his fleet across the Indian Ocean, it was this very same Ibn Majid. The Portuguese captain did not know how lucky he was. Nor could Ibn Majid have realized, as they sailed into Calicut harbor, that they were enacting one of the majestic ironies of history. The great Arab master of navigation was unwittingly guiding the great European sea captain to a success that meant the defeat of Arab navigation in the Indian Ocean.

Later Arab historians have tried to explain away Ibn Majid's role by saying he must have been drunk to confide to Vasco da Gama the information that would guide him safely to his Indian destination.[46]

In fact malicious gossips, as Arab gossips are always regarded in the eyes of Boorstin, say that Vasco da Gama had sought Ibn Majid for months before finding him. He took him on board, got him drunk against his will, and extracted from him the secret of the route of the Indies. Other more spiteful gossips say that there were loads of men like Ibn Majid. We know this one only because he guided Vasco da Gama on the route to the Indies long known and used by the Arabs.

By way of conclusion of this part, let us say that arguing with Boorstin over who, Ibn Majid or Vasco da Gama, discovered the route to the Indies is not the purpose of our momentary pause in his book. Nor is it a question of lamenting over the ruins of a civilization that can no longer beget men like Ibn Majid, Ibn Khaldūn, or Ibn Haytam.

The Arab genius is no more in question. It is true that there remain only echoes of it. Yet even today, a love of research is manifest among the children of *islam*. A large number of researchers and discoverers of Arab origins populate the laboratories of the West. The dynamics of the mass appearance of distinguished minds in the Muslim world of yesteryear ends up today in the scattering of our gray matter in the service of a kind of science that is engendered and animated by defiance and violence: defiance of God and violence against man.[47]

One is almost tempted to support the thesis of the Western science's affiliation to that of the Greeks. In the chapter titled "Rerouting History," I denounced this argument as a falsification and the result of a determination to exclude Muslim contribution in the progress of history. Judging by the spirit of the Islamic science and that of the modern West, the link seems to be subtle indeed. It is true that the Muslim world took up some Greek and Indian knowledge. In a perspective of faith, the Muslim world gave it an end and a meaning, and fit it into the scope of a certain code of ethics. The West inherited this knowledge, polished and tamed to serve man. The West took this oil, which ought to nurture man's wisdom, and threw it on the torch of Prometheus, rekindling thus the flame of rebellious science, often destructive, seldom constructive.

The Message encouraged the Muslim mind to see the world with eyes which are human-oriented, not utilitarian. The challenge to come will be to put Prometheus back in chains, and to link the sciences again to the Supreme Science which Revelation alone dispenses.

NOTES

1. Mohammed Chafik, Moroccan politician, writer, bard of Amazighism, and 2002 Prince Claus Laureate. In the early 1970s he wrote a veritable gem titled *Ce que dit le muezzin* [what the Muezzin says], published by Librairie-papeterie des écoles, Rabat. He is also author of a Tamazight/Arabic Dictionary.

2. Cited in Hunke (1963), p. 126.

3. Hunke (1963).

4. I would remind the reader that the order in which the *Sūras* and verses are organized is not that of their revelation—a divine way of saying that the Qur'ān is not a prisoner of time, but speaks of the universal and the essential.

5. Translation of the Arabic word *alaq*. The Qur'ān, sparing the ignorance of mankind at those times about the human gestation, alludes to the fetus clinging to the womb. Bucaille is filled with wonder at this notion. He points out that the secret of the nidation of the impregnated ovum that hangs from the womb was only discovered in the beginning of the twentieth century.

6. Qur'ān: S. XCV. 1–5.

7. Qur'ān: S. XXI. 21–22.

8. Qur'ān: S. LV. 1–9.

9. Qur'ān: S. LV. 33.

10. Invisible entities which according to the Qur'ān have a conscience. We know nothing else about them from the Qur'ān.

11. Hunke (1963), pp. 235, 245.

12. In speaking of such knowledge, I am alluding to what is related to the exact sciences. As regards philosophy and theology, the situation is not so fortunate. The desire to surpass the Greeks in speaking their philosophical language led to the logic of the biter being bit. The Mutazilites, intending to defend *islam* with the weapons of a pagan philosophy, found themselves caught in the intellectual turbulence that the inexact sciences always produce.

13. Hunke (1963), p. 211.

14. Hunke (1963), pp. 242–3.

15. TN: Also known as the Index; cf. www.muslimphilosophy.com/ei/nadim.htm.

16. The Prophet (grace and peace be upon him), as we have already mentioned, said: "God will inflict a harness of fire on whoever acquires knowledge and fails to instruct it."

17. When speaking of books and volumes, we must indicate that these may be bound chapters. Yet the figures are nonetheless significant.

18. Qur'ān: S. L. 6.

19. Al Battani (877–918) is a giant of astronomy and the worthy heir of the theses of that other giant, Khawarizmi. He is the first scientist to have calculated the inclination of the

ecliptic and the precession of the equinoxes. Known as Albategnus in the Middle Ages and in the Renaissance, he was illustrious for his Sabean Tables, translated into Latin and presented in his Introduction to Astronomy.

20. Idem, p. 84.

21. Hadith reported by Abu Darda.

22. Or the science of the shape and dimensions of earth. In the 9th century A.D. Ibn Hawqal took up the atlas of the Muslim world, inaugurated by Balkhi and then resumed by Istakhri, to develop it and correct it. Cf. *Dictionnaire de l'Islam,* Albin Michel, 1997, p. 386.

23. Hunke (1963), p. 197.

24. TN: cf. "Avicenna (Abu Ali al Hossin ibn Abdallah ibn Sina)" in *Runes* (1960), p. 31.

25. The practice, unfairly attributed to Ambroise Paré (who practiced it six centuries later), avoided hemorrhaging in cases of amputation.

26. Michel Servet (1511–53), Spanish physician and theologian who took refuge in Geneva, fleeing from the Spanish Inquisition. He was recaptured and burnt at the stake.

27. William Harvey (1578–1657), English physician to whom is attributed the discovery of the blood circulation.

28. *Dictionnaire de l'Islam.*

29. George Sarton, *Introduction to the History of Science,* Washington, 1927. In this work Sarton introduces Khayān as one of the great mathematicians of the Middle Ages.

30. *Dictionnaire de l'Islam,* p. 474.

31. Cited in Hunke (1963), p. 262.

32. André Miquel, *L'Islam et sa civilization: VIIIe siècle–XXe siècle* [Islam and its civilization, 8th to 20th centuries], Armand Colin, [s.d.], p. 138.

33. G. Wiet, *Les pays* [French translation of the *Kitāb al-Buldān* of Ya'qūbī], Cairo, 1937.

34. *Dictionnaire de l'Islam,* p. 847.

35. *Les atours précieux* [French translation of the *Kitāb al-A'lāq an-Nafīsa* of Ibn Rusteh] by G. Wiet, (Ed. Le Caire, 1955).

36. *Livre de la configuration de la terre* [Book of the Earth's configuring].

37. TN: The book is known in Arabic as *nuzhat al-mushtāq fi'khtirāq al-āfāq.*

38. *Dictionnaire de l'Islam,* p. 404.

39. Ibn Khaldūn, *The Muqaddimah, an Introduction to History,* trans. (from the Arabic) Franz Rosenthal, NY, Pantheon, 1958.

40. Yves Lacoste, *Ibn Khaldoun: naissance de l'histoire, passé du Tiers-Monde* [Ibn Khaldūn: Birth of history, the Third World's past], François Maspero, 1973, preface.

41. Lacoste (1973).

42. Lacoste (1973).

43. Lacoste (1973).

44. Op. cited, p. 303.

45. Daniel Boorstin, *The Discoverers: A History of Man's Search to Know His World and Himself*, Random House, 1985, pp. 181–82.

46. Ibid.

47. Mehdi Mandjra (eminent futurist and man of good will) stated in 1982: "Everyone knows that scientific research for military purposes in the industrialized countries is the main source of advances in the high-tech disciplines. We know that 60% of research workers in the world work for the military sector. According to Robert Hollomon, three quarters of R&D expenditure in the United States is devoted to defense, astronautics, and nuclear energy." Cited in *Nord-Sud, prélude à l'ère post-coloniale* [north/south: prelude to the post-colonial era], Casablanca, Toubkal, 1992, p. 179. For background cf. www.elmandjra.org/livre2/introd.htm.

EPILOG

IN THIS BOOK I have endeavored to cast light on the shadows that have sullied the image of *islam*. I hope I have begun to convince a few open minded readers that *islam* is not a life of incurable quietism or unfathomable barbarity, but rather one of fulfilling peace of mind and universal mercy. In delineating the long and turbulent history of the Islamic community, I hope I have indicated with sufficient force and clarity the rupture at the level of power that has been a determining factor in our increasingly evident inability to communicate the Qur'ānic Message to the rest of humanity.

Effectively deposed, our community is today little more than the faint impression of an attractive civilization whose discourse once was credible. Made deliberately illiterate by regimes intent on holding a monopoly on education and information, we have definitely lost our art of persuasion, our *balāgha*.[1] How could we have preserved it, since the great majority among us scarcely have the right to whisper?

Those of our children who have been privileged enough to preserve our *balāgha* and combine it with the languages of the conquerors have had, as their lot, the misfortune of being "deculturated."[2] Too often they have resigned their role of arousing consciences to become even more lost in the paths of nonsense than those they were supposed to inform. They themselves often need to be reminded that Descartes was a one-eyed masquerader, that Darwin was a upside-down crusader, that the continuous flow of information that bombards us causes brain cancer in the long run, that globalization is a hell paved with good intentions, that our forbears are not French, that our history is not golden blond, that death is not the end but the beginning—and so much more!

Who will tell humanity that the Qur'ānic Message offers vital information about human nature and destiny?

The pious Muslim? How would he do it, having lost all his means, and living in the grip of merciless poverty? The Friday sermons he hears deaden his mind more than they motivate it. They no longer revive the flame; instead, they manipulate consciences in the service of political propaganda, when they are not occasions for irascible preachers to rain threats of eternal punishment upon the heads of the faithful for the least trivial matter.

The wealthy Muslim? Obsessed as he is by his unconditional admiration for a civilization that sparkles with its goods (while withholding them), he too has lost the means to bring the Message to others.

There will of course always be some veiled woman or bearded man who may try to speak out. But what is such speech worth in the face of the media's hostility to whatever such "terrorists" might think or write? The "ratings god" has already condemned their speech, consigning it to the category of utopian, violent, or outmoded notions, out of touch with reality. Enlightening the inhabitants of modernity—who are not necessarily all Northeners—is too great a challenge, as long as we remain underdeveloped and miserable. Material civilization needs material arguments before lending an ear.

Meanwhile, few will have the chance to know what *islam* really is. For most it will continue to remain the religion of the Arabs, a fatalist religion made of bowing and scraping and prostrations in the style of Iznogood the vizier.[3]

For those more attuned to profundity of knowledge than to comic strips, *islam* is a set of original prescriptions and abstentions intended to vex the faithful throughout their lives.

Others, fellow members of the clubs attended by Monsieur del Valle, will continue to regard it as a turbaned history, written at sword-point, that dreams of restarting the Battle of Poitiers.

The world's supervisors, living in the centers of strategic studies, will see it as a federating force that is at all cost to be curbed, by means of nationalism, Wahhabism, feminism, dervishism, journalism, and many other "aberrationisms."

Who then, on a large scale, will make known and demonstrate, in practice, the definition the Prophet of *islam* (grace and peace be upon him) gave to *islam,* which has no connection with the standard Western notions of religion? *Islam* is a *dīn,* a whole set of acts and exercises by which we progress as much in our spiritual intimacy as in our relationship with others, society, and the world at large.

I do not pretend to be able in the space of a single book to give an exhaustive image of the Qur'ānic Message. I have merely cleared the ground a little. May the information that follows give my reader yet another reason for reconsidering *islam,* for *islam* is neither the historical private property of the Muslims nor my own, for that matter, but the heritage of all humankind which underestimates and ignores God's Message destined for man.

Let us listen to the *hadīth* which the Muslims call *hadīth ad dīn,* the *hadīth* that defines the Islamic faith: Omar (God bless him) relates:

One day as we were in company with the Messenger of God (grace and peace be upon him), a man came towards us. His dress was spotlessly white and his hair was very black. No one knew him, and he bore no sign of traveling. He came and knelt down in front of the Prophet (grace and peace be upon him)—he himself was seated in a kneeling position—put his hands on his own thighs and then asked, "O Muhammad, what is *islam?*" The Prophet (grace and peace be upon him) replied, "*Islam* is to bear witness that There is no god but God and that Muhammad is His Messenger, to perform the prayer, to do *zakat,*[4] to keep the Ramadan fast, to make the pilgrimage if you can afford it." "You are correct," [the foreigner replied].

272

Omar further relates:

> We were then amazed at the way he proceeded, asking him questions and replying that he was right. The foreigner continued, "What is *Imān* [faith]?" "*Imān* is believing in God, in His angels, in His Books, in His Messengers, in the Day of the Last Judgment, in predestination in Good as well as in Evil." "You are correct! And what is *Ihsān?*" "*Ihsān*[5] is worshiping God as if you saw Him, or considering that if you do not see Him, He indeed sees you." "You are correct! Tell me about the Hour!"[6] "The one questioned is no more learned in the matter than the questioner," [replied the Prophet]. "Tell me about the signs [of the End]!" [continued the foreigner]. "(It will occur) when a mother brings forth her mistress, and when you see the barefooted, the homeless, the poor and the goatherds[7] vie among one another in raising edifices." "You are correct!" [the foreigner replied].

Then, Omar says, the foreigner took his leave, leaving us intrigued.

> The Messenger (grace and peace be upon him) then asked us, "Do you know who the questioner is? It is the angel Gabriel, who came to teach you your *dīn*."

This *hadīth* informs us therefore that *islam* is not that stationary state confined within a frame of legality accredited by the power in office as we know it today. It is an aspiration, a life, a continuous movement, a radiant promise given to mankind.

Other *hadīth*s perfect our perception of the *dīn:*

The Prophet (grace and peace be upon him) says, "The *dīn* goes apace with good behavior (towards others)." He adds, "Those among you who will be the closest to God (in the Last Life) are those who will have been the most amiable in their behavior with others."

Islam is thus a continuous quest of human perfection, since it is the human qualities that are the focus in the process of development. It is a question of remaining human and becoming increasingly so through taming our instincts and channeling our passions in favor of virtue.

Spirituality in *islam* is tailor-made for man and takes into account all his dimensions. The ascent through the three stages of the *dīn* is not a solitary one towards ethereal summits. Progress towards God obliges us to progress with regard to our neighbor. To worship God as if we saw Him certainly means faithfulness at prayer and the cultivation of actions beyond those that are required, but valuing our neighbor is no less decisive in our Final Destiny.

The Messenger (grace and peace be upon him) specifically teaches that God pardons our weaknesses in practicing what He has prescribed; but His pardon for the wrongs we do to others depends on the pardon of our victims. This indicates the extent to which the spiritual element in *islam* is linked to the social element, and the degree to which the saintliness ardently aspired to by any Muslim depends on citizenship and good behavior. Michel Chodkiewicz tells us something about this in his book on Emir Abd el Kader (God bless him):

> As there is no place where God is not, there is no place where saintliness does not have room. Anchorite or gyrovagues, princes who retire to the desert, shopkeepers who abandon their shops and go and beg along the roads: such vocations are not lacking in Islam. They gather momentum when denied and blossom in exile. Yet perfection is not to be sought in such aberrations. The best remain where they are, because *He is with you wherever you are* (Qur'ān: S. LVII. 4). Caliphs or waterbearers, they do not flee their condition; it is their condition that sometimes quits them. Their retreat is the crowd, their desert is the public arena; conformity is their ascetism, the ordinary is their miracle. "The lesser holy war"[8] against the external enemy does not divert them from the great war against the infidel that each bears in himself, nor the greater from the lesser. With no regrets, if not without effort, their life combines the affairs of the world with those of eternity. They are similar to that "excellent tree" mentioned by the Qur'ān (S. XIV. 28) *whose root is firm and whose foliage is in the sky,* a symbol of the *axis mundi,* that is, the perfect man who, by virtue of the divine proxy, joins in his person the realities above to those below. Such saintliness has neither uniform nor emblem.[9]

Because saintliness has neither uniform nor emblem, the people of the West could very well take part in the reawakening of man. In this depraved and hard-hearted era they could give humanity another chance to rediscover the meaning of being virtuous and saintly by making themselves the champions of an Islamic faith awaiting to be reborn in the hearts of individuals and in the behavior of societies.

"I have a dream" of having convinced one single man or woman on earth to read the Qur'ān with new eyes and a ready heart. For this reason, I have written this book to "combine the affairs of the world with those of eternity." For this man, for that woman, I have a little too sharply criticized the "modernicious" world, since I have seen how the turbulence of our globalized era has generated a mental and social imbalance that is fatal for the personal Destiny of us all.

Still, the reader must not think that this book is a plea for obtaining a sentence that would pronounce the death penalty against any contact between Islam and modernity.

Moreover, I have in no way accused those who populate the West of being all horrible creatures engaged in leading the world astray. I hope the reader of this heartfelt cry will have sufficient intelligence not to read the book in that sense.

I would simply say that I would love it if everybody might have the chance to know that life has a meaning and that Messengers have been charged with making that known to us. When I set out in all simplicity to write this book, I came up against a fog so dense that I feared my voice would fade before reaching its destination—that my signals would find poor reception. Cartesian mentality has had its part in the forming that dense fog; Darwinist culture has aggravated its density; disinformation has impeded communication; and globalization has shuffled all the cards.

The good behavior prescribed by the Qur'ānic Teaching encompasses every human brother and sister. Good behavior may be expressed in the political domain in the form of alliances with any sincere partner. God knows that the future of our Muslim peoples is in desperate need of partnerships. For all of us, Muslims and non-Muslims alike, the future depends on our lucidity and moderation. The "affairs of the world" say that the twenty-first century will either be a century of harmony and understanding between peoples, or it will not.

NOTES

1. TN: Eloquence, rhetoric, art of persuasion.

2. Jacques Berque's expression, signifying the loss of one's cultural identity.

3. TN: Iznogood, another cartoon character invented by Goscinny, symbolizes the slyness and servility of sycophants in the court of "caliphs."

4. *Zakat,* translated as legal charity, is in fact an act of faith that the owner of a capital is required to perform so as to purify his money by paying a particular tax. Such an act requires the presence of intention. It does not by any means rule out other taxes adjudged as necessary by the community, should the need arise.

5. Literally, the word *Ihsān* has three accepted meanings: 1. The accomplishment of a thing or an act in its most possible perfect form; 2. Charity; 3. The meaning given by the *hadīth,* i.e., improvement of faith.

6. That is, the end of the world.

7. The Prophet (grace and peace be upon him) ascribes these three attributes to the Arabs. The description bears no derogatory connotation but is merely a statement of fact, since the Prophet (grace and peace be upon him) was himself an indigent shepherd who walked barefooted.

8. We have already explained that *jihād* is not a "holy war," but rather "effort," "resistance." Still, the beauty of Chodkiewicz's text excuses him for this small inaccuracy.

9. Abdel Kader, *Ecrits spirituels* [spiritual writings], introduced and translated by Michel Chodkiewicz, Éditions du Seuil, Paris, 1982, p. 15.

BIBLIOGRAPHY OF WORKS CITED
IN THE TEXT AND NOTES

Books

Abdel Kader. *Écrits spirituels,* intro. and trans. by Michel Chodkiewicz, Éditions du Seuil, Paris, 1982.

Ali, A. Yūsuf. *The Holy Qur'ān: Translation and Commentary*, Amana Corp., Brentwood, Md., 1983.

Arnold, Sir Thomas. *The Spreading of Islam in the World: A History of Peaceful Preaching,* Good-word Books, New Delhi, 2001 (first pub. London, 1896).

Baubérot, Jean. *La Laïcité: quel héritage?,* Labor et Fides, Paris, 1990.

Berque, Jacques. *Les Arabes,* Sindbad, Paris, 1979.

Berque, Jacques. *Une cause jamais perdue,* A. Michel, Paris, 1956.

Blachère, Régis. *Le Coran: Traduction,* G. P. Maisonneuve & Larose, 1966.

Boisard, Marcel. *L'Humanisme et l'islam,* A. Michel, Paris, 1980.

Bombardier, Claire. *Lettre ouverte aux Français qui se prennent pour le nombril du monde,* A. Michel, Paris, 2001.

Boorstin, Daniel. *The Discoverers: A History of Man's Search to Know His World and Himself,* Random House, NY, 1985.

Bourin, François. *Le contrat naturel,* Paris, 1990.

Braudel, Fernand. *Grammaire des civilisations,* Flammarion, Paris, 2nd ed., 1993.

Braudel, Fernand. *La Méditerranée: L'Espace et l'histoire,* v. I, *Arts et métiers graphiques,* Paris, 1977.

Brown, Michael H. *The Search of Eve,* Harper and Row, NY, 1990.

Brunot, Louis. *Premiers conseils,* École du livre, Rabat 1934.

Bucaille, Maurice. *The Bible, the Qur'ān and Science: The Holy Scriptures Examined in the Light of Modern Knowledge*, trans. Alastair D. Pannell and the author, Seghers, Paris, 1976.

Chaunu, Pierre. *Histoire et science sociale, la durée, l'espace et l'homme à l'époque moderne,* Sedes, Paris, 1974.

Comte-Sponsville, André. *Impromptus,* PUF, 1996.

Comte-Sponsville, André. *Petit traité des grandes vertus,* PUF, 1995.

Comte-Sponsville, André. *Valeur et Vérité,* PUF, 1994.

Cote, Roch. *Drogue: la guerre chimérique,* Les Belles Lettres, Paris, 1996.

Daoud, Zakia. *Féminisme et politique au Maghreb: sept décennies de lutte,* EDDIF, Casablanca, 1996.

del Valle, Alexandre. *Islamisme et États-Unis, une alliance contre l'Europe,* L'Age d'Homme, Paris, 1997.

Dictionnaire de l'Islam, A. Michel, Paris, 1997.

Djait, Hichem. *L'Europe et l'Islam,* Le Seuil, Paris, 1978.

Dozy, Reinhart. *Histoire des musulmans d'Espagne jusqu'à la conquête de l'Andalousie par les Almoravides,* Leiden (1861), 1932.

Dupuy, J. P., in *La société en quête de valeurs,* Maxima, Paris, 1996.

Ellul, Jacques. *Propagandes,* Economica, Paris, 1990.

Forrester, Viviane. *L'Horreur économique,* Fayard, Paris, 1996.

Foulquier, Jean-Michel. *Arabie Saoudite: La dictature protégé,* A. Michel, Paris, 1995.

Friedman, Georges. *La puissance et la sagesse,* Gallimard, Paris, 1970.

Gafouri, Abdul Hadi. *Islam et économie: réflexion sur les principes fondamentaux de l'économie islamique,* Al Bouraq, Paris, 2000.

Gennep, A. V. *Traité comparatif des nationalités*, Payot, Paris, 1922.

Gide, André. *Les nourritures terrestres*, Gallimard, Paris, 1897.

Grand, P.M. *Découverte de la préhistoire*, Club Français du livre, Paris, 1960.

Guéhenno, Jean-Marie. *La fin de la démocratie,* Flammarion, Paris, 1995.

Guitton, Jean, & Grichka and Igor Bogdanov, *Dieu et la science,* Grasset et Fasquelle, Paris, 1991.

Halimi, Serge. *Les nouveaux chiens de garde,* Raisons d'agir, Paris, 1997.

Heraclitus, *Fragments,* Text and Trans., with a Commentary by T. M. Robinson. University of Toronto Press, Toronto, Buffalo, London, 1987.

Hobsbawn, Eric J. *L'âge des extrêmes, histoire du court XXe siècle,* Complexe, Paris, 1994.

Hodgson, Marshall G. S. *L'Islam dans l'histoire mondiale*, trans. with a preface by Abdesselam Cheddadi, Sindbad, Actes Sud, Paris, 1998.

Hodgson, Marshall G. S. *Rethinking World History: Essays on Europe, Islam, and World History,* Cambridge University Press, Cambridge, 1996.

Hoffman, Stanley. *Gulliver enchaîné: essai sur la politique étrangère des États-Unis,* Éditions du Seuil, Paris, 1971.

Hugo, Victor. *Les Orientales,* Flammarion, Paris, 1968.

Hunke, Sigrid. *Le soleil d'Allah brille sur l'Occident,* A. Michel (*Espaces libres*), Paris, 1963.

Huntington, Samuel. *The Clash of Civilization and the Remaking of World Order.* Simon & Schuster, NY, 1996.

Ibn Khaldūn, *The Muqaddimah: An Introduction to History,* trans. (from the Arabic) Franz Rosenthal, Pantheon, NY, 1958.

Johnson, P. E. *Darwin on Trial,* Regnery Gateway, Washington, 1991.

Jordan, Michael. *Les sectes, prophéties, pratiques et personnalités,* PML, Paris, 1996.

Kassab, Muhammad. *Gloire à Dieu ou les milles vérités scientifiques du Coran,* Salam & Sarri, Algiers, 1990.

Lacoste, Yves. *Ibn Khaldoun: naissance de l'histoire, passé du Tiers-Monde,* François Maspero, Paris, 1973.

Laïdi, Zaki. *Le temps mondial,* Complexe, Paris, 1997.

Laoust, Henri. *Les schismes dans l'islam,* Payot, Paris, 1977.

Laroui, Abdallah. *L'Histoire du Maghreb, esssai de synthèse,* F. Maspero, Paris, 1975.

Laroui, Abdellah. *Islam et histoire,* A. Michel (*Idées*), Paris, 1999.

Latouche, Serge. *La planète des naufragés, essai sur le sous-développement,* La Découverte/ essais, Paris, 1993.

Liauzu, Claude. *Race et civilisation, l'Autre dans la culture occidentale, anthologie critique,* Syros, Paris, 1992.

Miquel, André. *L'Islam et sa civilisation: VIIIe–XXe siècle,* A. Colin, Paris, 2002.

Morin, Edgar & Sami Naïr. *Une politique de civilisation,* Arléa, Paris, 1997.

Morin, Edgar. *Introduction à la pensée complexe,* E.S.F., Paris, 1990.

Neirynck, Jacques & Tariq Ramadan. *Peut-on vivre avec l'Islam?* Favre, Paris, 1999.

Nord-Sud, prélude à l'ère post-coloniale, Casablanca, Toubkal, Casablanca, 1992.

Olaguë, Ignacio. *Les Arabes n'ont jamais envahi l'Europe,* Flammarion, Paris, 1969.

Johnson P. E. *Le darwinisme en question* [Fr. trans. of *Darwin on Trial*], preface by Anne Dambricourt Malassé, P. d'Angle, Paris, 1996.

Peyrefitte, Alain. *La France en désarroi,* Éditions de Fallois, Paris, 1992.

Peyrefitte, Alain. *Le mal français,* Plon, Paris, 1976.

Pilot, Albert. *L'art, la science et l'argent,* La Lyre, Rabat, 1998.

Pirenne, Henri. *Mahomet et Charlemagne,* Paris, Bruxelles, 1937.

Plato. *Complete Works,* ed. John M. Cooper. Hackett, Indianapolis, Cambridge, 1997.

Popper, Karl. *Conjectures et réfutations,* Payot, Paris, 1985.

Quellien, Alain. *La politique musulmane dans l'Afrique occidentale,* Larose, Paris, 1910.

Ramadan, Tariq. *Etre musulman européen, étude des sources islamiques à la lumière du context européen,* Tawhid, Lyon, 1999.

Ramadan, Tariq. *Les musulmans dans la laïcité: responsabilités et droits des musulmans dans les sociétés occidentales,* Tawhid, Lyon, 1994.

Raux, Jean-François. *La société en quête de valeurs,* Maxima, Paris, 1996.

Rodinson, Maxime. *Islam et capitalisme,* Éditions du Seuil, Paris, 1966.

Runes, Dagobert D. *Dictionary of Philosophy,* Philosophical Library, NY, 1960.

Sarton, George. *Introduction to the History of Science,* Washington, 1927.

Stendhal. *De l'amour,* Garnier-Flammarion, Paris, 1965.

Stengers, Isabelle. *L'invention des sciences modernes*, Flammarion, Paris, 1995.

Thiesse, Anne-Marie. *La création des identités nationales, Europe XVIIe–XXe siècles*, UH, Éditions du Seuil, Paris, 1997.

Thuilier, Pierre. *La grande implosion: rapport sur l'effondrement de l'Occident 1999–2002*, Fayard, Paris, 1995.

Vergez, André & Denis Huisman. *Nouveau cours de philosophie: La connaissance et la raison*, F. Nathan, 1988.

Wiet, G. *Les pays* [Fr. trans. the *Kitāb al buldân* of Ya'qūbī], Cairo, 1937.

Wolton, Dominique. *Penser la communication,* Flammarion, Paris, 1997.

Yassine, Abdessalam. *Islamiser la modernité,* al Ofok, Rabat, 1998.

Yassine, Abdessalam. *Winning the Modern World for Islam,* Justice & Spirituality, Iowa City, 2000.

Articles, Entries

Achcar, Gilbert. "Les Nations-Unis au fil des objectifs américains," *Le Monde diplomatique,* Oct 1995.

Bayrou, Francois. "L'école et l'argent," *Le Monde diplomatique,* July 1994.

Berque, Jacques. "Refuser la tentation de l'insularité," *Le Monde diplomatique,* March 1991.

Berque, Jacques. "Un monde à refaire," *Panoramiques* no. 2, Jan 1994.

Bougnoux, Daniel. "La Science au risque des médias," *Le Monde diplomatique,* Sept 1995.

Bourdieu, Pierre. "La tradition 'd'ouvrir sa gueule,'" in "Horizons, entretiens," *Le Monde,* Dec 3, 1999, p. 16.

Calmard, Jean. "Ghazali" in *Dictionary of Islam: Religion and Civilization,* A. Michel, Paris, 1997.

Charles, Raymond. *L'âme musulmane,* Flammarion, Paris, 1958.

Costa-Lascoux, Jacqueline. "Les trois âges de la laïcité," *Question politiques,* Hachette, 1996.

Cullman, Oscar. *The Christology of the New Testament,* London, SCM, 1959.

de Libéria, Alain. "Fracture en Méditerranée: une double amnésie nourrit le discours xéno-phobe," *Le Monde diplomatique,* Sept. 1993.

Decornoy, Jacques. "Communication et eugénisme pornographique," *Le Monde diplomatique,* Dec 1992.

Fottorino, Eric. "Naufrages et boussoles," *Le Monde,* Feb 1998.

Goldman, S. L., ed. *Science, Technology and Social Progress,* Lehigh University Press, Bethlehem, PA, 1989.

Golub, Philip S. "Rêves d'empire de l'administration américaine," *Le Monde diplomatique,* July 2001.

Guislain, Pierre. "Le spectacle de la propagande," *Le Monde diplomatique,* May 1991.

Guisnel, Jean. "L'Internet, ça sert aussi à faire la guerre," *Le Monde diplomatique,* May 1996.

Ilibert, Robert. "L'histoire du monde arabe et musulman dans l'enseignement," AFEMAM Issue 2, Dec 1987.

Jobert, Michel. "L'Islam et sa modernité," *Revue du Tiers-Monde* no. 92, Oct–Dec 1982, PUF.

Julien, Claude. "Le monde des extrêmes," *Le Monde diplomatique,* March 1995.

Lelong, Pierre. "L'islam et l'Occident," *Revue du Tiers-Monde* no. 92, Oct–Dec 1982.

Liauzu, Claude. "Jalons pour un état des lieux," AFEMAM Issue 2, Dec 1987.

Mahdi al Mandjra, "Nord/Sud," *Repères,* Toubkal, Casablanca, 1992.

Mattelart, Armand. "Dangereux effets de la globalisation des réseaux, les nouveaux scénarios de la communication mondiale," *Le Monde diplomatique,* Aug 1995.

Ramonet, Ignacio. "La télévision loin des fronts," *Le Monde diplomatique,* Feb 1991.

Ramonet, Ignacio. "Stratégies de la faim," *Le Monde diplomatique,* Nov 1998.

Roskis, Edgar. "Journalisme et vérité: images truquées," *Le Monde diplomatique,* Jan 1995.

Triaud, Jean-Louis. "L'Islam vu par les historiens français," *Esprit,* Nov 1998.

"Voyage au bout du cerveau," *Le Monde,* Feb 3–7, 1998.

Warde, Ibrahim. "Du sectarisme et comment le dépasser," *Le Monde diplomatique,* Jan 1994, p. 29.

Websites

Latouche, Serge. Text published, Feb 27, 1998, on the site "Terminal," http://weblifac .ens-cachan.fr/Terminal/texts/forum64.html.

Nord-Sud conferences: www.elmandjra.org/livre2/introd.htm.

Thèmes: Religions et modernité, Géoscopie review, February 1998, on the site www. geoscopie.com.